Impact of Artificial Intelligence in Business and Society

Belonging to the realm of intelligent technologies, it is increasingly accepted that artificial intelligence (AI) has evolved from being merely a development standpoint in computer science. Indeed, recent reports and academic publications show that we are clearly on the path toward pervasive AI in both business and society. Organizations must adopt AI to maintain a competitive advantage and explore opportunities for unprecedented innovation. This book focuses on understanding the wide range of opportunities as well as the spectrum of challenges AI brings in different business contexts and society at large.

The book highlights novel and high-quality research in data science and business analytics and examines the current and future impact of AI in business and society. The authors bridge the gap between business and technical perspectives and demonstrate the potential (and actual) impact on society. Embracing applied, qualitative, and quantitative research as well as field experiments and data analysis, the book covers a broad range of topics including but not limited to human-centered AI, product and process innovation, corporate governance, AI and ethics, organizational performance, and entrepreneurship.

This comprehensive book will be a valuable resource for researchers, academics, and postgraduate students across AI, technology and innovation management, and a wide range of business disciplines.

Francesco Paolo Appio is a Full Professor of Innovation at Paris School of Business, Paris, France. He earned his Ph.D. in Management from Scuola Superiore Sant'Anna in Italy. He has recently visited important international academic institutions such as Bocconi University (Italy), MIT Sloan School of Management (USA), and K.U. Leuven (Belgium). His research is interdisciplinary in nature and mainly revolves around the impact of digital transformation on innovation at multiple levels (ecosystems, city, organization, teams), taking into account different perspectives such as sustainability, socio-technical systems, technological change, and innovation capabilities. He has recently been appointed as a member of the Editorial Board for the journals like *Journal of Product Innovation Management, Technological Forecasting* *and Social Change*, and *IEEE Transactions on Engineering Management*. His research has been published in *Journal of Product Innovation Management, Long Range Planning, Technological Forecasting and Social Change, International Journal of Production Research, Industrial Marketing Management*, among others. He is guest editor of multiple special issues in journals like *Journal of Product Innovation Management, Organization Studies, Technological Forecasting and Social Change, IEEE Transactions on Engineering Management*, and *Journal of Urban Technology*.

Davide La Torre, Ph.D., HDR, is a Mathematician and Full Professor of Applied Mathematics and Computer Science at SKEMA Business School, Sophia Antipolis Campus, France. He is qualified in the French national university system as Professeur des Universités in Applied Mathematics (CNRS 26), Computer Science (CNRS 27), and Economics (CNRS 5) as well as in the Italian national university system as Professore Ordinario in Mathematical Methods for Economics (13 D4), Political Economy (13 A2), and Public Economics (13 A3).

His research and teaching interests include Applied Mathematics, Artificial Intelligence, Business Analytics, Mathematical Modeling, and Operations Research. He got his HDR (Habilitation à Diriger des Recherches) in Applied Mathematics from the Université Côte d'Azur, Nice, France (2021) and a Doctorate in Computational Mathematics and Operations Research from the University of Milan, Milan, Italy (2002) as well as professional certificates in Analytics from the Massachusetts Institute of Technology, USA. In the past, he held permanent and visiting university professor positions in Europe, Canada, Middle East, Central Asia, and Australia. He also served as Associate Dean, Departmental Chair, and Program Head at several universities. He has more than 190 publications in Scopus, most of them published in high IF journals ranging from Engineering to Business.

Francesca Lazzeri, Ph.D., is a data and machine learning scientist with extensive experience in academic research, tech innovation, and engineering team management. She is the author of a few books on machine learning and applied data science, and many other publications, including technology journals and conferences. Francesca is a Professor of Python for machine learning and AI at Columbia University and Principal Data Scientist Director at Microsoft Cloud + AI, where she leads an organization of data scientists and machine learning engineers building intelligent applications on the Cloud, utilizing data and techniques spanning from generative AI, time series forecasting, experimentation, causal inference, computer vision, natural language processing, reinforcement learning. Before joining Microsoft, she was a Research Fellow at Harvard University in the Technology and Operations Management Unit. Francesca is also Advisory Board Member of the AI-CUBE (Artificial Intelligence and Big Data CSA for Process Industry Users, Business Development and Exploitation) project, the Women in Data

Science (WiDS) initiative, machine learning mentor at the Massachusetts Institute of Technology, and active member of the AI community.

Hatem Masri is a Professor of Business Analytics and Vice President for Academic Affairs and Development at the Applied Science University, Kingdom of Bahrain. He received a Ph.D. in Management Science in 2004 and Master's in Operations Research in 1999 from the University of Tunis, Tunisia. His research interests include business analytics, supply chain management, financial engineering, and Islamic finance. He published more than 30 articles and six books among them a textbook on Islamic business administration. Hatem is founder and chair of the INFORMS Bahrain International Group, past president of the African Federation of Operational Research Societies, general secretary of the Tunisian Decision Aid Society, member of INFORMS and IEEE, and volunteer/mentor with the AACSB.

Francesco Schiavone is a Full Professor of Management at University Parthenope, Naples, Italy. He received Ph.D. degree in Network Economics and Knowledge Management from the Ca' Foscari University of Venice (Italy) in 2006. He is also an Affiliated Professor at Emlyon and Paris School of Business (France) and University of South Pacific (Fiji Island). Currently, his main research areas are technology management, strategic innovation, communities of practice, and healthcare management and innovation. Prof. Schiavone is the scientific director of VIMASS, the research lab in healthcare management and innovation, established at University Parthenope.

Routledge Studies in Innovation, Organizations and Technology
Public Innovation and Digital Transformation
Edited by Hannele Väyrynen, Nina Helander and Harri Jalonen

Advancing Big Data Analytics for Healthcare Service Delivery
Tiko Iyamu

Open Labs and Innovation Management
The Dynamics of Communities and Ecosystems
Edited by Valérie Mérindol and David W. Versailles

Technology Brands in the Digital Economy
Edited by Wioleta Kucharska and Ewa Lechman

Business Models for Industry 4.0
Concepts and Challenges in SME Organizations
Sandra Grabowska and Sebastian Saniuk

Innovation in the Digital Economy
New Approaches to Management for Industry 5.0
Edited by Agnieszka Rzepka

Information Technology in Contemporary Organizations
Redefining IT Management for Organizational Reliability
Katarzyna Tworek

Impact of Artificial Intelligence in Business and Society
Opportunities and Challenges
Edited by Francesco Paolo Appio, Davide La Torre, Francesca Lazzeri, Hatem Masri and Francesco Schiavone

For more information about this series, please visit: www.routledge.com/Routledge-Studies-in-Innovation-Organizations-and-Technology/book-series/RIOT

Impact of Artificial Intelligence in Business and Society

Opportunities and Challenges

Edited by
Francesco Paolo Appio, Davide La Torre, Francesca Lazzeri, Hatem Masri and Francesco Schiavone

LONDON AND NEW YORK

First published 2024
by Routledge
4 Park Square, Milton Park, Abingdon, Oxon OX14 4RN

and by Routledge
605 Third Avenue, New York, NY 10158

Routledge is an imprint of the Taylor & Francis Group, an informa business

British Library Cataloguing-in-Publication Data
A catalogue record for this book is available from the British Library

ISBN: 978-1-032-30341-3 (hbk)
ISBN: 978-1-032-30342-0 (pbk)
ISBN: 978-1-003-30461-6 (ebk)

DOI: 10.4324/9781003304616

Typeset in Bembo
by codeMantra

Contents

List of contributors   ix

Introduction   1
FRANCESCO PAOLO APPIO, DAVIDE LA TORRE, FRANCESCA
LAZZERI, HATEM MASRI AND FRANCESCO SCHIAVONE

PART 1
**Artificial Intelligence: Technological Advancements
and Methodologies**   13

1 **Artificial Intelligence and Machine Learning:
   Definitions and Applications**   15
   CINZIA COLAPINTO, RIADH KSANTINI, DAVIDE LA TORRE,
   HATEM MASRI AND MARCO REPETTO

2 **Adopting Machine Learning and AI for Data-driven
   Decisions**   33
   FRANCESCA LAZZERI

3 **Neural Networks and Deep Learning**   58
   CHIARA GALIMBERTI AND MARCO REPETTO

PART 2
**Artificial Intelligence in Business: Opportunities
and Challenges**   83

4 **Artificial Intelligence in Human Resource
   Management: Objectives and Implications**   85
   ALESSIA BERNI, LUIGI MOSCHERA, AND AIZHAN TURSUNBAYEVA

5 **Methodology for Evaluating the Appropriateness of a Business Process for Robotic Process Automation** 105
ABHISHTA ABHISHTA, LARS BERGHUIS, WOUTER VAN HEESWIJK AND AIZHAN TURSUNBAYEVA

6 **Startups and Artificial Intelligence: Insights from Italy** 134
IRENE DI BERNARDO AND FABIO GRECO

7 **Integrating AI to Blockchain and Cryptocurrency: A Case Study** 153
MOHAMED BECHIR CHENGUEL

PART 3
The Societal Impact of Artificial Intelligence 169

8 **AI Human Capital, Jobs and Skills** 171
LEA SAMEK AND MARIAGRAZIA SQUICCIARINI

9 **AI for Sustainability: A Dangerous Fantasy or an Unfulfilled Potential** 192
DANIELA INCLEZAN AND LUIS I. PRÁDANOS

10 **AI-Based Technologies in the Phygital Care Journey** 212
IRENE DI BERNARDO, MARIALUISA MARZULLO, CRISTINA MELE AND TIZIANA RUSSO SPENA

11 **AI Technologies and Hospital Blood Delivery in Peripheral Regions: Insights from Zipline International** 231
VALENTINA CUCINO AND GIULIO FERRIGNO

12 **Improving Healthcare by Designing AI-Human-Centered Systems** 250
GAETANO CAFIERO, MICHELA DE ROSA AND FRANCESCO SCHIAVONE

Index 271

Contributors

Abhishta Abhishta is an Assistant Professor at the High-tech Business and Entrepreneurship Department at the University of Twente. His research focuses on empirically measuring the economic/financial impact of cyberattacks. To do so, he devises/adapts data-driven economic impact assessment techniques. He looks to help organizations make well-measured investments in security. His current research is supported by two NWO grants, one aimed at cloud security (MASCOT) and the other at building a first prototype of the Responsible Internet (CATRIN). He serves on the program committee of ACM/IEEE/IFIP conferences aimed at network measurements and responsible internet (TMA, PAM, TAURIN).

Lars Berghuis received his M.Sc. in Business Administration from the University of Twente, The Netherlands, in 2021. His master focused on the digitalization of businesses, which included the implementation of IT within organizations, data science, and information system for the financial service industry and smart industry. He currently works as an IT Auditor at the Technology Risk Department of EY. His interests go out to helping organizations to explore and exploit new technologies and optimizing processes.

Irene di Bernardo is a Ph.D. candidate in Management at the University of Naples Federico II. Her research interests are in the field of services marketing and service innovation. Her most recent studies concern silver economy, smart technologies, and human actors well-being in highly sensitive service contexts such as healthcare. She collaborates with international universities and research centers. She attended several conferences and doctoral consortiums related to service science. She is currently researching on service and social robotics, well-being, customer and patient journey.

Alessia Berni is an Associate Professor of Organizational Studies at the University of Naples "Parthenope" (Italy). She has Ph.D. in "Organizational Design and Human Resource Management" from the University of Molise (Italy). She is a member of the Faculty of the Ph.D. program in Economics, Management, and Accounting at the University of Naples "Parthenope". She teaches Organizational Studies and Project Management. Her research focuses on organizational design, human research management, and new institutional theory.

Gaetano Cafiero is an entrepreneur, founder, and CEO of Kelyon. Prior to this, he served as consultant and then as sales manager for a number of multinational and SME ICT companies. He currently serves as board member of Campania Bioscience – the Technological District for Life Sciences companies – and Compagnia delle Opere Campania – an association representing manufacturing and service companies in Campania – and other associations in the field of open innovation and open source. He is a member of the Address Committee of the degree courses in computer science and engineering at Uniparthenope University of Naples.

Mohamed Bechir Chenguel is an Associate Professor of Finance at University of Kairouan, Tunisia. He holds a Ph.D. in Finance from University of Faculty of Management and Economics University Tunis Al manar and an HDR degree (Habilitation for Supervising Doctoral Research) from the University of Kairouan. He has published many academic papers in international refereed journals. His research interests include Cryptocurrency, Financial Crisis, Islamic banking, banking risk, and corporate governance. Active in research, he is reviewer in many indexed peer-reviewed journals based (Scopus, Francis Taylor, Emerald, Springer, etc.).

Cinzia Colapinto, Ph.D., in Business History and Corporate Finance (University of Milan, Italy), is an Associate Professor in the Department of Management, and a Senior Researcher in Strategy and Entrepreneurship at IPAG Business School (France). Her research interests focus on Entrepreneurship, Innovation, Strategy. In particular, she is interested in the role played by digital technologies on business model transformations and on their impact on the achievement of sustainable development goals by SMEs. Her main publications are in *Management International Review, Management Decision,* and *European Journal of Operational Research.* She is the author of several monographs, including *Adaptive Decision Making and Intellectual Styles* (Springer).

Valentina Cucino is a Postdoctoral Scholar at Scuola Superiore Sant'Anna, Pisa. She received her Ph.D. in Management Innovation, Sustainability, and Healthcare from Scuola Superiore Sant'Anna, Pisa. She has published in *Technological Forecasting and Social Change, R&D Management, Total Quality Management, Journal of Knowledge Management, European Journal of Innovation Management,* and *Studies in Higher Education.* Her research interest deals with technology transfer process, innovation management, and hybrid organizations.

Giulio Ferrigno is an Assistant Professor at the Catholic University of the Sacred Heart (Milan). He was a Postdoctoral Scholar at Scuola Superiore

Sant'Anna (Pisa). He received his Ph.D. from the University of Catania. He held visiting positions at University of Cambridge (United Kingdom), Tilburg University, and University of Umea. His works have been published in *International Journal of Management Reviews, Technological Forecasting and Social Change, Small Business Economics, R&D Management, Review of Managerial Science, Total Quality Management, Journal of Business and Industrial Marketing,* and *Technology Analysis & Strategic Management.* His research interests include strategic alliances, innovation management, and Industry 4.0.

Chiara Galimberti, Ph.D., is a Statistician and Data Scientist working for a company in the industrial sector. She received a Ph.D. degree in Statistics and Economics from the University of Milano-Bicocca (Italy) within a joint program in collaboration with Siemens Italy. She contributed with a novel approach in Bayesian graphical modeling for mixed data. She is also an Adjunct Lecturer at the University of Milan (Italy) for courses and laboratories on statistics and quantitative methods. Currently, her main research interests are Bayesian inference, graphical models, variational modeling together with topics related to the ethics of Artificial Intelligence solutions.

Fabio Greco is an Assistant Professor in Management at University of Naples Federico II and Founder of a start-up and Academic Spin-off. He was awarded a Ph.D. in Management. His main research topics are Entrepreneurship, Startup Ecosystems, Food Innovation, and the Management of Cultural Organizations. He wrote a doctoral thesis on the elements and main characteristics of Startup ecosystems, and the judgment from the commission was excellent. Among the main publications in international journals include "It gives you wheels: the university-based accelerators in start-up ecosystems" in the *International Journal of Entrepreneurship and Small Business.*

Wouter van Heeswijk is an Assistant Professor at the University of Twente, the Netherlands. He holds a Master's degree in Financial Engineering and a Ph.D. degree in Operations Research. As a researcher, he has been affiliated to the National Research Center for Mathematics and Computer Science (CWI) in Amsterdam and to the Technical University of Denmark (DTU) in Kongens Lyngby. Wouter is currently active in the domains of Financial Engineering and Operations Research, focusing his research activities primarily on the application of reinforcement learning in aforementioned domains.

Daniela Inclezan is an Associate Professor in Computer Science and Software Engineering at Miami University. Her area of research is artificial intelligence with a focus on knowledge representation and reasoning. Besides technical courses, Daniela teaches classes at the intersection of computer science and the humanities, on topics related to socio-environmental responsibility in computer science and engineering, and the relationship between ethics, global society, and technology. Daniela also serves as the chair of the committee that oversees the Humanitarian Engineering and Computing minor at Miami University.

Riadh Ksantini received the Bachelor's degree in Applied Mathematics and Computer Science from the Faculte des Sciences, Monastir, Tunisia, in 2000 and the M.Sc. and Ph.D. degrees in Computer Science from the Universite de Sherbrooke, Sherbrooke, QC, Canada, in 2003 and 2007, respectively. He is currently an Associate Professor in the Department of Computer Science, University of Bahrain, Kingdom of Bahrain. His research interests include Machine/Deep Learning, Pattern Recognition, and Computer Vision.

Marialuisa Marzullo (Ph.D.) holds a grant at the University of Naples Federico II. Her research interests are in the field of service innovation, service research, customer and patient experience, case theory, and digital transformation. Her most recent studies concern the application of smart technologies and customer engagement in the healthcare sector. She collaborates with international research centers, and she participated in numerous conferences on service innovation. Her articles have been published in the *Journal of Service Theory and Practice, Service Science, Journal of Service Management, Journal of Business Research, Journal of Business and Industrial Marketing,* and *Journal of Creating Value.*

Cristina Mele (Ph.D.) is a Full Professor of Service Innovation and the coordinator of the Ph.D. in Management in the Department of Economics, Management and Institutions at the University of Naples Federico II. She is delegated of Innovation and Third Mission at University. Her main research interests are innovation and smart technologies, value creation, markets, and service ecosystems. She has more than 270 publications. Her articles have appeared in the *Journal of The Academy of Marketing Science, Marketing Theory, Industrial Marketing Management, Journal of Business Research, Journal of Service Management,* and *Journal of Service Theory and Practice.* Cristina is one of co-chairs of The Naples Forum on Service. She is the recipient of the Service-dominant Logic Award (2019).

Luigi Moschera is a Full Professor of Organization Studies at the University of Naples "Parthenope" (Italy). He teaches Business Organization, Inter-firm Network Design, and HRM. His most recent research focuses on technology, contingent/alternative employment arrangements, and their implications for employees' attitudes, well-being, and behavior. He authored several international publications on organizational change in the temporary work agency sector in Italy and Europe.

Luis I. Prádanos (Iñaki) is a Professor of Contemporary Hispanic Cultural Studies at Miami University. He is the author of *Postgrowth Imaginaries*

(Liverpool UP, 2018) and the editor of *A Companion to Spanish Environmental Cultural Studies* (Tamesis, 2023). Iñaki's research and teaching interests include environmental humanities, political ecology of technology, critical energy studies, regenerative design, and postgrowth studies. His teaching approach is based on "The Pedagogy of Degrowth".

Marco Repetto is a Data Scientist and AI Assessor at CertX with a Ph.D. in Economics and Statistics from the University of Milano-Bicocca. He has contributed substantially to the field of Artificial Intelligence, focusing on Explainable AI and Federated Learning in various applications. Marco has been a visiting scholar at the AI Institute at SKEMA Business School, working on knowledge injection in Artificial Neural Networks. His analytical skills were honed during his tenure at Siemens, focusing on forecasting and prescriptive algorithms. As an educator, he has taught subjects such as mathematics and programming in Italy and France.

Michela De Rosa is Marketing and Business Development Specialist in Kelyon, a company specialized in design and development of Digital Health solutions. She earned a Bachelor's degree in Economics and Business Management, a Master's degree in Economics, and an Industrial Ph.D. in Big Data Management at the University of Salerno. She has collaborated with several research projects in the Digital Health field, focusing her research on the exploration of innovative solutions supported by sustainable business models and value creation processes, considering the efficiency and effective allocation of time, resources, and technologies in the patient-centered ecosystem.

Tiziana Russo Spena is a Full Professor of Management. She obtained her Ph.D. in Management and Economics in 2002. Her main areas of interest are innovation management, service innovation, and digital marketing. She has attended several international conferences and has co-authored over 100 refereed articles in journals and six books on innovation topics. She has written many articles and books and published in Italian and International journals, including the *Industrial Marketing and Management, Journal of Business Ethics, Journal of Service Management*, Journal of Business Research, Journal of Service Management*, and *Journal of Business and Industrial Marketing*. She is member of Reser – European Research Network on Services.

Lea Samek is an Economist at the Organisation for Economic Co-operation and Development (OECD) in the Science, Technology and Innovation (STI) Directorate. Her work encompasses a wide array of innovation and industry-policy-related topics including knowledge-based capital, the link between innovation and productivity, jobs and skills in digital transformation and Artificial Intelligence. She is also a Research Associate at the Economic Statistics Centre of Excellence (ESCoE). Previously Lea worked at the National Institute of Economic and Social Research in London and as a Visiting Lecturer at King's College London, from where she also obtained her Ph.D.

Mariagrazia Squicciarini is Chief of Executive Officer and Director a.i. at UNESCO's Social and Human Sciences Sector, where she leads policy-focused programs mainly related to Artificial Intelligence (AI) and neurotechnology; digital anthropology; futures and anticipatory approaches; and inequalities, inclusion, and gender. Before joining UNESCO, she was Senior Economist and Head of Unit at the OECD Directorate for Science, Technology and Innovation, where she led analysis on Intellectual Property Rights; knowledge-based capital, growth and productivity; digitalization and AI; job and skill dynamics; and the digital gender divide. She holds a Ph.D. in Economics from the University of Essex (UK).

Aizhan Tursunbayeva is an Assistant Professor at the University of Naples "Parthenope" (Italy). Her previous professional roles include Assistant Professor at the University of Twente (The Netherlands), Management Consultant at KPMG Advisory (Italy), and Manager at HSBC Bank (Canada, UK, Poland, and Kazakhstan). She teaches Organizational Design, Human Resource Management (HRM), and People Analytics. Her research lies at the intersection of HRM, technology, and innovation.

Introduction

Francesco Paolo Appio, Davide La Torre, Francesca Lazzeri, Hatem Masri and Francesco Schiavone

Artificial intelligence (AI hereafter) can be thought of as the "ability of a machine to perform cognitive functions that we associate with human minds, such as perceiving, reasoning, learning, interacting with the environment, problem-solving, decision-making, and even demonstrating creativity"(Rai et al., 2019, p. iii). Belonging to the realm of intelligent technologies (Bailey and Barley, 2020), it is increasingly accepted that AI has evolved from being merely a "development standpoint in computer science" (Skilton and Hovsepian, 2018, p. 269). Indeed, recent reports and academic publications (e.g., Ransbotham et al., 2017; Garbuio and Lin, 2019) show that we are clearly on the path towards pervasive AI and business is one of the macro areas in which AI is showcasing the wider range of applications and implications (Mikalef et al., 2021; Correia Loureiro et al., 2020; Akerkar, 2019).

More than 100 literature reviews[1] have been published in the last two decades, with 87 of them published in the last five years alone. They cover business topics that are closely related to sustainability (Kar et al., 2022; Bhagat et al., 2020; Vinuesa et al., 2020), healthcare (Tran et al., 2021; Secinaro et al., 2021), retail (Heins, 2022), digital technologies (Ashok et al., 2022), human resource management (Al Mubarak, 2022), accounting (Shaffer et al., 2020), project management (Elmousalami, 2021), supply chain management (Pournader et al., 2021), space industry (Izzo et al., 2019), among many others. In fact, potentially all sectors – i.e. healthcare (Leone et al., 2020; Stern et al., 2017), automotive (Liu, 2021), energy (Yue and Han, 2019), fintech (Hu, 2020) – as well as organizational functions – i.e. marketing (Huang and Rust, 2021), R&D (Viberg and Eslami, 2020), operations (Ontañón and Meseguer, 2015), accounting (Kokina and Davenport, 2017), logistics (Klumpp, 2018), human resource management (Pessach et al., 2020) – seem to be impacted.

Such a trend does not only concern the academic publications. Rather, it is something that reverberates in technological production. In 2021, the US Patent Office created a dedicated database of AI inventions (Giczy et al., 2022) called the Artificial Intelligence Patent Dataset (AIPD)[2] with the aim to "assist researchers and policymakers focusing on the determinants and impacts of artificial intelligence (AI) invention." A thorough overview of current trends in the AI patent landscape is provided in the WIPO report

DOI: 10.4324/9781003304616-1

on AI published in 2019[3]. The WIPO research revealed that half of the inventions had only recently been granted. Furthermore, the overall increase rate of patent activity from 2013 to 2016 was 10%. In contrast, the growth rate of AI-related patent activity across other technical fields is significantly higher; for instance, it reached 55% for robotics and control methods. The majority of AI patents cover multiple fields, with almost 70% of AI-related inventions including a combination of different AI techniques or functional applications (e.g., planning/scheduling, computer vision, among others). Telecommunications (15%), transportation (15%), life and medical sciences (12%), personal devices, computing, and human–computer interaction (11%), are the top industries patenting heavily in AI. The top patent assignees for AI technology typically have broad portfolios covering a variety of methods and applications. The top five leaders by portfolio size, as indicated by the WIPO data, are IBM (8,290 patents), Microsoft (5,930 patents), Toshiba (5,223 patents), Samsung (5,102 patents), and NEC (4,406 patents). By looking at the specific field of AI, the WIPO reports that the top patent assignees are Baidu (deep learning), Toyota and Bosch (transportation), Siemens, Philips, and Samsung (Life and medical sciences), and Facebook and Tencent (networks and social networks). China, United States, and Japan lead the race.

This brief overview illustrates how technology and science interact to influence the direction of AI development. But it is also fascinating to see how AI is affecting business and society.

Focusing on the business side, top reasons why organizations adopt AI (Ransbotham et al., 2017; Elmousalami, 2021; Muhlroth and Grottke, 2020; Davenport, 2018) involve maintaining a competitive advantage, entering new businesses, identifying new trends, coping with the threat of new entrants adopting AI as well as existing competitors using AI, pressure to reduce costs, suppliers offering – and customers asking for – AI-driven products and services. AI also offers business organizations unprecedented innovative opportunities (Rai et al., 2019; Akerkar, 2019; Mikalef and Gupta, 2021). For instance, AI technologies are critical in bringing about innovation (Haefner et al., 2021), providing new business models (Garbuio and Lin, 2019), reshaping the way organizations implement business intelligent systems (Arnott et al., 2017), rethinking collaborative strategies (Andres and Poler, 2016), designing intelligent products (Sohn and Kwon, 2020), devising novel service offerings (Huang and Rust, 2018), using differently existing business tools and inventing new forms of governance (Hilb, 2020), imagining and fostering new human-machine interactions to change the way we work (Davenport and Miller, 2022, and staying competitive on the market (Davenport, 2018).

However, does AI pervasiveness in business mean that it is getting better? Unfortunately, this is not clear at this stage. AI is becoming a prominent business buzzword (Akerkar, 2019) and many organizations continue to fail to effectively apply it to solve specific business cases (Davenport, 2018). And this is so for a number of reasons. For instance, business managers tend to consider AI as a technological panacea, neglecting the role of humans in the entire process (Shneiderman, 2020) and taking for granted widespread consensus when it comes to its acceptability and implementation. In addition, an important characteristic of AI is that it is not static, it learns and adapts (Akerkar, 2019); on this point, business organizations do not seem to keep up with the same pace, falling short in continuously learning and adapting their routines. AI can take a managerial role, either in itself or in conjunction with human managers. These new forms of agency can challenge long-held notions about how work routines form, how outcomes from work are produced, or what the role of a manager entails (Pentland et al., 2020). Furthermore, the difficult part is integrating AI into existing systems and business processes (Davenport, 2018). It is also possible that AI investments are prohibitively expensive, or that managers do not understand what AI is and how it works, or that there is a lack of expertise to fully exploit such technologies (Davenport, 2018).

Overall, the business adoption of AI is at a very early stage but growing at a significant rate (Akerkar, 2019). According to Davenport (2018), companies are now taking a cautious approach to AI, with many companies experimenting with AI technologies and investing financial and non-financial resources in a few pilots. However, AI is steadily passing into everyday business use. From workflow management to trend predictions and from customer service to dynamic price optimization, AI has many different usages in business. What makes things uncertain is that accompanying the horizon of possibilities are a host of multidisciplinary and complex challenges around business strategies (Borges et al., 2021), human-machine interfaces (Shneiderman, 2020; Colapinto et al., 2021; Najmaei and Kermani, 2011; Knott and Vlugter, 2008; Davenport and Miller, 2022), data privacy and security (Cheng et al., 2021), and ethics (Bench-Capon, 2020), labor (Flanagan and Walker, 2020; Bailey and Barley, 2020). Furthermore, while there are many aspects of a business that can be automated (Davenport, 2018; Davenport and Miller, 2022), and should be automated, tasks that require judgment, prioritization, and trade-offs still require human intelligence. Today's managers need to deal with both opportunities and challenges that accompany widespread AI. This is why it is of utmost importance to not neglect the relevance of contextualization, communication, and practice of AI in business (Ågerfalk, 2021; Davenport, 2018).

As previously stated, AI has the potential to impact society. What AI does is amplify the impact of certain issues, primarily those concerning misuse, privacy, bias, safety and security, transparency, and sustainability. About misuse, deepfakes are created by using AI techniques to craft or manipulate audio and visual content to make it appear authentic. Deepfakes, a hybrid of "deep learning" and "fake media," are ideal for future disinformation campaigns because they are difficult to distinguish from legitimate content, even with the use of technological solutions. Deepfakes can reach millions of people in different parts of the world at unprecedented speeds due to the widespread use of the internet and social media (Floridi, 2018; Karnouskos, 2020). Users' password guessing supported by AI poses another set of challenges (Xia et al., 2020; Guembe et al., 2022). Using neural networks and Generative Adversarial Networks (GANs), cybercriminals would be able to analyze large password datasets and generate password variations that fit the statistical distribution. This may lead to more accurate and targeted password guesses, as well as increased profit potential. Cybercriminals are also using AI to mimic human behavior (Tubaro et al., 2020, Yang et al., 2019). They can, for example, successfully fool bot detection systems on social media platforms like Spotify by mimicking human-like usage patterns. Cybercriminals can then monetize the malicious system by generating fraudulent streams and traffic for a specific artist using AI-assisted impersonation. An AI-powered Spotify bot on the forum *nulled[.]to* claims to be capable of simulating multiple Spotify users at the same time. It employs multiple proxies to avoid detection. This bot boosts streaming counts (and thus monetization) for specific songs. To avoid detection even further, it creates playlists with other songs that reflect human-like musical tastes rather than playlists with random songs, as the latter may indicate bot-like behavior.

Furthermore, AI can jeopardize privacy in a variety of ways (Manheim and Kaplan, 2019; Qiu et al., 2020). There may be exploitation of data taken without consent. In fact, most people have no idea how much data their software and devices generate, process, or share; and as we become more reliant on digital technology in our daily lives, the opportunity for exploitation will grow. AI can be also used to identify, track, and monitor people across multiple devices, whether they are at work, at home, or in public (Almeida et al., 2022). This means that even if your personal data is anonymized once it is included in a large data set, an AI can de-anonymize it using inferences from other devices. This blurs the line between personal and non-personal data, which is required by current legislation. Voice recognition and facial recognition are two methods of identification that AI is getting better at (Jan et al., 2018). These methods have the potential to severely jeopardize anonymity in public. For example, law enforcement agencies can use facial recognition and voice recognition to locate individuals who do not have probable cause or reasonable suspicion, thereby avoiding legal procedures that they would otherwise have to follow. AI can also utilize sophisticated machine learning algorithms to infer or predict sensitive information from non-sensitive forms of data (Sağbaş et al., 2020). For instance, someone's keyboard typing patterns can be utilized to deduce their emotional states such as nervousness, confidence, sadness, and anxiety. Even more alarming, a person's political views, ethnic identity, sexual orientation, and even overall health can also be determined from data such as activity logs, location data, and similar metrics. AI is not limited to information-gathering tasks. It can also use data as input for sorting, scoring, classifying, evaluating, and ranking people. This is frequently done without people's consent, and they frequently lack the ability to influence or challenge the outcomes of these tasks. China's social scoring system (implemented in 2018 after city trials) (Creemers, 2018) exemplifies how this information can be used to restrict access to things like credit, employment, housing, and social services.

Another class of issues may stem from bias. AI bias is a deviation in the output of machine learning algorithms caused by biased assumptions made during the algorithm development process or biases in the training data. Biases exist in AI systems for two reasons: cognitive biases and lack of complete data (Kliegr et al., 2021). Cognitive biases are unconsciously held beliefs that influence people's judgments and decisions. The brain's attempt to simplify processing information about the world results in these biases. Psychologists have defined and classified over 180 human biases. Cognitive biases may infiltrate machine learning algorithms through either designers unknowingly introducing them to the model or a training data set containing those biases. If the data is incomplete, it may not be representative and thus may contain bias. Most psychology research studies, for example, include results from undergraduate students, who are a specific group that does not represent the entire population. As a consequence, there are no quick fixes for eliminating all biases. You can build an AI system that makes unbiased data–driven decisions if you can clean your training dataset of conscious and unconscious assumptions about race, gender, or other ideological concepts. However, behind AI are humans, who can be deeply biased in their own right.

Another way AI can pose risks to society is when it is programmed to do something dangerous, such as autonomous weapons programmed to kill (Gómez de Ágreda, 2020). It is even possible that the nuclear arms race will be replaced by a global autonomous weapons race. Moreover, not only is it critical to have cybersecurity systems in place to defend against and prevent threats, but it is also critical to have the right one that synergizes with your company's needs. Manual document classification for documents, emails, and text messages is difficult and necessitates technical knowledge. Deep-learning transformers simplify those tasks and, when used correctly, can be used to save money and time. However, an AI model with incorrect settings can generate false positives and, as a result, too many alerts, causing security teams headaches. As a result, when selecting products with AI components, one should always seek expert advice. Next-generation AI tools will be capable of automating your business processes with minimal setup, human intervention, rules, and so on.

AI has two issues with transparency (Haibe-Kains et al., 2020). The first is concerned with public perception and understanding of how AI works, while the second is concerned with how much developers actually know about their own AI. When you ask people from various backgrounds about the current state of AI, you will hear responses pointing to its uselessness or the fear of robots taking control. Many people may be interacting with AI without realizing it. Many times, developers have no idea how a machine learning algorithm works, even in closed systems where identifying logic flaws appears to be nearly impossible. Trust is founded on historical accuracy and probability, not on a formula that can be audited for accuracy and predictability.

When it comes to sustainability, from recent research, it emerges that combining AI and sustainable development can assist all industries in designing a better planet that meets current needs without jeopardizing future generations due to climate change or other major challenges (Nishant et al., 2020; Khakurel et al., 2018). AI's emergence is reshaping a growing number of industries. For example, AI is expected to have a short and long-term impact on global productivity (Acemoglu and Restrepo, 2018), equality and inclusion (Bolukbasi et al., 2016), environmental outcomes (Norouzzadeh et al., 2018), and several other areas (Tegmark, 2017). AI is the ally that sustainable development requires to more effectively design, execute, advise, and plan the future of our planet and its sustainability. AI, for example, will help us build more efficiently, use resources more sustainably, and reduce and manage waste more effectively, among other things. The reported potential impacts of AI on sustainable development indicate both positive (Neal et al., 2016) and negative (Courtland, 2018) impacts. According to a study published in Nature (Vinuesa et al., 2020), AI could help achieve 79% of the Sustainable Development Goals (SDGs). The researchers point out that it is imperative to strengthen the links between science and engineering, industry and governments, to reinforce dialog and expand the different avenues toward achieving SDGs (Nilsson et al., 2016; Truby, 2020). However, the research mentioned above does not consider AI as part of the problem. In fact, to seriously address the SDGs, we must consider AI as a non-neutral technology. Recent research shows that AI can also be an inhibitor for SDGs (Gupta et al., 2021; Vinuesa et al., 2020). Furthermore, as clearly stated in the recently published book "Atlas of AI" (Crawford, 2021), AI is not sustainable in and of itself (Van Wynsberghe, 2021; Robbins and Van Wynsberghe, 2022). AI does not (in its current state) exhibit virtuous signs, whether viewed from an environmental (Brevini, 2020; Hao, 2019; Lin, 2021; Strubell et al., 2019; Yu et al., 2022), labor, data, political, social, or ethical (Floridi et al., 2018) standpoint. Rather, AI is defined as a novel "extractive industry": the development of modern AI systems is dependent on the extraction of energy and mineral resources from the planet, as well as cheap labor and data at scale. According to Strubell et al. (2019), training AI models for natural language processing (NLP) can produce 5× the lifetime emissions of an American car, or the equivalent of 300 round-trip flights between San Francisco and New York. Large AI model training can generate over 626,000 pounds of CO_2 equivalent - nearly five times the lifetime emissions of the average American car (and that includes manufacture of the car itself). What is critical today is that there are very few studies that help companies understand what the carbon impact of AI is. Furthermore, we do not yet know the carbon footprint of all types of AI. We must connect AI to socio-technical systems rather than relegating AI to a purely technical domain. And in so doing, we must consider what is being optimized, for whom, and who has the final say. Then we need to trace the implications of those choices. Nowadays, there is a tendency to over trust AI technologies, considering their supply chain and life cycles as a black box. We need an AI theory that takes into account the states and corporations that drive and dominate it, the extractive mining that harms the environment, mass data collection, and the profoundly unequal and increasingly exploitative labor practices that sustain it. We must trace the supply chain of AI technologies used by businesses, determine whether more sustainable alternatives exist, and opt for them. Furthermore, we must conduct life cycle assessments of AI technologies in order to understand their impact from conception to disposal.

The chapters in this Handbook attempt to shed light on some of these numerous aspects. We hope that the issues they address will inspire future researchers to take a serious look at the challenges and opportunities of AI for business and society.

Notes

1 Scopus extraction date: 30 November 2022. Query: TITLE ("artificial intelligence") AND (LIMIT-TO (DOCTYPE, "re")) AND (LIMIT-TO (SUBJAREA, "BUSI"))
2 https://www.uspto.gov/ip-policy/economic-research/research-datasets/artificial-intelligence-patent-dataset
3 https://www.wipo.int/publications/en/details.jsp?id=4386

References

Acemoglu, D., Restrepo, P. (2018). The race between man and machine: Implications of technology for growth, factor shares, and employment. *American Economic Review*, 108 (6): 1488–1542.

Ågerfalk, P.J. (2021). Artificial intelligence as digital agency. *European Journal of Information Systems*, 29: 1–8.

Akerkar, R. (2019). *Artificial Intelligence for Business*. SpringerBriefs in Business. Springer.

Al Mubarak, M. (2022). Sustainably developing in a digital world: Harnessing artificial intelligence to meet the imperatives of work-based learning in Industry 5.0. *Development and Learning in Organizations*, in Press.

Almeida, D., Shmarko, K. Lomas, E. (2022). The ethics of facial recognition technologies, surveillance, and accountability in an age of artificial intelligence: A comparative analysis of US, EU, and UK regulatory frameworks. *AI and Ethics*, 2: 377–387.

Andres, B., Poler, R. (2016). A decision support system for the collaborative selection of strategies in enterprise networks. *Decision Support Systems*, 91: 113–123.

Arnott, D., Lizama, F., Song, Y. (2017). Patterns of business intelligence systems use in organizations. *Decision Support Systems*, 97: 58–68.

Ashok, M., Madan, R., Joha, A., Sivarajah, U. (2022). Ethical framework for Artificial Intelligence and Digital technologies. *International Journal of Information Management*, 62: 102433.

Bailey, D.E., Barley, S.R. (2020). Beyond design and use: How scholars should study intelligent technologies. *Information and Organization*, 30 (2): 100286.

Bench-Capon, T.J.M. (2020). Ethical approaches and autonomous systems. *Artificial Intelligence*, 281: 103239.

Bhagat, S.K., Tung, T.M., Yaseen, Z.M. (2020). Development of artificial intelligence for modeling wastewater heavy metal removal: State of the art, application assessment and possible future research. *Journal of Cleaner Production*, 250: 119473.

Bolukbasi, T., Chang, K.-W., Zou, J.Y., Saligrama, V., Kalai, A.T. (2016). Man is to computer programmer as woman is to homemaker? Debiasing word embeddings. In D. Lee, M. Sugiyama, U. Luxburg, I. Guyon, and R. Garnett (eds.), *Advances in Neural Information Processing Systems*, 4349–4357.

Borges, A.F.S., Laurindo, F.J.B., Spinola, M.M., Goncalves, R.F., Mattos, C.A. (2021). The strategic use of artificial intelligence in the digital era: Systematic literature review and future research directions. *International Journal of Information Management*, 57: 102225.

Brevini, B. (2020). Black boxes, not green: Mythologizing artificial intelligence and omitting the environment. *Big Data & Society*, 7(2), 1–5.

Cheng, X., Su, L., Luo, X.R., Benitez, J., Cai, S. (2021) The good, the bad, and the ugly: Impact of analytics and artificial intelligence-enabled personal information collection on privacy and participation in ridesharing. *European Journal of Information Systems*, 31, 339–363.

Colapinto, C., Durosini, I., La Torre, D., Triberti, S. (2021). Team formation for human-artificial intelligence collaboration in the workplace: A goal programming model to foster organizational change. *IEEE Transactions on Engineering Management*, 70, 1966–1976.

Correia Loureiro, S.M., Guerreiro, J., Tussyadiah, I. (2020). Artificial intelligence in business: State of the art and future research agenda. *Journal of Business Research*, 129, 911–926.

Courtland R. (2018). Bias detectives: The researchers striving to make algorithms fair. *Nature*, 558: 357–360.

Crawford, K. (2021). *Atlas of AI*. Yale University Press.

Creemers, R. (2018). China's social credit system: An evolving practice of control (May 9, 2018). Available at SSRN: https://ssrn.com/abstract=3175792.

Davenport, T.H. (2018). *The AI Advantage: How to Put the Artificial Intelligence Revolution to Work*. MIT Press.

Davenport, T.H., Miller, S.M. (2022). *Working with AI: Real Stories of Human-Machine Collaboration*. MIT Press.

Elmousalami, H.H. (2021). Comparison of artificial intelligence techniques for project conceptual cost prediction: A case study and comparative analysis. *IEEE Transactions on Engineering Management*, 68 (1): 183–196.

Flanagan, F., Walker, M. (2020). How can unions use artificial intelligence to build power? The use of AI chatbots for labour organising in the US and Australia. *New Technology, Work and Employment*, 36, 159–176.

Floridi, L. (2018). Artificial intelligence, deepfakes and a future of ectypes. *Philosophy & Technology*, 31: 317–321.

Floridi, L., et al. (2018). AI4People—An ethical framework for a good AI society: opportunities, risks, principles, and recommendations. *Minds and Machines*, 28: 689–707.

Garbuio, M., Lin, N. (2019). Artificial intelligence as a growth engine for health care startups: Emerging business models. *California Management Review*, 61 (2): 59–83.

Giczy, A.V., Pairolero, N.A., Toole, A.A. (2022). Identifying artificial intelligence (AI) invention: A novel AI patent dataset. *Journal of Technology Transfer*, 47: 476–505.

Gómez de Ágreda, A. (2020). Ethics of autonomous weapons systems and its applicability to any AI systems. *Telecommunications Policy*, 44 (6): 101953.

Guembe, B., Azeta, A., Misra, S., Osamor, V.C., Fernandez-Sanz, L., Pospelova, V. (2022) The emerging threat of Ai-driven cyber attacks: A review. *Applied Artificial Intelligence*, 36: 1.

Gupta, S., Langhans, S.D., Domisch, S., Fuso-Nerini, F., Felländer, A., Battaglini, M., Tegmark, M., Vinuesa, R. (2021). Assessing whether artificial intelligence is an enabler or an inhibitor of sustainability at indicator level. *Transportation Engineering*, 4: 100064.

Haefner, N., Wincent, J., Parida, V., Gassmann, O. (2021). Artificial intelligence and innovation management: A review, framework, and research agenda. *Technological Forecasting and Social Change*, 162: 120392.

Haibe-Kains, B., et al. (2020). Transparency and reproducibility in artificial intelligence. *Nature*, 586: E14–E16.

Hao, K. (2019). Training a single AI model can emit as much carbon as five cars in their lifetimes. *MIT Technology Review*. Available at: https://www.technologyreview.com/2019/06/06/239031/training-a-single-ai-model-can-emit-as-much-carbon-as-five-cars-in-their-lifetimes/

Heins, C. (2022). Artificial intelligence in retail – A systematic literature review. Foresight, in Press.

Hilb, M. (2020). Toward artificial governance? The role of artificial intelligence in shaping the future of corporate governance. *Journal of Management and Governance*, 24 (4): 851–870.

Hu, Z. (2020). Research on fintech methods based on artificial intelligence. *Journal of Physics: Conference Series*, 1684 (1): 012034.

Huang, M.-H., Rust, R.T. (2018). Artificial intelligence in service. *Journal of Service Research*, 21 (2): 155–172.

Huang, M.-H., Rust, R.T. (2021). A strategic framework for artificial intelligence in marketing. *Journal of the Academy of Marketing Science*, 49 (1): 30–50.

Izzo, D., Märtens, M., Pan, B. (2019). A survey on artificial intelligence trends in spacecraft guidance dynamics and control. *Astrodynamics*, 3: 287–299.

Jan, A., Meng, H., Gaus, Y.F.B.A., Zhang, F. (2018). Artificial intelligent system for automatic depression level analysis through visual and vocal expressions. *IEEE Transactions on Cognitive and Developmental Systems*, 10 (3): 668–680.

Kar, A.K., Choudhary, S.K., Singh, V.K. (2022). How can artificial intelligence impact sustainability: A systematic literature review. *Journal of Cleaner Production*, 376: 134120.

Karnouskos, S. (2020). Artificial intelligence in digital media: The era of deepfakes. *IEEE Transactions on Technology and Society*, 1 (3): 138–147.

Khakurel, J., Penzenstadler, B., Porras, J., Knutas, A., Zhang, W. (2018). The rise of artificial intelligence under the lens of sustainability. *Technologies*, 6 (100): 1–18.

Kliegr, T., Bahník, S., Fürnkranz, J. (2021). A review of possible effects of cognitive biases on interpretation of rule-based machine learning models. *Artificial Intelligence*, 295: 103458.

Klumpp, M. (2018). Automation and artificial intelligence in business logistics systems: Human reactions and collaboration requirements. *International Journal of Logistics Research and Applications*, 21 (3): 224–242.

Knott, A., Vlugter, P. (2008). Multi-agent human–machine dialogue: Issues in dialogue management and referring expression semantics. *Artificial Intelligence*, 172 (2–3): 69–102.

Kokina, J., Davenport, T.H. (2017). The emergence of artificial intelligence: How automation is changing auditing. *Journal of Emerging Technologies in Accounting*, 14 (1): 115–122.

Leone, D., Schiavone, F., Appio, F.P., Chiao, B. (2020). How does artificial intelligence enable and enhance value co-creation in industrial markets? An exploratory case study in the healthcare ecosystem. *Journal of Business Research*, 129, 849–859.

Lin, H.Y. (2021). Colors of artificial intelligence. *Computer*, 54 (11): 95–99.

Liu, L. (2021). Artificial intelligence in the field of driverless cars. *Advances in Intelligent Systems and Computing*, 1303: 794–799.

Manheim, K., Kaplan, L. (2019). Artificial intelligence: Risks to privacy and democracy. *Yale Journal of Law and Technology*, 106 (21): 108–185.

Mikalef, P., Gupta, M. (2021). Artificial intelligence capability: Conceptualization, measurement calibration, and empirical study on its impact on organizational creativity and firm performance. *Information and Management*, 58 (3): 103434.

Mikalef, P., Pappas, I.O., Krogstie, J., Jaccheri, L., Rana, N. (2021). Editors' reflections and introduction to the special section on 'artificial intelligence and business value'. *International Journal of Information Management*, 57: 102313.

Muhlroth, C., Grottke, M. (2020). Artificial intelligence in innovation: How to spot emerging trends and technologies. *IEEE Transactions on Engineering Management*, 69, 493–510.

Najmaei, N., Kermani, M.R. (2011). Applications of artificial intelligence in safe human-robot interactions. *IEEE Transactions on Systems, Man, and Cybernetics, Part B: Cybernetics*, 41 (2): 448–459.

Neal, J., Burke, M., Xie, M., Davis, W.M., Lobell, D.B., Ermon, S. (2016). Combining satellite imagery and machine learning to predict poverty. *Science*, 353 (6301): 790–794.

Nilsson, M., Griggs, D., Visbeck, M. (2016). Map the interactions between sustainable development goals. *Nature*, 534: 320–322.

Nishant, R., Kennedy, M., Corbett, J. (2020). Artificial intelligence for sustainability: Challenges, opportunities, and a research agenda. *International Journal of Information Management*, 53: 102104.

Norouzzadeh, M.S., Nguyen, A., Kosmala, M., Swanson, A., Palmer, M.S., Packer, C., Clune, J. (2018). Automatically identifying, counting, and describing wild animals in camera-trap images with deep learning. *PNAS*, 115 (25): E5716–E5725.

Ontañón, S., Meseguer, P. (2015). Speeding up operations on feature terms using constraint programming and variable symmetry. *Artificial Intelligence*, 220: 104–120.

Pentland, B.T., Liu, P., Kremser, W., Hærem, T. (2020). The dynamics of drift in digitized processes. *MIS Quarterly*, 44, 19–47.

Pessach, D., Singer, G., Avrahami, D., Chalutz Ben-Gal, H., Shmueli, E., Ben-Gal, I. (2020). Employees recruitment: A prescriptive analytics approach via machine learning and mathematical programming. *Decision Support Systems*, 134: 113290.

Pournader, M., Ghaderi, H., Hassanzadegan, A., Fahimnia, B. (2021). Artificial intelligence applications in supply chain management. *International Journal of Production Economics*, 241, 108250.

Qiu, M., Dai, H.-N., Sangaiah, A.K., Liang, K., Zheng, X. (2020). Guest editorial: Special section on emerging privacy and security issues brought by artificial intelligence in industrial informatics. *IEEE Transactions on Industrial Informatics*, 16 (3): 2029–2030.

Rai, A., Constantinides, P., Sarker, S. (2019). Editor's comments: Next-generation digital platforms: Toward human–AI hybrids. *MIS Quarterly*, 43 (1): iii–ix.

Ransbotham, S., Kiron, D., Gerbert, P., Reeves, M. (2017). Reshaping Business with Artificial Intelligence. MIT Sloan Management Review and The Boston Consulting Group. Available at: https://sloanreview.mit.edu/projects/reshaping-business-with-artificial-intelligence/

Robbins, S., Van Wynsberghe, A. (2022). Our new artificial intelligence infrastructure: Becoming locked into an unsustainable future. *Sustainability*, 14: 1–11.

Sağbaş, E.A., Korukoglu, S. Balli, S. (2020). Stress detection via keyboard typing behaviors by using smartphone sensors and machine learning techniques. *Journal of Medical Systems*, 44: 68.

Secinaro, S., Calandra, D., Secinaro, A., Muthurangu, V., Biancone, P. (2021). The role of artificial intelligence in healthcare: A structured literature review. *BMC Medical Informatics and Decision Making*, 21: 125.

Shaffer, K.J., Gaumer, C.J., Bradley, K.P. (2020). Artificial intelligence products reshape accounting: Time to re-train. *Development and Learning in Organizations*, 34 (6), 41–43.

Shneiderman, B. (2020). Human-centered artificial intelligence: Reliable, safe & trustworthy. *International Journal of Human–Computer Interaction*, 36 (6): 495–504.

Skilton, M., Hovsepian, F. (2018). *The 4th Industrial Revolution: Responding to the Impact of Artificial Intelligence on Business*. Palgrave Macmillan.

Sohn, K., Kwon, O. (2020). Technology acceptance theories and factors influencing artificial Intelligence-based intelligent products. *Telematics and Informatics*, 47: 101324.

Stern, R., Kalech, M., Rogov, S., Feldman, A. (2017). How many diagnoses do we need? *Artificial Intelligence*, 248: 26–45.

Tegmark, M. (2017). *Life 3.0: Being Human in the Age of Artificial Intelligence*. Vintage Books.

Tran, T.Q.B., du Toit, C., Padmanabhan, S. (2021). Artificial intelligence in healthcare-the road to precision medicine. *Journal of Hospital Management and Health Policy*, 5: 29.

Truby, J. (2020). Governing artificial intelligence to benefit the UN sustainable development goals. *Sustainable Development*, 28: 946–959.

Tubaro, P., Casilli, A.A., Coville, M. (2020). The trainer, the verifier, the imitator: Three ways in which human platform workers support artificial intelligence. *Big Data & Society*, 7 (1), 1–12.

Van Wynsberghe (2021). Sustainable AI: AI for sustainability and the sustainability of AI. *AI and Ethics*, 1: 213–218.

Viberg, D., Eslami, M.H. (2020). The effect of machine learning on knowledge-intensive R&D in the technology industry. *Technology Innovation Management Review*, 10 (3): 87–97.

Vinuesa, R., Azizpour, H., Leite, I., Balaam, M., Dignum, V., Domisch, S., Felländer, A., Langhans, S.D., Tegmark, M., Fuso Nerini, F. (2020). The role of artificial intelligence in achieving the sustainable development goals. *Nature Communications*, 11 (1): 233.

Xia, Z., Yi, P., Liu, Y., Jiang, B., Wang, W., Zhu, T. (2020). GENPass: A multi-source deep learning model for password guessing. *IEEE Transactions on Multimedia*, 22 (5): 1323–1332.

Yang, K.-C., Varol, O., Davis, C.A., Ferrara, E., Flammini, A., Menczer, F. (2019). Arming the public with artificial intelligence to counter social bots. *Human Behavior and Emerging Technologies*, 1 (1): 48–61.

Yu, J.-R., Chen, C.-H., Huang, T.-W., Lu, J.-J., Chung, C.-R., Lin, T.-W., Wu, M.-H., Tseng, Y.-J., Wang, H.-Y. (2022). Energy efficiency of inference algorithms for clinical laboratory data sets: Green artificial intelligence study. *Journal of Medical Internet Research*, 24 (1): 1–17.

Yue, D., Han, Q.-L. (2019). Guest editorial special issue on new trends in energy internet: Artificial intelligence-based control, network security, and management. *IEEE Transactions on Systems, Man, and Cybernetics: Systems*, 49 (8): 1551–1553.

Part 1

Artificial Intelligence

Technological Advancements and Methodologies

1 Artificial Intelligence and Machine Learning

Definitions and Applications

*Cinzia Colapinto, Riadh Ksantini, Davide La Torre,
Hatem Masri and Marco Repetto*

1.1 Introduction

What is Artificial Intelligence (AI)? Nowadays, it is broadly accepted that this label identifies an interdisciplinary area and is based on the ability of a machine to learn from experience, simulate human intelligence, adapt to new scenarios, and get engaged in human-like activities. Indeed, AI is an interdisciplinary field that attempts to create machines that act rationally in response to their environment. The world of AI is booming, and it seems no industry or sector has remained untouched by its impact and prevalence.

The goal of AI is to allow computers to learn and work on their own, just like humans. Many experts and academics maintain that AI is the future, and it is improving our everyday lives. Companies such as Google and Facebook have invested a lot of money in AI research and are constantly working on new ways to integrate AI to improve their services. AI can analyze data from obvious sources, add value by assimilating patterns of images, voice, video, and text, and transform them into meaningful, actionable information for decision-making. Trends, outliers, and patterns are determined using Machine Learning (ML)-based algorithms that help guide a travel or hospitality company to make informed decisions. AI is playing a more and more crucial role in the economic, social, and scientific areas of business and society. It is well recognized that AI will be outperforming humans on most cognitive tasks in this century as well as it will be more disrupting than any previous technological revolution.

According to the *United Nations Conference on Trade and Development*, AI is already having a significant impact on the economy and the labor market. Projections show that AI will increase labor productivity by up to 40% and create $13 trillion in additional wealth by 2030 (McKinsey Global Institute, 2019): AI economic impact will be driven by consumer surplus—the value consumers derive from using a good or service over and above the price they pay—and labor-productivity gains.

In general, AI is a broad term that includes everything that computers can do that normally cannot be done by humans. In the strict sense, AI involves machines that can perform tasks beyond the capability of humans. A specific

DOI: 10.4324/9781003304616-3

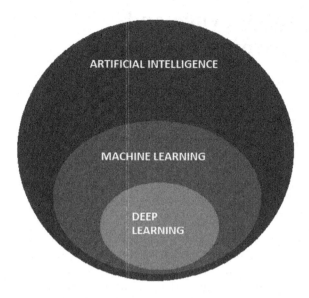

Figure 1.1 Relationships between the three concepts.

subset of AI is ML. ML uses algorithms to learn from data to make future decisions or predictions. Machines are trained to solve problems without explicitly programming them to do so. Instead, the expression Deep learning, denotes a specific subset of ML using artificial neural networks (ANNs), which are layered structures inspired by the human brain. Figure 1.1 represents these three different levels.

This chapter is organized as follows: Section 2 introduces the main definitions while Section 3 reviews some applications of AI techniques and technologies to different domains. Section 4 draws our conclusion.

1.2 Artificial Intelligence

As just mentioned, AI refers to an interdisciplinary field–encompassing biology, computer science, philosophy, mathematics, engineering, and robotics, and cognitive science-concerned with simulating human intelligence using computer-based technologies (Figure 1.2).

AI domains are split into two major domains: data versus human-centric AI. Data-centric AI refers to any AI methods and techniques that need data to be trained and therefore able to make forecasting and predictions.

Most data-centric methods define visual qualities using volumetric data information. For instance, early studies only used 1D Transfer Functions (TFs), which were created solely using the histogram of voxel intensity values (i.e. Khan *et al.*, 2018). However, it was challenging to distinguish

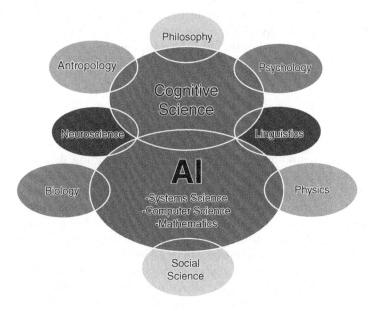

Figure 1.2 Interdisciplinary AI.

between various materials only based on scalar values, particularly when they had comparable intensities. The concept of creating multidimensional TFs based on scalar value and derivative information was initially used by (Kindlmann and Durkin, 1998). They considered the resulting histogram to design a model to emphasize borders between homogenous zones, which are known as arches. Other approaches are instead image-centric and they are developed using rendered images rather than volume attributes. They assess projective images and automatically modify parameters based on the initial data until a good rendering outcome is obtained. A well-liked image-centric strategy is the Marks *et al.* (1997) design gallery method. In this procedure, a set of input parameters that produce dissimilar output values at the optimal level are varied to produce several different TFs. The user just makes a choice from the options that are offered to optimize the final visualization results.

By contrast, human-centric AI comprises any AI system that amplifies and augments rather than displaces human abilities. Human-centric AI seeks to preserve human control in a way that ensures AI meets needs while also operating transparently and ethically, delivering equitable outcomes, respecting privacy, and showing fairness in ML predictions. One of the main goals of human-centric AI is to make sure that AI technologies are designed and used in ways that support and empower humans. To achieve this, human-centric AI systems need to be transparent and explainable (explainable AI, or XAI), so that humans can understand how they work and why they make the decisions they do and, even more important, trust results. Indeed, explanations in XAI should provide the reasons why managers and professionals should rely on the system in practice—that is, they should address the epistemic concerns of those using the system in specific contexts and specific occasions.

1.2.1 Machine Learning

The sub-field of AI, ML can be divided into two primary families of ML algorithms: supervised and unsupervised learning. The former refers to the process of learning an unknown function using labeled training data and example input-output pairs. In contrast, unsupervised learning refers to the detection of previously unnoticed patterns and information in an unlabeled data set. Both have their own advantages and disadvantages. Supervised learning is typically more accurate than unsupervised learning, but it can be more difficult to train supervised learning algorithms on large data sets. In contrast, unsupervised learning algorithms can be easier to train on large data sets, but they may be less accurate than supervised learning algorithms.

There are many different types of ML algorithms, but some of the most common include support vector machines (SVMs), decision trees, ANN, and k-means clustering.

Many current ML applications, aided by the quantity of data, necessitate a significant amount of training. Local rules, on the other hand, posed severe limitations in terms of data transfer in distributed systems. As quite recently the notion of Federated Learning (FL) has been proposed. FL is a distributed learning methodology that allows model training on decentralized data. With dispersed data across multiple nodes, the decision maker must deal with opposing node objectives as well as potential hostile threats. This last one is also known as adversarial training.

1.2.1.1 Regression Vs Classification

Problems with classification predictive modeling are distinct from those with regression predictive modeling. Regression is the challenge of forecasting a continuous quantity, whereas Classification is the task of predicting a discrete class label. However, the algorithms for classification and regression have some overlaps, for instance: A continuous value may be predicted by a classification algorithm, and the continuous value will take the form of a probability for a class label; a discrete value may be predicted by a regression technique, but it would be an integer number.

With little adjustments, some algorithms (such as decision trees and ANN) can be utilized for both classification and regression. On the contrary, some techniques, such as linear regression for regression predictive modeling and logistic regression for classification predictive modeling, cannot be applied to both types of problems.

1.2.1.2 Incremental Learning Vs Batch Learning

Implementations of the existing classical classification algorithms typically presumptively assume that all the data are given upfront and that the learning process is completed in a single step. Consequently, batch learning is the name given to these methods. Due to this restriction, batch approaches suffer a significant performance hit in real-world applications when data are not immediately available. A fresh approach to learning is necessary in this circumstance. When working with non-stationary or very large amounts of data, incremental learning is superior to batch learning. As a result, it is used in a wide range of contexts, including visual tracking, software project estimation, brain computer interface, surveillance systems, cybersecurity, online shopping, etc. Without access to the original data, incremental models should be able to learn new information from fresh data. They should also keep track of previously learned information and apply it to improve an existing classifier.

1.2.1.3 One-Class Classification

The primary responsibility of One-Class Classification is to identify unusual or flawed behavior. It is usually assumed that information from normal operation is easy to collect during a training process, but most faults do not, or rarely appear. Therefore, there are two main causes:

1   It is either impossible or extremely expensive to measure outlier data objects. For instance, it is feasible to quantify the attributes required for a nuclear power plant to operate normally. In the event of an accident, it is either too risky or impossible to measure the same features. In this case, a classifier must be trained solely using data from the target class of normal circumstances.

2   There are target items and a small number of skewed outliers available for training. This typically occurs in unusual medical conditions or tumor identification, where there is a dearth of non-target data available during training. In these circumstances, outliers cannot always be trusted because of their poor representation.

1.2.2 Reinforcement Learning

Reinforcement learning (RL) is an area of ML concerned with how intelligent agents take actions in an environment by maximizing some notion of reward. RL is one of three basic ML paradigms, alongside supervised learning, and unsupervised learning. RL differs from supervised learning in not needing labeled input/output pairs to be presented. The focus is on finding a balance between exploration and exploitation. The environment is typically based on Markov Decision Process because many RL algorithms for this context use dynamic programming techniques. Essentially there are three main types of RL:

1   Positive RL: where a reward is given for a desired action.
2   Negative RL: where punishment is given for an undesired action.
3   Extrinsic RL: the agent is rewarded based on the actions of another agent(s).

Because of its flexibility, RL has been used in a variety of domains, including but not limited to gaming, robotics, and control systems.

1.2.3 Ethics and Human–Machine Interaction AI

As said above, with the word Human-machine interaction AI we define any AI system that amplifies and augments rather than displaces human abilities. In this sense, human-centered AI is more oriented toward augmented intelligence rather than AI. One of the main goals of human-centered AI is to make sure that AI technologies are designed and used in ways that support and empower humans. To achieve this, these AI systems need to be transparent and explainable, so that humans can understand how they work and why they make the decisions they do. Additionally, these AI systems need to be designed with human values in mind, so that they can be trusted to act in ways that are ethical and fair.

1.2.4 Quantum Machine Learning

Quantum ML (or quantum-enhanced ML) is the integration of quantum algorithms within ML techniques and algorithms. The most common use of the term refers to ML algorithms and software that make use of quantum algorithms or quantum computers to process information.

Its main advantage is that it can potentially provide speedups over classical ML algorithms. For example, a quantum computer can exploit the fact that quantum information can be processed in parallel, whereas classical information can only be processed sequentially: thus, a quantum computer presents a significant speed advantage over a classical computer. In addition, quantum ML algorithms have the potential to be more accurate than classical algorithms. This is because quantum computers can store and process information in a way that is fundamentally different from classical computers. Indeed, a quantum computer can store information in superposition, which means that it can effectively store multiple pieces of information at the same time.

There are several different ways in which quantum ML algorithms can be used. Quantum computers can perform the computationally intensive task of training an ML model; once the model is trained, it can then be run on a classical computer. This approach can provide a speedup over classical training algorithms, as well as potentially improve the accuracy of the trained model. Quantum ML is still in its early stages of development. However, there is already a significant amount of research being conducted in this area. In addition, several companies are beginning to develop quantum ML algorithms and software. As quantum computing technology continues to develop, it is likely that quantum ML will become more widely used.

1.2.5 Facial Recognition and Image Analysis

Facial recognition is a subarea of image analysis, and it encompasses techniques and algorithms used to identify or confirm an individual's identity using their face. Facial recognition systems can be used to identify people in photos, videos, or in real-time. And it is also used as a tool for biometric security.

There are a few different ways that facial recognition systems work, but they all typically involve extracting unique facial features from an image and then comparing those features to a database of known faces. The comparison can be done using different techniques, but the most common method is to use a mathematical algorithm. Facial recognition systems are not perfect, and they can sometimes make mistakes. However, they are getting better all the time, and they are becoming increasingly common in both the public and private sectors. The most well-known facial recognition database is probably the one maintained by the US government, which is known as the National Security Entry-Exit Registration System (NSEERS). NSEERS was created in the aftermath of the 9/11 attacks, and it was used to track people from countries that were at high-risk for terrorism. The program was eventually discontinued, but not before it generated a lot of controversies. Other facial recognition databases are maintained by private companies, and they are often used for marketing purposes. For example, Facebook has a facial recognition system that is used to suggest friends to users.

1.2.6 Bias in Data and Big Data

Recently a lot of attention has been devoted to potential bias in data that can affect the ML process and, more in general, any analytics. And while there can be advantages to intentional bias in areas such as target marketing, where a bias in data can provide more direct insight, bias in big data can quickly become an issue for business (Joyce, 2021).

This issue has been brought to the forefront due to the US presidential election. The role that social media played in the election has been widely discussed, with a lot of focus on the way that Facebook and Twitter can be used to spread fake news and other forms of misinformation. There is a lot of concern that the way that these platforms are designed can amplify the effects of bias, and that this can have a major impact on the way that people vote (Aggarwal *et al.*, 2020). Bias in big data can also have a major impact on the way that businesses operate. For example, if a company is using big data to make decisions about which products to stock, and the data is biased towards certain types of products, then the company may end up stocking products that are not in demand. This can affect sales and customer trust.

The issue of bias in big data is not new, but it is becoming more important as the use of big data grows. It is important for businesses to be aware of the potential for bias in their data, and to take steps to mitigate their effects. There are a few ways to do this, including using data from: multiple sources; different time periods; different geographical regions; different demographic groups; and different industries. Taking these steps can help to reduce the impact of bias in big data, including different multiple biases. However, it is important to remember that no data set is completely free of bias.

1.2.7 Explainable and Interpretable AI

Explainable AI is AI in which the results of the solution can be understood and interpreted by humans. That is the ability to explain a model after it has been developed and providing transparent model architectures, which allows human users to both understand the data and trust results. This term is used in contrast with the concept of the "black box" in ML in which even computer scientists and programmers cannot explain why an AI arrived at a specific decision. Explanations should aim to satisfy three properties, namely, accuracy, comprehensibility, and justifiability.

Additionally, Interpretable AI, or glass box AI, focuses on the identification of the patterns a model has learned and why it produces certain results. The difference between the two of them is the following: XAI tells why a certain decision was made, but not how the decision maker arrived at that decision. Interpretable AI, instead, tells how the decision was made, but not why the criteria it used are sensible.

There are many benefits to XAI. First, it can help ensure that AI solutions are fair and unbiased. If a computer scientist (or programmer) cannot understand why AI arrived at a specific decision, it may be difficult to identify and correct any biases in the decision-making process. Additionally, XAI can help build trust between humans and AI systems. If humans can understand why an AI system made a particular decision, they are more likely to trust the system. Finally, explainable AI can improve the usability of AI systems. If humans can understand how an AI system works, they are more likely to be able to use the system effectively. There are several challenges to developing XAI. One challenge is that it can be difficult to create explanations that are both comprehensible and accurate. Additionally, the explanations produced by XAI systems may be too simplistic to be useful. Finally, XAI systems may be less efficient than traditional AI systems because they require additional resources to generate explanations.

1.2.8 Deep Learning

Deep Learning (DL) is an AI discipline and a type of ML technique aimed at developing systems that can operate in complex situations and focuses on ANNs. ANNs (Figure 1.3) are networks composed of many interconnected processing nodes or neurons that can learn how to recognize complex patterns from data. ANNs are used for different applications, mostly for image recognition and classification, pattern recognition, and time series prediction. In Deep Learning, the so-called deep architectures are combinations of different ANNs.

One of the first ANN architectures that were trained is the Multilayer Perceptron (MLP). The MLP is inspired by the brain's essential functioning and emulates a simple feedforward network of neurons, historically called perceptron. From a modeling perspective, the main activity of a neuron is described by means of an activation function that can either be linear, sigmoidal, or piecewise.

Although they are time consuming, feature engineering and feature extraction are essential steps in the ML workflow. They focus on transforming training data and enhancing it with new features to improve the performance of ML algorithms. Deep learning's proponents claim that this is changing. With DL, one can begin with unprocessed data because as the neural network learns, features will be formed automatically.

Another architecture well known for its relevant applications to image processing is the Convolutional Neural Network (CNN). With respect to the MLP architecture, a classical CNN does not rely only on fully connected layers, even if feature extraction through filtering is performed by convolution layers. The main advantage of CNN is that it performs features engineering and classification, simultaneously, which allows high classification performance, comparatively, to classical ML models.

With the renewed interest in ANNs and DL, more advanced and sophisticated architectures have been proposed to overcome the problems presented in earlier ANNs as, for instance, the problem of the vanishing gradient. ResNet differs from the canonical MLP architecture in that, it allows for

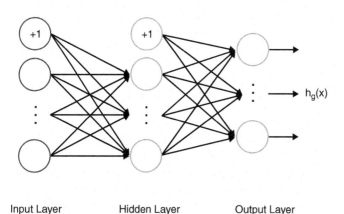

Input Layer   Hidden Layer   Output Layer

Figure 1.3 Neural Network Architecture.

shortcut connections that mitigate the problem of degradation in the case of multiple layers.

1.2.9 Natural Language Processing

Natural Language Processing (NLP) allows machines to break down and interpret human language by identifying words, bag of words, and more in general structured sentences. NLP is at the core of recent AI tools and technologies that are used for translation, chatbots, spam filters, and search engines, to grammar correction software, voice assistants, and social media monitoring tools.

1.3 AI Applications

No matter the AI industry has become commonplace and is emerging as a new engine of growth by providing useful insights and intelligence. In this section, we present some of the most interesting applications of AI to different areas and domains.

1.3.1 AI in Finance: Prediction and Forecasting

Financing and banking industries have been leveraging the power of AI technologies and algorithms as AI has automated routine tasks, streamlined procedures, and improved the customer service experience. The AI revolution has pushed the financial industry to embrace more and more the digital experience: cost savings are expected as AI technologies might save banks and financial institutions $447 billion by 2023 (Business Insider, 2022). This is because AI can free up personnel, improve security measures and ensure that the business is moving in the right technology-advanced, innovative direction. According to Columbus (2020), 70% of financial firms are using ML to predict cash flow events, adjust credit scores and detect fraud.

Risk refers to the degree of uncertainty and/or potential financial loss inherent in an investment decision. AI is used to determine whether someone is eligible for a loan. More and more ML algorithms are used not only to determine a person's loan eligibility but also to provide personalized options, and their results are rapid and more accurate. Predictions are crucial when we talk about risk: AI can analyze a customer's spending patterns and actions, which can predict loan borrowing behavior; or can identify trends and risks and ensure better information for future planning. Moreover, thanks to AI, fraud detection systems analyze a person's buying behavior and trigger an alert if something seems out of the ordinary or contradicts traditional spending patterns. From the financial institution's perspective, AI can automate repetitive mundane, time-consuming tasks, and this will free up employees to tackle other projects and reduce costs.

1.3.2 AI in Medicine: Medical Imaging and Drug Discovery

AI has enormous potential to improve healthcare systems, for instance by fostering preventative medicine and new drug discovery. AI technologies and models can compete and sometimes surpass clinician performance in a variety of tasks and support the decision-making process in multiple medical domains. Indeed, AI techniques and technologies are used to search medical data, to discover insights, to uncover hidden patterns, and to help the decision-making process, the patient-doctor interaction, the health outcome, the medical diagnosis, and the overall patient experience (Schmitt, 2022). For instance, in oncology, MLP architecture is used for breast cancer detection (Figure 1.4) achieving remarkable accuracy and relatively low training time. And the more medical data will be digitalized, the more AI can help to find valuable patterns and cost-effective decisions in complex analytical processes.

Saving lives requires an efficient and correct diagnosis that takes years of medical training. Even then, diagnostics is often an arduous, time-consuming process. In many fields, the demand for experts far exceeds the available supply. This puts doctors under strain and often delays life-saving patient diagnostics. ML and DL algorithms have recently made huge advances in automatically diagnosing diseases, making diagnostics cheaper and more accessible. ML algorithms can learn to see patterns similar to the way doctors see them. A key difference is that algorithms need a lot of concrete examples – many thousands – to learn. And these examples need to be neatly digitized – machines cannot read between the lines in textbooks. ML is particularly helpful in areas where the diagnostic information a doctor examines is already digitized, such as detecting lung cancer or strokes based on CT scans, assessing the risk of sudden cardiac death or other heart diseases based on electrocardiograms and cardiac MRI images, classifying skin lesions in skin images, finding indicators of diabetic retinopathy in eye images, and others. The application of ML in diagnostics is just beginning and more and more ambitious systems involve the combination of multiple data sources (CT, MRI, genomics and proteomics, patient data, and even handwritten files) in assessing a disease or its progression. Despite the growth of AI in diagnosis, AI will not replace doctors anytime soon but will allow them to focus on interpretation.

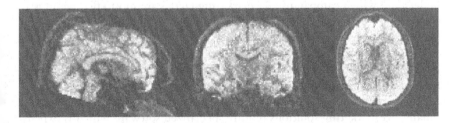

Figure 1.4 Medical Images.

AI can sustain efficient innovation and the development of drugs, which is a notoriously expensive process. Indeed, AI has already been used successfully in all four main stages of drug development: Identifying targets for intervention, discovering drug candidates, speeding up clinical trials, and finding biomarkers for diagnosing the disease. Within this area, ML algorithms can analyze all the available data and even learn to automatically identify good target proteins. ML can also learn to predict the suitability of a molecule based on structural fingerprints and molecular descriptors. ML can speed up the design of clinical trials by automatically identifying suitable candidates as well as ensuring the correct distribution for groups of trial participants. AI can automate a large portion of the manual work and speed up the process, so that clinicians can focus on analyzing the best prospects.

AI can personalize treatment, discovering which characteristics indicate that a patient will have a particular response to a particular treatment. Indeed, different patients respond to drugs and treatment schedules differently, and personalized treatment has enormous potential to increase patients' lifespans. In the same way, ML models have been proven to produce the best results when it comes to predicting the degree of both guide-target interactions and off-target effects for a given sgRNA, speeding up the development of guide RNA for every region of human DNA.

1.3.3 AI in Marketing: Customer-Centric Perspectives

Companies strive to exceed customer expectations throughout the entire customer journey while maintaining operational efficiency. Marketers constantly look for a more nuanced, comprehensive understanding of their target audiences: AI and ML use customer data from online and offline sources coupled with ML algorithms to predict what users will do on websites or apps for instance. AI marketing tools can suggest how to best communicate with customers, then serve them tailored messages at the right time via the right channel. The expansion of AI marketing offers the potential for improvements in outcomes and puts marketers in a position to make informed and cost-effective decisions faster. Potential benefits range from increased ROI to better and hyper-personalized customer experience. AI helps marketers understand which campaigns and marketing tactics are most effective in real time, so they can immediately replicate (or interrupt) those tactics across different campaigns or channels.

There are, however, some potential drawbacks. Obviously, if we deal with incomplete or inconsistent data AI tools cannot produce meaningful insights for marketing campaigns. AI needs to comply with laws and rules regarding how data associated with individuals is stored, processed, and managed. Finally, AI marketing solutions require specialized software which is expensive to acquire, deploy, and maintain (lack of budget) and skilled people (lack of talent).

1.3.4 AI in Tourism and Hospitality

The proliferation of AI in the travel and hospitality industry can be attributed to the enormous amount of data generated today. AI can help to design personalized packages that include discounts, programs, and benefits by using behavioral science and social media information.

Soon more and more travel and hospitality organizations will use AI for intelligent recommendations and their own chatbots. Before the travel, customers can rely on Intelligence travel search using AI. Flight and hotel rates are dynamic and vary in real-time, depending on the provider; AI smart algorithms that monitor and send timely alerts on the most attractive deals are currently in high demand. AI can create a self-learning algorithm, capable of forecasting future price movements based on several factors, such as seasonal trends, demand growth, airline specials, and deals. Additionally, consumers can rely on Intelligent travel assistants. Chatbots can help to find flights, to request travel recommendations and unplanned suggestions: Consumers are overwhelmed with different choices to take and a chatbot can help to cut through the noise, and organizations can connect with consumers at their own pace and in social media spaces they frequent most often. AI is also of great help in avoiding a repetitive process, to answer common and repetitive questions about fares.

AI allows to offer tailored experiences. Many hotel chains have started using an AI-powered bot. For instance, robots are used to speed up the check-in process and to provide customers with succinct information about local attractions, places to visit, etc. Since the AI is driven by a self-learning capability, it can learn and adapt and respond to each guest in a personalized manner. AI gathers individual preferences and generates personalized suggestions to provide a tailored, streamlined experience and properly address any issues encountered.

Finally, automated disruption management is a different application of AI in this area. AI aims to solve real-world problems that a traveler might encounter while traveling to a destination point. The risk of travel disruption is still quite high: there are thousands of delays and several hundred canceled flights every day. With recent advances in AI, it has become possible to predict such disruptions and effectively mitigate losses for both the traveler and the carrier.

1.3.5 AI in Supply Chain Management: Shipping and Delivery

AI and ML tools are used in supply chain to increase efficiency, reduce the impact of a worldwide worker shortage, and discover better, safer ways to move goods from one point to another. AI applications can be found throughout supply chains, from the manufacturing floor to front-door delivery. For instance, shipping companies are using Internet of Things (IoT) sensors to gather and analyze data about goods in shipment and track the mechanical health and constant location of expensive vehicles and related transportation tools. Customer-facing retailers are using AI to gain a better understanding of their key demographics to make better predictions about future behavior. Some of the benefits derived from AI in supply chains are less tangible and visible than others. For instance, predictive analytics has a direct impact on increased revenues and decreased costs. Advantages of applying AI to modern supply chain challenges include end-to-end visibility enhanced with near real-time data, actionable analytic insights based on pattern identification, reduced manual human work, informed decision-making augmented by ML, AI-driven predictions, and recommendations. Beyond, AI is optimizing routing efficiency and delivery logistics, answering customers' expectations about quick and accurate shipping; AI is also improving the health and longevity of transportation vehicles thanks to IoT device data. ML makes maintenance recommendations and failure predictions based on past and real-time data, allowing companies to take vehicles out of the chain before performance issues create a cascading backlog of delays (Hunt, 2021). Finally, AI insights are adding efficiency and profitability to loading processes. Supply chain management includes a great deal of detail-oriented analysis, including how goods are loaded and unloaded from shipping containers.

1.3.6 AI in Remote Sensing and Landmine Detection

Landmine explosions result in the death or injury of people every day during and after wartime. The *International Campaign to Ban Landmines* has stated that the high number of casualties in 2017 include at least 7,239 people killed or injured by landmines, with 87% (47% children) of those being civilian casualties. The remaining 13% of the overall casualties are made up of security personnel and deminers.

To clear the existing minefields and save lives, it is required to build automatic detection and discrimination systems. The most popular methods for finding landmines rely on electromagnetic induction, like a metal detector, or on sending an electromagnetic wave to the target and then using radar to measure the returned wave. Ground Penetrating Radar (GPR), the most popular of these approaches, is a geophysical technique used to find objects buried in the ground that is mostly based on soil scanning. However, GPR captures noise (clutter) (Daniels, 2004): Any type of buried object, including metal or plastic mines, wood sticks, stones, etc., is detectable by the GPR. However, to clear the clutter and properly distinguish between landmines and harmless objects, this technology does not make use of any data processing algorithms or classification methods.

As a result, a variety of clutter reduction strategies have been created to address the demining issue. These techniques can be divided into two groups. The first category pertains to signal processing procedures to boost the signal-to-clutter ratio (i.e., Daniels, 2004; Zoubir *et al.*, 2020). The second category relates to methods for image processing. The delay-and-sum (DAS) algorithm is the most used picture reconstruction technique for reducing clutter (Wang *et al.*, 2005). Although it is quick and easy to execute, the latter produces photos with poor quality and significant side lobes. To accomplish picture reconstruction while minimizing clutter, the recursive side-lobe minimization (RSM) algorithm (Nguyen, 2009) is a unique variant of the DAS algorithm. Although the clutter RSM technique does not improve image resolution, it outperforms DAS in terms of noise and side lobe reduction. Time–domain SLIM (TD-SLIM) and frequency-domain SLIM are two methods (Lim *et al.*, 2015) based on the sparse learning via iterative minimization (SLIM) approach to increase image resolution (FD-SLIM). These algorithms reduce side lobes and clutter, but because of their high computational complexity, they might not be suitable for real-time applications. Another emerging method for identifying and distinguishing between land-mines and unimportant things is image-based classification. We specifically point to Lameri *et al.* (2017) who provide a system based on convolutional neural networks and GPR imagery (CNNs). The faster R-CNN has been suggested by Kafedziski *et al.* (2018) to distinguish between the hyperbolic signatures of anti-personnel (AP) mines and anti-tank (AT) mines.

CNN's objective function is neither convex nor concave, though. Finding the best solution is not an easy task because it offers multiple solutions connected to local minima. Additionally, it performs poorly at finding tiny mines (Giovanneschi *et al.*, 2018), and the training step necessitates the use of very big datasets. These factors have led several academics to employ multi-class SVM for the detection and discrimination of landmines (Jose *et al.*, 2013; Park *et al.*, 2014). In reality, because of the convex nature of its objective function, SVM has the benefit of offering a distinctive solution. Additionally, SVM makes use of non-linear kernel functions, which may handle highly overlapping and nonlinearly separable data. Giovanneschi *et al.* (2017, 2018) propose Online Dictionary Learning (ODL) approaches for landmine detection using GPR data, namely the classical ODL technique and the Drop-Off MINI-batch Online Dictionary Learning (DOMINODL) technique for GPR data sparse representation (SR), to improve the accuracy of the landmine detection SVM is then utilized to classify the samples. Asserting that ODL approaches handle small mines better than CNNs, Giovanneschi *et al.* (2018) have demonstrated that the ODL methods combined with the SVM classifier outperform the CNNs in terms of landmine classification.

1.3.7 *AI for Quality of Service and Quality of Experience*

Over 80% of all internet traffic in recent years has been attributed to the growing popularity of video streaming. Network Applications like YouTube and Netflix have a thorough understanding of the caliber of their network services for video transmission by managing the video quality of experience (QoE), which is used as an actual evaluation of clients' experiences in mobile video dissemination. Real-time video QoE assessment enables network operators to dynamically enhance their traffic routing and network capacity provisioning methods (Ananthanarayanan *et al.*, 2017). The quality of video streaming has been extensively researched in the literature (Huynh-Thu and Ghanbari, 2008; Tasaka 2017), but it is still difficult to measure, analyze, and anticipate video streaming QoE. Influence Factors (IFs), often referred to as system IFs, context IFs, and human Ifs (Zhao *et al.*, 2017), are a series of interconnected variables that have an impact on the QoE of video streaming. Traditional techniques IF modeling focus on system variables like the Peak Signal-to-Noise Ratio (PSNR) (Deng *et al.*, 2014). Since these strategies fall short in assessing human perceptual participation, methodologies that rely on context Ifs (Li *et al.*, 2013) and human IFs (Song *et al.*, 2016) are rapidly replacing them. There are two main categories for the QoE prediction: subjective methods and objective methods, which can be used to quantify the two kinds of IFs listed above in situations where human cognition is not fully understood. Maia *et al.* (2015) suggest to use subjective models to obtain evaluation scores from customers in a thoroughly controlled setting to measure consumer QoE directly. Comparing techniques is the foundation of objective models, which forecast perceived quality and offer an understandable score. Objective results are verified using subjective testing.

For the perception of users' QoE, numerous researchers have used ML techniques in the literature. For instance, Aroussi and Mellouk (2014) provide an overview of ML techniques used to automatically identify the relationship between Quality of Service (QoS) metrics and QoE values, including the random forest model (RF), SVM model, naive Bayes model, and K-nearest neighbors' model. Additionally, Bampis and Bovik (2007) suggest a model for assessing the quality of video streaming utilizing a variety of regression techniques, such as ridge and lasso regression, as well as ensemble techniques, such as RF, gradient boosting, and additional trees.

A framework for predicting video quality of experience utilizing optimized learning models (OLMs) based on multi-feature fusion (MFF) was also introduced by Ghosh and Singhal (2022). The OLMs are neural network optimization methods created for QoE estimation. In addition, a transfer learning-based ML model for video QoE estimate is provided in Tasaka (2017) who combines predictions from two different trained models to increase overall accuracy. Both the source domain and the target domain have seen application of the XGBoost (XGB) and Neural Network (NN) techniques. Despite the possibility of using conventional ML techniques to improve user QoE, these models require expert feature engineering that requires manual intervention, which is time-consuming and expensive. Additionally, because wireless network conditions change so quickly, they are hardly ever reusable.

1.4 Conclusion

AI technology and creative intelligence have made rapid progress in recent years by changing and transforming business models and every segment of all industries. In the years to come, AI will contribute to business and society through the large-scale implementation and adoption of AI technologies such as IoT, smart speakers, chat-bots, cybersecurity, 3D printing, drones, face emotions analysis, sentiment analysis, NLP, human resources, and many others. AI-powered computers can shift through data faster than humans, which expedites the entire process and saves large chunks of time. This chapter presented a narrative review to identify how different organizations can deploy AI, after tackling definitions and technicalities about the AI context and jargon.

References

Aggarwal, S., Sinha, T., Kukreti, Y., Shikhar, S. (2020), 'Media bias detection and bias short term impact assessment', *Array*, 6, 100025.

Ananthanarayanan, G., Bahl, V., Bodik, P., Chintalapudi, K., Philipose, M., Ravindranath Sivalingam, L., Sinha, S. (2017), 'Real-time video analytics: The killer app for edge computing', *Computer*, 50(10), 58–67.

Aroussi, S., Mellouk, A. (2014), 'Survey on machine learning-based QoE-QoS correlation models,' *2014 International Conference on Computing, Management and Telecommunications (ComManTel)*, Da Nang, Vietnam, 200-204, doi: 10.1109/ComManTel.2014.6825604

Bampis, C.G., Bovik, A.C. (2017), 'Learning to predict streaming video QoE: Distortions, rebuffering and memory', *arXiv [cs.MM]*. https://arxiv.org/pdf/1703.00633.pdf

Columbus, L. (2020), 'The state of AI adoption in financial services', Forbes.

Daniels, D.J. (2004), *Ground Penetrating Radar-2nd Edition*, The Institution of Electrical Engineers, London.

Deng, X., Chen, L., Wang, F., Fei, Z., Bai, W., Chi, C., Han, G., Wan, L. (2014), 'A novel strategy to evaluate QoE for video service delivered over HTTP adaptive streaming', *2014 IEEE 80th Vehicular Technology Conference* (VTC2014-Fall), 1–5.

Ghosh, M., Singhal, C. (2022), 'MO-QoE: Video QoE using multi-feature fusion based optimized learning models', *Signal Processing: Image Communication*, 107(116766), 116–766.

Giovanneschi, F., Mishra, K.V., Gonzalez-Huici, M.A, Eldar, Y.C., Ender, J.H. (2017), 'Online dictionary learning aided target recognition in cognitive GPR', IEEE International Geoscience and Remote Sensing Symposium (IGARSS). July, 4813–4816. https://doi.org/10.1109/IGARSS.2017.8128079

Giovanneschi, F., Mishra, K.V., Kumar, M.A., Gonzalez-Huici, M.A., Eldar, Y.C., Ender, J.H. (2019), 'Dictionary learning for adaptive GPR target classification', IEEE International Geoscience and Remote Sensing Symposium (IGARSS), May, 1–20.

Hunt, S. (2021), Artificial Intelligence (AI) in Supply Chains, October 25, 2021, [online]. Available at: https://www.datamation.com/artificial-intelligence/artificial-intelligence-in-supply-chains (Accessed: 14 September 2022)

Huynh-Thu, Q., Ghanbari, M. (2008), 'Temporal aspect of perceived quality in mobile video broadcasting', *IEEE Transactions on Broadcasting,* 54(3), 641–651.

Jose, M., Murillo, L., Chova, G.L., Valls, G.L. (2013), 'Multitask remote sensing data classification', *IEEE Transactions on Geoscience and Remote Sensing*, 51(1), 151–161.

Joyce, K. (2021) Bias in Big Data: How to Find it and Mitigate Influence, [online]. Available at: https://www.techtarget.com/searchdatamanagement/feature/Bias-in-big-data-How-to-find-it-and-mitigate-influence (Accessed: 29 September 2022)

Kafedziski, V., Pecov, S., Tanevski, D. (2018), 'Detection and classification of landmines from ground penetrating radar data using faster R-CNN', *2018 26th Telecommunications Forum (TELFOR)*, 1–4, IEEE. November.

Khan, N.M., Ksantini, R., Guan, L. (2018), 'A novel image-centric approach toward direct volume rendering', *ACM Transactions on Intelligent Systems and Technology (TIST)*, 9(4), 1–18.

Kindlmann, G., Durkin, J.W. (1998), 'Semi-automatic generation of transfer functions for direct volume rendering', *IEEE Symposium on Volume Visualization* (Cat. No. 989EX300), 79–86. IEEE.

Lameri, S., Lombardi, F., Bestagini, P., Lualdi, M., Tubaro, S. (2017), 'Landmine detection from GPR data using convolutional neural networks', *Proceedings of the 25th European Signal Processing Conference (EUSIPCO)*, Kos, Greece, 28 August–2 September 2017, 508–512.

Li, J., Kaller, O., De Simone, F., Hakala, J., Juszka, D., Le Callet, P. (2013), 'Cross-lab study on preference of experience in 3DTV: Influence from display technology and test environment', *2013 Fifth International Workshop on Quality of Multimedia Experience (QoMEX)*, 46–47.

Lim, D., Xu, L., Gianelli, G., Li, J., Nguyen, L., Anderson, J. (2015), 'Time-and frequency-domain MIMO FLGPR imaging', *IEEE National Radar Conference – Proceedings*, 1305–1310, IEEE, May.

Maia, O.B., Yehia, H.C., Errico, d.L. (2015), 'A concise review of the quality of experience assessment for video streaming', *Computer Communications,* 57, 1–12.

Marks, J., Andalman, B., Beardsley, P.A., Freeman, W., Gibson, S., Hodgins, J., Kang, T., Mirtich, B., Pfister, H., Ruml, W., *et al.* (1997), 'Design galleries: A general approach to setting parameters for computer graphics and animation', *Proceedings of the 24th Annual Conference on Computer Graphics and Interactive Techniques*, 389–400. ACM Press/Addison-Wesley Publishing Co.

Nguyen, L. (2009), 'Signal and image processing algorithms for U.S. Army Research Laboratory Ultra-Wideband (UWB) Synchronous Impulse Reconstruction (SIRE) radar', *Army Research Laboratory*, 35–38.

Park, S., Kim, K., Ko, K.H. (2014), 'Multi-feature based multiple landmine detection using ground penetration radar', *Radio Engineering*, 23(2), 643–651.

Schmitt, M. (2022) Artificial Intelligence in Medicine [online]. Available at: https://www.datarevenue.com/en-blog/artificial-intelligence-in-medicine (Accessed: 14 September 2022)

Song, J., Yang, F., Zhou, Y., Wan, S., Wu, H.R. (2016), 'QoE evaluation of multimedia services based on audiovisual quality and user interest', *IEEE Transactions on Multimedia,* 18(3), 444–457.

Tasaka S. (2017), 'Bayesian hierarchical regression models for QoE estimation and prediction in audiovisual communications', *IEEE Transactions Multimedia,* 19(6), 1195–1208.

Wang, Y., Li, X., Sun, Y., Li, J. (2005), 'Adaptive imaging for forward-looking ground penetrating radar', *IEEE Transactions on Aerospace and Electronic Systems,* 41(3), 922–936.

Zhao, T., Liu, Q., Chen, C.W. (2017), 'QoE in video transmission: A user experience-driven straegy', *IEEE Communications Surveys and Tutorials,* 19(1), 285–302.

Zoubir, A.M., Chant, I.J., Brown, C.L., Barkat, B., Abeynayake, C. (2020), 'Signal processing techniques for landmine detection using impulse ground penetrating radar', *IEEE Sensors Journal*, 2(1), 41–51.

2 Adopting Machine Learning and AI for Data-driven Decisions

Francesca Lazzeri

In the last few decades, data from different sources have become more accessible and consumable, and companies have started looking for ways to use machine learning techniques to optimize business metrics, pursue new opportunities, and grow revenues (Lazzeri, 2019). Not only has data become more available, but there has also been an explosion of machine learning applications that enable companies to build sophisticated and intelligent solutions.

Not only has the sheer volume of available data grown exponentially over the past years and is expected to continue to do so, but also have new tools been developed for turning this flood of raw data into insights and eventually into profitable actions for companies. Machine learning, a term that encompasses a range of algorithmic approaches from statistical methods like regressions to neural networks, has rapidly advanced to the forefront of analytics (Tambe, 2012).

Machine learning is a set of algorithms that can be applied to multiple data and generates predictive results (Lazzeri, 2019). Machine learning is also a subfield of artificial intelligence (AI), which is broadly defined as the capability of a machine to imitate intelligent human behavior: for this reason, machine learning is very often defined as a method of data analysis that automates analytical model building. It is a branch of AI based on the concept that systems can learn from data, identify patterns, and make decisions with minimal human intervention (Tambe, 2012). But what does it really mean to adopt machine learning for data-driven decisions and how can companies take advantage of it to improve processes and add value to their business?

In this chapter, you will learn what machine learning is and how being a machine learning organization implies embedding machine learning teams to fully engage with the business and adapting the operational support of the company (techniques, processes, infrastructures, culture) (Lazzeri, 2019).

In the next few paragraphs, you will learn the following four dimensions that companies can leverage to become machine learning-driven (Figure 2.1):

1 Understanding Algorithms and the Business Questions that Algorithms can answer
2 Defining Business Metrics and Business Impact

DOI: 10.4324/9781003304616-4

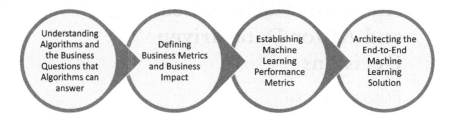

Figure 2.1 Machine learning adoption process by companies.

3   Establishing Machine Learning Performance Metrics
4   Architecting the End-to-End Machine Learning Solution

Given the rapid evolution of this field, companies typically need guidance on how to apply the latest machine learning techniques to address their business needs or to pursue new opportunities.

2.1 Literature Review

Machine learning models have become increasingly prevalent in virtually all fields of business and research in the past decade. With all the research that has been done on the training and evaluation of machine learning models, the difficulty for most companies and practitioners now is not to find new algorithms and optimizations in training, but rather how to actually deploy models to production in order to deliver tangible business value (Bijamov et al., 2011). Most companies are still in the very early stages of incorporating Machine Learning into their business processes (Lushan et al., 2019)

Software engineering for Machine Learning systems is still a young and immature knowledge area. Traditional software systems are largely deterministic, computing-driven systems whose behavior is purely code-dependent. Machine learning models have an additional data dependency, in the sense that their behavior is learned from data, and they have even been characterized as non-deterministic (Dhankhad et al., 2018). The additional data dependency is one of the factors contributing to the fact that Machine Learning systems require a great amount of supporting infrastructure (Herath et al., 2018).

DevOps for Machine Learning, named MLOps or AIOps, is a subset of Machine Learning and an extension of DevOps (Mishu et al., 2016), focusing on adopting DevOps practices when developing and operating Machine Learning systems (Robles–Durazno et al., 2018). Moh et al. (2015) define that "MLOps is a cross-functional, collaborative, continuous process that focuses on operationalizing data science by managing statistical, data science, and machine learning models as reusable, highly available software artifacts, via a repeatable deployment process.").

In recent years, many innovations have been created using machine learning and MLOps systems: autonomous vehicles, data mining, biometrics, among other solutions. As a result, the demand for intelligent systems had a relevant growth in the market and the scientific field (Lushan et al., 2019). These systems use algorithms for pattern detection that involve various other disciplines. According to Moh et al. (2015), machine learning occurs when the computer learns by improving the performance of a class of tasks, which are measured statistically. The process of learning a computer program involves three steps:

1   The first step is about defining the labels that will be learned.
2   The second step is the measurement definition that will be performed to identify whether there was an improvement in the performance of the model.
3   The third step is about training, evaluating, and deploying the model.

Thus, the implementation of machine learning involves a set of tasks, performance measurement of these tasks, and a set of training to obtain experience in performing these tasks (Herath et al., 2018). Software engineering used in the development of information systems has brought many benefits to companies (Robles-Durazno et al., 2018). However, only a few areas of software engineering have benefited from using machine learning approaches in their tools and processes (Robles-Durazno et al., 2018).

2.2 Understanding Algorithms and the Business Questions that Algorithms Can Answer

Today, with the rise of big data, IoT, and ubiquitous computing, machine learning has become essential for solving problems across numerous areas (Brynjolfsson et al., 2011), such as:

*   Computational finance (credit scoring, algorithmic trading)
*   Computer vision (facial recognition, object detection)
*   Computational biology (DNA sequencing, drug discovery)
*   Automotive, aerospace, and manufacturing (predictive maintenance)
*   Natural language processing (speech recognition and topic modeling)

Machine Learning is a field of computer science that was born from pattern recognition and the theory that computers can learn without being programmed to perform specific tasks; computer science researchers interested in machine learning wanted to see if computers could learn from data and generate predictions based on that data. The iterative aspect of machine learning is important because as models are exposed to new data, they can predict (Davenport et al., 2012). They learn from previous computations to produce results.

While many machine learning algorithms have been around for a long time, the ability to automatically apply mathematical functions to big data is a recent development (Brynjolfsson et al., 2011). Data scientists usually divide the learning and automatic logic of a machine learning algorithm into three main parts, as listed below:

1   *A Decision Process*: In general, machine learning algorithms are used to make a prediction or classification. Based on some input data, which can be labeled or unlabeled, your algorithm will produce an estimate about a pattern in the data.
2   *An Error Function*: An error function evaluates the prediction of the model. If there are known examples, an error function can make a comparison to assess the accuracy of the model.
3   *A Model Optimization Process*: If the model can fit better to the data points in the training set, then weights are adjusted to reduce the discrepancy between the known example and the model estimate. The algorithm will repeat this "evaluate and optimize" process, updating weights autonomously until a threshold of accuracy has been met (Brynjolfsson et al., 2011).

From a data point of view, the machine learning process is usually structured in a few standard phases:

1   The machine learning algorithms are fitted on a training dataset to create a model.
2   As a new testing input dataset is introduced to the trained machine learning algorithm, it uses the developed model to make a prediction.
3   The prediction is then checked for accuracy.
4   Based on its accuracy, the machine learning algorithm is either deployed or trained repeatedly with an augmented training dataset until the desired accuracy is achieved.

Based on these phases of learning, machine learning is broadly categorized into four main types. Machine learning models fall into three primary categories (Tambe, 2012):

1   *Supervised machine learning*: Supervised learning is a kind of machine learning approach that uses labeled datasets to train algorithms to classify data or predict outcomes accurately. As input data is fed into the model, the model adjusts its weights until it has been fitted appropriately (Tambe, 2012). This occurs as part of the cross-validation process to ensure that the model avoids overfitting or underfitting. Supervised learning helps companies solve a variety of real-world problems at scale,

such as classifying spam in a separate folder from your inbox. Some methods used in supervised learning include neural networks, Naïve Bayes, linear regression, logistic regression, random forest, and support vector machine (SVM).

The primary objective of the supervised learning technique is to map the input variable with the output variable. Supervised machine learning is further categorized into two broad categories:

- Classification: These refer to algorithms that address classification problems where the output variable is categorical. Some known classification algorithms include the Random Forest Algorithm, Decision Tree Algorithm, Logistic Regression Algorithm, and SVM Algorithm (Brynjolfsson et al., 2011).
- Regression: Regression algorithms handle regression problems where input and output variables have a linear relationship. These are known to predict continuous output variables. Popular regression algorithms include the Simple Linear Regression Algorithm, Multivariate Regression Algorithm, Decision Tree Algorithm, and Lasso Regression.
- *Unsupervised machine learning*: Unsupervised learning uses machine learning algorithms to analyze unlabeled datasets. These algorithms discover hidden patterns or data groupings without the need for labeled data. This method is often used for exploratory data analysis, cross-selling strategies, customer segmentation, and image and pattern recognition. It is also utilized to reduce the number of features in a model through the process of dimensionality reduction.

Unsupervised machine learning is further classified into two types:

- Clustering: Clustering is the method of dividing the data sets into a certain number of clusters in such a manner that the data points belonging to a cluster have similar characteristics. Clusters are groups of data points such that the distance between the data points within the clusters is minimal. Some known clustering algorithms include the K-Means Clustering Algorithm, Mean-Shift Algorithm, Principal Component Analysis, and Independent Component Analysis.
- Association: The task of association rule learning is to discover this kind of relationship and identify the rules of their association. Association learning refers to identifying typical relations between the variables of a large dataset. It determines the dependency of various data items and maps associated variables. Typical applications include web usage mining and market data analysis. Popular algorithms obeying association rules include the Eclat Algorithm and FP-Growth Algorithm.
- *Reinforcement Learning*: The Reinforcement Learning problem involves a model ingesting an unknown set of data to achieve a goal or to

produce an accurate prediction. Reinforcement Learning is based on the hypothesis that all the predictions can be described by the maximization of predicted cumulative rewards. The model must learn to learn from the state of the environment and external data points using its actions to derive a maximal reward. The formal framework for Reinforcement Learning borrows from the problem of optimal control of Markov Decision Processes. Reinforcement Learning is applied across different fields such as game theory, information theory, and multi-agent systems (Brynjolfsson et al., 2011) and it is divided into two types of methods:

- Positive reinforcement learning: This refers to adding a reinforcing weight after a specific behavior of the agent, which makes it more likely that the behavior may occur again in the future. Positive reinforcement is the most common type of reinforcement used in reinforcement learning, as it helps models maximize performance on a given task.
- Negative reinforcement learning: It is a particular type of reinforcement learning algorithm that helps the learning process avoid a negative outcome, it learns from it (through historical data) and improves its future predictions.

Industry verticals handling large amounts of data have realized the significance and value of machine learning technology (Tambe, 2012). As machine learning derives insights from data in real time, companies using it can work efficiently and gain an edge over their competitors. In the next paragraphs, the most common machine learning algorithms are listed and explained:

- *Linear regression*: Linear regression reveals the linear relationship between two features. It models the correlation between two features by fitting a linear equation to the collected data. One feature is an explanatory variable, and the other is a dependent variable (Brynjolfsson et al., 2011).
- *Logistic regression*: This type of machine learning algorithm is often used for classification and predictive analytics. Logistic regression estimates the probability that a future event will happen. Since the result is a probability, the dependent variable is bounded between 0 and 1.
- *Decision tree*: Decision tree builds regression or classification models in the form of a tree structure. The learning process divides the original dataset into smaller and smaller subsets and the result is a tree with decision nodes and leaf nodes. A decision node has two or more branches, each representing values for the tested variable. The leaf node represents a decision on the numerical target. The topmost decision node in a tree corresponds to the best predictor and it is called root node.
- *Support vector machine*: SVM is a machine learning algorithm that creates the best decision boundary to segregate n-dimensional space into classes so that we can easily input the new data in the correct category in the

future. This best decision boundary is called a hyperplane. SVM chooses the extreme points/vectors that help in creating the hyperplane. These extreme cases are called support vectors, and hence algorithm is termed SVM (Brynjolfsson et al., 2011).

- *K Nearest Neighbors*: The K Nearest Neighbors algorithm is used for both classification and regression problems. It stores all the known use cases and classifies new data points by segregating them into different classes. This classification is accomplished based on the similarity score of the recent use cases to the available ones. The K Nearest Neighbors is a supervised machine learning algorithm, wherein "K" refers to the number of neighboring points we consider while classifying and segregating the known n groups (Tambe, 2012).

- *K-means*: K-means is a clustering algorithm that computes the centroids and iterates until it finds optimal centroid. It assumes that the number of clusters is already known. In this algorithm, the data points are assigned to a cluster in such a manner that the sum of the squared distance between the data points and centroid would be minimum (Brynjolfsson et al., 2011). It is to be understood that less variation within the clusters will lead to more similar data points within the same cluster.

- *Random forest algorithm*: A random forest is a machine learning technique that is used to solve regression and classification problems. It utilizes ensemble learning, which is a technique that combines many classifiers to provide solutions to complex problems. A random forest algorithm consists of many decision trees, and it establishes the outcome based on the predictions of the decision trees. It predicts by taking the average or mean of the output from various trees. Increasing the number of trees increases the precision of the outcome (Tambe, 2012).

- *Artificial neural networks*: Artificial neural networks are machine learning algorithms that have three or more interconnected layers in their computational model that process the input data. The first layer is the input layer or neurons that send input data to deeper layers. The second layer is called the hidden layer. The components of this layer change or tweak the information received through various previous layers by performing a series of data transformations (Tambe, 2012). The third layer is the output layer that sends the final output data for the problem.

- *Recurrent neural networks*: Recurrent neural networks refer to a specific type of artificial neural networks that processes sequential data. Here, the result of the previous step acts as the input to the current step. This is facilitated via the hidden state that remembers information about a sequence. It acts as a memory that maintains the information on what was previously calculated (Tambe, 2012).

The Machine Learning Algorithm diagram below helps you choose the right algorithm to build a predictive analytics model (Figure 2.2):

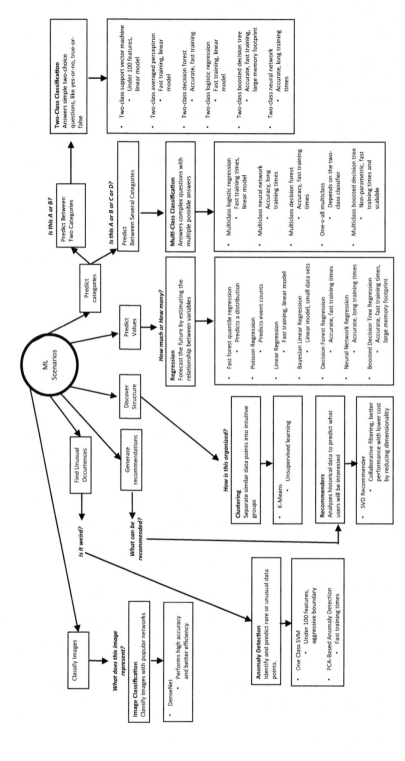

Figure 2.2 Machine learning algorithm diagram.

2.3 Defining Business Metrics and Objectives

For most companies, lack of data is not a problem. In fact, it is the opposite: there is often too much information available to make a clear decision (Lazzeri, 2019). With so much data to sort through, companies need a well-defined strategy to clarify the following business aspects:

- How can machine learning help companies transform business, better manage costs, and drive greater operational excellence?
- Do companies have a well-defined and clearly articulated purpose and vision for what they are looking to accomplish?
- How can companies get support of C-level executives and stakeholders to take that data-driven vision and drive it through the different parts of a business?

In short, companies need to have a clear understanding of their business, decision-making process, and a better machine learning strategy to support that process (Lazzeri, 2019). With the right machine learning mindset, what was once an overwhelming volume of disparate information becomes a simple, clear decision point. Driving transformation requires that companies have a well-defined and clearly articulated purpose and vision for what they are looking to accomplish. It often requires the support of a C-level executive to take that vision and drive it through the different parts of a business.

Companies must begin with the right questions. Questions should be measurable, clear and concise, and directly correlated to their core business. In this stage, it is important to design questions to either qualify or disqualify potential solutions to a specific business problem or opportunity. For example, start with a clearly defined problem: a retail company is experiencing rising costs and is no longer able to offer competitive prices to its customers (Lazzeri, 2019). One of many questions to solve this business problem might include: can the company reduce its operations without compromising quality?

There are two main tasks that companies need to address to answer these types of questions:

- Define business goals: companies need to work with business experts and other stakeholders to understand and identify business problems.
- Formulate right questions: companies need to formulate tangible questions that define the business goals that the machine learning teams can target.

2.4 Establishing Machine Learning Performance Metrics

To successfully translate this vision and business goals into actionable results, it is important to establish clear performance metrics. In the table below, we provide a summary of 20 metrics used for evaluating machine learning models (Table 2.1). We group these metrics into different categories based on the machine learning application they are mostly used for:

Table 2.1 Machine Learning Performance Metrics

Machine learning problem	Performance metric	Description
Classification models	Classification accuracy	It is the number of correct predictions divided by the total number of predictions
Classification models	Precision	It is the metric that is calculated in the following way: True Positive/(True Positive + False Positive)
Classification models	Recall	It is the metric that is calculated in the following way: True Positive/(True Positive + False Negative)
Classification models	F1 Score	It is the percentage of correct predictions that a machine learning model has made
Classification models	Sensitivity	It is the metric that evaluates a model's ability to predict true positives of each available category
Classification models	Specificity	It is the proportion of actual negatives, which got predicted as the negative (or true negative)
Classification models	Receiver operating characteristic curve	It is a plot which shows the performance of a binary classifier as a function of its cut-off threshold. It essentially shows the true positive rate against the false positive rate for various threshold values
Classification models	Area under the curve	It is the metric that calculates the area under the ROC curve, and therefore it is between 0 and 1. One way of interpreting AUC is as the probability that the model ranks a random positive example more highly than a random negative example
Regression	Mean squared error	It is the average squared error between the predicted and actual values
Regression models	Mean absolute error	It is the average absolute distance between the predicted and target values

(Continued)

Table 2.1 (Continued)

Machine learning problem	Performance metric	Description
Regression models	Inlier ratio metric	It is the percentage of data points which are predicted with an error less than a margin
Regression models	Root mean squared error	It is the square root of the average of the squared difference between the target value and the value predicted by the regression model
Ranking models	Mean reciprocal rank	It is the average of the reciprocal ranks of the first relevant item for a set of queries
Ranking models	Precision at k	It is the proportion of recommended items in the top-k set that are relevant
Ranking models	Normalized discounted cumulative gain	It is the metric of measuring ranking quality
General Statistical Models	Pearson correlation coefficient	It is the metric that measures the strength of the association between two continuous variables
General statistical models	Coefficient of determination	It is the proportion of the variance in the dependent variable that is predictable from the independent variable

In order to identify the right set of metrics, it is important for companies to focus on these analytical aspects:

a Decide what to measure

Let's take Predictive Maintenance, a technique used to predict when an in-service machine will fail, allowing for its maintenance to be planned well in advance. As it turns out, this is a very broad area with a variety of end goals, such as predicting root causes of failure, which parts will need replacement and when, providing maintenance recommendations after the failure happens, etc.

Many companies are attempting predictive maintenance and have piles of data available from all sorts of sensors and systems. But, too often, customers do not have enough data about their failure history and that makes it very difficult to do predictive maintenance – after all, models need to be trained on such failure history data in order to predict future failure incidents (Lazzeri, 2019). So, while it's important to lay out the vision, purpose, and scope of any analytics project, it is critical that you start off by gathering the right data.

b　*Decide how to measure it*

Thinking about how companies measure their data is just as important, especially before the data collection and ingestion phase. Key questions to ask for this sub-step include:

- What is the time frame?
- What is the unit of measure?
- What factors should be included?

A central objective of this step is to identify the key business variables that the analysis needs to predict. We refer to these variables as the *model targets*, and we use the metrics associated with them to determine the success of the project. Two examples of such targets are sales forecasts or the probability of an order being fraudulent.

c　*Define the success metrics*

After the key business variables identification, it is important to translate your business problem into a machine learning question and define the metrics that will define your project's success. Companies typically use machine learning or machine learning to answer five types of questions:

- How much or how many? (regression)
- Which category? (classification)
- Which group? (clustering)
- Is this weird? (Anomaly detection)
- Which option should be taken? (recommendation)

Determine which of these questions companies are asking and how to answer them achieves business goals and enables measurement of the results (Lazzeri, 2019). At this point, it is important to revisit the project goals by asking and refining sharp questions that are relevant, specific, and unambiguous. For example, if a company wants to achieve a customer churn prediction, it will need an accuracy rate of "x" percent by the end of a three-month project. With this data, companies can offer customer promotions to reduce churn.

2.5　Architecting the End-to-End Machine Learning Solution

In the era of Big Data, there is a growing trend of accumulation and analysis of data, often unstructured, coming from applications, web environments, and a wide variety of devices. In this third step, companies need to think more organically about the end-to-end data flow and architecture that will support their machine learning solutions (Lazzeri, 2019). Data architecture is the process of planning the collection of data, including the definition of the information to be collected, the standards and norms that will be used for its structuring, and the tools used in the extraction, storage, and processing of such data.

This stage is fundamental for any project that performs data analysis, as it is what guarantees the availability and integrity of the information that will be explored in the future (Lazzeri, 2019). To do this, you need to understand how the data will be stored, processed, and used, and which analyses will be expected for the project. It can be said that at this point there is an intersection of the technical and strategic visions of the project, as the purpose of this planning task is to keep the data extraction and manipulation processes aligned with the objectives of the business.

There are mainly seven stages of building an end-to-end pipeline in machine learning (Figure 2.3):

1   Data Ingestion: The initial stage in every machine learning workflow is transferring incoming data into a data repository. The vital element is that data is saved without alteration, allowing everyone to record the original information accurately. You can obtain data from various

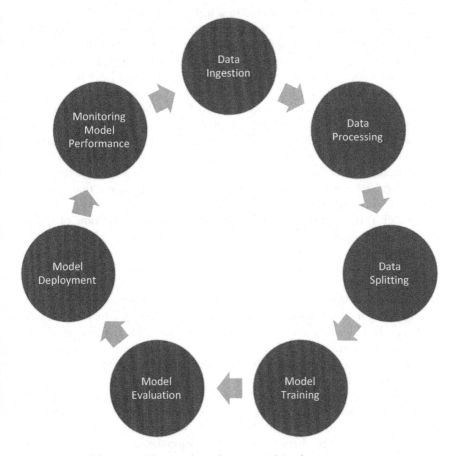

Figure 2.3 Building an end-to-end pipeline in machine learning.

sources, including pub/sub requests. Also, you can use streaming data from other platforms. Each dataset has a separate pipeline, which you can analyze simultaneously. The data is split within each pipeline to take advantage of numerous servers or processors. This reduces the overall time to perform the task by distributing the data processing across multiple pipelines. For storing data, use NoSQL databases as they are an excellent choice for keeping massive amounts of rapidly evolving organized/unorganized data. They also provide storage space that is shared and extensible (Lazzeri, 2019).

2   Data Processing: This time-consuming phase entails taking input, unorganized data and converting it into data that the models can use. During this step, a distributed pipeline evaluates the data's quality for structural differences, incorrect or missing data points, outliers, anomalies, etc., and corrects any abnormalities along the way (Lazzeri, 2019). This stage also includes the process of feature engineering. Once you ingest data into the pipeline, the feature engineering process begins. It stores all the generated features in a feature data repository. It transfers the output of features to the online feature data storage upon completion of each pipeline, allowing for easy data retrieval.

3   Data Splitting: The primary objective of a machine learning data pipeline is to apply an accurate model to data that it hasn't been trained on, based on the accuracy of its feature prediction. To assess how the model works against new datasets, you need to divide the existing labeled data into training, testing, and validation data subsets at this point. Model training and assessment are the next two pipelines in this stage, both of which should be likely to access the API used for data splitting. It needs to produce a notification and return with the dataset to protect the pipeline (model training or evaluation) against selecting values that result in an irregular data distribution (Lazzeri, 2019).

4   Model Training: This pipeline includes the entire collection of training model algorithms, which you can use repeatedly and alternatively as needed. The model training service obtains the training configuration details, and the pipeline's process requests the required training dataset from the API (or service) constructed during the data splitting stage. Once it sets the model, configurations, training parameters, and other elements, it stores them in a model candidate data repository which will be evaluated and used further in the pipeline. Model training should take error tolerance, data backups, and failover on training segments. For example, you can retrain each split if the latest attempt fails, owing to a transitory glitch.

5   Model Evaluation: This stage assesses the stored models' predictive performance using test and validation data subsets until a model solves the business problem efficiently. The model evaluation step uses several criteria to compare predictions on the evaluation dataset with actual values. A notification service is broadcast once a model is ready for deployment,

and the pipeline chooses the "best" model from the evaluation sample to make predictions on future cases. A library of multiple evaluators provides the accuracy metrics of a model and stores them against the model in the data repository (Lazzeri, 2019).

6 Model Deployment: Once the model evaluation is complete, the pipeline selects the best model and deploys it. The pipeline can deploy multiple machine learning models to ensure a smooth transition between old and new models; the pipeline services continue to work on new prediction requests while deploying a new model.

7 Monitoring Model Performance: The final stage of a pipeline in machine learning is model monitoring and performance scoring. This stage entails monitoring and assessing the model behavior on a regular and recurring basis to gradually enhance it. Models are used for scoring based on feature values imported by previous stages. When a new prediction is issued, the Performance Monitoring Service receives a notification, runs the performance evaluation, records the outcomes, and raises the necessary alerts. It compares the scoring to the observed results generated by the data pipeline during the assessment. You can use various methods for monitoring, the most common of which is logging analytics.

It is now necessary to select the right tools that will allow an organization to actually build an end-to-end machine learning solution. Factors such as volume, variety of data, and the speed with which they are generated and processed will help companies identify which types of technology they should use (Lazzeri, 2019). Among the various existing categories, it is important to consider:

• Data collection tools: These are the ones that will help us in the extraction and organization of raw data.
• Storage tools: These tools store data in either structured or unstructured form, and can aggregate information from several platforms in an integrated manner
• Data processing and analysis tools: With these, we use the data stored and processed to create a visualization logic that enables the development of analyses, studies, and reports that support operational and strategic decision-making.
• Model operationalization tools: After a company has a set of models that perform well, they can operationalize them for other applications to consume. Depending on the business requirements, predictions are made either in real time or on a batch basis. To deploy models, companies need to expose them to an open API interface. The interface enables the model to be easily consumed from various applications (Lazzeri, 2019).

The tools can vary according to the needs of the business but should ideally offer the possibility of integration between them to allow the data to be used in any of the chosen platforms without needing manual treatments (Lazzeri, 2019). This end-to-end architecture will also offer some key advantages and values to companies, such as:

- Accelerated Deployment and Reduced Risk: An integrated end-to-end architecture can drastically minimize cost and effort required to piece together an end-to-end solution, and further enables accelerated time to deploy use cases
- Modularity: Allows companies to start at any part of the end-to-end architecture with the assurance that the key components will integrate and fit together
- Flexibility: Runs anywhere including multi-cloud or hybrid-cloud environments
- End-to-End Analytics and Machine Learning: Enables end-to-end analytics from edge-to-cloud, with the ability to push machine learning models back out to the edge for real-time decision making
- End-to-End Data Security and Compliance: Pre-integrated security and manageability across the architecture including access, authorization, and authentication
- Enabling Open-Source Innovation: Built off open-source projects and a vibrant community innovation model that ensures open standards

AI offers companies the possibility to transform their operations: from applications able to predict and schedule equipment's maintenance to intelligent R&D systems able to estimate the cost of new drug development, until HR AI-powered tools are able to enhance the hiring process and employee retention strategy. However, to be able to leverage this opportunity, companies must learn how to successfully build, train, test, and push hundreds of machine learning models in production, and to move models from development to their production environment in ways that are robust, fast, and repeatable (Lazzeri, 2022).

Nowadays data scientists and machine learning developers have a much easier experience when building AI-based solutions through the availability and accessibility of data and open-source machine learning frameworks. However, this process becomes a lot more complex when they need to think about model deployment and pick the best strategy to scale up to a production-grade system (Lazzeri, 2022).

In this chapter we will introduce some common concepts and challenges of machine learning model deployment and AI application building process; in particular, we will discuss the following points to enable organizations to tackle some of those challenges:

1   What AI is
2   Why successful model deployment is fundamental for AI-driven companies

3   How to select the right tools to succeed with model deployment and AI adoption
4   Why AIOps is critical for successful maintenance of AI applications

2.6 What AI Is

AI is a field which combines computer science, big data, and machine learning, to enable problem-solving. These disciplines are comprised of machine learning algorithms which seek to create trained models which make predictions or classifications based on input data (Russell, 2010). Both deep learning and machine learning are sub-fields of AI, and deep learning is a sub-field of machine learning. Deep learning is comprised of neural networks (Bose, 2007). Machine learning is a subset of AI that uses statistical learning algorithms to build smart systems. Machine learning systems can learn from historical data, be deployed, and automatically learn and improve without explicitly being programmed again. Machine learning algorithms are classified into three categories: supervised, unsupervised, and reinforcement learning.

Deep Learning is a subset of machine learning, and it is a technique that is inspired by the way a human brain filters data and external input. In simple terms, deep learning models filter the input data through layers of mathematical and optimization functions to predict and classify information. Deep learning network architectures are classified into Convolutional Neural Networks, Recurrent Neural Networks, and Recursive Neural Networks (Russell, 2010).

In the table below (Table 2.2), we summarize some of the most innovative AI applications in recent years, divided by business areas:

Companies are increasingly recognizing the competitive advantage of applying AI insights to business objectives and are making it a business-wide priority. For example, targeted recommendations provided by AI can help

Table 2.2 Innovative AI Applications

Industry	AI application
Retail and E-commerce	Personalized shopping, AI-powered assistants, virtual fitting rooms
Education	Voice assistants, personalized learning, machine translation (speech to text and text to speech)
Healthcare	Clinical trials for drug development, robotic surgeries, virtual nursing assistants
Manufacturing	Steel quality inspection, predictive maintenance, food waste reduction
Transportation	Self-driving vehicles, pedestrian detection, computer vision-powered parking management
Finance	Fraud detection, commercial lending operations, investment robo-advisory

businesses make better decisions faster. Many of the features and capabilities of AI can lead to lower costs, reduced risks, faster time to market, and much more (Bahrammirzaee, 2010).

2.7 Why Successful Model Deployment is Fundamental for AI-Driven Companies

Machine learning model deployment is the process by which a machine learning algorithm is converted into a web service. We refer to this conversion process as *operationalization*: operationalizing a machine learning model means transforming it into a consumable service and embedding it into an existing production environment.

Model deployment is a fundamental step of the Machine Learning Model Workflow. Through machine learning model deployment, companies can begin to take full advantage of the predictive and intelligent models they build, develop business practices based on their model results and, therefore, transform themselves into actual AI-driven businesses (Lazzeri, 2022).

When we think about AI, we focus our attention on key components of the machine learning workflow such as data sources and ingestion, data pipelines, machine learning model training and testing, how to engineer new features and which variables to use to make the models more accurate. All these steps are important; however, thinking about how we are going to consume those models and data over time is also a critical step in every machine learning machine learning pipeline. We can only begin extracting real value and business benefits from a model's predictions when it has been deployed and operationalized.

We believe that successful model deployment is fundamental for AI-driven enterprises for the following key reasons:

- Deployment of machine learning models means making models available to external customers and/or other teams and stakeholders in a company.
- By deploying models, other teams in a company can use them, send data to them and get their predictions, which are in turn populated back into the company systems to increase training data quality and quantity.
- Once this process is initiated, companies will start building and deploying higher numbers of machine learning models in production and master robust and repeatable ways to move models from development environments into business operations systems.

Many companies see AI-enablement efforts as a technical practice. However, it is more of a business-driven initiative that starts within the company; to become an AI-driven company, it is important that the people, who today successfully operate and understand the business, collaborate closely with those teams that are responsible for the machine learning deployment workflow (Lazzeri, 2022).

Right from the first day of an AI application process, machine learning teams should interact with business counterparts. It is essential to maintain constant interaction to understand the model *experimentation* process parallel to the model *deployment* and *consumption* steps. Most organizations struggle to unlock machine learning's potential to optimize their operational processes and get data scientists, analysts, and business teams speaking the same language.

Moreover, machine learning models must be trained on historical data which demands the creation of a prediction data pipeline, an activity requiring multiple tasks including data processing, feature engineering, and tuning. Each task, down to versions of libraries and handling of missing values, must be exactly duplicated from the development to the production environment. Sometimes, differences in technology used in development and in production contribute to difficulties in deploying machine learning models.

Companies can use machine learning pipelines to create and manage workflows that stitch together machine learning phases. For example, a pipeline might include data preparation, model training, model deployment, and inference/scoring phases. Each phase can encompass multiple steps, each of which can run unattended in various computer targets. Pipeline steps are reusable and can be run without rerunning subsequent steps if the output of that step hasn't changed. Pipelines also allow data scientists to collaborate while working on separate areas of a machine learning workflow (Lazzeri, 2022).

2.8 How to Select the Right Tools to Succeed with Model Deployment and AI Adoption

Building, training, testing and finally deploying machine learning models is often a tedious and slow process for companies that are looking at transforming their operations with AI. Moreover, even after months of development, which delivers a machine learning model based on a single algorithm, the management team has little means of knowing whether their data scientists have created a great model and how to scale and operationalize it.

Below we share a few guidelines on how a company can select the right tools to succeed with model deployment. The model deployment workflow should be based on the following simple steps:

1   Register the model
2   Prepare to deploy (specify assets, usage, compute target)
3   Deploy the model to the compute target
4   Register the model

A registered model is a logical container for one or more files that make up the model. For example, if data scientists and Machine Learning developers have a model that is stored in multiple files, data scientists and ML developers can register them as a single model in the workspace. After registration, data scientists and ML developers can then download or deploy the registered model and receive all the files that were registered.

To deploy a model as a web service, data scientists and ML developers must create an inference configuration and a deployment configuration. Inference, or model scoring, is the phase where the deployed model is used for prediction, most commonly on production data. In the inference config, data scientists and ML developers specify the scripts and dependencies needed to serve the model. In the deployment config data scientists and ML developers specify details of how to serve the model on the compute target (Lazzeri, 2022).

The entry script receives data submitted to a deployed web service and passes it to the model. It then takes the response returned by the model and returns that to the client. The script is specific to the model; it must understand the data that the model expects and returns. When data scientists and ML developers register a model, data scientists and ML developers provide a model name used for managing the model in the registry (Bose, 2007).

Finally, before deploying, data scientists and ML developers must define the deployment configuration. The deployment configuration is specific to the compute target that will host the web service. For example, when deploying locally data scientists and ML developers must specify the port where the service accepts requests.

2.9 Why AIOps is Critical for Successful Maintenance of AI Applications

AIOps is important for several reasons. First, machine learning models rely on huge amounts of data, and it is very difficult for data scientists and engineers to keep track of it all. It is also challenging to keep track of the different parameters that can be tweaked in machine learning models. Sometimes small changes can lead to very big differences in the results that data scientists and ML developers get from the machine learning models. Data scientists and ML developers also must keep track of the features that the model works with; feature engineering is an important part of the machine learning lifecycle and can have a large impact on model accuracy.

Once in production, monitoring a machine learning model is not really like monitoring other kinds of software such as a web app, and debugging a machine learning model is complicated. Models use real-world data for generating their predictions, and real-world data may change over time. As it changes, it is important to track the model performance and, when needed, update the model. This means that data scientists and ML developers have to keep track of new data changes and make sure that the model learns from them (Lazzeri, 2022).

There are many different AIOps capabilities to consider before deploying to production. First is the capability of creating reproducible machine learning pipelines. Machine learning pipelines allow data scientists and ML developers to define repeatable and reusable steps for the data preparation, training, and scoring processes. These steps should include the creation of reusable software environments for training and deploying models, as well as the ability to register, package, and deploy models from anywhere. Using pipelines allows to frequently update models or roll out new models alongside the other AI applications and services.

Data scientists and ML developers also need to track the associated metadata required to use the model and capture governance data for the end-to-end machine learning lifecycle. In the latter case, lineage information can include, for example, who published the model, why changes were made at some point, or when different models were deployed or used in production (Lazzeri, 2022).

It is also important to notify and alert people to events in the machine learning lifecycle. For example, experiment completion, model registration, model deployment, and data drift detection. Data scientists and ML developers also need to monitor machine learning applications for operational and ML-related issues. Here it is important for data scientists to be able to compare model inputs from training-time vs. inference-time, to explore model-specific metrics, and to configure monitoring and alerting on machine learning infrastructure.

The second aspect that is important to consider before deploying machine learning in production is open-source integration. Here, there are three different open-source technologies that are extremely important. First, there are open-source training frameworks, which are great for accelerating machine learning solutions. Next are open-source frameworks for interpretable and fair models. Finally, there are open-source tools for model deployment (Lazzeri, 2022).

There are many different open-source training frameworks. Three of the most popular are PyTorch, TensorFlow, and RAY. PyTorch is an end-to-end machine learning framework, and it includes TorchServe, an easy-to-use tool for deploying PyTorch models at scale. PyTorch also has mobile deployment support and cloud platform support. Finally, PyTorch has C++ frontend support: a pure C++ interface to PyTorch that follows the design and the architecture of the Python frontend.

TensorFlow is another end-to-end machine learning framework that is very popular in the industry. For AIOps, it has a feature called TensorFlow Extended (TFX) that is an end-to-end platform for preparing data, training, validating, and deploying machine learning models in large production environments. A TFX pipeline is a sequence of components which are specifically designed for scalable and high-performance machine learning tasks.

RAY is a reinforcement-learning (RL) framework, which contains several useful training libraries: Tune, RLlib, Train, and Dataset. Tune is great for hyperparameter tuning. RLlib is used for training RL models. Train is for distributed deep learning. Dataset is for distributed data loading. RAY has two additional libraries, Serve and Workflows, which are useful for deploying machine learning models and distributed apps to production (Lazzeri, 2022).

For creating interpretable and fair models, two useful frameworks are InterpretML and Fairlearn. InterpretML is an open-source package that incorporates several machine learning interpretability techniques. With this package, data scientists and ML developers can train interpretable glass box models and explain black box systems. Moreover, it helps data scientists and ML developers understand the model's global behavior, or understand the reason behind individual predictions.

Fairlearn is a Python package that can provide metrics for assessing which groups are negatively impacted by a model and can compare multiple models in terms of their use of fairness and accuracy metrics. It also supports several algorithms for mitigating unfairness in a variety of AI and machine learning tasks, with various fairness definitions (Lazzeri, 2022).

Our third open-source technology is used for model deployment. When working with different frameworks and tools, data scientists and ML developers have to deploy models according to each framework's requirements. In order to standardize this process, data scientists and ML developers can use the ONNX format.

ONNX stands for Open Neural Network Exchange. ONNX is an open-source format for machine learning models which supports interoperability between different frameworks. This means that data scientists and ML developers can train a model in one of the many popular machine learning frameworks, such as PyTorch, TensorFlow, or RAY. Data scientists and ML developers can then convert it into ONNX format and it in different frameworks; for example, in ML.NET.

The ONNX Runtime (ORT) represents machine learning models using a common set of operators, the building blocks of machine learning and deep learning models, which allows the model to run on different hardware and operating systems. ORT optimizes and accelerates machine learning inferencing, which can enable faster customer experiences and lower product costs. It supports models from deep learning frameworks such as PyTorch, and TensorFlow, but also classical machine learning libraries, such as Scikit-learn.

There are many different popular frameworks that support conversion to ONNX. For some of these, such as PyTorch, ONNX format export is built in. For others, like TensorFlow or Keras, there are separately installable packages that can process this conversion. The process is very straightforward: First, data scientists and ML developers need a model trained using any framework that supports export and conversion to ONNX format. Then data scientists and ML developers load and run the model with ONNX Runtime. Finally, data scientists and ML developers can tune performance using various runtime configurations or hardware accelerators (Lazzeri, 2022).

The third aspect that data scientists and ML developers should know before deploying machine learning in production is how to build pipelines for the machine learning solution. The first task in the pipeline is data preparation, which includes importing, validating, cleaning, transforming, and normalizing the data.

Next, the pipeline contains training configuration, including parameters, file paths, logging, and reporting. Then there are the actual training and validation jobs that are performed in an efficient and repeatable way. Efficiency might come from specific data subsets, different hardware, compute resources, distributed processing, and also progress monitoring. Finally, there is the deployment step, which includes versioning, scaling, provisioning, and access control.

Choosing a pipeline technology will depend on the particular needs; usually, these fall under one of three scenarios: model orchestration, data orchestration, or code and application orchestration. Each scenario is oriented around a *persona* who is the primary user of the technology and a *canonical pipeline*, which is the scenario's typical workflow (Lazzeri, 2022).

In the model orchestration scenario, the primary persona is a data scientist. The canonical pipeline in this scenario is from data to model. In terms of open-source technology options, Kubeflow Pipelines is a popular choice for this scenario. For a data orchestration scenario, the primary persona is a data engineer, and the canonical pipeline is data to data. A common open-source choice for this scenario is Apache Airflow. Finally, the third scenario is code and application orchestration. Here, the primary persona is an app developer. The canonical pipeline here is from code plus model to a service. One typical open-source solution for this scenario is Jenkins.

Then the service determines the dependencies between steps, resulting in a very dynamic execution graph. When each step in the execution graph runs, the service configures the necessary hardware and software environment. The step also sends logging and monitoring information to its containing experiment object. When the step is complete, its outputs are prepared as inputs to the next step. Finally, the resources that are no longer needed are finalized and detached (Lazzeri, 2022).

2.10 General Remarks and Future Directions

The goal of this chapter is to guide every company throughout the AI life-cycle and adoption. While the specifics will vary based on the organization, scope, and skills, the strategy should clearly define how a model can become an AI solution and can move from stage to stage, designating responsibility for each task along the way. The following questions (Ajgaonkar, 2021) can also help to guide conversations as companies build the AIOps strategy:

- What are the company goals with AI?
- What performance metrics will be measured when developing models?
- What level of performance is acceptable to the business?
- Where will data scientists test and execute the machine learning model?

- How will the company create alignment between the development and production environments?
- How will data ultimately be ingested and stored?
- Who is responsible for each stage in the lifecycle?
- Who will build the AIOps pipeline?
- Who will oversee implementation?
- Who will be responsible for ongoing performance evaluation and maintenance?
- How can visibility, collaboration, and handoffs be improved across these different roles?
- How will models be monitored over time?
- How frequently will models be audited?
- How will models be updated to account for deterioration or anomalous data?
- How will you gather feedback from users to improve results?

Several impressive documentations of established research methods and philosophy have been discussed in print for several years. Unfortunately, little comparison and integration across studies exist. In this chapter, we have set out to create a common understanding of AI research.

References

Ajgaonkar, A. (2021). MLOps: The key to unlocking AI operationalization, *Insight Tech Journal, 2*, 42–46.

Bahrammirzaee, A. (2010). A comparative survey of artificial intelligence applications in finance: Artificial neural networks, expert system and hybrid intelligent systems, *Neural Computing and Applications*, 19(8), 1165–1195.

Bijamov, A., Shubitidze, F., Fernández, J. P., Shamatava, I., Barrowes, B., & O'Neill, K. (2011). Comparison of supervised and unsupervised machine learning techniques for UXO classification using EMI data, *Proceedings of SPIE – The International Society for Optical Engineering*, 801706, 1–11.

Bose, B. K., (2007). Neural network applications in power electronics and motor drives-an introduction and perspective, *IEEE Transactions on Industrial Electronics*, 54(1), 14–33.

Brynjolfsson, E., Hitt, L. M., & Kim, H. H. (2011). Strength in numbers: How does data-driven decision making affect firm performance? Working paper. SSRN working paper. Available at SSRN: http://ssrn.com/abstract=1819486

Davenport, T. H., & Patil, D. J. (2012). Data scientist: The sexiest job of the 21st century, *Harvard Business Review*, 90(10), 70–76.

Dhankhad, S., Mohammed, E., & Far, B. (2018). Supervised machine learning algorithms for credit card fraudulent transaction detection: A comparative study. *2018 IEEE International Conference on Information Reuse and Integration*, 122–125.

Herath, H. M. M. G. T., Kumara, J. R. S. S., Fernando, M. A. R. M., Bandara, K. M. K. S., & Serina, I. (2018). Comparison of supervised machine learning techniques for PD classification in generator insulation. *2017 IEEE International Conference on Industrial and Information Systems*, 1–6.

Lazzeri, F. (2019). The data science mindset: Six principles to build healthy data-driven companies, InfoQ.

Lazzeri, F. (2022). What you should know before deploying ML in production, InfoQ.

Lushan, M., Bhattacharjee, M., Ahmed, T., Rahman, M. A., & Ahmed, S. (2019). Supervising vehicle using pattern recognition: Detecting unusual behavior using machine learning algorithms. *2018 IEEE Region Ten Symposium*, 277–281.

Mishu, S. Z., & Rafiuddin, S. M. (2016). Performance analysis of supervised machine learning algorithms for text classification. *2016 19th International Conference on Computer and Information Technology*, 409–413.

Moh, M., Gajjala, A., Gangireddy, S. C. R., & Moh T.-S. (2015). On multi-tier sentiment analysis using supervised machine learning. *2015 IEEE/WIC/ACM International Conference on Web Intelligence and Intelligent Agent Technology*, 341–344.

Robles-Durazno, A., Moradpoor, N., McWhinnie, J., & Russell, G. (2018). A supervised energy monitoring-based machine learning approach for anomaly detection in a clean water supply system. *2018 International Conference on Cyber Security and Protection of Digital Services (Cyber Security)*, 1–8.

Russell, S. J. (2010). *Artificial Intelligence: A Modern Approach*, Upper Saddle River, NJ, Prentice Hall.

Tambe, P. (2012). Big data know-how and business value. Working paper. New York, NYU Stern School of Business.

3 Neural Networks and Deep Learning

Chiara Galimberti and Marco Repetto

3.1 Introduction

Artificial Intelligence (AI) and all its related fields are in the midst of an optimism cycle called AI Summer (Mitchell, 2021). The term describes the current period of increased investment and activity in AI following the AI winter that happened in the late 1990s.

One way to measure the level of investment in AI is to look at the amount of venture capital funding that goes into AI startups. This metric has been increasing steadily over the past few years, from $2.4 billion in 2016 to $9.3 billion in 2019 (CBinsights, 2021). Another way to measure AI activity is to look at the number of papers published on the topic. According to the Web of Science database, the number of papers published on AI has been increasing rapidly, from just over 3,000 in 2010 to over 25,000 in 2020. The increased investment and activity in AI are leading to higher expectations for the technology. In a survey of AI experts, 62% said they believe AI will "substantially transform" society by 2030, and 18% said AI will "transform" or "revolutionize" society (Anderson, 2018).

The present AI boom began about in the 10s with no signs of abating. The use of AI is becoming increasingly popular among big technology corporations, with Google, Meta, IBM, and Microsoft among those making significant investments. Manufacturing companies are not lagging in AI adoption. According to the research report by the International Data Corporation (IDC), worldwide spending on AI and cognitive services in manufacturing companies is expected to reach 26.6 billion dollars in 2025 (IDC, 2022). AI is expected to bring about significant changes in manufacturing. Some companies are using AI to help with product design. For example, Autodesk offers a program called Autodesk Fusion 360 that uses AI to help designers create products. The program can recommend designs based on what has been designed before, and it can also suggest changes to a design based on customer feedback. Other companies are using AI to help with production. A worth noting example is the MindSphere platform owned by Siemens that enables companies to use AI to optimize their production processes (Lichtenthaler, 2018). Several alternative tasks can be performed using

DOI: 10.4324/9781003304616-5

built-in applications or developing new ones. For example, it is possible to build a recommender system to suggest optimal settings for production processes based on data collected from machines. In addition to these projects run by well-established companies, there is an emerging ecosystem of startups. These companies are developing AI technologies on par with their larger competitors and are receiving record amounts of investments. For example, in the car industry, Comma AI aims to build a full self-driving system like the one provided by Tesla (Santana & Hotz, 2016). What is setting the difference in comparison to the previous AI summers is the pervasive usage of Deep Learning (DL) techniques. In fact, during this time, DL techniques experienced a significant expansion. DL is a subset of AI that is concerned with algorithms that can learn to represent and model data through multiple layers of abstraction, resulting in systems that can learn to perform tasks that are difficult to explicitly program. In DL, artificial neural networks (ANNs) are an essential component. Originally ANNs were modeled after the human brain in that they are composed of a vast number of interconnected nodes, also called neurons. Given this complex structure, an ANN is capable of recognizing highly nonlinear patterns in the input data (Ciampi & Gordini, 2013). Moreover, ANNs can learn faster than canonical Expert Based Systems since they require less human intervention (LeCun et al., 1990). Nowadays we know that ANNs are by no means mimicking the inner working of a biological brain. In fact, ANNs take from the biological brain only two components: neurons and axons. The first difference resides in how biological neurons work, which is more similar to the Perceptron as proposed by Rosenblatt than the current activation functions, exposed in Section 0. Another worth noting difference is the learning process. As surveyed by Lillicrap et al. (2020), there is no scientific evidence that the brain uses a backpropagation algorithm for learning. Regardless of these considerations, there has been an increase in the number of ANN applications to provide services and produce goods that we use daily due to the vast amount of data generated daily and the need to analyze it quickly and accurately. Another critical factor to consider from a practitioner's perspective is the democratization of such technology. ANNs were formerly reserved for specialists only. As new software is developed, they are becoming more user-friendly, which is encouraging. It means that a more significant number of people will be able to use them and benefit from their features. Furthermore, recent advances in software have established an environment that allows non-expert programmers to design and deploy complicated ANN structures without the need for specialized knowledge. This software comprehends ANN frameworks such as Tensorflow (Abadi et al., 2015), Pytorch (Paszke et al., 2019), and Flux (Innes et al., 2018). As well as models and results management tools, such as Weights and Biases, for managing the distribution and reproducibility of such models as well as their findings (Biewald, 2020). Several companies have started to use ANNs in their daily operations. Services such as Spotify, which employs an ANN to locate tunes that best match users' preferences are a good illustration of this pervasiveness in practice (Dieleman, 2014). Another example is Tesla's Autopilot, which is capable of providing an aided self-driving experience and has been available in cars since 2015 (Dikmen & Burns, 2016). The above are only a few examples of how ANNs are becoming increasingly popular. They are often utilized to know how to serve the customers and improve their overall experience effectively. More specifically, ANN usage is becoming increasingly popular in a wide range of business fields. For example, ANNs are used to assess credit risk for both consumers and enterprises to predict whether or not a borrower will default on a loan (Lessmann et al., 2015). This is accomplished by teaching the network to recognize patterns in historical data about defaulting borrowers. Another application of ANN in business is in the prediction of consumer behavior (Khodabandehlou & Zivari Rahman, 2017). Consumers' potential interests in products, websites they might visit, and types of advertisements they might click on can all be predicted using DL techniques. Customers' preferences can be used to create more targeted advertisements and to improve the overall customer experience. ANN is also used in business to improve decision-making. ANN can be used to improve the accuracy of algorithmic predictions, to improve the accuracy of forecasts, and to improve the accuracy of risk assessments, among other things. When businesses have better data, they can make better decisions about where to allocate their resources, how to respond to changing market conditions, and how to reduce the risk of making bad decisions (Mosavi et al., 2020). Finally, ANN can be applied to business processes in order to increase their efficiency. Besides to numerical application of ANN, they can also be used to improve the accuracy of data entry, translations, and text recognition, to name a few applications. Businesses can save time and money by reducing the amount of human error that occurs during business processes as a result of this information. Additionally, to business advice in the broad field of DL, the purpose of this chapter is to provide the reader a practical introduction to the basic principles of ANNs. Specifically, the reader will become acquainted with the structural elements that are shared by all the different DL architectures, such as the activation functions of the neurons. Following that, a comprehensive overview of the most relevant architectures will be provided. Every DL architecture has its own set of characteristics and is designed to address a certain use case, such as image recognition, object detection, and time series analysis. The most well-known architectures are Feedforward Networks, Convolution Neural Network (CNN), Recurrent Neural Network, and Generative Neural Network. In addition to the basic architecture of Feedforward Networks, a Section of the chapter is dedicated to CNNs, which are frequently used in Computer Vision applications due to their particular structures and properties. The architectures presented are by no means exhaustive. The selection, on the other hand, was based on the popularity of the topic among researchers and practitioners, as well as the prevalence of practical application situations. Another selection factor was the simplicity with which the ideas in the book could be implemented so that the reader could put them into practice during reading.

3.2 History of Artificial Neural Networks and Deep Learning

The history of DL can be traced back to the early days of AI and cognitive science. In 1943, Warren McCulloch and Walter Pitts published a paper that introduced the concept of ANNs (McCulloch & Pitts, 1943). During the 1950s Marvin Minsky and Dean Edmonds created the first neural network simulator called Stochastic Neural Analog Reinforcement Calculator (SNARC). McCulloch and Pitts' work was later extended by Frank Rosenblatt, who developed the first neural network machine, the Perceptron, in the late 1950s (Rosenblatt, 1958). The Perceptron was capable of simple learning tasks, but it was limited in its ability to learn more complex patterns. The first AI winter happened at the end of the 1950s. This was a time when the field of AI was just getting started. Some early successes in the field led to a lot of hype and excitement. But then, a series of setbacks and disappointments caused many people to lose interest in AI. Funding for AI research dried up and the field went into a long period of decline. In the 1960s and 1970s, neural networks were developed more formally and widely used, but there were few successful applications. In 1960, Bernard Widrow and Marcian Hoff created the Adaline which is an early single-layer neural network (Widrow & Hoff, 1960). In the 1970s, a number of researchers began exploring ways to overcome the limitations of the Perceptron. In the 1980s, one of the most influential figures in this effort was Geoffrey Hinton, who developed a technique called backpropagation (Rumelhart et al., 1986). In the 1990s, advances in computer hardware made it possible to train larger neural networks. This led to the development of more sophisticated algorithms such as support vector machines. With backpropagation, neural networks could be trained to perform more complex tasks, such as image recognition and classification. This led to a resurgence of interest in DL in the 1990s. These algorithms were able to learn complex patterns in data and were able to outperform traditional neural networks at the time. However, they were not widely adopted at the time due to the lack of computing power and data. It was not until the early 2000s that DL began to gain traction, due to the advent of more powerful computers and large amounts of data. In the 2000s, new types of neural networks were developed that could learn from data more effectively. These included CNNs and RNNs. In the 2010s, Yann LeCun, Yoshua Bengio, and Geoffrey Hinton published a paper outlining a new way of training neural networks, known as Deep Learning (LeCun et al., 2015). This paper proved to be highly influential, and DL began to gain popularity among researchers in the field of artificial intelligence. In 2012, a team of researchers from the University of Toronto created a neural network that could identify objects in images with high accuracy (Krizhevsky et al., 2017). This breakthrough demonstrated the potential of DL to revolutionize the field of computer vision. In 2015, Google released its own DL software library, TensorFlow, which has been used to develop some of the most advanced AI applications in the world.

3.3 ANN Architectures

ANNs architectures share common elements, such as input and output layers, hidden layers, nodes, and activation functions.

The specification of the structure, on the other hand, is important, and it can be optimized depending on the purpose and the type of data that a particular application deals with. In this section, we will identify more suited architectures for specific use cases such as time series analysis, image analysis, text corpora analysis, casting predictions, and performing data augmentation tasks.

However, before discussing the various architectures, it is necessary to examine the fundamental aspects that all of them have in common, which is the activation functions. Therefore, the following subsection is devoted to explaining all of the various activation functions, along with the implications that they have on the mapping of input to output. In particular, it is considered the distinction between scale variant and scale invariant activation functions, as well as the issues of convergence in specific functions and the problem of the saturating gradient in sigmoidal functions and how to counter them.

The remainder of the section presents the most prevalent types of networks, as well as instances of their use, and is organized as follows. Subsection 0 exposes one of the most common types of ANN, which is the Feedforward Artificial Neural Network (FANN). Subsection 0 exposes the CNN, a special type of neural network designed to extract features from images.

3.4 Activation Functions

An activation function is a mathematical function that is used to map the values of input variables to their corresponding values of output variables. Activation functions are crucial because they enable neural network models to learn complex patterns of data from a variety of sources. More precisely the output of a neuron is determined by the total of all of the neuron's inputs multiplied by the weights of the connections between the neuron and the inputs and shifted by a bias factor. We will generalize it to x. The activation function is used to decide how a neuron should fire (i.e., having an output different from zero) based on the input and the weight of the signal received.

When it comes to neural networks, there are a variety of different activation functions that may be utilized, and the choice of activation function can have an impact on the overall performance of the network. As previously stated, the Perceptron was the first activation function to be suggested. Essentially, the Perceptron is a step function of the following type:

$$f(x) = \begin{cases} 0 & x \le 0 \\ 1 & x > 0 \end{cases}$$

exposed in Figure 3.1a. The Perceptron belongs to the family of thresh-old-based activation functions which differ based on the spiking threshold as well as its amplitude of it. With the introduction of backpropagation, Percep-tron's application began to wane. By examining the first-order derivative of a type of activation function of this nature, it becomes clear why that has hap-pened. As a result of using such an activation function, the ANN will have no way of learning how to alter its weights in order to minimize any given loss function. Aside from the Perceptron activation function, the scale-invariant activation functions are a common family of activation functions. We say that a certain activation function is scale-invariant if the following equality holds:

$$f(\alpha x) = \alpha f(x)$$

The linear activation function is a member of this family of functions, and it is defined as follows:

$$f(x) = x$$

depicted in Figure 3.1b. The Rectified Linear Unit (ReLU), whose func-tional form is

$$f(x) = max(0, x)$$

belongs to this family and is one of the most commonly utilized activation functions (Zhou et al., 2018). Figure 3.1c portrays the ReLU as well as its first-order derivative. The ReLU has the advantages of being linear and scale-invariant, but it also has the disadvantage of providing no significant gradient for half of the function's length. It is possible that if this condition is not dealt with properly, networks will be unable to learn because gradients will be destroyed in all of the weights and no updating will take place as a result. The Leaky ReLU was presented as a solution to this issue in the liter-ature. In the Leaky ReLU function, we have:

$$f(x) = \begin{cases} \alpha x & x \le 0 \\ x & x > 0 \end{cases}$$

where α is the negative slope. Assuming $\alpha = 0.1$ then the function and its derivative become the one depicted in Figure 3.1d. In the Leaky ReLU formulation, the α parameter is not learned but imposed by the modeler. Conversely, in the Parametric ReLU, the α is also a learnable parameter. All the activation functions so far, with the exception made of the linear one, are non-differentiable at zero. This is not a big limitation, however, since one can either apply a clip function or take the right or left derivative. Instead, if we want to revert differentiability in functions like ReLU, we need to give up on scale invariance. A typical scale invariant but a fully differentiable alternative to the ReLU is the Softplus activation function. Softplus is defined as follows:

$$f(x) = \log\left(e^x + 1\right)$$

and it is illustrated in Figure 3.1e. From this activation function is worth noting its first-order derivative:

$$f'(x) = \frac{e^x}{e^x + 1} = \sigma(x)$$

where σ(x) is the logistic function. The Exponential Linear Unit (ELU) function is another differentiable variation of the ReLU function, and it has the following representation:

$$f(x) = \begin{cases} \alpha\left(e^x - 1\right) x \le 0 \\ \\ xx > 0 \end{cases}$$

depicted in Figure 3.1f, for α = 1. The most significant difference between the ELU and the Softplus is that the former may produce negative outputs as well as positive outputs, which allows for faster convergence (Clevert et al., 2015). Another popular scale variant function, implemented in many statistical libraries such as nnet in R (Venables & Ripley, 1999), is the sigmoid activation function. The following is the definition of the sigmoid activation function:

$$f(x) = \frac{1}{1 + e^{-x}}$$

and depicted in Figure 3.1g. Hyperbolic tangent is another prominent scale variant activation function that may be expressed as follows:

$$f(x) = \frac{e^x - e^{-x}}{e^x + e^{-x}}$$

which, despite having twice the amplitude and being centered in zero, essentially behaves like a sigmoid. The chief advantage of hyperbolic tangent is given by the fact that the output might be negative, allowing for faster convergence, as for the case of ELU. A common issue of both the hyperbolic tangent and sigmoid function is the saturating gradient problem. Namely, as the function value approaches 1 or −1, the gradient approaches 0, and the training of the neural network might be hindered. As a result of this problem, after a few epochs of training, the linear part of each neuron, denoted by x, will be located on the periphery of the activation functions. In other words, regardless of the linear portion's sign, the linear part's output value will be considerable. As a result, the input of such functions in each neuron that contributes to defining the nonlinearity will be located at a distance from the center of these functions. In some regions, the gradient/derivative value is extremely tiny compared to the surrounding areas. As a result, even after several iterations, the weights are updated at a snail's pace due to the modest magnitude of the gradient. In other words, saturating in this context means that after a few epochs during which learning occurs relatively quickly, the value of the linear part will be far from the center of the activation function. It will have saturated, and it will take an excessive amount of time to update the weights because the gradient value will be small. To counteract this problem Turian et al. (2009) proposed the Soft Sign activation function defined as

$$f(x) = \frac{x}{1+|x|}$$

and depicted in Figure 3.1i.

So far, we considered functions of the type $f : R^N \to R$. In the final segment of this section, we will go over some vector-valued functions that are commonly used in ANNs. These functions are of the type $f : R^N \to R^N$. The Softmax activation function is one of the most commonly utilized vector-valued activation functions. Essentially Softmax turns the input x into pseudo-probabilities summing to one. Because of that, it is generally used as the output layer activation function in classification tasks with multiple categories. The functional form of Softmax is the following:

$$f_i(x) = \frac{e^{x_i}}{\sum_j e^{x_j}}$$

A second, although more uncommon, vector-valued activation function is the Softmin, defined as Softmax($-x$), in other words:

$$f_i(x) = \frac{e^{-x_i}}{\sum_j e^{-x_j}}$$

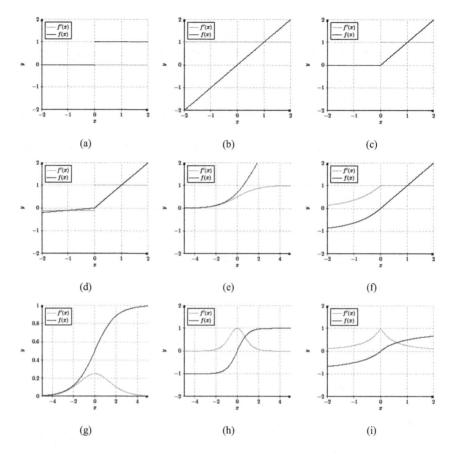

Figure 3.1 Various Artificial Neural Network activation functions. Each activation function (solid line) is plotted against its first-order derivative (dashed line). The figure represent: (a) Perceptron, (b) Linear, (c) Rectified Linear Unit, (d) Leaky Rectified Linear Unit, (e) Soft plus, (f) Exponential Linear Unit, (g) Sigmoid, (h) Hyperbolic Tangent, (i) SoftSign activation functions.

in essence, the following formulation reverses the rank order of its inputs instead of preserving it (Romdhane, 2006)

3.5 Feedforward Neural Network

FANNs are the simplest type of architecture in ANNs. Moreover, FANNs are very common in DL and are powerful prediction models, making them the general off-the-shelve solution for many use cases (Ciampi & Gordini, 2013). A term used frequently to identify FANNs is Multi-Layer Percep-tron (MLP) (Goodfellow et al., 2016). The name is due to the fact that in its origin, FANNs were orchestrated as a stack of Perceptrons organized in different layers. FANNs are composed of a series of layers, where each layer is formed of a series of neurons. The layers that exist between the input and the output are referred to as hidden layers. FANNs that do not have a hidden layer do not fall under the domain of DL. The linear regression model and the logistic regression model are examples of FANNs that are not considered DL architectures. In fact, both are single-layer dense architectures with only one activation function, respectively, the linear and the sigmoidal one. Clearly, it is not efficient to train these models using stochastic gradient descent. Especially in the case of a linear regression model, there is a closed-form solution to the resulting quadratic loss minimization problem, which is the Ordinary Least Square (OLS) estimator.

Speaking about the overall architecture, we have that the information goes in just one direction from the input layer to the output one. Because of that, FANNs are referred to as feedforward networks. In other words, a FANN is a direct acyclic dense graph in its most basic form. The term "direct graph" refers to a graph in which each edge connects one vertex to another, with no vertex having more than one edge flowing into it or leaving it at any given time. An acyclic graph is a graph that does not contain any cycle. In more detail, there are no self-loops of neurons in the network graph in question. A dense graph is a graph in which the number of edges is close to the maximum number of edges that could exist between the number of vertices. FANNs, in particular, are considered dense since each neuron is connected to all of the other neurons in each subsequent layer of the FANN. Each neuron takes a set of values and produces a scalar output value that serves as input to subsequent layer neurons. When a neuron is activated, its output is a function of its input values, the weights of the connections between its neurons, as well as an activation function. Once the inputs have been weighted and moved by a bias term, they are fed to an activation function that scalarizes the distinct contributions of the different inputs. The activation function discussed thoroughly in Subsection 0 of a neuron is an essential component of the neuron since it controls whether or not the neuron will fire. During the training phase, the network learns the weights of the connections as well as the bias term. In a supervised learning framework, this is accomplished by minimizing a given differentiable loss function, which can be either the Root Mean Squared Error (RMSE) in the case of regression or the Crossentropy in the case of classification, depending on the application. A general graphical representation of a FANN is the one proposed in Figure 3.2a. In particular, this model contains three hidden layers, each one constituted by seven neurons. The number of features is six, whereas the output is only one. The primary disadvantages of this representation are essentially two. The first is that this sort of representation is prohibitively expensive in the case of really complicated networks. Second, no information is available regarding the activation functions that have been applied in each neuron. As a result,

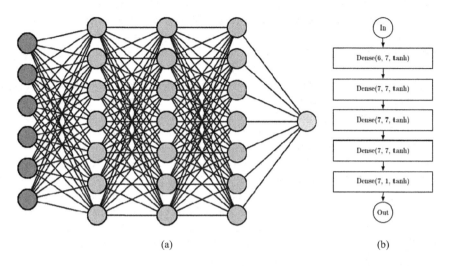

(a)   (b)

Figure 3.2 Different representations of a Feedforward Artificial Neural Network.
(a) Feedforward Artificial Neural Network using network representation. (b) Feedforward Artificial Neural Network using the flowchart
representation.

one frequent method of describing a FANN architecture is through the
use of flowcharts, which indicate the composition of each layer and define
the inputs, outputs, and activation functions for each layer. The following
form is more compact than the preceding one since it more closely reflects
the output of numerous differentiable programming frameworks, such as
Tensorflow and Pytorch, than the prior one.

In mathematical terms FANNs are deep architectures of the type:

$$F = \{f(\cdot, w), w \in W\}$$

where $f(\cdot, w)$ is a shallow architecture, in other words, an activation function, adding some sort of nonlinearity (Bengio, 2009). More specifically, in
a binary classification task, the output of a single hidden layer FANN can be
described as in Arifovic and Gencay by

$$f(x) = \phi\left(\beta_0 + \sum_{j=1}^{d} \beta_j G\left(\gamma_{j0} + \sum_{i=1}^{p} \gamma_{ji} x_i\right)\right)$$

where ϕ and G define the activation functions employed and β and γ the set
of parameters, namely weights and biases. Even though this notation may
seem compelling, FANN can have many layers; therefore, it is necessary to

represent it in a recursive format. Following Roberts et al. (2021), we can define the first input layer as:

$$z_i^{(1)}(x_\alpha) \equiv b_i^{(1)} + \sum_{j=1}^{n_0} W_{i,j}^{(1)} x_{j;\alpha}, \forall i = 1, \cdots, n_1$$

and the successive layers, including the output one as:

$$z_i^{(l+1)}(x_\alpha) \equiv b_i^{(l+1)} + \sum_{j=1}^{n_l} W_{ij}^{(l+1)} \sigma\left(z_j^{(l)}(x_\alpha)\right), \forall i = 1, \cdots, n_{(l+1)}; l = 1, \cdots, L-1$$

In this notation, L describes the number of layers in the network, where each layer l is composed of n_l neurons. The number of layers L defines the depth of the network and the different number of neurons in each layer $n_l = 1, \ldots, L-1$ define the widths of the layers. The depth and hidden-layer widths are variable architecture hyper parameters that define the shape of the network, while the values of n_0 and n_L are set by input and output dimensions of the task, respectively.

As mentioned in Subsection 0, the first FANN architectures used the Perceptron. Nowadays, these architectures are rarely used as they are not trained efficiently under the differentiable programming paradigm that made DL the pervasive technology it is nowadays. Current FANNs require activation functions that provide meaningful information during the backpropagation pass. Complete differentiability of the activation function is not a requirement. Functions like the rectifier units are used extensively, despite being not differentiable in zero. Recent advances in FANNs entail many different innovations impacting different aspects, ranging from learning to architecture design (Almási et al., 2016). Some of the most spread innovations are the usage of dropout regularization and residual connections. Dropout is a regularization technique, initially proposed by Hinton et al. (2012). Such a technique consists in randomly omitting hidden units in each training epoch. By doing this, the subsequent hidden units cannot rely on the units being omitted. In other words, dropout is an efficient way of performing model bagging, where bagging consists of training multiple models and evaluating numerous models on each test example. Performing bagging is impractical in a vast neural network since training these models is time-consuming. In Hinton et al. (2012), dropout has been applied to Convolutional Neural Networks (CNNs) at the level of feature detectors. Nowadays, dropout in FANNs produced staggering results in many fields (Addo et al., 2018; Piotrowski et al., 2020). Contrary to dropout that acts on the layers' connections, residual connections constitute an additional building block of the FANN architecture. They were initially proposed by He et al. (2015). In the paper, the authors used residual connections in computer vision on CNN architectures. While the original implementation of ResNet was CNNs, nowadays, they have been applied to other domains and architectures. ResNets proved to be a parsimonious yet effective architecture in several tasks (Canziani et al., 2017; Chen et al., 2019; Wu & Yan, 2019). A FANN with residual connections differs from the canonical FANN architecture in that it allows for "shortcut connections" that mitigate the problem of degradation in the case of multiple layers. Although the usage of per se of shortcut connection is not new in the literature (Venables & Ripley, 1999), the key proposal of He et al. (2015), was to use identity mapping instead of any other nonlinear transformation.

Figure 3.3 shows the smallest building block of the ResNet architecture in which both the first and the second layers are shortcutted, and the inputs x are added to the output of the second layer. The rationale behind ResNet is that by residual learning, the solvers will be able to capture identity mappings that otherwise will be lost in multiple nonlinear layers. With shortcuts, identity mapping is achieved by simply annihilating the weights of the input layers that have been shortcutted. In practical terms implementing a shortcut connection *à-là* ResNet on a FANN implies the change of the previous formulation as follows:

$$z_i^{(l+1)}(x_\alpha) \equiv \lambda_1 \left[b_i^{(l+1)} + \sum_{j=1}^{n_l} W_{ij}^{(l+1)} \sigma \left(z_j^{(l)}(x_\alpha) \right) \right] + \lambda_2 z_i^{(l)}(x_\alpha)$$

where λ_1 and λ_2 are tunable hyperparameters.

In conclusion, despite their longevity, FANNs are generally the out-of-shelve technique in many fields. In recent years this architecture has been used in many business applications ranging from Management to Economics. Their conceptual simplicity made them one of the pillars of DL. Moreover, given their flexibility, many novelties have been applied to them, making this architecture still a powerful one. Possible research avenues are trying

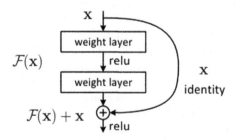

Figure 3.3 A shortcut connection layer with identity mapping characterizing the Residual Network architecture.

to implement the features common to biological brains, as in the case of Chavlis & Poirazi (2021). Other strands of literature instead focus on making them on par with more complex architectures with the advantage of being easier to optimize.

3.6 Convolutional Neural Network

CNNs are widely used in computer vision applications such as image classification, face recognition, and object detection. In general, the common ground for application is any grid-structured inputs and the strength lies in the identification of strong spatial dependencies in local regions of the grid. Despite their complexity, they are considered the most performing networks for solving difficult tasks. Their name refers to convolution-like mathematical operations performed in at least one layer of the network, substituting the basic matrix multiplication present in FANN architectures. Moreover, the peculiarity of CNN architectures is to increase layers' structure to three dimensions, extending the notion of network depth not only to the number of layers but also to the *volume* of layers.

Before introducing the general architecture of a CNN, a short explanation of convolution may be beneficial to the reader. Convolution is a crucial mathematical operation for signal processing and computer vision procedures. Generally speaking, this operation involves two different functions, and it is represented by the asterisk symbol; in particular, given f two functions f and g convolution is defined as the integral of the product of the two functions after one is reversed and shifted:

$$f(t) * g(t) = \int_{-\infty}^{\infty} f(\tau) g(t-\tau) d$$

In the case of CNN, this operation is computed between matrices meaning that the input matrix of features is transformed into a smaller and compact representation through convolution with a kernel matrix, see Figure 3.4. The kernel matrix K can be treated as a mask moving upon the input matrix I and the output matrix is obtained by summing at each step the results of element-wise multiplications. For instance, the ij-th element of the output matrix is obtained as:

$$(I \star K)_{ij} = \sum_{i'=1}^{k} \sum_{j'=1}^{k} I(i-i', j-j') K(i'.j')$$

where k is the dimension of the kernel matrix K. By doing so, it is possible to verify that the output matrix (also called feature map) has a smaller dimension

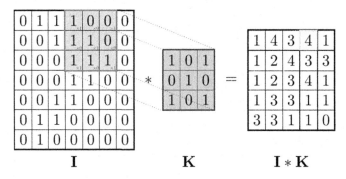

Figure 3.4 An example of the convolution operation between a two-dimensional array with a 3 × 3 kernel matrix.

concerning I. However, it may be necessary to have the output of the same dimension as the input. In that case, the most common approach is named "padding" and it consists to add imaginary zeros around the input matrix in order to match kernel dimensions.

Moreover, an important characteristic of convolution is that is based on the dot product. This product can be considered as a correlation measure since it involves a cosine operation. As a consequence, it is possible to retrieve from the output matrix which elements are correlated with the adjacent ones.

As an example to understand convolution operations in practice, we can consider applications to images. Images can be represented as matrices since they are defined by two properties (height and width) and one optional additional dimension (color). Instead, a kernel matrix can be defined to act as a filter to modify the image (e.g., add blurring effects) or a way to detect shapes (e.g., edge detector). Thus, this operation allows to create feature maps between the input and the set of patterns of interest for the image classification or analysis.

Given the definition of convolution, it is possible to embed it into a NN node as the argument of non–linear activation functions as for matrix multiplication in dense layers:

$$Convolution\,layer : \sigma\left(K * x + b\right) \quad Dense\,layer : \sigma\left(W^T x + b\right)$$

where x is the input of the node, W is the weights matrix, K is the kernel matrix and b is the bias term.

Convolution layers are the core of CNN architectures; however, the structure is more complex with respect to FNN and other elements need to be considered. Starting from a basic and generic architecture, a CNN can be divided into two major stages: image transformation and classification/regression (according to the scope of the analysis) as in Figure 3.5. The first

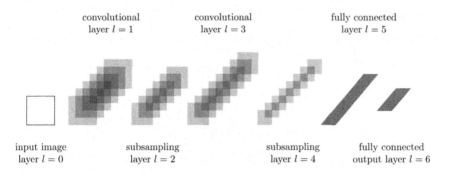

Figure 3.5 Architecture of a traditional convolutional neural network, alternating between convolutional layers and subsampling layers. The feature maps of the final subsampling layer are the input of the second stage consisting of an arbitrary number of fully connected layers.

stage is composed of two different alternating layers: each convolution layer is followed by a pooling layer, see Figure 3.6.

The convolution layers are the portion of a CNN where the mapping across subsequent layers is performed maintaining their spatial structure. The pooling layers are introduced to compress and average the operations performed in the previous layers. To figure out the sequence of these layers, in the case of an image recognition task lower-level layers are able to capture primitive shapes or lines from the input and higher-level ones detect more complex patterns. Therefore, this structure leads to the CNN learning hierarchical features of the input. Pooling stages enable to resize images in order to be smaller and this operation can be done in different ways. Recalling the idea that adjacent pixels in images are very similar to each other and the fact that convolution can be considered also as a map for correlation, down sampling images can be a helpful step to shrink the number of data and computations to be performed at each step losing only spatial information. As a consequence, pooling can be done by defining the size of the sampling and then averaging the value in that area. An alternative to this approach is to select the maximum value in the area.

The second stage is a series of dense (fully connected) layers, as for FNN, to combine the information from all previous levels and elaborate a result. However, this type of layer requires vectors as input data. Therefore, between the first and second steps, we need to flatten the matrix of the last pooling step into a vector. For this stage, it is only needed to define the number of hidden dense layers and the activation functions, especially for the output layer whose choice depends on the task being done by the CNN. In general, image processing can be treated as a regression problem, instead, of object recognition as a classification problem.

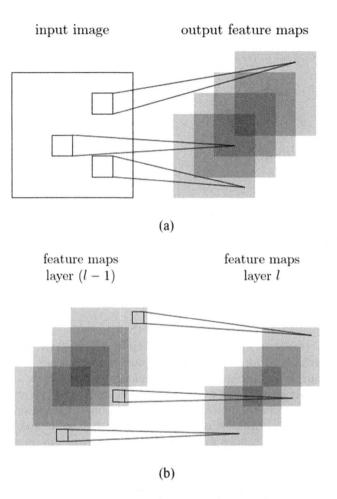

(a)

(b)

Figure 3.6 Layer types in the first stage of a Convolution Neural Network architecture: respectively, (a) convolution and (b) pooling.

In general, the advantage of using convolution in this structure mainly resides in its flexible and adaptive behavior based on the following characteristics: sparse interactions, parameters sharing, and equivariant representations. First, sparsity allows to significantly reduce the total number of weights (parameters) involved in the neural network architecture, improving statistical efficiency and computational effort. Compared to FANN, CNN architectures avoid matrix multiplication describing interactions between each input and output unit by defining the kernel matrix as smaller than the input. This property is intimately related to the idea of parameter sharing due to the convolution between the input layer and kernel matrix. Instead of having each weight used one time to compute an output, convolution enables the combination of each element of the kernel with almost every value of input data (except for elements on boundaries). Therefore, CNNs learn a unique set of parameters, instead of separate sets related to the combination of input and output. This is a crucial advantage in terms of storage requirements during the execution of the algorithm. Finally, the characteristics of equivariance to translation follow the property of parameter sharing. This means that if the input is shifted, the output will be the same after convolution. Thus, it is a favorable condition in computer vision because, for example, it implies that CNNs are able to identify an object in an image disregarding its location. However, if the object appears scaled or rotated, it is necessary to use more specific mechanisms to also ensure these types of equivariance.

Therefore, even complex structures and tasks can be easily addressed by continuous alternating convolution and pooling steps that allow resizing the analysis by focusing on finding the relevant patterns and details. However, with respect to FNN, CNNs have more hyperparameters to define. When defining the architecture, in addition to activation functions and the number of layers we have also to specify the dimension of the kernel function and the pooling methodology. In the literature, several suggestions and conventions can be found on how to set all those parameters, accordingly to computation time, statistical performance, and tuning.

Nonetheless, an advantage of the well-known outstanding results provided by CNNs is that there exist lots of pre-trained CNN that can enable their usage in new applications without major changes. As described before, the core power of CNNs is in the first stage where convolution and pooling layers are: there the complex task of finding patterns, detecting objects, and extrapolating details are performed. Therefore, it is beneficial to use a pre-trained first stage to reduce computation time whilst being sure of a good performance, but it is advisable to train the second stage in order to tune the architecture to the specific use case of interest. The motivation lies in the fact that the original CNN may have been defined for a different task or a classi-fication problem with a different size of class label.

The first generalized pre-trained CNN architecture proposed by (LeCun et al., 1990) is called *LeNet-5*, see Figure 3.7. The development of this archi-tecture was related to a practical application of handwritten digit recognition provided by the US Postal Service. This CNN considers as input a grey-scale (one channel) image of size 32×32 pixels and seven layers: the first stage is composed of two pairs of convolution (C) and pooling (S) layers and the sec-ond stage contains three dense layers. The activation function is the sigmoid and it is the same along all steps. We can notice how the dimension of the input image is shrunken in the first stage and how the convolution leads to including volume in the layers. Instead, in the output layer, it is possible to recognize the classification task of predicting the digit since 10 output class labels are defined. This architecture is very simple and easy to understand, but its definition created the basis for the development of more powerful CNNs in the next decades. The first improvement is the so-called *AlexNet* designed

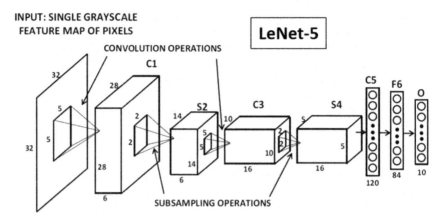

Figure 3.7 Structure of the original LeNet-5 Convolutional Neural Network as proposed by LeCun et al. in their paper "Handwritten Digit Recognition
with a Back-Propagation Network".

by (Krizhevsky et al., 2017) which outperformed the original *LeNet-5*. The
proposed architecture modifies the previous structure by adding more convolutional layers and using a ReLu activation function to solve vanishing
gradient issues on convergence. Specifically, the additional convolution step
is performed sequentially without pooling steps in between leading to the
detection of more nonlinear patterns. Increasing the depth of the network
also introduced a computational challenge, but it was solved by using GPU
computation. This work is considered one of the most influential papers for
computer vision and it reached a high number of citations in related work on
CNNs. More recent and worth mentioning CNNs architectures are *Goog-
LeNet, Inception-V3,* and *ResNet*, see (Alzubaidi et al., 2021) for more details.

3.7 Conclusions

According to CBinsights 2021 report the last decade showed a significant and
continuous increase in investment in Artificial Intelligence. Starting from the
biggest technology companies, the popularity of this topic spreads to other
sectors leading to the inclusion of AI features also in very specific-purpose
software uses, enabling the usage of recommender systems for several applications. Moreover, advances in software have established an environment
that allows non-expert programmers to design and deploy complicated ANN
structures without the need for specialized knowledge, such as Tensorflow or
Pytorch. Regarding Tensorflow, the developers produced also the so-called
"Tensorflow playground" where users can do some experiments on Neural
Networks in a web-based and no-code environment. This open-source tool
is very helpful at a learning stage when it is relevant to visualize the effects

of changes in NN architectures, leading to a concrete comprehension of the mathematical model definition.

The goal of this chapter is to introduce the reader to some fundamental concepts about Neural Networks and Deep Learning. The main advantage of including Neural Networks in machine learning research and industrial applications is mainly related to their performance and flexibility, also in complex contexts. Starting from the intuition of biology, Neural Networks allow building a structure able to discover connections between units (e.g., neurons) and transfer the information along the layers. At the final stage, the processed information from input data is transformed into knowledge through the final activation function, defined accordingly to the task required (classification or regression).

In general, ANNs architectures share common elements, such as input and output layers, hidden layers, nodes, and activation functions. However, the choice of the overall architecture and its elements is mostly related to the current data type involved in a use case. In literature, many references and conventions on how to proceed may be found, but the tuning of some hyper-parameters can be optimized also during computational steps. Furthermore, it is worth mentioning that there exist several pre-trained Neural Networks of different architectures that can be adjusted with a minor effort to similar applications, as mentioned in Section 3.3.

Nevertheless, in Section 3.1 an extensive introduction to activation functions is included with also a discussion of related aspects that should be considered. Activation functions are the core of neural networks, especially FANN. The reason is that they directly affect the performance of output estimates and how the information is transmitted along the layers. Therefore, particular attention should be paid to their choice, especially considering the problem of the vanishing gradient that has been briefly introduced.

In Sections 3.2 and 3.3, FANN and CNN are respectively extensively described. FANNs are the simplest architecture of Neural Networks, but they are still very powerful in solving regression problems. In this architecture, the information only moves from input to output through (optional) hidden layers without the possibility of having recursive loops inside. Additionally, they have a dense structure, and it could be a limitation to their computation in the case of use-case with a large number of neurons. Instead, CNNs are a more recent architecture introduced to deal more efficiently with tasks related to image processing or object detection. The major novelty introduced in their definition is the use of a convolutional layer in the substitution of matrix multiplication. This mathematical operation introduces several advantages, strongly related to its properties. For example, it allows recognizing an object disregarding its location because it is invariant to translation. Moreover, convolution allows to shrink of the size of the input image (data) simplifying complex tasks also through a small number of layers.

Finally, we would like to mention other wide-spread used architecture and we leave it to the reader to investigate further into their mathematical definition. Recurrent Neural Networks (RNNs) are specific architecture designed to extract information from sequential data such as text sentences or time series. RNNs layers convert input data into hidden states to map the implicit sequence encoded in the input. Different from FANNs, RNNs allow having a self-loop cycle within their structure to include interactions also between the current input and corresponding hidden state and inputs at previous timestamps. Therefore, a hidden state is a function of the input vector and the previous hidden state and the output value is determined through another function that learns the probability based on the current state. Thus, RNNs are time-layered architectures, and they embed also a time dimension in the algorithm of backpropagation that is called "backpropagation through time" (BPTT). This definition is functional to the analysis of sequential data because it is typically relevant to predict what is the next value of a variable of interest given its current value. In a time-series setting, the output might be the forecasted prediction in the next timestamp; instead in the text setting, the task may be to predict the next word in a sentence (also known as language modeling). The most structures for RNNs are the so-called Long short-term memory (LSTM) and Gated Recurrent Unit (GRU). The other two relevant architectures are Autoencoders and Generative Adversarial Networks (GANs). Even if they are differently defined, they both are used in tasks when there is the need to create a "copy" of input data and possibly generate new data that are very similar to the original ones. An example of use-cased may be anomaly detection or data augmentation. The former requires the model to be able to reproduce a benchmark situation and detect whether new input data are outliers to the standard condition. The latter falls in the situation of a strongly imbalanced dataset; therefore the model should be able to produce synthetic data for the minority class that are very close to real available data. Thus, both architectures in a different way use the operation of compression and mapping to reproduce as output data the input data.

References

Abadi, M., Agarwal, A., Barham, P., Brevdo, E., Chen, Z., Citro, C., ... Zheng, X. (2015). TensorFlow: Large-scale machine learning on heterogeneous systems. Retrieved from https://www.tensorflow.org/

Addo, P., Guegan, D., & Hassani, B. (2018, April). Credit risk analysis using machine and deep learning models. *Risks, 6,* 38. doi:10.3390/risks6020038

Almási, A.-D., Woźniak, S., Cristea, V., Leblebici, Y., & Engbersen, T. (2016, January). Review of advances in neural networks: Neural design technology stack. *Neurocomputing, 174,* 31–41. doi:10.1016/j.neucom.2015.02.092

Alzubaidi, L., Zhang, J., Humaidi, A. J., Al-Dujaili, A., Duan, Y., Al-Shamma, O., ... Farhan, L. (2021, March). Review of deep learning: Concepts, CNN architectures, challenges, applications, future directions. *Journal of Big Data, 8,* 53. doi:10.1186/s40537-021-00444-8

Anderson, J. A. (2018). Artificial intelligence and the future of humans. Washington, DC: *Pew Research Center,* 10.

Arifovic, J., & Gencay, R. (2001). Using genetic algorithms to elect architecture of a feedforward artiÿcial neural network. *Physica A, 289*(2001), 574–594.

Bengio, Y. (2009). Learning Deep Architectures for AI. doi:10.1561/9781601982957

Bengio, Y., & LeCun, Y. (n.d.). *Scaling Learning Algorithms towards AI.* Cambridge, MA: MIT Press. 41.

Biewald, L. (2020). Experiment Tracking with Weights and Biases. Retrieved from https://www.wandb.com/

Canziani, A., Paszke, A., & Culurciello, E. (2017). An analysis of deep neural network models for practical applications. *arXiv.* Retrieved from http://arxiv.org/abs/1605.07678

CBinsights. (2021). Retrieved from www.cbinsights.com: https://www.cbinsights.com/research/report/ai-trends-2021/

Chavlis, S., & Poirazi, P. (2021, October). Drawing inspiration from biological dendrites to empower artificial neural networks. *Current Opinion in Neurobiology, 70,* 1–10. doi:10.1016/j.conb.2021.04.007

Chen, F., Chen, N., Mao, H., & Hu, H. (2019). Assessing four neural networks on handwritten digit recognition dataset (MNIST). *arXiv.* Retrieved from http://arxiv.org/abs/1811.08278

Ciampi, F., & Gordini, N. (2013). Small enterprise default prediction modeling through artificial neural networks: An empirical analysis of italian small enterprises. *Journal of Small Business Management, 51,* 23–45.

Clevert, D.-A., Unterthiner, T., & Hochreiter, S. (2015). Fast and accurate deep network learning by exponential linear units (ELUs). *arXiv.*

Dieleman, S. (2014). Recommending music on Spotify with deep learning. *Abgerufen von.* http://benanne.github.io/2014/08/05/spotify-cnns.html

Dikmen, M., & Burns, C. M. (2016, October). Autonomous driving in the real world. *Proceedings of the 8th International Conference on Automotive User Interfaces and Interactive Vehicular Applications.* doi:10.1145/3003715.3005465

Goodfellow, I., Bengio, Y., & Courville, A. (2016). *Deep Learning.* Cambridge, MA: MIT Press.

He, K., Zhang, X., Ren, S., & Sun, J. (2015). Deep residual learning for image recognition. *arXiv.* Retrieved from http://arxiv.org/abs/1512.03385

Hinton, G. E., Srivastava, N., Krizhevsky, A., Sutskever, I., & Salakhutdinov, R. R. (2012). Improving neural networks by preventing co-adaptation of feature detectors. *arXiv.*

IDC. (2022). www.idc.com. Retrieved from https://www.idc.com/getdoc.jsp?containerId=prAP49010122

Innes, M. (2018). Flux: Elegant machine learning with Julia. *Journal of Open Source Software, 3*(25), 602. doi:10.21105/joss.00602

Innes, M., Saba, E., Fischer, K., Gandhi, D., Rudilosso, M. C., Joy, N. M., ... Shah, V. (2018). Fashionable modelling with flux. *arXiv,* abs/1811.01457. Retrieved from https://arxiv.org/abs/1811.01457

Khodabandehlou, S., & Zivari Rahman, M. (2017, March). Comparison of supervised machine learning techniques for customer churn prediction based on analysis of customer behavior. *Journal of Systems and Information Technology, 19,* 65–93. doi:10.1108/jsit-10-2016-0061

Krizhevsky, A., Sutskever, I., & Hinton, G. E. (2017). ImageNet classification with deep convolutional neural networks. *Communications of the ACM, 60*(6), 84–90. https://doi.org/10.1145/3065386

LeCun, Y., Bengio, Y., & Hinton, G. (2015). Deep learning. *Nature, 521*(7553), 436–444. doi:10.1038/nature14539

LeCun, Y., Boser, B., Denker, J., Henderson, D., Howard, R., Hubbard, W., & Jackel, L. (1990). Handwritten digit recognition with a back-propagation network. *Advances in Neural Information Processing Systems, 2*, 396–404. Retrieved from https://proceedings.neurips.cc/paper/1989/hash/53c3bce66e43be4f209556518c2fcb54-Abstract.html

Lessmann, S., Baesens, B., Seow, H.-V., & Thomas, L. C. (2015). Benchmarking state-of-the-art classification algorithms for credit scoring: An upyear of research. *European Journal of Operational Research, 247*, 124–136. doi:10/gffd5q

Lichtenthaler, U. (2018, September). Substitute or synthesis: The interplay between human and artificial intelligence. *Research-Technology Management, 61*, 12–14. doi:10.1080/08956308.2018.1495962

Lillicrap, T. P., Santoro, A., Marris, L., Akerman, C. J., & Hinton, G. (2020, April). Backpropagation and the brain. *Nature Reviews Neuroscience, 21*, 335–346. doi:10.1038/s41583-020-0277-3

McCulloch, W. S., & Pitts, W. (1943, December). A logical calculus of the ideas immanent in nervous activity. *The Bulletin of Mathematical Biophysics, 5*, 115–133. doi:10.1007/bf02478259

Mitchell, M. (2021, June). Why AI is harder than we think. *Proceedings of the Genetic and Evolutionary Computation Conference*. doi:10.1145/3449639.3465421

Mosavi, A., Faghan, Y., Ghamisi, P., Duan, P., Ardabili, S. F., Salwana, E., & Band, S. S. (2020). Comprehensive review of deep reinforcement learning methods and applications in economics. *Mathematics, 8*(10), 1640. doi:10.3390/math8101640

Paszke, A., Gross, S., Massa, F., Lerer, A., Bradbury, J., Chanan, G., … Chintala, S. (2019). PyTorch: An imperative style, high-performance deep learning library. In H. Wallach, H. Larochelle, A. Beygelzimer, F. dAlché-Buc, E. Fox, & R. Garnett (Eds.), *Advances in Neural Information Processing Systems 32* (pp. 8024–8035). Red Hook, NY: Curran Associates, Inc. Retrieved from http://papers.neurips.cc/paper/9015-pytorch-an-imperative-style-high-performance-deep-learning-library.pdf

Piotrowski, A. P., Napiorkowski, J. J., & Piotrowska, A. E. (2020, February). Impact of deep learning-based dropout on shallow neural networks applied to stream temperature modelling. *Earth-Science Reviews, 201*, 103076. doi:10.1016/j.earscirev.2019.103076

Roberts, D. A., Yaida, S., & Hanin, B. (2021). The principles of deep learning theory. *arXiv.*

Romdhane, L. B. (2006). A softmin-based neural model for causal reasoning. *IEEE Transactions on Neural Networks, 17*, 732–744. doi:10.1109/tnn.2006.872350

Rosenblatt, F. (1958). The perceptron: A probabilistic model for information storage and organization in the brain. *Psychological Review, 65*, 386–408. doi:10.1037/h0042519

Rumelhart, D. E., Hinton, G. E., & Williams, R. J. (1986, October). Learning representations by back-propagating errors. *Nature, 323*, 533–536. doi:10.1038/323533a0

Santana, E., & Hotz, G. (2016). Learning a driving simulator. *arXiv.* https://arxiv.org/abs/1608.01230

Turian, J., Bergstra, J., & Bengio, Y. (2009). Quadratic features and deep architectures for chunking. *Proceedings of Human Language Technologies: The 2009 Annual*

Conference of the North American Chapter of the Association for Computational Linguistics, Companion Volume: Short Papers (pp. 245–248). Toronto: Association for Computational Linguistics.

Venables, W. N., & Ripley, B. D. (1999). *Modern Applied Statistics with S-PLUS* (3 ed.). New York: Springer-Verlag. doi:10.1007/978-1-4757-3121-7

Widrow, B., & Hoff, M. E. (1960, June). Adaptive Switching Circuits. 96–104. doi:10.21236/ad0241531

Wu, Q., & Yan, X. (2019). Capturing deep tail risk via sequential learning of quantile dynamics. *Journal of Economic Dynamics and Control, 109*, 103771. doi:10.1016/j.jedc.2019.103771

Zhao, G., Zhang, Z., Guan, H., Tang, P., & Wang, J. (2018, August). Rethinking ReLU to Train Better CNNs. *2018 24th International Conference on Pattern Recognition (ICPR).* doi:10.1109/icpr.2018.8545612

Part 2

Artificial Intelligence in Business

Opportunities and Challenges

4 Artificial Intelligence in Human Resource Management

Objectives and Implications

Alessia Berni, Luigi Moschera, and Aizhan Tursunbayeva

4.1 Introduction

Labor costs in many sectors can account for as much as 60–80% of total business costs (Choi, 2018). Thus, organizations of different types and sizes and from different sectors worldwide carry out Human Resource (HR) management (HRM) practices aimed at efficiently and effectively designing jobs, employing, training, and compensating people, and developing strategies to retain them (Minbaeva, 2021). In principle, all such HR processes/practices can be supported by technology (Ruel et al., 2004). Indeed, modern HR professionals widely use multi-modular or standalone HR information systems (HRIS) or ones embedded into broader enterprise resource planning systems (Harris, 2020) capable of collecting, storing, and reporting data on a rich, wide-ranging, and constantly increasing database of people (Tursunbayeva et al., 2018).

A recent report suggested that organizations use eight types of HR technologies on average, spending circa $274 on them for each employee (Harris, 2020). The relevant worldwide market of HR technologies has been estimated at around $158 billion (Bersin, 2021). Overall, such technologies and systems are extensively used beyond HR departments as well. Candidates, employees, managers, and organizational leaders are all users of HR technologies for their day-to-day needs and interactions (Bersin, 2021).

Recently, organizations worldwide have also started adopting specific advanced technologies such as artificial intelligence (AI) (e.g., machine learning (Albert, 2019), chatbots, social robots (Molitor, 2020) or their convergences in addition to existing organizational HR technologies or systems, throughout the HR life cycle (Khan, 2021) (Figure 4.1). The term AI refers in general to using human intelligence in machines through technological innovations. It was first coined in 1956 by John McCarthy, who proposed the possibility of computers becoming as intelligent as humans (Garg et al., 2021).

The worldwide spending on AI has been projected to reach $110 billion in 2024 (IDC, 2020), and AI in HRM was labeled as "necessary to employ" and no longer as "nice to have" (Black & van Esch, 2020). Indeed, many

DOI: 10.4324/9781003304616-7

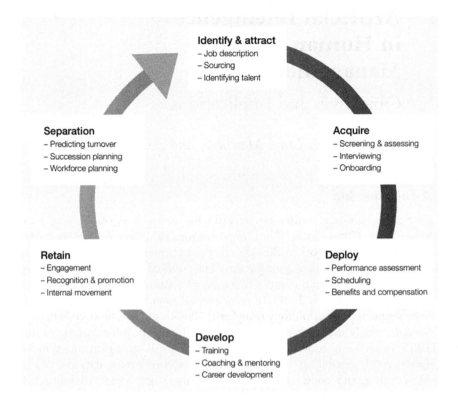

Figure 4.1 HR life cycle stages supported by AI (Khan, 2021).

EU countries are setting strategic objectives to expand AI use, particularly for operational applications (e.g., Italian Government, 2021) – under which HRM tasks and processes fall – labeling them a "lower-hanging fruit" (European Commission, 2020).

There are already 250 HR tools that use AI for all aspects of HRM (Khan, 2021), which are quickly diffusing in organizations due to their numerous expected benefits (Kurter, 2021). However, AI for HRM in the form of automated HRM, People Analytics, or algorithmic management practices (Tursunbayeva et al., 2021) is also highly debated due to the potential consequences for employees' privacy and monitoring, and organizations' reputation, among others.

Despite all this, AI applications in/for HRM have received relatively little scholarly attention, compared to other areas with a strong focus on the use of AI and data analytics such as education or medicine (Tursunbayeva et al., 2021). The existing attempts so far have had a rather limited legal (e.g., Borgesius, 2020) or technical (e.g., Lokman & Ameedeen, 2019) focus, or were practitioner-led investigations suggesting, for example, the number of jobs (Manyika et al., 2017) to be affected by AI in different sectors. Existing research on AI in HRM has also been fragmented and rather detached from previous research on HR technologies such as HRIS (e.g., Tursunbayeva et al., 2018) or electronic-HRM (e.g., Ruel et al., 2004). This might be the reason why it is often referred to as a theoretical and practice-driven emerging innovation with as-yet-unknown consequences, and organizations need to envision and mitigate risks as AI development or implementation is happening (Tursunbayeva et al., 2021). Thus, understanding whether and how AI is currently being or can be embedded for different HRM practices within organizations and the objectives behind their adoption is absolutely imperative to support the informed, explainable, and accountable use of high-risk AI applications for HRM, which differentiate it from many other areas where AI has been applied (Tambe et al., 2019).

This study aims to address such an important literature gap. Specifically, this chapter builds on established research on the use of technologies in HRM to present and discuss the objectives and consequences of AI use for different HRM practices. In doing so, it fashions a conceptual framework on AI use throughout the HR lifecycle and presents illustrative AI applications from the scholarly and socially curated literature, as well as among the existing vendor solutions of AI for HRM.

By studying the objectives/consequences of AI for HRM throughout the HR lifecycle, this study can help to provide the best match between them, facilitate AI's ethical and human-centered design, implementation, and use (World Economic Forum, 2021), and shed important light on the approaches for evaluating impacts, interactions, and unanticipated complex consequences of AI for HRM (Orlikowski & Scott, 2008). More broadly, this research will also contribute to the emerging multi-disciplinary discourses on the future of work and address the need for research on the assumptions and rationalizations driving the decisions to develop, implement, or use AI, as well as on the evaluations of their outcomes.

The chapter starts by introducing the concepts used in this research, recognizing the efforts of other scholars on AI and HRM, and explains how it provides new insights into the effects of AI for HRM. The objectives/consequences of AI for different HRM practices throughout the HR life cycle will then be discussed. Finally, the chapter concludes with suggestions for future research, practice, and policy.

4.2 Towards a Theoretical Framework

The application of technology to HRM has been extensively studied within the HRIS and e-HRM literature streams (hereinafter to be used interchangeably) by drawing on interdisciplinary theoretical frameworks from HR, innovation and change, information systems, and other broad management corpora of literature(Tursunbayeva et al., 2017). Recent advances in emerging technology such as AI and the growing availability of the data it can analyze have given rise to evolving applications of AI to HRM in the form of machine learning (Albert, 2019), chatbots, and social robots (Molitor, 2020), or their convergences. Such applications consequently have given rise to independent research streams that have been conceptualized and operationalized as HR analytics (e.g., Tursunbayeva et al., 2018), HRM algorithms (e.g., Cheng & Hackett, 2021), algorithmic management (e.g., Meijerink et al., 2021), or AI deployed in HRM (e.g., Vrontis et al., 2021), which have even further fragmented the relevant scholarly research on HR and technology across terminology and concepts.

These later studies have already provided valuable insights into which HRM practices AI can be used for (e.g., Garg et al., 2021; Qamar et al., 2021). However, many of them are atheoretical as they do not build on or advance existing theoretical frameworks established within e-HRM/HRIS literature streams. Hence, although AI is a specific type of HRIS/e-HRM (e.g., Prikshat et al., 2021), it is still unknown whether the objectives that drive the adoption of AI or their consequences are the same as those that characterize the adoption of legacy technologies. Last but not least, existing theoretically informed studies on AI and HRM have mostly been conceptual (e.g., Prikshat et al., 2021), thus not connecting to real-life AI uses.

In our chapter, we would like to address such important knowledge gaps by building on the proficiency accumulated in the HRIS/e-HRM literature streams and drawing on illustrative real-life AI applications. We will be using inclusive terminology such as AI use in HRM while drawing on the established classification of the objectives and consequences of e-HRM and HRIS that have been grouped as operational, relational, and transformational (Lepak & Snell, 1998).

Operational outcomes refer to the efficiency and effectiveness of HR technologies (Prikshat et al., 2021), such as reducing costs and alleviating administrative burdens. Operational HRM activities typically include personnel record keeping and administration, payroll, time management, or access control (Ruel et al., 2004).

Initially, relational outcomes referred to the use of HR technologies for supporting basic business processes including recruiting, training, and performance appraisal, and remuneration of employees (Ruel et al., 2004). More recently, the relational category has started to emphasize the interactions and networking of different actors in sustaining the relationships with an employee by improving HR services to internal clients and empowering employees (Prikshat et al., 2021), including internal communication, team building, information management, knowledge sharing, and collaboration (Martini et al., 2020).

Finally, transformational outcomes comprise improving strategic orientation towards HRM (Prikshat et al., 2021). This category was originally reported to include strategic competence management and strategic knowledge management (Ruel et al., 2004). Recently, it was described as consisting of HRM practices such as recruitment, compensation, training and

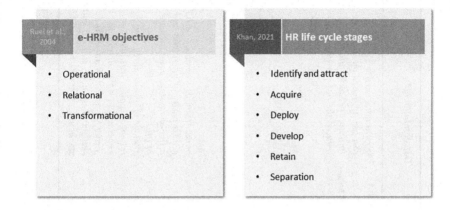

Figure 4.2 Integrated framework.

development, and performance management (Martini et al., 2020). It was also noted that such consequences can refer to broader transformations in terms of doing business and business models (Vrontis et al., 2021) which go beyond traditional HRM boundaries.

Considering that the operational, relational, and transformational objectives of HR technologies are mostly discussed in relation to classical(e.g., recruitment and selection or performance management) and emerging (e.g., knowledge sharing, collaboration, or team building) HRM practices, and the fact that so far only one study has tried to impose an e-HRM consequences framework broadly to the application of AI in HRM (Prikshat et al., 2021), we will also draw on the HR life cycle stages that were recently reported to be supported by AI (see Figure 4.1). These stages include identify and attract (e.g., job description, sourcing, and identifying talent); acquire (e.g., screening and assessing, interviewing, and onboarding); deploy (e.g., performance assessment, scheduling, and benefits and compensation); develop (e.g., training, coaching and mentoring, and career development); retain (e.g., engagement, recognition and promotion, and internal movement); and separation (e.g., predicting turnover, succession planning, and workforce planning). In Figure 4.2 we visually represent the integrated framework that we built, drawing on the generic three HRIS/e-HRM objectives and specific HR life cycles that can be supported by AI.

4.3 Application of the Theoretical Framework

This section elaborates on the operational, relational, and transformational objectives/consequences of AI for HRM and organizations (Lepak & Snell, 1998) throughout the HR life cycle by presenting existing knowledge and illustrative examples from a recent report (Garr & Jackson, 2019) (see Table 4.1).

Table 4.1 Integrated Framework with Illustrative Examples

HR life cycle stages/ e-HRM objectives	Operational★	Relational★	Transformational★
Identify and attract (job description, sourcing, and identifying talent)	www.wonderkind.com Offers automated job ads targeted at passive and active job candidates from all backgrounds, by passions/ interests www.eightfold.ai Makes hiring more efficient using an AI platform to match people and roles www.visage.jobs Combines crowdsourcing, advertising and AI to provide a list of passive and active candidates for a job and engages candidates via a multichannel approach (e.g., email and LinkedIn).	www.gender-decoder.katmatfield. com Identifies gender biased language in job descriptions—free online tool	"Accenture has seen a $2.1M in cost savings based on time spent (minutes per task) and it has reduced the cost-per-hire by 55%"
Acquire (screening and assessing, interviewing, and onboarding)	www.checkr.com Allows for standardization of criteria for what screens out candidates during background check to increase consistency; criteria can be customized for specific roles www.knockri.com Uses video analysis and AI to screen candidate soft skills www.pymetrics.ai Predicts candidates that fit jobs using behavioral analysis and AI	www.gapjumpers.me Assesses and reduces bias through blind hiring practices www.fortay.co Helps screen candidates for cultural team fit, nurture and improve company culture, engagement and employee retention with actionable insights	"Tata Communications was able to achieve gender parity in interviews and a five-percentage point increase in the percentage of women hired. Further, the organization was able to experience a 45% increase in hiring for critical, hard-to-find skills and estimates it saved four to six hours per recruiter per week"

(Continued)

Table 4.1 (Continued)

HR life cycle stages/ e-HRM objectives	Operational★	Relational★	Transformational★
	www.greenhouse.io *Includes "nudges" within its technology system to remind recruiters and interviewers of bias-reducing behaviors* www.mya.com *Uses an AI chatbot to interview candidates, potentially reducing bias*		
Deploy (performance assessment, scheduling, and benefits and compensation)	www.cultureamp.com *Provides structure to performance feedback*	www.cornerstoneondemand.com *Offers a library of comments and coaching tips for managers to provide more accurate, meaningful and unbiased feedback* www.sap.com *Uses gender indicators to show where bias might exist in performance scores, removes photos during calibration sessions, provides exception flags when talent actions vary from expectations*	*"With Affirmity, we have access to experienced, knowledgeable people, which keeps us prepared with the right audit-ready data and reports," explains the energy company's HR Director. "That means saved time and money, and compliance with federal regulations."* *The energy company has seen several benefits from their partnership with Affirmity such as saved time, more efficient use of internal resources, improved audit readiness, and access to accurate compensation data that is readily available for analysis"*

(Continued)

Table 4.1 (Continued)

HR life cycle stages/ e-HRM objectives	Operational★	Relational★	Transformational★
Develop (training, coaching and mentoring, and career development)	www.beingvr.io *Uses virtual reality and immersive storytelling for experiential learning and bias awareness* www.glassbreakers.co *Offers mentor matching software* www.landit.com *Offers personalized career pathing and development, executive coaching and targeted skill development*	www.crescendowork.com *Delivers personalized unconscious bias training within employee communication platforms (e.g., Slack or Microft Teams)*	*"By creating a career mentoring program for high-potential women, Paychex has raised the retention rate for participating employees to 94% (14% higher than company average). "By pairing high-potential women with mentors who could help them apply for and reach new management levels, we knew we could build a stronger pipeline of female leaders," says a senior project manager of leadership and organizational development at Paychex"*
Retain (engagement, recognition and promotion, and internal movement)	www.alliebot.com *Uses a Slack chatbot to collect demographic data and understand employee experience* www.cultureamp.com *Allows customization of questions on its employee experience platform to focus on diversity, inclusion, and intersectionality within organizations*	www.trustsphere.com *Uses passive organizational network analysis to identify employees who build networks that are indicative of good high-potential candidates* www.cultureamp.com *Uses organizational network analysis to identify feedback networks*	*"OurOffice has a toolkit module that enables users to see the link between D&I and business and financial KPIs and quantify the D&I business case for specific activities. Pipeline focuses on gender equity and estimates the financial impact of achieving it for each client organization"*

(Continued)

Table 4.1 (Continued)

HR life cycle stages/ e-HRM objectives	Operational*	Relational*	Transformational*
Separation (predicting turnover, succession planning, and workforce planning)	www.trustsphere.com *By automatically ingesting the metadata from digital interactions across corporate communication and collaboration systems (e.g., email, voice, and instant messaging), TrustSphere then used real-time organizational network analytics to generate insights into the working networks employees built, their collaboration, and influence over others*		*"By measuring their networks and collaboration, Ramco identified that trainees who were high in social capital were able to share knowledge and information faster. For an innovation-intensive company like Ramco this meant that trainees could have strong networks that would enable speed-to-market strategies and deliver value to the organization"*

*Examples are adopted from Garr & Jackson (2019)

*Examples are adopted from Garr & Jackson (2019)

4.3.1 Operational

4.3.1.1 Identify and Attract

AI (e.g., in the form of machine learning) promises speedy and improved matching between candidates and jobs and facilitates process efficiency (Garg et al., 2021). For instance, a recent review reported that AI can automate the process of extracting candidates' information from their resumes (Garg et al., 2021). AI also promises to help companies to search and access a diverse pool of candidates (e.g., in terms of backgrounds, passions, and interests) via automated job ads targeted at both passive and active job candidates (e.g., Garr & Jackson, 2019).

AI seems to entail time efficiencies not only for HR professionals but also for candidates in the management of their applications, and that support can be available 24/7.

4.3.1.2 Acquire

AI is also envisioned to identify attributes to be used as selection criteria or for the subsequent development of selection models (standardized) (Garg et al., 2021). AI seems to be already diffused for assessing candidates' suitability for vacant job positions. For example, to assess their personality traits based on social media data usage (e.g., Twitter, LinkedIn, or GitHub), to measure their skills, qualifications, and achievements against job requirements (Garg et al., 2021). Even the classical face-to-face interview process has now been replaced by internet-based interviews (e.g., asynchronous video interviews) (Torres & Mejia, 2017) or interviews with chatbots (e.g., Albert, 2019).

4.3.1.3 Deploy

In the performance management process, AI promises to provide structure to performance feedback (e.g., Garr & Jackson, 2019). AI can also automate current manual performance evaluation by, for example, clustering employees into distinct groups on the basis of their performance or job satisfaction levels (Aktepe & Ersoz, 2012).

Meanwhile, automation in payroll systems can enable efficient handling of all relevant payroll activities (Budhwar et al., 2022) because AI can track all types of employee data and any relevant changes (Bussler & Davis, 2002), as well as calculate and determine salary parameters (Mehrabad & Brojeny, 2007).

4.3.1.4 Develop

AI is also reported to assist with the automation of the analysis of the organizational training and skills needs and provide relevant training recommendations based on the results (Garg et al., 2021). It can also assist with assessing such training effectiveness (Budhwar et al., 2022) and optimize training resource allocation (Beane, 2019). Finally, with AI and other convergent technologies (e.g., virtual reality), organizations can embrace fully immersive trainings, as well as enable matching between mentors and employees (Garr & Jackson, 2019).

4.3.1.5 Retain

AI promises to enable the customization of questions on employee experience platforms, while chatbots can be specifically used to gather such employee experiences automatically, even in different languages (Garr & Jackson, 2019).

4.3.1.6 Separation

Some studies pertaining to AI applications in HRM decision-making highlight the ability of AI to process large amounts of data at high speeds, which can help to effectively evaluate and manage employee turnover risk (e.g., Vrontis et al., 2021), as well as to identify high-performing employees in the succession planning process(Garr & Jackson, 2019).

4.3.2 Relational

4.3.2.1 Identify and Attract

AI tools for verifying the "language" used in job descriptions to check for potential biases (e.g., gender bias) promise to make this HR lifecycle phase more inclusive and eliminate the occurrence of recruiters' biases (Sajjadiani et al., 2019).

4.3.2.2 Acquire

Applying AI to attract and acquire employees is believed to reduce the risk of human errors and ensure that employee data is adequately safeguarded (Kaushal et al., 2021). Anonymized or blinded approaches to the identification and evaluation of candidates are expected to make the selection process more systematic and fairer by eliminating potential biases or even applicants' influences on the selection process (Sajjadiani et al., 2019). This can also improve the candidates' perceptions of organizations. The matching tools that can assess candidates' fit with jobs (e.g., based on their skills or psychometric assessment), teams, or organizations are envisioned to improve company culture, employee engagement, and retention (Garr & Jackson, 2019).

Other parties claim that applications of AI in this HR life cycle can instead operationalize gender bias and discrimination (e.g., Amazon's gender-biased algorithm) resulting from poorly trained algorithms or those that inherit human bias (Giermindl et al., 2021) and permit psychologically or socially profiling candidates (Tursunbayeva et al., 2021). The substitution of human recruiters byAI (e.g., chatbots) in previously human processes (e.g., candidates' interviewing) envisions removing the human touch from HRM practices (e.g., Tursunbayeva et al., 2021), thus potentially also affecting the relationship between HR and candidates.

4.3.2.3 Deploy

AI is claimed to be a potent instrument to gather and review information relating to employees' job performance. Some feel that this can lead to a fairer evaluation of employees (e.g., Budhwar et al., 2022) by flagging potential biases or offering tips for managers to provide more meaningful feedback (Garr & Jackson, 2019). Others have raised the point that such approaches could reduce the performance of people to numbers and threaten privacy or autonomy through tracking and surveillance (Giermindl et al., 2021; Tursunbayeva et al., 2021), which can change the trust relationship between employees and organizations.

4.3.2.4 Develop

About a decade ago, organizations were advised to assess the personal development needs of each employee and develop tailored individual training plans (D'Netto et al., 2014) rather than conducting a standardized gap analysis. AI is already delivering on this promise by identifying what the workforce is required to learn in a particular situation and offering employees an individualized curriculum (Kaushal et al., 2021).

Technology giants such as IBM are reported to be assisting multinational companies such as the Royal Bank of Scotland in deploying chatbots to act as personal career coaches for employees instead of humans (e.g., Castellanos, 2019), suggesting relevant training, jobs, or career advancement opportunities within the organization. Bots in other contexts such as India are employed to provide personalized responses to HR queries.

4.3.2.5 Retain and Separation

Castellacci & Viñas-Bardolet (2019) argue that automation-based communication technologies like AI in organizations can facilitate communication and informal networks, enrich the information flow between candidates, employees, and organizational managers, create new bonds with external agents (Budhwar et al., 2022), as well as facilitate valuable internal service interactions (Vrontis et al., 2021) by, for example, complementing human interactions (Singh et al., 2017).

Data analysis capabilities of AI are envisioned to permit the analysis of different employee-related qualitative and quantitative data, listen to employees, and analyze their engagement. For example, analyzing employees' social media data may allow us to grasp their brand engagement (Pitt et al., 2018), sentiment (Strohmeier & Piazza, 2015), or job stress (Lee & Shin, 2010).

4.3.3 Transformational

4.3.3.1 Identify and Attract

By delivering the aforementioned operational objectives, AI promises to free up recruiters to work on higher-value tasks (Cathey & Prabhakar, 2021), engage in opportunities to use their skills more effectively (Lindsay et al., 2014), and even make them less prone to human errors (Black & van Esch, 2020). The time-efficiency benefits for candidates are also frequently mentioned. For example, now the candidates do not need to go to the physical office for their interviews. They can be interviewed regardless of their temporal and spatial location (Vrontis et al., 2021). What is neglected is what the candidates could/ should be doing in this time gained (e.g., applying for more jobs).

4.3.3.2 Acquire

AI applications are also transforming the candidate's journey. However, it is still unclear how applicants perceive the use of AI or the replacement of humans with AI in the broader process of recruitment and selection. For example, does the presence of AI alter the candidates' perceptions about the organizational attractiveness or employer branding? Meanwhile, there are already some hints that people prefer human to algorithmic decision-making during selection (e.g., Narayana et al., 2018) because they believe algorithms are less fair or trustworthy (e.g., Lee, 2018).

4.3.3.3 Deploy

The application of AI for reward and compensation has been recently reported as a blind spot in the literature (Kaushal et al., 2021), though it has also been acknowledged that AI can be inconvenient for employees or create income insecurity by, for example, altering work schedules in the sector with fluid workforces (Tursunbayeva et al., 2021). Overall, it can be suggested that the application of AI to scheduling has in a sense embraced pure algorithmic management without the involvement of humans, and more broadly the emergence of the gig economy.

4.3.3.4 Develop

AI's capability to analyze large amounts of data helps to provide actionable insights throughout the employee life cycle. Specifically, in the development phase, AI was reported as helping with the analysis of the training effective-ness of trainees' performance and learning behaviors (Wang et al., 2015). One of the biggest transformations with regard to organizational training is that

AI in e-learning platforms enabled Netflix to personalize training and make recommendations, which considered the employees' preferences or preferred career paths (Garr & Jackson, 2019).

Advanced algorithms are also claimed to have predictive power that forecasts the occupational level of employees at different time intervals during their career or their performance level on the basis of their background and performance characteristics (Garg et al., 2021). There are AI applications aiming to detect potential subjectivity in performance appraisal (Garg et al., 2021), estimate the expertise level of employees, analyze the impact of financial incentives on the efficiency of employees (Massrur et al., 2014), or develop customized incentives (Petruzzellis et al., 2006).

4.3.3.5 Retain

AI applications are also transforming the management of people in organizations by moving the focus from the management of individuals to the management of teams (Tursunbayeva, 2019). With AI, organizations are now enabled to grasp a "mood" of a team as a whole (in comparison to only individual sentiment or opinion), as well as collaboration and interaction patterns within the teams (see Garg et al., 2021 for discussion).

More than 100 applications listed in the report on AI applications for Diversity and Inclusion (D&I) (Garr & Jackson, 2019) imply that AI could potentially help organizations to increase the diversity of their staff and enable all employees to be fully included in organizations, which has been on the organizations' strategic management agenda for a long time. Some of the existing AI applications promise to quantify the D&I business case or relevant financial KPIs (Garr & Jackson, 2019).

4.3.3.6 Separation

AI in the form of predictive algorithms is used to foresee employee turnover intentions (e.g., Sandhya & Sulphey, 2020), as well as to estimate the value of employees for organizations (Saradhi & Palshikar, 2011).

4.4 Conclusions, Limitations, and Future Research

This chapter aimed to build on the established research on the use of technologies in HRM (Ruel et al., 2004) to present and discuss the objectives/consequences of AI use throughout the HR lifecycle (Khan, 2021). It proposes a conceptual framework intersecting these two dimensions and discusses existing knowledge of AI in HRM together with illustrative AI applications from the scholarly and socially curated literature, as well as among the existing vendor solutions of AI for HRM (i.e., Garr & Jackson, 2019). In comparison to previous research that narratively discussed potential benefits (e.g., Prikshat et al., 2021) or challenges from AI separately (e.g., Tursunbayeva et al., 2022), this chapter has brought such discussions together and enriched them with illustrative real-life examples of AI for HRM vendor solutions. Their applications thus indirectly contribute to knowledge on how to diminish negative consequences due to the technology adaptions in HRM functions (Budhwar et al., 2022).

This chapter reveals that AI for HRM can have all three objectives/consequences for employees and organizations. The objectives are always positioned as positive, while the consequences could also be negative. AI applications can help HR departments and professionals to achieve operational objectives by easing the administrative burden, though for full assimilation of AI in HRM, reaching only such objectives might not be enough (Galanaki et al., 2019). It was also noted that the objectives/consequences of AI could be achieved through its different approaches to adoption in HRM, including data handling and analysis, or as a means of communication with employees. While AI can help to achieve some positive operational objectives in terms of time efficiency(e.g., because of chatbot interviews), such applications can have other crucial negative consequences (e.g., relational) as a result of an increasing lack of direct contact between the various stakeholders (Vrontis et al., 2021) and inhibited interpersonal interaction and emotional support (Chao & Kozlowski, 1986).

As evident from such illustrative examples, AI applications to HRM enabled HR to embrace new HRM practices such as employee listening or engagement, which are not usually classified within traditional HRM practices (e.g., D'Netto et al., 2014). It is also evident that the consequences of AI for HRM are not sequential (e.g., first operational, then relational, and finally transformational). Some AI applications can be directly transformational, as in the case of "predictive" actionable insights that AI can provide HR departments and organizational leaders (e.g., Prikshat et al., 2021) that can transform HR departments from being traditional and reactive to agile and proactive (Garg et al., 2021)and permit them to perform HRM practices also at the team level.

Thus, AI is already a critical component in the future of HRM, yet there are more paths still to be uncovered and a number of challenges still to be addressed (Vrontis et al., 2021). To fully convert the objectives of AI into positive consequences, many "dark-side" issues related to the application of AI for HRM still need to be solved. These include trust, transparency, opacity, ethics, and human-centeredness in AI applications for HRM (Omrani et al., 2022). It has already been noted by many that employees do not understand how decisions have been made using AI-based systems or cannot accept those decisions, which leads them to adversarial behavior in organizations (Tambe et al., 2019).

This chapter has some limitations. It extensively discusses the potential impact of AI on HRM and organizations but does not consider socio-technical people, organizational or technological factors of influence (e.g., Prikshat et al., 2021) on AI development, implementation, or use. Nor does it consider the context in which AI applications have been adopted (Bondarouk et al., 2017) that could impact the transition of the AI objectives into potentially realized outcomes. Nevertheless, we believe the chapter still has important *theoretical, practical,* and *policy* implications.

4.4.1 Research Implications

From a theoretical perspective, in terms of existing knowledge gaps, this study contributes to the corpus of research on AI for HRM, as well as to the independent streams of literature on AI and HRM. To the best of our knowledge, it is the first scholarly publication to propose a conceptual framework on how the objectives and consequences of AI could be grasped throughout the HR life cycle. Thus, it advances the existing knowledge of AI applications for separate HRM practices significantly further. The conceptual framework and some of the organizational challenges and dilemmas discussed in this chapter make a conceptual contribution to the HRM literature (Klein & Potosky, 2019) and build a strong agenda for future multi-practice, -level, -disciplinary, and -stakeholder research by revealing existing AI applications for future empirical investigation. This study is also one of the very few on AI for HRM which builds on the extensive literature on e-HRM/HRIS, thus addressing existing criticisms about the atheoretical nature of studies on AI for HRM. Finally, this chapter contributes to the emerging multi-disciplinary discourses on the future of work in the data- and algorithm-driven society.

From a practical perspective, this study can also guide organizations considering the implementation of AI for HRM or already doing it. Given the limited and fragmented nature of existing knowledge on AI for HRM, it is challenging for organizations to build a holistic picture of the existing state-of-the-art or potential consequences. This chapter offers this precious information, thus supporting the informed and responsible adoption of high-risk AI applications for HRM, which differentiate it from many other areas where AI has been applied (Tambe et al., 2019). It can also equip organizations with a starting point for assessing the impact, interactions, and unanticipated complex consequences of AI for HRM (Orlikowski & Scott, 2008). Finally, it can also be of interest to entrepreneurs to inform the human-centered design of AI for HRM, as we may witness with the proliferation of relevant spinoffs and startups (As & Basu, 2022).

From a policy perspective, the chapter can enlighten policymakers about the extent of diffusion of AI for HRM in organizations, or its potential impact, which is invaluable considering the ongoing work in many contexts on AI-related legislations (AI act in the European Union or the US).

References

Aktepe, A., & Ersoz, S. (2012). A quantitative performance evaluation model based on a job satisfaction–performance matrix and application in a manufacturing company. *International Journal of Industrial Engineering: Theory, Applications, and Practice,* *19*(6), 637. https://doi.org/10.23055/ijietap.2012.19.6.637

Albert, E. T. (2019). AI in talent acquisition: A review of AI-applications used in recruitment and selection. *Strategic HR Review, 18*(5), 215–221. https://doi.org/10.1108/SHR-04-2019-0024

As, I., & Basu, P. (2022). *The Routledge Companion to Artificial Intelligence in Architecture.* Routledge. https://www.routledgse.com/The-Routledge-Companion-to-Artificial-Intelligence-in-Architecture/As-Basu/p/book/9780367424589

Beane, M. (2019). Shadow learning: Building robotic surgical skill when approved means fail. *Administrative Science Quarterly, 64*(1), 87–123. https://doi.org/10.1177/0001839217751692

Bersin, J. (2021). *HR Technology 2021: The Definitive Guide: Everything You Want to know about Buying, Implementing, and Investing in HR Technology.*

Black, J. S., & van Esch, P. (2020). AI-enabled recruiting: What is it and how should a manager use it? *Business Horizons, 63*(2), 215–226. https://doi.org/10.1016/j.bushor.2019.12.001

Bondarouk, T., Parry, E., & Furtmueller, E. (2017). Electronic HRM: Four decades of research on adoption and consequences. *The International Journal of Human Resource Management, 28*(1), 98–131. https://doi.org/10.1080/09585192.2016.1245672

Borgesius, F. J. Z. (2020). Strengthening legal protection against discrimination by algorithms and artificial intelligence. *The International Journal of Human Rights, 24*(10), 1572–1593. https://doi.org/10.1080/13642987.2020.1743976

Budhwar, P., Malik, A., De Silva, M. T. T., & Thevisuthan, P. (2022). Artificial intelligence – challenges and opportunities for international HRM: A review and research agenda. *The International Journal of Human Resource Management, 33*(6), 1065–1097. https://doi.org/10.1080/09585192.2022.2035161

Bussler, L., & Davis, E. (2002). Information systems: The quiet revolution in human resource management. *Journal of Computer Information Systems, 42*(2), 17–20. https://doi.org/10.1080/08874417.2002.11647482

Castellacci, F., & Viñas-Bardolet, C. (2019). Internet use and job satisfaction. *Computers in Human Behavior, 90*, 141–152. https://doi.org/10.1016/j.chb.2018.09.001

Castellanos, S. (2019). HR departments turn to AI-enabled recruiting in race for talent. *Wall Street Journal.* https://www.wsj.com/articles/hr-departments-turn-to-ai-enabled-recruiting-in-race-for-talent-11552600459

Cathey, G., & Prabhakar, A. (2021). Ethical AI: A new strategic imperative for recruiting and staffing. *MIT Sloan Management Review.* https://sloanreview.mit.edu/sponsors-content/ethical-ai-a-new-strategic-imperative-for-recruiting-and-staffing/

Chao, G. T., & Kozlowski, S. W. (1986). Employee perceptions on the implementation of robotic manufacturing technology. *Journal of Applied Psychology, 71*(1), 70. https://doi.org/10.1037/0021-9010.71.1.70

Cheng, M. M., & Hackett, R. D. (2021). A critical review of algorithms in HRM: Definition, theory, and practice. *Human Resource Management Review, 31*(1), 100698. https://doi.org/10.1016/j.hrmr.2019.100698

Choi, S. (2018). Enhancing Customer Response Capability through Organizational Knowledge Resources in Service Encounters. *PACIS 2018 Proceedings.* https://aisel.aisnet.org/pacis2018/233

D'Netto, B., Shen, J., Chelliah, J., & Manjit, M. (2014). Human resource diversity management practices in the Australian manufacturing sector. *The International Journal of Human Resource Management, 25*(9), 1243–1266. https://doi.org/10.1080/09585192.2013.826714

European Commission. (2020). *WHITE PAPER on Artificial Intelligence – A European Approach to Excellence and Trust*. https://eur-lex.europa.eu/legal-content/EN/TXT/?qid=1603192201335&uri=CELEX:52020DC0065

Galanaki, E., Lazazzara, A., & Parry, E. (2019). A cross-national analysis of E-HRM configurations: Integrating the information technology and HRM perspectives. In A. Lazazzara, R. C. D. Nacamulli, C. Rossignoli, & S. Za (Eds.), *Organizing for Digital Innovation* (pp. 261–276). Springer International Publishing. https://doi.org/10.1007/978-3-319-90500-6_20

Garg, S., Sinha, S., Kar, A. K., & Mani, M. (2021). A review of machine learning applications in human resource management. *International Journal of Productivity and Performance Management, 71*(5), 1590–1610. https://doi.org/10.1108/IJPPM-08-2020-0427

Garr, S. S., & Jackson, C. (2019). *Diversity & Inclusion Technology: The Rise of A Transformative Market*. Mercer. https://www.mercer.com/our-thinking/career/diversity-and-inclusion-technology.html

Giermindl, L. M., Strich, F., Christ, O., Leicht-Deobald, U., & Redzepi, A. (2021). The dark sides of people analytics: Reviewing the perils for organisations and employees. *European Journal of Information Systems*, 1–26. https://doi.org/10.1080/0960085X.2021.1927213

Harris, S. (2020). *Sierra-Cedar 2019–2020. HR Systems Survey Findings*. Sierra-Cedar. https://cdn.ymaws.com/www.clevelandshrm.com/resource/collection/09E0F41E-BD60-41C0-A2FD-AAD4D5A44B59/The_Future_of_HR_Technology_Virtual_Learning-_February_2020_.pdf

IDC. (2020). *Worldwide Spending on Artificial Intelligence Is Expected to Double in Four Years, Reaching $110 Billion in 2024, According to New IDC Spending Guide*. IDC. https://www.idc.com/getdoc.jsp?containerId=prUS46794720

Italian Government. (2021). *Strategic Programme on Artificial Intelligence 2022-2024*. Italian Government.

Kaushal, N., Kaurav, R. P. S., Sivathanu, B., & Kaushik, N. (2021). Artificial intelligence and HRM: Identifying future research Agenda using systematic literature review and bibliometric analysis. *Management Review Quarterly*. https://doi.org/10.1007/s11301-021-00249-2

Khan, S. (2021). *Artificial Intelligence for Human Resources Toolkit Helps Organizations Overcome Implementation Challenges*. World Economic Forum. https://www.weforum.org/press/2021/12/artificial-intelligence-for-human-resources-toolkit-helps-organizations-overcome-implementation-challenges/

Klein, H. J., & Potosky, D. (2019). Making a conceptual contribution at Human Resource Management Review. *Human Resource Management Review, 29*(3), 299–304. https://doi.org/10.1016/j.hrmr.2019.04.003

Kurter, H. L. (2021). *4 Top HR Trends and Predictions For 2022*. Forbes. https://www.forbes.com/sites/heidilynnekurter/2021/12/28/5-top-hr-trends-and-predictions-for-2022/

Lee, M. K. (2018). Understanding perception of algorithmic decisions: Fairness, trust, and emotion in response to algorithmic management. *Big Data & Society, 5*(1), 205395171875668. https://doi.org/10.1177/2053951718756684

Lee, Y., & Shin, S. (2010). Job stress evaluation using response surface data mining. *International Journal of Industrial Ergonomics, 40*(4), 379–385. https://doi.org/10.1016/j.ergon.2010.03.003

Lepak, D. P., & Snell, S. A. (1998). Virtual HR: Strategic human resource management in the 21st century. *Human Resource Management Review, 6*(3), 215–234.

Lindsay, C., Commander, J., Findlay, P., Bennie, M., Dunlop Corcoran, E., & Van Der Meer, R. (2014). 'Lean', new technologies and employment in public health services: Employees' experiences in the National Health Service. *The International Journal of Human Resource Management*, 25(21), 2941–2956. https://doi.org/10.1080/09585192.2014.948900

Lokman, A. S., & Ameedeen, M. A. (2019). Modern chatbot systems: A Technical Review. In K. Arai, R. Bhatia, & S. Kapoor (Eds.), *Proceedings of the Future Technologies Conference (FTC) 2018* (pp. 1012–1023). Springer International Publishing. https://doi.org/10.1007/978-3-030-02683-7_75

Manyika, J., Chui, M., Miremadi, M., Bughin, J., George, K., Willmott, P., & Dewhurst, M. (2017). *A Future that Works: Automation, Employment, and Productivity.* McKinsey Global Institute.

Martini, M., Cavenago, D., & Marafioti, E. (2020). Exploring types, drivers and outcomes of social e-HRM. *Employee Relations: The International Journal*, 43(3), 788–806. https://doi.org/10.1108/ER-10-2019-0404

Massrur, R., Nejad, A. F., & Sami, A. (2014). The surveying of the effect of the incentive pays to the degree of the attraction of resources in bank branches through the data mining technique. *2014 Iranian Conference on Intelligent Systems (ICIS)*, 1–6. https://doi.org/10.1109/IranianCIS.2014.6802590

Mehrabad, M. S., & Brojeny, M. F. (2007).The development of an expert system for effective selection and appointment of the jobs applicants in human resource management. *Computers & Industrial Engineering*, 53(2), 306–312. https://doi.org/10.1016/j.cie.2007.06.023

Meijerink, J., Boons, M., Keegan, A., & Marler, J. (2021). Algorithmic human resource management: Synthesizing developments and cross-disciplinary insights on digital HRM. *The International Journal of Human Resource Management*, 32(12), 2545–2562. https://doi.org/10.1080/09585192.2021.1925326

Minbaeva, D. (2021). Disrupted HR?. *Human Resource Management Review*, 31(4), 100820. https://doi.org/10.1016/j.hrmr.2020.100820

Molitor, M. (2020). *Effective Human-Robot Collaboration in the Industry 4.0 Context – Implications for Human Resource Management* [Masters Business Administration, University of Twente]. http://essay.utwente.nl/82586/1/Molitor_MA_BMS.pdf

Omrani, N., Rivieccio, G., Fiore, U., Schiavone, F., & Agreda, S. G. (2022). To trust or not to trust? An assessment of trust in AI-based systems: Concerns, ethics and contexts. *Technological Forecasting and Social Change*, 181, 121763. https://doi.org/10.1016/j.techfore.2022.121763

Orlikowski, W. J., & Scott, S. V. (2008). Sociomateriality: Challenging the separation of technology, work and organization. *Academy of Management Annals*, 2(1), 433–474. https://doi.org/10.5465/19416520802211644

Petruzzellis, S., Licchelli, O., Palmisano, I., Semeraro, G., Bavaro, V., & Palmisano, C. (2006). Personalized Incentive Plans through Employee Profiling. *ICEIS*. https://doi.org/10.5220/0002493401070114

Pitt, C. S., Botha, E., Ferreira, J. J., & Kietzmann, J. (2018). Employee brand engagement on social media: Managing optimism and commonality. *Business Horizons*, 61(4), 635–642. https://doi.org/10.1016/j.bushor.2018.04.001

Prikshat, V., Malik, A., & Budhwar, P. (2021). AI-augmented HRM: Antecedents, assimilation and multilevel consequences. *Human Resource Management Review*, 33, 100860. https://doi.org/10.1016/j.hrmr.2021.100860

Qamar, Y., Agrawal, R. K., Samad, T. A., & Chiappetta Jabbour, C. J. (2021). When technology meets people: The interplay of artificial intelligence and human resource management. *Journal of Enterprise Information Management, 34*(5), 1339–1370. https://doi.org/10.1108/JEIM-11-2020-0436

Ruël, H., Bondarouk, T., & Looise, J. K. (2004). E-HRM: Innovation or Irritation. An explorative empirical study in five large companies on web-based HRM. *Management Revue, 15*(3), 364–380. https://www.jstor.org/stable/41783479

Sajjadiani, S., Sojourner, A. J., Kammeyer-Mueller, J. D., & Mykerezi, E. (2019). Using machine learning to translate applicant work history into predictors of performance and turnover. *The Journal of Applied Psychology, 104*(10), 1207–1225. https://doi.org/10.1037/apl0000405

Sandhya, S., & Sulphey, M. M. (2020). Influence of empowerment, psychological contract and employee engagement on voluntary turnover intentions. *International Journal of Productivity and Performance Management, 70*(2), 325–349. https://doi.org/10.1108/IJPPM-04-2019-0189

Saradhi, V. V., & Palshikar, G. K. (2011). Employee churn prediction. *Expert Systems with Applications, 38*(3), 1999–2006. https://doi.org/10.1016/j.eswa.2010.07.134

Singh, J., Brady, M., Arnold, T., & Brown, T. (2017). The emergent field of organizational frontlines. *Journal of Service Research, 20*(1), 3–11. https://doi.org/10.1177/1094670516681513

Strohmeier, S., & Piazza, F. (2015a). Artificial intelligence techniques in human resource management—A conceptual exploration. In C. Kahraman, & S. Çevik Onar (Eds.), *Intelligent Techniques in Engineering Management: Theory and Applications* (pp. 149–172). Springer International Publishing. https://doi.org/10.1007/978-3-319-17906-3_7

Tambe, P., Cappelli, P., & Yakubovich, V. (2019). Artificial intelligence in human resources management: Challenges and a path forward. *California Management Review, 61*(4), 15–42. https://doi.org/10.1177/0008125619867910

Torres, E. N., & Mejia, C. (2017). Asynchronous video interviews in the hospitality industry: Considerations for virtual employee selection. *International Journal of Hospitality Management, 61*, 4–13. https://doi.org/10.1016/j.ijhm.2016.10.012

Tursunbayeva, A., Bunduchi, R., Franco, M., & Pagliari, C. (2017). Human resource information systems in health care: A systematic evidence review. *Journal of the American Medical Informatics Association: JAMIA, 24*(3), 633–654. https://doi.org/10.1093/jamia/ocw141

Tursunbayeva, A., Di Lauro, S., & Pagliari, C. (2018). People analytics—A scoping review of conceptual boundaries and value propositions. *International Journal of Information Management, 43*, 224–247. https://doi.org/10.1016/j.ijinfomgt.2018.08.002

Tursunbayeva, A., Pagliari, C., Di Lauro, S., & Antonelli, G. (2021). The ethics of people analytics: Risks, opportunities and recommendations. *Personnel Review*, ahead-of-print. https://doi.org/10.1108/PR-12-2019-0680

Vrontis, D., Christofi, M., Pereira, V., Tarba, S., Makrides, A., & Trichina, E. (2022). Artificial intelligence, robotics, advanced technologies and human resource management: A systematic review. *The International Journal of Human Resource Management, 33*(6), 1237–1266. https://doi.org/10.1080/09585192.2020.1871398

Wang, J., Lin, Y. I., & Hou, S. Y. (2015). A data mining approach for training evaluation in simulation-based training. *Computers & Industrial Engineering, 80*, 171–180. https://doi.org/10.1016/j.cie.2014.12.008

World Economic Forum. (2021). *Human-Centred Artificial Intelligence for Human Resources*. World Economic Forum. https://www.weforum.org/reports/human-centred-ai-for-hr-state-of-play-and-the-path-ahead/toolkit/

5 Methodology for Evaluating the Appropriateness of a Business Process for Robotic Process Automation

Abhishta Abhishta, Lars Berghuis, Wouter van Heeswijk and Aizhan Tursunbayeva

5.1 Introduction

Robots ensure that work, previously done by humans, is replaced by machines consisting of mechanical parts representing the human body and transistors symbolising electronic network as the human brain. Where production lines were previously occupied by people, machines are frequently reported to take their place. Self-driving cars and e-invoicing did not seem possible until 20 years ago and could now replace taxi drivers and bookkeepers. Frey and Osborne (2017) discuss the effect of automation on the current job market. They write about the susceptibility of jobs to computerisation in their paper and calculated the probability of jobs that are most at risk of automation replacement.

They predict that 47% of the current jobs will be replaced within the upcoming 20 years by machines and software. Furthermore, Frey and Osborne predict that among the jobs with the highest probability are jobs such as accounting workers and auditors, with a probability of 94%, compared to engineers and sales managers only having a 1% chance of being replaced by technology (Frey and Osborne, 2017).

A recently introduced technology that contributes to this automation and intents to reduce workload is 'Robotic Process Automation' (hereafter RPA). RPA is software that automates tasks, previously executed by humans. The software allows, via a script, to let a digital robot access websites and system applications to read, extract or fill in data (Van der Aalst et al., 2018). This automation of processes may lead to many benefits, such as increasing the efficiency and quality of processes, by reducing Full Time Equivalent (FTE) and preventing manual errors. Furthermore, compared to traditional process automation – which may require substantial software development skills – RPA does not change any of the underlying IT systems. This increases accessibility and reduces risks during implementations (Van der Aalst et al., 2018). While RPA technology already exists for a number of years, it has recently received a surge in attention due to organisations recognising its potentials, vendors adding features and more user-friendly RPA products.

DOI: 10.4324/9781003304616-8

Although RPA has much to offer, it also poses challenges. A survey done by Deloitte found that out of 400 firms, 63% did not meet the RPA project deadlines (Trefler, 2018). Furthermore, they found that 30 to 50% of firms failed their initiative project. Rutaganda et al. (2017) state that the reason many RPA initiatives fail is because of the difficulties in finding processes fitting the RPA solution. One of the key challenges organisations face when initiating RPA projects is to effectively identify RPA-suited processes (Leopold et al., 2018, Moffitt et al., 2018, Van der Aalst et al., 2018). Geyer-Klingeberg et al. (2018) mention that RPA is not a technology applicable to each process and rather requires a careful analysis of the automation potential as well as its benefits and risks. Selecting the wrong processes could lead to excessive bot maintenance and unexpected risks (Van der Aalst et al., 2018). Risks such as updates or failures of systems could result in bots processing data wrongly or disrupting bot activities (Van der Aalst et al., 2018), hence leading to longer and more costly implementations than expected, lowering the initial expectations of businesses and therefore missing out on promising automation opportunities (Syed et al., 2020).

In the past few years, methods have been created to address the challenges of selecting RPA-suitable processes. Whereas some methods addressed the identification problems via semi-structured interviews with process experts (Agaton and Swedberg, 2018, Syed et al., 2020), others created methods involving calculations via scorecards or extracting user interface logs to apply process mining algorithms (Leshob et al., 2018, Wanner et al., 2019). However, issues are faced when using such methods.

Interviewing people to extract suitable business processes for RPA can be quite time consuming. Conducting more than five interviews to obtain multiple views takes considerable time, especially if people are not familiar with RPA. In addition, conducting interviews only considers the view of an individual. As processes need to be carefully analysed, multiple viewpoints may be required to avoid misconceptions. Individuals can easily misjudge processes' RPA suitability by misunderstanding RPA or omitting activities that require human thinking.

The use of process mining might be a solution to these issues, due to the use of algorithms to extract a process and calculate RPA suitability (Wanner et al., 2019). However, Dumas et al. (2013) describe that for most organisations such a project requires quite some effort, as process mining relies on the availability of event logs. Many organisations, especially smaller or medium-sized ones, do not possess the necessary architecture and expertise to implement process mining, making process mining a rather context-specific option. Besides issues such as complexity, dependency on individuals and large time consumption, none of the methods show a systematic approach of the steps to be taken during process selection. While most literature refers to establishing a "process-selection method", Wanner et al. (2019) identify a lack of any systematic selection of processes. Even though frameworks (Agaton and

Swedberg, 2018) and scorecards with calculations (Leshob et al., 2018) have been introduced as solutions, there are no empirical examples with procedural steps given, making such solutions unsuitable for practitioners.

This work is primarily based on the master thesis of the first author (Berghuis, 2021). It contributes to literature by addressing the identification phase of RPA, integrating brainstorming techniques and business process management (BPM), and providing a concrete and comprehensive workshop format for RPA process identification.

5.2 RPA: Tools and Functions

A literature review collects background information about RPA and current criteria for selecting relevant business processes for automation. The search term focuses on "Robotic Process Automation" within the Title or Abstracts of papers. The term "RPA" is not used, as a preliminary search showed that many unrelated fields and subject areas use "RPA" as an abbreviation. Only Scopus is used during the initial searches for relevant literature, being preferred over alternatives such as Web of Science or IEEE. Scopus has a larger publication body while incorporating most of the peer-reviewed literature from other databases. Particularly in terms of contemporary literature, it is known to be a richer source than Web of Science (Stahlschmidt and Stephen, 2020). However, papers that are selected from the Scopus database might contain relevant references not found on Scopus. These papers are added manually via the so-called snowballing method, where references from sources are deemed relevant to add within the SLR. No publication date limit was set, as RPA is a relatively novel topic, with one of the pioneering papers on RPA dating back to 2014. Inclusion criteria are mainly aimed at other process selection methods, as these are likely to contain process criteria to evaluate whether processes are suitable for RPA. In addition, as mentioned in the Design Science framework by Wieringa (2014), these methods help with using tooling or elements from other process-selection methods to potentially integrate within the workshop.

Besides scientific literature, so-called 'grey literature' is consulted to glean more detailed and state-of-the-art information about the primary functions of RPA. The grey literature approach is adopted, as it is "suited to emerging areas of innovation where formal research lags behind evidence from professional or technical sources" (Tursunbayeva et al., 2021). Like other technologies, RPA is being innovated continuously, such that academic sources may lag behind. RPA's primary functions are projected to rapidly develop and are more likely to be found on websites from vendors and consultants than in academic literature. For this reason, sources from the Internet, such as tooling, and consultancy websites are approached to include recent developments regarding RPA functions. This grey literature was found via references of other academic sources (snowballing) and by searching for "Robotic Process Automation" using the Google search engine. In addition, most RPA vendors give potential buyers the opportunity to explore the functionalities of their RPA product. For this reason, software from the most popular vendor, UIpath, was downloaded and tested to better grasp RPA's capabilities.

To analyse the data, a literature matrix is deployed to conceptualise RPA. This matrix helps structuring the content found within the literature, setting up questions such as, "How does RPA work?", "How is AI involved in RPA?", "What RPA products/tooling is used" and extracting answers to these questions from different authors of both academic and grey literature.

The primary functions and process criteria are analysed by extracting different sentences, concepts and keywords from the collected literature. After extracting all data, keywords are used to categorise both the primary functions and the process criteria. Keywords are either qualitatively created or derived from external sources. Each category is re-assessed by evaluating non-frequent criteria and determining whether to merge them with other criteria or exclude them.

5.3 Selection of Relevant Literature

The first search within Scopus, based on the previously described review protocol, resulted in 294 articles of which first all titles were evaluated. Based on the titles, the abstracts of 68 articles were assessed. This assessment resulted in a selection of 43 papers suitable for initial screening. Five of these papers were excluded due to access constraints. The remaining 38 were read in order to evaluate whether the papers defined RPA or not.

A Google advanced search was done to find relevant grey literature. Specifically, articles from the biggest RPA vendors – such as UiPath, Blue Prism and Automation Anywhere – were included, as well as articles from major consultancy firms such as Accenture and Deloitte, having assisted many organisations with their RPA journeys. The grey literature search yielded 15 articles (primarily web pages) for further analysis.

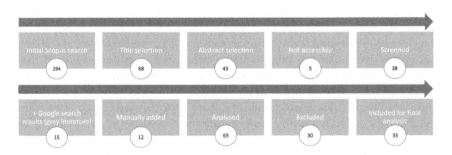

Figure 5.1 Process for selecting relevant literature.

In addition to the aforementioned literature, 12 more articles from other scientific databases were manually added as snowball references. This leads to a total of 65 articles, comprising both grey literature and scientific literature, to be fully analysed. The analysis showed that many sources refer back to earlier published sources about RPA, its primary functions and the process criteria. For instance, Wanner et al. (2019) re-used the criteria described by authors such as Asatiani and Penttinen (2016) and Willcocks et al. (2017) and transformed these criteria into quantitative measurements. To avoid duplicates, only papers describing unique criteria are added to the list. As a result, 30 papers were eventually not included. Ultimately, the literature review resulted in the selection of 35 papers that were fully analysed, with the results being presented next (see Figure 5.1).

5.4 What is Robotic Process Automation?

RPA is software that automates tasks previously executed by humans. Via a script, the software enables a digital robot to access websites and system applications to read, extract and process data (Van der Aalst et al., 2018). While RPA already exists for some years, a generally accepted definition has not yet emerged. Literature gives multiple, but overlapping, meanings to RPA.

Van der Aalst et al. (2018), for instance, describe RPA as an umbrella term for tools that operate on the user interface of computer systems in the same way a human would do this, in contrast to other automation initiatives it operates via an "outside-in" manner. Tools in this case refer to various techniques that are integrated with the RPA technology, such as Image Recognition and Optical Character recognition to handle and execute tasks previously performed by humans. Cewe et al. (2017) state that RPA can be regarded as a special kind of Business Process Management System (BPMS) that uses the Graphical User Interface (GUI) as an automation adaptor instead of regular interfaces for inter-system communication. Syed et al. (2020) describe "RPA as a technology comprising software agents called "bots" that mimic the manual path taken by a human through a range of computer applications when performing certain tasks in a business process". These bots can be seen as software robots programmed by the RPA developer to perform various actions within different web- and desktop applications.

RPA performs actions directly on the GUI (Cewe et al., 2017), thereby distinguishing itself from other automation initiatives. RPA sets itself apart from other more traditional BPM tools that are automated via interactions with the back end and its data layers (Willcocks et al., 2017). A typical approach for automating processes is via BPMS (Cewe et al., 2017). Cewe et al. (2017) state that within such systems, processes are defined as rule-based workflows that are executed in a process engine, with communication between these applications taking place via Application Programming Interfaces (APIs). However, the deployment of an API requires substantial development effort. When contrasting RPA to more non-robotic automation and BPM automation initiatives, it can be considered as a more lightweight solution for innovations (Mendling et al., 2018, Penttinen et al., 2018), which does not invade existing IT infrastructures (Bygstad, 2017, Penttinen et al., 2018). As Van der Aalst et al. (2018) state, innovating processes with RPA happens via an "outside-in" manner. RPA uses an approach of integrating the bot with the presentation layer by interacting with the user interface (Cewe et al., 2017). As a result, underlying IT applications do not have to be adjusted, making RPA an easier-to-implement alternative than other automation initiatives.

5.5 Which Tools Can Be Used to Implement RPA?

Leno et al. (2021) mention that an RPA tool operates by mapping a process to the RPA language, which is subsequently translated into a script that can be carried out. Currently, there are multiple vendors offering RPA tooling. To this day the most famous RPA tooling providers are UiPath, Blue Prism and Automation Anywhere (Gotthardt et al., 2020, Leno et al., 2021, Van der Aalst et al., 2018), see Figure 5.2. These vendors offer organisations RPA tools in the form of product licenses. Most vendors allow organisations to build one bot for free (using a community version) that can be extended to multiple bots via the purchase of a license. Furthermore, while these vendors offer the most capabilities regarding RPA, there are also open-source RPA tools available that provide libraries which can be called via R or Python as programming language. This allows the more experienced programmer to develop multiple bots without licensing costs and to integrate the programmer's own machine learning algorithms to operate within an RPA script. However, it may be questioned whether open-source tooling is scalable, as one of the strengths of RPA is the easy creation of scripts via drag-and-drop activities by non-programmers.

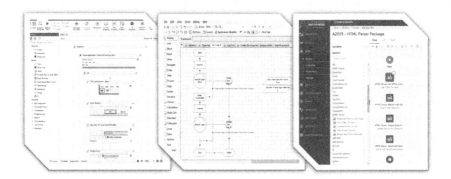

Figure 5.2 Process mapping interfaces of RPA respectively UiPath, Blue Prism and Automation Anywhere.

Attended and Unattended Bots: The execution of a script produced by RPA tooling can be triggered via two ways, namely an attended trigger or an unattended trigger (Wanner et al., 2019). The trigger types also distinguish two types of bots. Mullukara and Asokan (2020) refer to these as attended bots and unattended bots. Unattended bots are bots that run autonomously (without any human interference) and are suitable for simple processes that do not vary between instances (Syed et al., 2020). Unattended bots are fit for executing deterministic routines that are easy to divide into steps and codify (Leno et al., 2021). In addition, unattended bots are often placed on a server together with a virtual machine where they perform actions in the background (Mullakara and Asokan, 2020, Jimenez-Ramirez et al., 2019). As an example, weekly updating source data for BI dashboards could be an action performed by an unattended bot, as such efficiently collecting up-to-date management information.

Attended bots are bots that must be triggered by individuals. Unlike unattended bots, they often fulfil part of the overall process and are actively monitored by the human user. Le Clair et al. (2017) describe this way of bot triggering as trigger points that commence processes after a specific event, such as pressing a hotkey or a file entering the database. An example of a routine process suitable for attended bots is the transfer of invoice data from a pdf to an Excel spreadsheet and subsequently to a financial system (Leno et al., 2021). In such a setting it might be important to have a human supervising the automated process to prevent accounting mistakes. Another example is hiring new employees. Whenever a new employee enters the organisations, accounts must be created, user access must be defined and personnel information needs to be obtained and updated. These activities are all very structured and easy to parse into steps, making them suitable candidates for RPA implementation. However, there are still processes that require human decision and judgement, such as the initial hiring of employees and evaluating due diligence, as a result composing a process with both manual and automated user activities.

Digital Colleagues and Twins: Once attended bots and unattended bots are developed, organisations need to remain in control of their automated processes. For process managers and auditors, it may be hard to detect and manage active bots within the process landscape of organisations. In addition, having robots as digital colleagues can be risky (González Enríquez et al., 2020, Gotthardt et al., 2020, Syed et al., 2020). A user has to step in if a robot fails (e.g., due to a data error or system failure) and manually complete the process.

Kokina and Blanchette (2019) describe that companies avoid these risks by including process monitoring and exception management within the implementation stages to control RPA governance. To assist this management, most vendors provide dashboards. Figure 5.3 shows a dashboard from the company UIpath, called UIpath Orchestrator. This dashboard shows data on bots running within an organisation and lets the user manage these processes

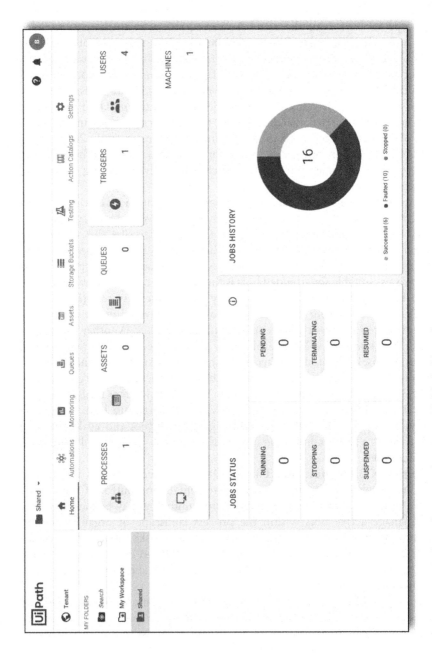

Figure 5.3 UiPath Orchestrator showing an RPA dashboard.

(Leno et al., 2021). The data includes, for instance, the number of successfully ran processes, failures of processes, and logging of processes. Furthermore, users can use the dashboard to schedule different processes to be run by the robot. Due to the existence of such process overviews, Reinkemeyer (2020) refers to digital twins arising within organisations. A digital twin is a virtual equivalent of a certain physical system. For instance, an engine of a car can be fully visualised in order to generate simulations and identify optimisation opportunities (Grieves and Vickers, 2017). In the case of RPA, its dashboard serves as a digital twin of the processes automated by RPA (Reinkemeyer, 2020). As such, organisations adopting RPA obtain both an overview of their processes and insights into potential optimisations.

Artificial Intelligence: RPA has made recent advances in capabilities, due to the addition of artificial intelligence (AI) features. Besides the basic functions of RPA, such as screen scraping, copy-pasting and filling in data, RPA has been upgraded with functionalities containing various AI solutions throughout the years. Most of these AI solutions help with processing unstructured data. Some AI techniques currently integrated within RPA tooling are Computer Vision (such as Optical Character Recognition and Image Recognition), Fuzzy Matching/Logic, Natural Language Processing, Statistical Methods and Neural Networks (Ribeiro et al., 2021). An example of AI being used in combination with RPA is the prediction of risk scores regarding Customer Due Diligence processes and evaluation. For instance, a bot collects risk factors (independent variables), by scraping Google searches and collecting other data, where a machine learning algorithm can subsequently calculate a score regarding the risk level. However, Cooper et al. (2019) describe that the majority of contemporary RPA work is still rule-based and requires little to no judgement, yet indicate that in the future RPA may display more.

5.6 Functions of RPA

For decision makers to assess whether RPA can be a viable solution to automate their processes, RPA's primary functions should be explained during the workshop. (Slack and Brandon-Jones, 2018), mention that the first step decision-makers should take is articulating the basic capabilities of a new process technology, demarcating what it can and cannot do.

Based on the literature review, 65 primary RPA functions were identified. Descriptions of RPA functionalities have first been categorised into functionalities described in one or two words, such as opening/closing application, logging in, copying/pasting data and saving/loading data. In addition, due to the large total number of functionalities, further categorisation was performed to help participants get a better understanding of where and how primary functions are used. This last categorisation eventually led to following category names: 'Application', 'Data', 'Desktop', Email', 'Programming functions', 'Web applications', 'Process', 'Triggers', 'User' and 'Advanced'.

Table 5.1 Categories Representing the Functionalities of RPA

Category	Description
Application	Automation activities that an RPA robot can perform within an (web) application.
Data	Activities the bot can perform related to processing data.
Desktop	Desktop, refers to activities the bot could perform on desktop level. This refers to general activities such as the robot typing, clicking or moving files from one folder to the other.
Email	Activities the bot can perform related to email.
Programming Functions	Just as program languages, RPA functions, such as for/while loops and if then else statements can be written. This makes is possible to automate some decision making.
Web Applications	Automation activities that an RPA robot can perform within a web application specifically.
Other	Some others mentioned functionalities that could be used within RPA tooling, such as auditing and logging processes. Or functionalities which triggers the bot by pressing hotkeys or the appearance of images. advanced intelligence.

The categories 'Process', 'Triggers' and 'User' were eventually classified under 'Other', as these were not frequently mentioned. Table 5.1 gives a short description of how each of the categories refers to the different functionalities of RPA. Considering the literature consensus that the focus should be on 'basic' functionalities of RPA, AI functionalities such as predictive analysis, email classification and computer vision were excluded.

Syed et al. (2020) mention that for organisations starting RPA projects, the focus should be on the basic capabilities of RPA. For this reason, the 17 AI functionalities resulting from the literature review were left out. As a result, a total of 48 primary functions were used, serving as the functionalities necessary for decision-makers to understand RPA's capabilities and therefore its business implications. Table 5.2 presents all the identified primary functions.

5.7 Criteria for Selecting a Process for RPA

Knowing the criteria for selecting business processes suitable for implementing RPA is crucial for the initial identification of suitable processes and is commonly one of the first activities being performed during BPM projects (Dumas et al., 2013). Collecting these criteria is therefore imperative, aiding workshop participants to select processes that fulfil most of these criteria. Again, relevant literature sources selected as described previously were analysed and then categorised into one or two words as initial criteria. These criteria were then evaluated again to combine criteria and remove duplicates.

Table 5.2 List of Primary Functions Split into 7 Categories.

Application	Data	Desktop	Email	Programming functions	Web application	Other
Opening/closing applications	Saving data	Extracting data	Typing	Open/closing emails & attachments	For/while loops	Opening/closing browsers
Logging in	Entering data	Validating data	Clicking	Reading emails	If-then-else rules or	Locating URL's
Logging off	Archiving	Dealing with structured data	Dragging	Generating sending emails	Moving mails to folder or	Exception handling
Expanding applications	Converting data	Calculations	Entering queries	Moving files/folders		Web recording
API integrations (SAP, Excel, Outlook, PDF)	Uploading files	Copy/pasting	Screen scraping	Generating sending emails		Auditing
Accessing databases	Encoding files	Collecting statistics	Storing files/folders			Logging
Reading databases	Detecting file changes		Updating data			Web scraping
Writing databases	Migrating data to					Trigger by hotkey
OCR						User interaction
						Trigger by image appearance

This list was eventually consolidated into a list of 18 entries and used for the interviews with the two RPA developers. During the interview, one of the developers mentioned that there were two criteria missing, which were in his opinion important to be added. These were added, resulting in a total of 20 criteria. Many literature sources present process criteria presented in a single list, not distinguishing between criteria with regard to the benefits of RPA and criteria determining automation potential. However, a list of 20 criteria might be too large to be properly assessed by participants. For this reason, the criteria are segregated into criteria related to 'Automation Potential' and criteria related to 'Business Value'.

This way, participants may assess (i) the complexity of a process to be automated and (ii) the benefits resulting from this automation, allowing informed trade-offs.

Automation potential: Given the established segregation of criteria, the first set refers to automation potential. This set (Table 5.3) contains criteria describing process aspects that relate to its automation potential. Example criteria of processes mentioned by different authors are 'Low cognitive', 'Standardised', 'Multiple Systems' and 'Structured data'

(Agaton and Swedberg, 2018, Asatiani and Penttinen, 2016, Lacity et al., 2015). A process is more suitable for RPA when it does not require too much thinking (personal judgement), follows a known path, accesses and uses multiple systems, and is only using structured digital data. However, a process does not need to fulfil every criterion to be a viable candidate for RPA. For example, if a process is mature and highly standardised, but only uses a single application, it can still be a viable option for RPA automation. For this reason, these criteria should be seen as guidelines rather than requirements.

Business Value: The other set of criteria is referred to as Business Value criteria. These criteria

Stable applications or systems or websites (1)

Interfaces will remain stable, so no changing interfaces due to updates

Stable applications or systems or websites (2)

No connection or capacity problems during the process

Are the applications within the organisation or external indicate how much value the business will receive once a process has been automated (Table 5.4). Compared to the Automation Potential criteria, these criteria cannot all be answered as binary by stating Yes or No. The Automation Potential criteria should also include interval or ratio variables. For instance, the criteria 'Duration' require a numerical value. The same goes for 'High in Volume'. This criterion should be evaluated on whether the process runs daily, weekly or monthly. If a process scores high on these criteria (e.g., a daily process that has an average duration lasting longer than one hour), has high chances of human error, requires substantial manual effort and will increase in compliance via RPA, a high value is gained when automated by RPA. However, just as with the Automation Potential criteria, the Business Value criteria are seen as guidelines rather than requirements.

Table 5.3 Criteria for RPA Process Selection (Automation Potential)

Automation Potential	Explanation
Mature	All ins and outs are known within the process No adjustments to the process are made/will be made (within the short term) every activity within the process is predictable (cause and effect are known)
Standardized	Process is executed the same by colleagues/ departments/business units The order of the process doesn't change no exceptions during the process minor difference between other process variants and happy path knows little to no different process variants
Rule-based	The process is easy to be written in steps the process is easy to be formulated in if-then-else statements the process is structured/well defined and non-subjective
Multiple systems	There are multiple applications/websites the user has to act on during the process
Few decision points	No or few decisions have to be made during the process
Structured digital data	Data is structured and digital
Low cognitive	Low cognitive activities within the process Decisions within the process are not based on intuition or experiences
Easy data access	Data is easily accessible
Lifetime (mentioned by developer)	The process should still exist after five years Internal/external (mentioned by developer)

Table 5.4 Criteria for RPA Process Selection (Business Value)

Business Value	Explanation
Duration	Average duration of the overall process
High in volume	Is the process executed weekly monthly, four time per week
Repetitive	The process returns frequently
Human errors	Human mistakes are made within the process
Manual effort	A lot of manual activities by the user
Essential business process	Without this process the business cannot operate
Increase in compliance	For example, data privacy, accuracy or due to a process being better logged
Trigger options	Attended: the user is present and watches the robot operate Unattended: the robot can perform on a virtual machine and the user doesn't have to present hybrid: the process can be executed within the background on the user's computer where the user can still take control if or once necessary

Tables 5.3 and 5.4 show the categorised criteria resulting from the SLR. These process criteria are shared with participants to recognise suitable RPA processes during the workshop.

5.8 Design of a Workshop

We propose a workshop format to help organisations to identify processes suitable for RPA adoption. Suitable processes should have enough automation potential for RPA software to be applied and add substantial business value once they are automated. Another requirement of the workshop is that it provides a systematic step-wise approach that enables organisations to identify processes from scratch, without having to use any documentation or other resources besides the knowledge of participants. A well-known model that can be used to systematically identify business processes is the BPM life cycle provided by Dumas et al. (2013).

BPM life cycle shows the overall management of business processes and uses a range of methods and tools to identify and manage business processes (Dumas et al., 2013). Organisations often deploy this framework to optimise business processes. In addition, Dumas et al. (2013) mention that an appropriate way to address this life cycle is by conducting 'workshops' to identify processes. They then state that the identification can utilise criteria in order to find appropriate processes. Recent literature has shown that the cycle can be helpful regarding RPA projects and also showed that using the BPMN language is a fitting approach to find suitable processes (Flechsig et al., 2019). This section describes the three phases from the BPM life cycle that are used as the framework for the workshop design: 'Process Identification', 'Process Discovery' and 'Process Analysis' (also see Figure 5.4).

These phases shape the design of the workshop.

While the BPM life cycle by Dumas et al. (2013) serves as a suitable framework for the steps to be taken within the workshop's design and the BPMN-R as a better way of modelling the processes, there are some crucial details left out that are relevant for the design of the workshop. Even though Dumas et al. (2013) mentions in their book that a workshop is an appropriate method to identify and manage business processes via the BPM life-cycle, only minor details are given and few suggestions are being made on how to organise one. For instance, they mention that for the modelling part, participants could make use of sticky notes in order to model processes. However, aspects such as generating ideas and guiding group discussions are left untouched. The ultimate goal of this study is to find suitable RPA processes based on the ideas of a group and a discussion to evaluate these ideas. Social factors – such as the number of participants, their experiences, the duration of the workshop, and whether ideas are generated and selected individually or as a group – are likely to influence the outcome of the workshop. These social factors are addressed next.

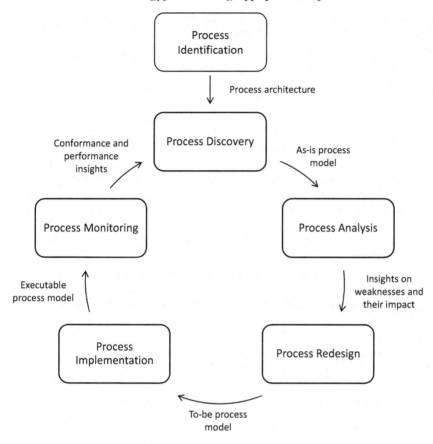

Figure 5.4 BPM life cycle (Dumas et al., 2013).

5.9 Brainstorming Technique for This Workshop

Most studies agree that nominal brainstorming (NBS) and electronic brain-storming (EBS) techniques outperform traditional brainstorming in both the quantity and quality of ideas (Dennis and Reinicke, 2004, Maaravi et al., 2021). Nearly all studies agree that standard brainstorming leads to fewer ideas than NBS and EBS (Maaravi et al., 2021), yet there is disagreement as to whether nominal- or EBS is more effective, with the most suitable method depending on the problem context.

For the design of the workshop in this study, the NBS technique is deemed the most suitable. There are two main reasons why the NBS technique is preferred over the EBS technique. First, an essential part of this approach towards process selection is the discussion between group members. For instance, process profiles gathered during the idea generation phase should be explained by each member. After the explanation, group members will give feedback to the idea. With EBS, the goal is to keep everyone anonymous by letting members type their explanation and feedback. A drawback is that this approach hampers communication, due to process profiles being rather extensive (Nunamaker et al., 1991). In contrast, NBS participants can verbally communicate ideas, comments and questions, making it more user-friendly and efficient.

The second reason for choosing NBS over EBS is the group sizes. EBS is more effective when the group is sufficiently large (>8 participants). However, group size becomes a bottleneck whenever arranging a workshop which not only includes a brainstorming session of approximately 40 minutes (Maaravi et al., 2021) but also a full presentation about RPA. As such, a minimum of nine participants should be available for a longer period of time. In conclusion, the NBS technique will likely lead to a less time-consuming and more user-friendly technique to be integrated within the workshop.

Key Takeaways: For decision makers it is important to be aware about specific process technology (e.g., RPA) and what it can and cannot do. Understanding RPA and its primary functions aids participants to grasp how RPA can be used for process automation. An SLR was conducted, which resulted in the analysis of 35 papers consisting of both scientific papers and grey literature. This literature described that RPA consists of software that helps to program digital bots, which operate on the GUI, automating processes and removing repetitive tasks from workers. Furthermore, it was found that the robot can be triggered either attended or unattended and that AI functionalities, such as Optical Character Recognition and Natural Language Processing, are becoming increasingly common within RPA tooling. The exact functionalities were obtained by consolidating primary functions from literature. The SLR findings and the findings from the interviews resulted in a total of 48 primary functions of RPA, which help participants (process experts) to understand RPA's capabilities.

In addition to an explanation of PRA and its primary functions, the literature search assessed process criteria, determining the feasibility and value of automating a process via RPA. The study identified 20 process criteria. A distinction was made between two sets of criteria, encompassing automation potential and business value. Automation potential criteria help participants assess whether a process can be automated via RPA. Business value criteria help participants to assess whether automating a process is sufficiently valuable.

The BPM life cycle serves as the foundation for the workshop design. This model presents systematic steps and helpful tools to identify processes, analyse them and use criteria to determine which process needs to be optimised. In particular the first three phases of this model – (i) Process Identification, (ii) Process Discovery and (iii) Process Analysis – are used as a funnel to filter out processes and retain the most suitable ones. To further structure the workshop and help participants generate sufficient high-quality ideas, the NBS technique complements the BPM life-cycle. The NBS technique has participants generate ideas individually, preventing free riding, production blocking and evaluation apprehension. Lastly, using a multidisciplinary approach, including external members, is likely to enhance idea generation and evaluation. These findings are used as building blocks for designing the workshop.

5.10 Workshop Structure and Group Composition

The framework presents the generic process to be taken when an organisation conducts the workshop and is split into two parts. Part 1 consists of the Process Identification phase and Part 2 of the Process Discovery and Process Analysis phase. The workshop design outlines the generic steps to be taken.

The coloured borders in the frame of Figure 5.5 synthesise the BPM Life-cycle, NBS and RPA. Each of the parts consists of three main phases, namely 'input', 'NBS' and 'output'. These three phases represent the funnel, where Part 1 of the workshop starts off with all processes in scope, using NBS to generate and evaluate ideas, and ends with a few selected processes filled in within the process profiles (i.e., the output). These process profiles then serve as input for Part 2 of the workshop, using NBS to model and evaluate the processes. The output of Part 2 consists of evaluating these modelled processes and positioning them into the process portfolio.

5.11 Roles, Group Composition and Setting

An appropriate group composition is important, influencing the generation of ideas as well as their evaluation. This section discusses the different roles that should be taken during the workshop, the group composition and the setting of the workshop.

5.11.1 Roles

Two roles should be present during the workshop: the facilitator and the participant. It is recommended to have two facilitators present during the workshop, to lead and assist the workshop participants. It is preferred to have at least one facilitator who is leading the RPA initiative, the RPA Business Champion, and one facilitator knowing the processes under a scope, a Process Expert. A Business Champion is motivated to automate processes and identifies opportunities with RPA, having knowledge about the concepts. A Business Champion's role is to take the lead in finding RPA-suitable processes. Their task is to lead, prepare and present the workshop and answer questions. Lastly, the Business Champion should have some basic understanding of the BPMN language, required for modelling during the second phase of the workshop. The Process Expert (the second facilitator) assists the Business Champion in preparing the workshop (for example creating the Process

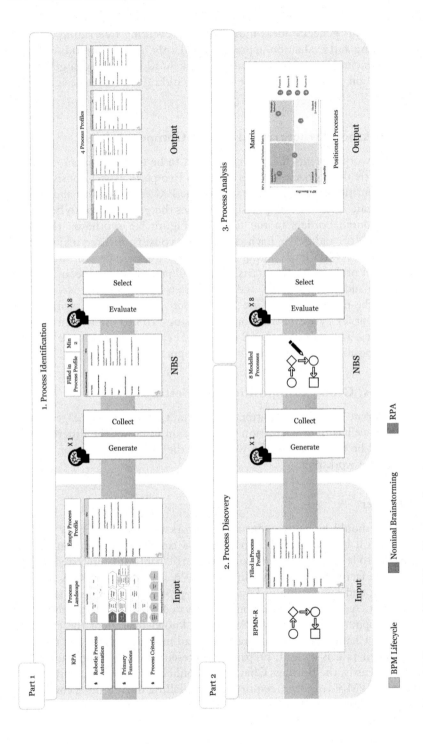

Figure 5.5 Proposed Workshop Framework.

Landscape) and helps with filtering unique ideas during the first phase of the workshop.

The participants' main task during the workshop is to evaluate processes they are experienced with through daily practice. Workshop participants are process experts working within the same department or business unit of the organisation. Their thinking and experiences are required for coming up with ideas and evaluating their colleagues' ideas.

5.11.2 Group Composition

The group composition during a brainstorm session influences the efficiency and effectiveness of the outcome. There are three important variables regarding the group composition during the workshop which are considered within the design of this workshop.

First, the number of participants needs to be carefully determined. Within the design of this workshop, the recommended number of participants is eight ($n = 8$). This number is chosen, as too many participants (>8) result in insufficient time for everyone to explain and discuss their ideas, whereas having only two to three participants takes away the dynamics of group discussions and reduces the number of generated ideas. Second, the participants should have different experiences regarding years of work and daily tasks performed. For instance, many companies have employees within a department or business unit having different rankings or specialities. This causes them to have different knowledge about processes. For instance, a manager of a department is likely to know more processes than staff employees and is therefore likely to come up with different ideas. In addition, they often have much experience with the processes and therefore know which generic paths most processes will go through. On the other hand, managers are less familiar with the operational details of the processes. For this reason, it is also important to include employees on the operational level because of their daily experiences and detailed process knowledge, which is important in assessing RPA viability. Third, it is preferred to include external employees to provide an outside perspective.

5.11.3 Setting

The workshop is recommended to be conducted virtually due to the use of digital tools during the workshop, such as Padlet, Draw.io and Excel files and also to face no limitations with regards to travelling by participants. On the other hand, being in front of a computer screen for several hours might decrease motivation and proactive behaviour faster than in a setting where everyone is physically present in one room. The Lorentz Center (2021) recommends conducting that virtual workshop last no longer than two hours. In line with this recommendation, the workshop is split up into two sessions. Having addressed the desired group composition and setting, the overall

Name Participant:

Process Information (General)	Fill In:	Automation Potential	Fill In: Yes or No	Business Value	Fill In	Prioritized
Name Process:		Low Cognitive?		Manual effort? (Low/Medium/High)		
Where in process landscape:		Rule-based Process?		Volume (Weekly/Monthly):		
Goal of the Process:		Standardized Process?		Repetitive? (Yes/No)		
Outcome:		No or few Decision Points?		Human Errors? (Yes/No)		
Trigger:		Stable Application/Systems/Websites 1?		Duration of process (average):		
End-to-end or sub-process?:		Stable Application/Systems/Websites 2?		Essential Business Process?		
First activity:		Mature Process?		Can RPA increase its compliance once automated?		
Last activity:		Structured Digital Data?		How can it be triggered? Attended/Unattended/Hybrid		
		Multiple Systems?		Potential to operate 24/7? (Yes/No)		
		Easy Data Access?		Long lifetime?		
		Internal?				

Figure 5.6 Process profile.

process of the workshop is explained, consisting of two parts. The design of Part 1 of the workshop consists of the Process Identification phase. The design of Part 2 consists of the Process Discovery and Process Analysis phase.

5.11.4 Process Identification

The first task to address during the workshop is to identify processes which have the potential for RPA automation. This is the first step of the BPM life cycle and the first part of the workshop. This section describes the design of this first part, see Figure 5.5, consisting of the Process Identification phase. The goal of Part 1 is to extract processes that have the highest probability of being automated via RPA. As output, these ideas are filled into Process Profile. This Process Profile is depicted in Figure 5.6. Note that this profile includes 'General Process Information', the 'Automation Potential' and the 'Business Value' as columns to be filled in. Process Information will help the other participants to get a better understanding of the process, whereas Automation Potential and Business Value will help determine whether a process can be suitable for RPA. However, before these Process Profiles can be filled in (the output), participants require input and perform the NBS technique.

5.11.5 Input Session 1

For participants to generate initial processes suitable for RPA, certain information is required to come up with good ideas and to fill them into the Process Profiles. As described by (Slack and Brandon-Jones, 2018), it is important for decision-makers to know what RPA is and what its Primary Functions are in order to evaluate whether a process technology, such as RPA, can be applied within the business and will also deliver value. An explanation of RPA and its 48 primary functions are input for participants to help identify suitable processes. Furthermore, Dumas et al. (2013) state that for finding the desired processes, the participants should receive a set of criteria.

These Process Criteria serve as input for identification. The framework in Figure 5.6 shows the green-coloured border within the 'input', representing RPA, its primary functions and the process criteria. An explanation of RPA, its primary functions and process criteria should first be explained within the first part of the workshop (see Figure 5.6, green-coloured borders represent RPA elements within the workshop).

In addition, a Process Landscape as described by Dumas et al. (2013) aids participants in recalling processes within the business. Figure 5.5 shows an example of a Process Landscape. This Process Landscape is given to the participants as a support tool, as suggested by Dumas et al. (2013), and used as input for participants to help them recall all processes in scope.

All these elements, including the Primary Functions, Process Criteria, Process Profile and Process Landscape, should be clarified by the facilitator before Brainstorming begins.

5.11.6 Nominal Brainstorming Session 1

The aim of brainstorming is for participants to generate ideas and discuss them with their colleagues. Based on the SLR, the Nominal Brainstorm (NBS) technique was chosen as the most suitable technique to let participants generate ideas and evaluate them effectively. The NBS is implemented according to the four steps of brainstorming (see Figure 5.7) and is represented by the blue-coloured borders within the framework. The brainstorming part of the Process Identification step consists of two phases. First, after participants received all the information (i.e., the input), they will each have a limited amount of time to come up with processes they think are suitable for automation via RPA. Within the scope of this workshop, the time to fill in the Process Profiles is set to 30 minutes and the minimum number of process profiles that must be filled in by participants is set to two, increasing stimulation and avoiding free-riding. Support items, such as the Process Landscape, the Primary Functions and Process Criteria are given to the participants before the idea generation step occurs. Moreover, the brainstorming rules should be mentioned by the facilitator to the participants before the session starts. Rule number 4 however, stated that ideas can be built on each other, is optional. This is due to the debate about the effect on the quality of ideas when applying this rule.

After time is over and participants individually filled in their ideas, the Process Profiles are collected by the facilitators. They filter the duplicate processes to determine how many unique ideas there are. Next, each unique Process Profile must be explained by the participant, stating why they think that the process is a good candidate for RPA automation. Then, the discussion on the answers provided in the Process Profile can commence. This part is important, as it shows who agrees or disagrees with the idea. The facilitator should lead this discussion by managing time, minimising critique and giving everyone the chance to speak. After each idea has been explained and discussed, participants will get the opportunity to vote for the processes they think are most suitable. Each participant must select their top four processes.

5.11.7 Output Session 1

Based on the final voting, the output is generated, consisting of four Process Profiles, see Figure 5.5. These four processes are further assessed regarding RPA suitability during the second part of the workshop including the Process Discovery and Process Analyses phases.

5.12 Process Discovery and Process Analysis

The second phase of the workshop consists out of the Process Discovery and Process Analysis steps. During the Process Discovery step, processes are visualised via a process modelling language to get a better understanding of the selected processes. After modelling, the processes are analysed to determine whether the Process Criteria still apply to them. The overall objective of this phase is to place the processes on the Process Portfolio, evaluating them based on their complexity and their added business value (Benefits of RPA). It then becomes clear whether RPA is a Quick Win or is too Limited for implementation. This phase follows the same steps as the previous phase, requiring input for participants to start modelling, NBS to generate and evaluate the ideas, and the output consisting of each process being positioned on the Process Portfolio.

5.12.1 Input Session 2

Process Modelling helps visualise the process and thereby discover its specific activities. It may identify activities overlooked during the Process Identification phase. In addition, it enhances understanding of activities requiring cognition or activities that involve decision-making too complex for a robot to perform. Therefore, the objective of the Process Discovery step is to increase understanding of the processes selected from the first phase, by explaining a BPMN language and letting the participants each model a Process Profile from the first phase. As mentioned previously, the BPMN-R language is explained to the participants and serves as input for the process discovery phase. After the BPMN-R language is explained to the participants, an example of a modelled process is shown as input. Figure 5.7 displays a process example of a Power BI dashboard being weekly updated. Each participant gets a Process Profile from Part 1 assigned in order to model. A standard template within Draw.io with the specific notation for the BPMN-R language can be set up by the facilitator and send to each participant together with the filled in Process Profile from Part 1 of the workshop.

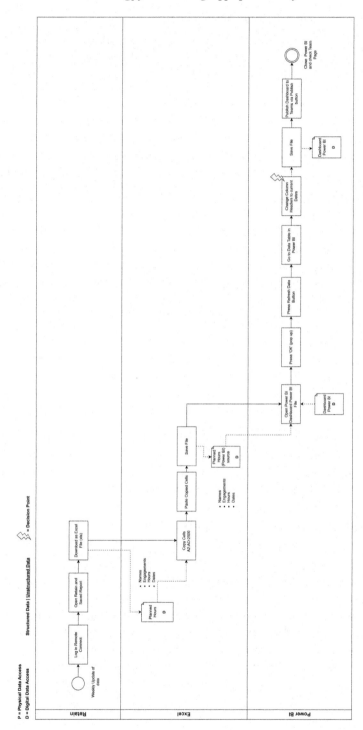

Figure 5.7 Example using BPN-R language.

5.12.2 Nominal Brainstorming Session 2

The NBS technique is also used during Part 2 of the workshop, see Figure 5.5. Each participant must first model a process individually for 30 minutes. The facilitators help participants with potential problems that may arise. The goal is to get the process visualisation as complete and detailed as possible. For this reason, participants should first model the general steps of the process and then add the additional steps including more detail. Again, the general brainstorming rules are explained to the participants. Once time is finished, the processes are collected. As a result, two models of each Process Profile have been created, as there are only four profiles from the first part and eight participants recommended to be present. The reason for having two participants model the same process is to have at least two persons think thoroughly about one process. This approach aims to stimulate discussion, as participants may have different perspectives.

Once time is finished, the participants all show their models for evaluation. All participants again explain their model, such that the group can discuss the model's completeness and representation. Once every model has been evaluated, the processes are positioned within the Process Portfolio, depending on the criteria re-evaluation by the participants. This positioning is discussed by the group, with each participant giving an opinion regarding the process's complexity and the benefits of its automation.

5.12.3 Output Session 2

The output of Part 2 consists of four modelled processes being positioned within the Process Portfolio, see Figure 5.8, and is the final workshop deliverable. The desired outcome for organisations wanting to assess RPA suitability is to identify processes that can be positioned as Quick Wins. However, the group should stay critical and try to position each process as representative as possible by re-evaluating the models and process criteria.

5.13 Tooling and Setting for the Workshop

The setup of the workshop is virtual. Therefore, the workshop can be joined by participants from every place. We prefer a virtual workshop over a physical one for two reasons. First, the workshop is more accessible to participants, due to the absence of travelling (Lorentz Center, 2021). Because it is recommended to include external participants, physical workshops may be harder to arrange. Second, the workshop could make use of digital artefacts and tooling, such as digital process profiles, Padlet and Draw.io. This requires participants to be behind a computer during most of the workshop. The Lorentz Centre (2021) presents a list of tips and tricks for conducting a virtual workshop. The following is relevant for the design of the workshop:

RPA Prioritisation and Selection Matrix

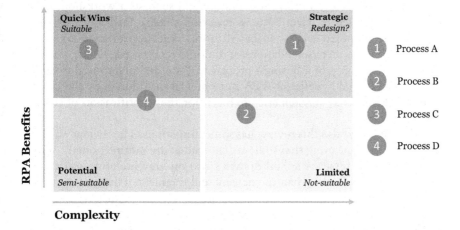

Figure 5.8 RPA process prioritisation and selection matrix.

1   It is recommended to limit the sessions to a maximum of two hours to avoid mental fatigue by participants.
2   Take breaks during the workshop, because participants have to look at a screen for quite a while.
3   Clearly state the goal and the outcome of the workshop (also mentioned by Boddy, 2012)
4   Explain how participants can ask questions and comment during the virtual workshop and how they should make use of tooling.
5   Strictly stick with the time planned.
6   Send around the program of the workshop as well as the platforms being used.
7   Consider creating couples, for instance, regarding exercises by creating breakout rooms.

Tooling: Because the workshop is held virtually, digital tooling can be used to optimise the brainstorming process. Offline brainstorming sessions often use sticky notes and whiteboards (Boddy, 2012). Participants can write their ideas on sticky notes and place them on a whiteboard. However, there are also options to use such items digitally. Siegle (2020) recommends to make use of Padlet for online brainstorming sessions. Padlet is a free online tool where everyone can join to share their ideas, comment on them, order them and vote.

5.14 Conclusion

This book chapter (chiefly based on Berghuis, 2021) discusses various process selection methods covered in the literature and suggests a workshop design that can be utilised to select business processes suitable for RPA implementation. The proposed workshop-based process selection method takes into consideration the recommendations of multiple process stakeholders to evaluate the complexity of a business process to RPA and gives insights on the potential expected benefits of RPA implementation. Moreover, the created framework serves as a systematic approach for the identification of suitable RPA processes.

Like any study, also this review has some limitations. The review was conducted in 2021 meaning that some recent studies are not integrated. Adopting the scoping review method drawing also on grey literature sources has enabled us to go further than the nascent and fragmented literature on RPA identification and selection. Though, as more relevant studies are available, the case for using comprehensive review methods will also increase. Nevertheless, we believe, that despite these limitations, our chapter has important scholarly and practical implications.

From a scholarly perspective, identifying RPA-suitable processes is one of the key challenges organisations face when they start their RPA journey. Still, so far, the literature was almost silent about the specific tools that can be used to implement RPA, criteria for selecting a process for RPA, or functions of RPA that we reveal in our chapter. Moreover, to the best of our knowledge, group-based RPA process identification and selection have not been previously described in detail in the literature. Thus, our study proposing a group-based approach for RPA identification and selection and describing in detail how such could/should be conducted significantly extends existing knowledge and responds to the calls for scholars from different disciplines to design a systematic approach for RPA process identification and selection that can enhance the implementation of RPA in organisations (Syed et al., 2020). In summary, the theoretical contributions of this study are as follows: (i) adding to the sparse body of literature on the identification phase of RPA (ii) an interdisciplinary combination of the BPM life cycle and NBS and (iii) proposing a concrete workshop format to guide users through the BPM life-cycle.

From a practical perspective, many organisations are looking into RPA as a potential solution for automating routine and monotonous processes, often not knowing where to start. Thus, the detailed descriptions provided in this chapter on the potential workshop design as well as its application proposes methodological and practical methods that can inform and support businesses in their nascent RPA journeys.

Building on this study, we identify four potential avenues for future research. First, the workshop format requires further testing within a variety of settings (e.g., sectors, companies, business teams, processes) to increase its external validity. Second, the effectiveness of the workshop approach can only be validated if identified processes are eventually automated via RPA. Follow-up studies should track progress after the workshop, validating whether the identified processes can indeed be successfully automated. Third, the effectiveness of the workshop may be compared to other process selection methods, critically comparing the selection performance and (dis)advantages of each method. Fourth, the proposed workshop format might also be suitable for assessing the adoption of other process technologies, such as process mining. Future research may assess this potential and verify whether the wisdom of the crowd will help them with digitising.

Bibliography

Agaton, B. and Swedberg, G. (2018). Evaluating and developing methods to assess business process suitability for robotic process automation-a design research approach. Master's thesis, University of Gothenburg.

Asatiani, A. and Penttinen, E. (2016). Turning robotic process automation into commercial success–case opuscapita. *Journal of Information Technology Teaching Cases*, 6(2):67–74.

Berghuis, L. (2021). Using the wisdom of the crowd to digitalize: Designing a workshop-based process selection method for the identification of suitable rpa processes. Master's thesis, University of Twente.

Boddy, C. (2012). The nominal group technique: An aid to brainstorming ideas in research. *Qualitative Market Research: An International Journal*, 15(1):6–18.

Bygstad, B. (2017). Generative innovation: A comparison of lightweight and heavyweight it. *Journal of Information Technology*, 32(2):180–193.

Cewe, C., Koch, D., and Mertens, R. (2017). Minimal effort requirements engineering for robotic process automation with test driven development and screen recording. In *International Conference on Business Process Management*, pages 642–648. Springer.

Cooper, L. A., Holderness Jr, D. K., Sorensen, T. L., and Wood, D. A. (2019). Robotic process automation in public accounting. *Accounting Horizons*, 33(4):15–35.

Dennis, A. R. and Reinicke, B. A. (2004). Beta versus VHS and the acceptance of electronic brainstorming technology. *MIS Quarterly*, 28:1–20.

Dumas, M., La Rosa, M., Mendling, J., Reijers, H. A., et al. (2013). *Fundamentals of business process management*, volume 1. Springer.

Flechsig, C., Lohmer, J., and Lasch, R. (2019). Realizing the full potential of robotic process automation through a combination with BPM. In Bierwirth, C., Kirschstein, T., and Sackmann, D. (eds), *Logistics Management*, Lecture Notes in Logistics. pages 104–119. Springer, Cham.

Frey, C. B. and Osborne, M. A. (2017). The future of employment: How susceptible are jobs to computerisation? *Technological Forecasting and Social Change*, 114:254–280.

Geyer-Klingeberg, J., Nakladal, J., Baldauf, F., and Veit, F. (2018). Process mining and robotic process automation: A perfect match. In *International Conference on Business Process Management (Dissertation/Demos/Industry)*, pages 124–131.

González Enríquez, J., Jiménez Ramírez, A., Domínguez Mayo, F. J., and García García, J. A. (2020). Robotic process automation: A scientific and industrial systematic mapping study. *IEEE Access*, 8:39113–39129.

Gotthardt, M., Koivulaakso, D., Paksoy, O., Saramo, C., Martikainen, M., Lehner, O., et al. (2020). Current state and challenges in the implementation of smart robotic process automation in accounting and auditing. *ACRN Journal of Finance and Risk Perspectives*, 9:90–102.

Grieves, M. and Vickers, J. (2017). Digital twin: Mitigating unpredictable, undesirable emergent behavior in complex systems. In *Transdisciplinary Perspectives on Complex Systems*, pages 85–113. Springer.

Jimenez-Ramirez, A., Reijers, H. A., Barba, I., and Valle, C. D. (2019). A method to improve the early stages of the robotic process automation lifecycle. In *International Conference on Advanced Information Systems Engineering*, pages 446–461. Springer.

Kokina, J. and Blanchette, S. (2019). Early evidence of digital labor in accounting: Innovation with robotic process automation. *International Journal of Accounting Information Systems*, 35:100431.

Lacity, M., Willcocks, L. P., and Craig, A. (2015). Robotic process automation at Telefonica O2. *The Outsourcing Unit Working Research Paper Series*, volume 15, pages 21–35.

Le Clair, C., Cullen, A., and King, M. (2017). The RPA market will reach $2.9 billion by 2021. https://www.forrester.com/report/The+RPA+Market+Will+Reach+29+Billion+By+2021/-/ERES137229. Accessed: 2021-10-2.

Leno, V., Polyvyanyy, A., Dumas, M., La Rosa, M., and Maggi, F. M. (2021). Robotic process mining: Vision and challenges. *Business & Information Systems Engineering*, 63(3):301–314.

Leopold, H., Aa, H. v. d., and Reijers, H. A. (2018). Identifying candidate tasks for robotic process automation in textual process descriptions. In Gulden, J., Reinhartz-Berger, I., Schmidt, R., Guerreiro, S., Guédria, W., and Bera, P. (eds) *Enterprise, Business-Process and Information Systems Modeling*, BPMDS EMMSAD 2018 2018. Lecture Notes in Business Information Processing, vol 318, pages 67–81. Springer, Cham. https://doi.org/10.1007/978-3-319-91704-7_5

Leshob, A., Bourgouin, A., and Renard, L. (2018). Towards a process analysis approach to adopt robotic process automation. In *2018 IEEE 15th International Conference on e-Business Engineering (ICEBE)*, pages 46–53. IEEE.

Lorentz Center. Virtual workshops. https://www.lorentzcenter.nl/virtual-workshops.html. Accessed: 2021-06-15.

Maaravi, Y., Heller, B., Shoham, Y., Mohar, S., and Deutsch, B. (2021). Ideation in the digital age: Literature review and integrative model for electronic brainstorming. *Review of Managerial Science*, 15(6):1431–1464.

Mendling, J., Decker, G., Hull, R., Reijers, H. A., and Weber, I. (2018). How do machine learning, robotic process automation, and blockchains affect the human factor in business process management? *Communications of the Association for Information Systems*, 43(1):19.

Moffitt, K. C., Rozario, A. M., and Vasarhelyi, M. A. (2018). Robotic process automation for auditing. *Journal of Emerging Technologies in Accounting*, 15(1):1–10.

Mullakara, N. and Asokan, A. K. (2020). *Robotic process automation projects: Build real-world RPA solutions using UiPath and automation anywhere*. Packt Publishing Ltd.

Nunamaker, J. F., Dennis, A. R., Valacich, J. S., Vogel, D., and George, J. F. (1991). Electronic meeting systems. *Communications of the ACM*, 34(7):40–61.

Penttinen, E., Kasslin, H., and Asatiani, A. (2018). How to choose between robotic process automation and back-end system automation? In *European Conference on Information Systems 2018*.

Reinkemeyer, L. (2020). *Process Mining in Action: Principles, Use Cases and Outlook.* Springer, Cham. https://link.springer.com/book/10.1007/978-3-030-40172-6

Ribeiro, J., Lima, R., Eckhardt, T., and Paiva, S. (2021). Robotic process automation and artificial intelligence in industry 4.0–a literature review. *Procedia Computer Science*, 181:51–58.

Rutaganda, L., Bergstrom, R., Jayashekhar, A., Jayasinghe, D., Ahmed, J., et al. (2017). Avoiding pitfalls and unlocking real business value with RPA. *Journal of Financial Transformation*, 46(11):104–115.

Siegle, D. (2020). I have an idea i need to share: Using technology to enhance brain-storming. *Gifted Child Today*, 43(3):205–211.

Slack, N. and Brandon-Jones, A. (2018). *Operations and process management: Principles and practice for strategic impact.* Pearson.

Stahlschmidt, S. and Stephen, D. (2020). Comparison of web of science, scopus and dimensions databases. *KB Forschungspoolprojekt. DZHW.*

Syed, R., Suriadi, S., Adams, M., Bandara, W., Leemans, S. J., Ouyang, C., ter Hofstede, A. H., van de Weerd, I., Wynn, M. T., and Reijers, H. A. (2020). Robotic process automation: Contemporary themes and challenges. *Computers in Industry*, 115:103162.

Trefler, A. (2018). The big RPA bubble. https://www.forbes.com/sites/cognitive-world/ 2018/12/02/the-big-rpabubble/#4dc3d91568d9. Accessed: 2021-04-26.

Tursunbayeva, A., Pagliari, C., Di Lauro, S., and Antonelli, G. (2021). The ethics of people analytics: Risks, opportunities and recommendations. *Personnel Review.*

Van der Aalst, W. M., Bichler, M., and Heinzl, A. (2018). Robotic process automation.

Wanner, J., Hofmann, A., Fischer, M., Imgrund, F., Janiesch, C., and Geyer-Klingeberg, J. (2019). Process selection in RPA projects-towards a quantifiable method of decision making.

Wieringa, R. J. (2014). *Design science methodology for information systems and software engineering.* Springer.

Willcocks, L., Lacity, M., and Craig, A. (2017). Robotic process automation: Strategic transformation lever for global business services? *Journal of Information Technology Teaching Cases*, 7(1):17–28.

6 Startups and Artificial Intelligence

Insights from Italy

Irene Di Bernardo and Fabio Greco

6.1 Introduction

The advent of new technologies and the greater ease of access to the use and development of the latter have practically changed traditional business paradigms (Massa and Tucci, 2013). New organizational roles are emerging, the need for a new entrepreneurial culture is growing, and the related ecosystem for innovation changes with new actors, such as startups and tools like Artificial Intelligence (AI) has advanced rapidly over the past decade. Several scholars assess that AI has the potential to boost human productivity and economic growth (Greco and Tregua, 2022; Furman and Seamans, 2019). However, for this macroeconomic growth to be realized, firms need to develop and implement AI-enabled products and services for their own or their customers' use. In this vein, the phenomenon of AI-related entrepreneurship is growing especially related to the changing scenario for startup founders (Kumar et al, 2021; Obschonka and Audretsch, 2020). Indeed, in these turbulent times, startups with technological and innovative natures are showing a good predisposition to adapt to difficulties such as the post-pandemic crisis (Pramono et al., 2021; Kuckertz et al., 2020). Shedding light on the Italian scenario, 2022 is a turning point for innovative startups. The National Fund for Innovation (FNI) has become operational; therefore, the Government can invest through venture capital operations, in companies and strategic startups, thus giving the great opportunity to generate new investments, a better way to align the interests of investors and Italian entrepreneurs towards the common goal of economic growth.[1]

Despite the increasing interest from scholars and practitioners (Garbuio and Lin, 2019; Bessen et al., 2018), literature on startups and AI is rather sparse. To the best of the authors' knowledge, there is still little scientific evidence on the subject, but the conditions are promising rather than merely positive (Bessen et al., 2018). Furthermore, the scalability of startups (Blank, 2013; Poole, 2012) may achieve even higher levels via novel technologies (Rizwana and Padmalini, 2019), but further clarifications are needed on how this effect may occur.

DOI: 10.4324/9781003304616-9

The remainder of this chapter first addresses scholarly contributions to startups and AI aiming to set the ground for research based on highlighting the tie between these two topics. The following sections present the methodology adopted in the empirical analysis and the results that allow the depiction of insights and outlooks on how AI can favor the emerging and the workability of new ventures. Finally, discussion and implications for both scholars and practitioners conclude the chapter.

6.2 Literature Review

6.2.1 Startups

Startups, as a form of entrepreneurship, play an important role in delivering solutions to both existing and emerging challenges in innovative manners and are crucial to the growth of both individual countries and global economies (Kuckertz et al, 2020; Colombo and Piva 2008; Davila et al., 2003). They are also provided solutions to "wicked" societal problems (Global Entrepreneurship Research Association, 2020). Steve Blank, the so-called "father of modern entrepreneurship", defined a startup as "a temporary organization in search of a scalable, repeatable, profitable business model" (Blank, 2013). The salient features of a startup lie in a temporary and scalable business model (Blank and Dorf, 2020). First, the term "temporary" is related to the future of a startup, which can, at best, be absorbed by a large enterprise or fail and move on to another opportunity (Blank, 2012). Indeed, the difference between a startup and a small business is that the latter is not capable of this type of rapid scale and probably does not even go towards this goal (Greco, 2021) Second, a "scalable business model" refers to a business that can increase its size exponentially, without using proportional resources (Cavallo et al., 2023). On a more abstract level, young firms have "liabilities of newness and smallness" so they fail at higher rates than their larger and older competitors (Freeman and Engel, 2007). Indeed, according to Walsh and Cunningham (2016) innovative startups that will shape future economic activity are one of the most vulnerable actors in any economy. The proliferation of technologies and the spread of the Internet have initiated "the productive or innovative wave of entrepreneurship" which allow the origination of the so-called "innovative startups" (Cavallo et al., 2021), introduced with law Decree 179/12 in October 2012 in Italy. An innovative startup is a new business structure that can generate knowledge and facilitate its transmission (Capocchi et al., 2020; Barboza and Capocchi, 2020; Matricano, 2019). They can contribute to broadening the country's entrepreneurial culture, by creating an environment more receptive to innovation and by attracting both investment and talented individuals (Barboza and Capocchi, 2020). In other words, an Innovative startup is a very high-tech or innovative enterprise with the credentials to grow quickly and generate lots of value, including for the entire country in which it operates (Greco, 2021).

To earn the status of "innovative startup", an enterprise has to meet two classes of requirements, that is, the objective and the subjective requirement. The following are all mandatory and necessary:

a   establishment for less than five years.
b   the total annual value of production is less than 5 million euros.
c   headquartered in Italy or in an EU country (in this case, a production site or branch in Italy is required).
d   does not distribute profits.
e   is not established because of a corporate merger or demerger.
f   does not have shares or capital stock on a regulated market.
g   has as its corporate subject the development, production, and marketing of a product or service with high technological or innovative value.

Focusing on the Italian scenario, scholars and practitioners increasingly consider the phenomenon of startup companies as a solution to the many problems of economic decline and unemployment (Matricano, 2019) and the technological aspect remains the main pivot (Colombelli, 2016).

More in general, an increasing number of studies are focusing on the advent of emerging technologies and the development of startup companies (Park et al., 2020; Balboni et al., 2019). In this vein, scholars highlighted different drivers of success from emerging technologies such as AI (Bessen et al., 2018) and financial instruments to systems to support startup growth through institutions like seed accelerators and their supportive instruments (Greco and Tregua, 2022). Regardless, it should be remembered that startups are not just based on technologies. A startup is a "human institution designed to deliver a new product or service under conditions of extreme uncertainty" (Ries, 2011, p.27). In this domain, technology is miraculous because it allows us to "do more with less". To accomplish this aim, we move to the literature on AI.

6.2.2 Artificial Intelligence

AI as a research topic gained interest in the early 1950. In his seminal book, McCarthy defined AI as "every aspect of learning or any other feature of intelligence can in principle be described so precisely that it can be simulated by a machine" (McCarthy et al. 1955, p.1). This elementary definition by McCarthy et al. (1955) broadly describes AI as the capability of a machine to act as intelligently as humans. More in detail, AI includes Machine Learning, an ability to automatically refine computational methods (Brynjolfsson and McAfee, 2014), Natural Language Processing designed to understand languages, and Image Processing which follows algorithmic inspection and analysis of the images (Brynjolfsson and McAfee, 2000). Along similar lines, other scholars define AI as "the ability of a machine to exhibit human capabilities such as reasoning, learning, planning and creativity" (Schulte-Althoff et al., 2021). From a practical point of view, AI has been also defined as the simulation of human intelligence processes by machines, especially computer systems. These processes include learning, reasoning, and self-correction (Nguyen, 2019). Academics, instead, framed it as "the study of complex information processing problems that often have their roots in some aspect of biological information processing" (Marr, 1977) or simply as "the intelligence exhibited by machines or software" (Pannu, 2015).

In substance, AI can emulate cognitive tasks and mimic human behavior. It stimulates the ability to learn and interpret external data to perform tasks through flexible adaptation (Haenlein and Kaplan, 2019).

In this regard, the debate on AI is still heated and debated. Indeed, there are fears of "putting the power of AI in the hands of the wrong people, and general concern and caution when it comes to new technologies" (Schmelzer, 2019). However, benefits can also be observed in business activities, as AI can influence the way "companies make decisions and interact with their external stakeholders (e.g., employees, customers)" (Haenlein and Kaplan, 2019, p. 11).

Therefore, many scholars are paying attention to what AI can do for businesses because of the nature of the challenges and opportunities it offers. For example, AI-based systems can perform thinking and routine tasks, while human employees can focus more on the "emotional side" of business (Huang et al., 2019). Especially in service research, AI is taking on a focal role, due to its characteristic ability to adapt to changing needs, foster customer engagement, enhance customer experience such as service quality, and reduce costs in every part of several stages of the service process (Huang and Rust, 2021; 2018; Wirtz et al., 2021; Davenport et al., 2020).

This can be a reason for major attention to startups using this technology and for researchers to investigate AI in startups. Due to this, further research is needed to better understand the contribution of AI in reshaping services and their provision by performing various tasks, constituting a major source of innovation (Rust and Huang, 2014).

6.2.2.1 *AI and Startups Development*

The distinctiveness of AI, as something intended to shape contexts, lies in its applicability to any domain, shaping itself as a pervasive technology (Huang and Rust, 2018). According to Huang et al. (2022; 2019), AI implementation is seen as the next source of competitive advantage and as a trigger for stimulating new investment and fostering entrepreneurial orientation (Baldegger et al., 2020). The burst of attention to AI is triggering a diversity of responses, ranging from the excitement that the capabilities can quickly scale up startup companies (Ebigbo et al., 2021) to making startups increasingly scale up (Rizwana and Padmalini, 2019). The ongoing debate shows AI as a general-purpose technology with new opportunities yet to be exploited as the efficiency of the decision-making process grows exponentially (Van Knippenberg et al., 2015). Innovative businesses are a rising trend in many countries around the world, with new technology-based companies arising year after year. Smart technologies are entering every organization, manufacturer, and service (Rippa and Secundo, 2018). In this context, startups can be described as companies that market, distribute, and support a digital product or service online. In this light, Schulte-Althoff et al. (2021) define an AI startup as a digital startup whose core element of its business model is AI. It uses digital technology as a context, enabler, or consequence of its activities (Recker and von Briel, 2019).

AI-based startups can increase knowledge by transferring powerful machine learning models to other business applications or by providing new services that transcend people in terms of cognition (Lehrer and Almor, 2021). Startups attract considerable and growing attention from both investors and corporations, as demonstrated by the massive amounts of investment in AI startups (Weber et al, 2021). According to Weber et al. (2021) startups have to find the right business model to ensure their long-term performance and survival (Weber et al., 2021). In this vein, Bessen et al. (2018) explain that "unlike large technology firms, AI startups do not have user-based platforms or other business lines that enable them to collect large amounts of data" (p.2). AI startups rely on information technology that is licensed internally or through a cloud service provider. This is important for startup survival, growth, and functionality (Jin and McElheran, 2019; Bessen et al., 2018).

Despite the growing interest, in literature few studies have investigated AI as a lever to boost startup companies (Agarwal et al., 2021; Filieri et al., 2021). However, there are several positive and promising contributions, such as the case studies analyzed, which increase the thesis according to which AI is a key, useful and successful engine for an innovative startup.

6.3 Methodology and Research Process

As suggested by Flick et al. (2004), to explore and highlight how AI is being implemented in startups, it was considered appropriate to adopt a qualitative research methodology in addressing emerging topics. We use multiple case studies that provide ample opportunity to observe and investigate the phenomenon in business realities (Yin, 2009). In particular, 12 case studies from different contexts characterized our research process; due to the early stage of this field of study and the need to adopt a wider perspective on the circumstances of startups that implement AI and its tools. According to Baker and Foy (2003), this methodology is useful for inductively advancing theory through the description and analysis of new phenomena.

6.4 Data Collection and Analysis

As proposed by Nieto and Pérez (2000) we collected data from multiple sources and cases due to the vagueness of the phenomenon and its context of observation. Data sampling was based on a ranking provided by Crunchbase. It is an online platform for gaining awareness about business information about private and public companies. The platform provides intelligent prospecting software powered by live company data, including the stock market.

The Crunchbase dataset was queried to list the top 12 funded startups in Italy through 2021. This enabled us to reach a privileged position to gather data from multiple sources and also to obtain triangulation as a way to strengthen the reliability and interpretation of the results (Yin, 2004). In addition, according to Flick et al. (2004) the multiple sources combination of empirical material is often identified as the best strategy for adding rigor, breadth, complexity, richness, and depth to a study. For this reason, we collect data from official websites, local media, additional websites, and other minor sources. The 12 Italian startups belonging to different industries and their variety in terms of age lead to a good balance between homogeneity and heterogeneity in the research context, thus further reducing the bias in case studies analysis. Furthermore, we also considered the fundraising criterion because the start-ups that manage to achieve the main scalability and repeatability objectives faster (Blank, 2013) are those that obtain copious venture capital funds (Thanapongporn et al., 2021). AI technological developments require robust investments to obtain future benefits in business management (Mou, 2019).

6.4.1 Findings

Based on the activity's target audience and primary impact, we divided the 12 case studies into three categories: (a) "Data for business," (b) "Data for marketing," and (c) "Implements".

The first two groups' instances are all business-to-business service providers, while the "implements" category can contain either business-to-consumer or business-to-business solutions. The 12 startups that were examined are summarized in Table 6.1, on which we based the categorization of our findings.

6.4.2 Data for Business

The first category, data for business, refers to the use of data to analyze key features in a market through the opportunities brought by AI (Bessen et al., 2018). With AI-based technological tools and algorithms, a company can derive a huge amount of data very quickly to make accurate decisions. Startups as Translated, Travel Appeal, MDTOM, and Ayxon AI fall under this first category (Figures 6.1–6.4).

Table 6.1 Key Information on Case Studies

Startup name	Headquarter	Industry/business	Funded achieved	Main activity	Category
Musixmatch	Bologna	Leisure – music	>1 mln euro	Natural language	Tools
Translated	Rome	Digital communication	>1 mln euro	Translation services processing	Data analysis for market
Userbot	Naples	Digital communication	>1 mln euro	Conversation Agent and Chatbot	Tools
Cogisen		Digital communication	>1 mln euro	Video compression	Tools
Travel appeal	Florence	Tourism	>1 mln euro	Travel	Data analysis for market
Thron	Padua	Digital communication	>1 mln euro	Marketing	Data analysis for marketing
ELSE Corp	Milan	Design and marketing solution	>1 mln euro	Fashion tech	Data analysis for marketing
MDOTM	Milan	Finance	>1 mln euro	Fintech	Data analysis for market
i Genius	Milan	Data analysis	>1 mln euro	Support information systems	Tools
Ayxon AI	Modena	Finance	>1 mln euro	Fintech	Data analysis for market
Kellify	Genoa	Finance	>1 mln euro	Fintech	Tools
World Lift		Digital communication	>1 mln euro	Marketing	Tools

Figure 6.1 Translated logo.

Translated provides companies and organizations with a translation service based on two AI systems. Among the main customers, it boasts Airbnb, Uber, and the European Parliament. Translated, which is based not only in Italy but also in the United States, has developed its end-to-end translation platform and, subsequently, ModernMT, proprietary neural adaptive machine translation software. Thanks to these technologies and the network of 200,000 professional translators, the company has recorded organic growth of 30% on an annual basis in recent years. This symbiosis between humans and AI now allows Translated to serve global technology platforms such as Airbnb, Google, and Uber, as well as thousands of international small and medium-sized enterprises.

Figure 6.2 Travel Appeal logo.

Travel Appeal collects data from over 500 sources to create the potentially biggest database in the tourism industry. The analysis of this data leads to the creation of various algorithms and consequently information offered through graphics, maps, and trends. The main aim of the expected information is to combine trends and predict prices, the number of tourists visiting a place, and expected revenues for hospitality firms. Due to this offering, the firm claims the opportunity to increase firms' revenue by up to 25%, increase employment, and favour a higher number of direct bookings by up to 7%, supporting more conspicuous margins for firms. Currently, almost 3,000 firms subscribed to this service, and some of them implemented even a chatbot to shape new tourism offerings to be proposed to tourists.

Figure 6.3 MDOTM logo.

MDOTM is a startup that develops investment ideas for the financial market using AI algorithms. Similar to the previous instance, gathering data and analyzing it are two crucial procedures since they enable the development of trends and the interaction between them and other influential factors, such as rumors. The major objective is to address market inefficiencies and develop practical tools that the banking and insurance sectors may utilize to provide investors with less hazardous and more effective financial products.

Figure 6.4 Ayxon AI logo.

Ayxon AI. Concerns themselves with the same sector as MDOTM. Since AI is used to evaluate the solvency of loans granted to businesses and merchant banks, financial data are even analyzed with different objectives. Since these loans are complicated in nature and based on various aims, the necessity for AI depends on the volume of data that must be taken into account. Axyon's main recommendations include long-term forecasts, performance studies, and trend assessments. The Axyon solution can also be used to help investors make investment decisions.

6.4.3 Data for Marketing

Data for Marketing proposes the use of AI in the marketing relationships a firm has with customers, thus changing the way a marketing action is performed (Huang and Rust, 2022; Huang et al., 2019). In a fiercely competitive market, AI-based solutions help in creating an outstanding customer experience, which contributes to increasing customer loyalty and boosting sales (Ameen et al., 2021; Verma et al., 2021). Innovative startups such as Thron and ELSE Corp shape this category (Figures 6.5 and 6.6).

Figure 6.5 Thron logo.

Thron A software-as-a-service called Thron offers a technique to categorize digital content to suggest the most appropriate options to consumers based on what is thought to be in line with their unique characteristics. To relate to all operations, but primarily with marketing as a solution for e-commerce, CRM, and online communication, the platform combines performance management tools with asset evaluation and service provision. Through AI that creates user profiles depending on the content that has been viewed, Thron personalizes communication. This service was chosen by several well-known businesses, and they have already acknowledged that cost savings are one of the major advantages.

Figure 6.6 ELSE Corp logo.

ELSE Corp. is comparable to Thron in some ways but embeds administration of distribution routes. The core of the product consists of design customization, order management, and novel approaches to encourage online purchasing; these services are based on client features and should enable businesses in the fashion industry to create offerings that are more suited to consumers. AI is utilized to further analyze the data from sales to update it for use in manufacturing; 3D printing and cloud production are other services that businesses can utilize.

6.5 Implements

The case studies shaping this group are iGenius, Userbot, Worldlift, Musixmatch, Cogisen, and Kellify. This last group consists of firms implementing AI to shape new implements, or tools, to be used in specific industries. New services or enriched ones may emerge from the infusion of these tools in business activities (Figures 6.7–6.12).

Figure 6.7 iGenius logo.

i Genius; iGenius is based on an intelligent interface that manages to bridge the technical skills gap that often separates people from business intelligence software. This start-up offers a system capable of querying, analyzing, and illustrating the data of company information systems in an effective, fast, and natural language way.

iGenius has developed Crystal, an AI advisor for business intelligence that can interface with any data source in real-time, to interpret the information contained in the data.

Figure 6.8 Userbot logo.

Userbot uses AI, Machine Learning, and Natural Language Processing to simplify numerous business processes, especially conversations between users and companies. In this way it automates repetitive processes, relieving man from boring and frustrating actions. Userbot announces that its AI and Machine Learning technologies will be used not only by companies but also by associations, organizations, and the Public Administration to make intervention processes more effective, promoting cooperation and offering better assistance, for example, during the humanitarian crisis currently underway in Ukraine.

Figure 6.9 WorldLift logo.

WorldLift: Thanks to the AI system used by WordLift, it is possible to improve and automate the SEO indexing of web marketing content. WordLift combines a linguistic analysis engine (NLP), which now supports over 100 languages, with a platform for publishing knowledge graphs (Knowledge Graph) that adopt the Linked Data standard. Web pages relating to commercial articles or products are analyzed by WordLift, enriched and transformed into a knowledge base that communicates with search engines (Google, Bing, and Yandex) and with the company's internal applications.

Figure 6.10 Musixmatch logo.

Musixmatch collects, disseminates, and reviews song lyrics from around the world. The company's mission is to create the world's largest set of song lyrics. The services are intended for both end users and other companies using machine learning. In the first scenario, users can search for song lyrics, and companies using this service can provide recommendations and further analyze the lyrics by looking for emotions, reactions, and relationships between songs.

6.6 Discussion and Implications

In addition, because some AI-based processes rely on a large scale of data and processes, scholars' considerations of the scalability of business models (Ruggieri et al., 2018; Thiel, 2017) may be expanded when considering AI. This leads to examining scalability as an inherent feature of new ventures

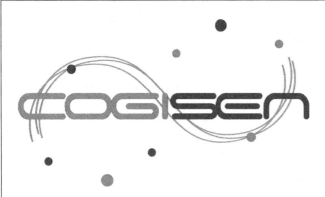

Figure 6.11 Cogisen logo.

The innovative eye-tracking software created by Cogisen enables the identification of a person's gaze direction and eye position. It provides a platform that can be used in a variety of ways, but the most popular application is related to video-sharing platforms because an algorithm can compress videos and encourage faster sharing and easier storage of videos than available technologies. AI is used to develop content that is thought to be secondary to the core, but, only essential information is retained. The same technique can also be used for streaming, and further applications are expected in cybersecurity and the operation of autonomous vehicles.

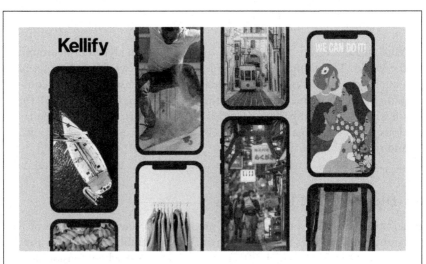

Figure 6.12 Kellify logo.

Kellify develops algorithms to link the value of commodities to everyday events. The main goals of this company are to provide price transparency and reduce inefficiencies, because some commodities may be considered useless or of little value, but for collectors and art enthusiasts, they may have significant economic value. The pillars of this system, which provide valuable information to all users, are machine learning, cognitive processes, data combination, and analytics.

deploying new processes, services, and products through AI. This proof adds to the analysis of AI's disruptive impact on goods, services, and startups themselves (Makridakis, 2017). AI seems to encourage new businesses and innovation as a way of expressing its performative influence. From a managerial perspective, this chapter shows some of the potentialities of AI in shaping markets, business activities, and ways of performing service actions for customers. Thus, the positive impacts the new technologies had on the Italian context should encourage interventions at both a micro- and a macro-level. Indeed, at a micro-level, new investments in startups can be partnered with AI as a carrier of new opportunities to be infused in new companies and create the chance to innovate markets and firms' processes. At a macro-level, national and supranational institutions should encourage changes through AI since the beneficial impacts on innovation, employment, and competitiveness are self-evident.

Since the diffusion of innovation through AI-driven processes is faster and can easily operate on a wider scale, as often large amounts of data are required, and a variety of applications - both in business-to-business and business-to-consumer markets - are achievable, AI has overall mirrored the opportunity to chase two key features of startups: rapidity and scalability (Bessen et al., 2018).

6.7 Conclusions, Limitations, and Further Research

In conclusion, this chapter describes how AI can act as a lever and driver of change in markets through the creation of startups. The features of AI are in line with the needs of startups, i.e., the ability to be a catalyst for innovation processes, to offer something completely new, or reshape existing services and processes in a more high-performance way.

Given the exploratory nature of this study, some limitations are evident. First, the companies taken into consideration are among the most established in Italy, but a broader sample could yield a more in-depth and more pertinent analysis. Moreover, the study was desk-based using a wide range of sources, thus the use of different approaches may lead to new results. Indeed, we believe that further research on these issues could strengthen the evidence presented in this paper by considering more Italian startups and broadening the scope to other nations to determine whether a country's context influences an entrepreneur's readiness. In addition, the examination of startups can be combined with surveys and interviews to support earlier findings and gain new perspectives on these fledgling enterprises, as well as through analysis of their performance as early as possible. To identify differences in economic success, customer perception, and business model quality, future studies could compare companies in the same industry, focusing on those that use AI and those that do not. Finally, the evaluation of users and their experience, satisfaction, and loyalty in both B2B and B2C markets could broaden the overview of AI as a driver of innovation and success for companies. For this purpose, future research would be required.

Note

1 https://www.mise.gov.it/en/

References

Ameen, N., Tarhini, A., Reppel, A., & Anand, A. (2021). Customer experiences in the age of artificial intelligence. *Computers in Human Behavior*, 114, 106548.

Balboni, B., Bortoluzzi, G., Pugliese, R., & Tracogna, A. (2019). Business model evolution, contextual ambidexterity and the growth performance of high-tech start-ups. *Journal of Business Research*, 99, 115–124.

Baldegger, R., Caon, M., & Sadiku, K. (2020). Correlation between entrepreneurial orientation and implementation of AI in human resources management. *Technology Innovation Management Review*, 10(4), 72–79.Baker, M.J. and Foy, A. (2003). Business and Management Research, Westburn Publishers, Helensburgh.

Bessen, J., Impink, S. M., Seamans, R., Reichensperger, L. (2018). The business of AI startups. Law and Economics Research Paper, Boston University School of Law.

Blank, S. (2013). Why the lean start-up changes everything. *Harvard Business Review*, 91(5), 63–72.

Brynjolfsson, E., & McAfee, A. (2014). The second machine age: Work, progress, and prosperity in a time of brilliant technologies. W W Norton & Co.

Capocchi, A., Barboza, G., DeMicco, F., Vallone, C. (2020). An empirical estimation of the value-added impact of Lucca Comics and Games festival on hotel performance. *Journal of Hospitality & Tourism Research*, 44(3), 523–546. https://doi.org/10.1177/1096348020901778

Cavallo, A., Cosenz, F., Noto, G. (2023). Business model scaling and growth hacking in digital entrepreneurship. *Journal of Small Business Management*, in Press. https://www.tandfonline.com/doi/full/10.1080/00472778.2023.2195463

Cavallo, A., Ghezzi, A., Colombelli, A. et al. (2020). Agglomeration dynamics of innovative start-ups in Italy beyond the industrial district era. *International Entrepreneurship* and *Management Journal*, 16, 239–262. https://doi.org/10.1007/s11365-018-0521-8

Colombelli, A. (2016). The impact of local knowledge bases on the creation of innovative startups in Italy. *Small Business Economics*, 47(2), 383–396.

Colombo, M.G., & Piva, E. (2008). Strengths and weaknesses of academic startups: A conceptual model. *IEEE Transactions on Engineering Management*, 55, 37–49.

Davila, A., Foster, G., Gupta, M. (2003). Venture capital financing and the growth of startup firms. *Journal of Business Venturing*, 18(6), 689–709.

Davenport, T., Guha, A., Grewal, D., Bressgott, T. (2020). How artificial intelligence will change the future of marketing. *Journal of the Academy of Marketing Science*, 48(1), 24–42.

Ebigbo, A., Palm, C., & Messmann, H. (2021). Barrett esophagus: What to expect from Artificial Intelligence? *Best Practice & Research Clinical Gastroenterology*, 52, 101726.

Flick, U., von Kardoff, E., Stenke, I. (2004). A Companion to Qualitative Research. Sage Publications.

Freeman, J., & Engel, J.S. (2007). Models of innovation: Startups and mature corporations. *California Management Review*, 50, 119–194.

Furman, J., Seamans, R. (2019). AI and the economy. *Innovation Policy and the Economy*, 19(1), 161–191.

Garbuio, M., & Lin, N. (2019). Artificial intelligence as a growth engine for healthcare startups: Emerging business models. *California Management Review*, 61(2), 59–83.

Global Entrepreneurship Research Association. (2020). Global entrepreneurship monitor 2019/2020 global report.

Greco, F. (2021). Start up Ecosystems: Features, Process and Actors, Phd Thesis Federico II of Naples.

Greco, F., & Tregua, M. (2022). It gives you wheels: The university-based accelerators in start-up ecosystems. *International Journal of Entrepreneurship and Small Business*, 45(2), 235–257.

Huang, A., Chao, Y., de la Mora Velasco, E., Bilgihan, A. & Wei, W. (2022). When artificial intelligence meets the hospitality and tourism industry: an assessment framework to inform theory and management. *Journal of Hospitality and Tourism Insights*, 5(5), 1080–1100. https://doi.org/10.1108/JHTI-01-2021-0021

Huang, M. H., & Rust, R. T. (2018). Artificial intelligence in service. *Journal of Service Research*, 21(2), 155–172.

Huang, M. H., & Rust, R. T. (2021). Artificial Intelligence in Service. *Journal of Service Research*, 24(2), 137–147.

Huang, M. H., Rust, R., & Maksimovic, V. (2019). The feeling economy: Managing in the next generation of artificial intelligence (AI). *California Management Review*, 61(4), 43–65.

Kuckertz, A., Brändle, L., Gaudig, A., Hinderer, S., Reyes, C. A. M., Prochotta, A., … & Berger, E. S. (2020). Startups in times of crisis–A rapid response to the COVID-19 pandemic. *Journal of Business Venturing Insights*, 13, e00169.

Kumar, I., Rawat, J., Mohd, N., & Husain, S. (2021). Opportunities of artificial intelligence and machine learning in the food industry. *Journal of Food Quality*, 13, 171–178.

Lehrer, M., & Almor, T. (2021). Startups internationalizing in quest of a business model: The global prospecting of process niche firms. *Journal of International Management*, 100906. doi:10.1016/j.intman.2021.100906.

Marr, D. (1977). Artificial intelligence—a personal view. *Artificial Intelligence*, 9(1), 37–48.

Matricano, D. (2019). Lo studio dell'imprenditorialità. Carocci Editore.

McCarthy, J., Minsky, M., Rochester, N., & Shannon, C. (1955). A Proposal for the Dartmouth Summer Research Project on Artificial Intelligence. http://www-formal.stanford.edu/jmc/history/dartmouth.html

Mou, X. (2019). Artificial intelligence: Investment trends and selected industry uses. *International Finance Corporation*, 1–8.

Nguyen, G., Dlugolinsky, S., Bobák, M., Tran, V., López García, Á., Heredia, I., … & Hluchý, L. (2019). Machine learning and deep learning frameworks and libraries for large-scale data mining: A survey. *Artificial Intelligence Review*, 52(1), 77–124.

Nieto, M., & Pérez, W. (2000). The development of theories from the analysis of the organisation: Case studies by the patterns of behaviour. *Management Decision*, 38(10), 723–734.

Obschonka, M., & Audretsch, D. B. (2020). Artificial intelligence and big data in entrepreneurship: A new era has begun. *Small Business Economics*, 55(3), 529–539.

Pannu, A. (2015). Artificial intelligence and its application in different areas. *Artificial Intelligence*, 4(10), 79–84.

Park, G., Shin, S. R., & Choy, M. (2020). Early mover (dis) advantages and knowledge spillover effects on blockchain startups' funding and innovation performance. *Journal of Business Research*, 109, 64–75.

Paternoster, N., Giardino, C., Unterkalmsteiner, M., Gorschek, T., Abrahamssonb, P. (2014). Software development in startup companies: A systematic mapping study. *Information and Software Technology*, 56(10), 1200–1218.

Poole, Robert. (2012). Global mindset: An entrepreneur's perspective on the born-global approach. *Technology Innovation Management Review*, 2, 10.

Pramono, C. A., Manurung, A. H., Heryati, P., & Kosasih, W. (2021). Factors affecting start-up behavior and start-up performance during the COVID-19 pandemic in Indonesia. *The Journal of Asian Finance, Economics and Business*, 8(4), 809–817.

Recker, J., & von Briel, F. (2019). The future of digital entrepreneurship research: existing and emerging opportunities. In: 40th international conference on information systems, Munich, pp. 1–9.

Ries, E. (2011). The Lean Startup. Rizzoli Etas.

Rippa, P., Secundo, G. (2018). Digital academic entrepreneurship: The potential of digital technologies on academic entrepreneurship. *Technological Forecasting and Social Change*, 146, 900–911.

Rust R. T., & Huang M.-H. (2014), The service revolution and the transformation of marketing science. *Marketing Science*, 33(2), 206–221.

Schmelzer, R. (2019). Should we be afraid of AI? Available at https://www.forbes.com/sites/cognitiveworld/2019/10/31/should-we-be-afraid-of- ai/?sh=235e12f04331.

Schulte-Althoff, M., Fürstenau, D., & Lee, G. M. (2021, January). A scaling perspective on AI startups. In Proceedings of the 54th Hawaii International Conference on System Sciences. 6515.

Thanapongporn, A., Ronnakorn, R., & Warayutt, C. (2021). Key success factors and framework of fundraising for early-stage startups in Thailand. *Academy of Strategic Management Journal*, 20, 1–16.

Van Knippenberg, D., Dahlander, L., Haas, M. R., & George, G. (2015). Information, attention, and decision making. *Academy of Management Journal*, 58(3), 649–657.

Verma, S., Sharma, R., Deb, S., & Maitra, D. (2021). Artificial intelligence in marketing: Systematic review and future research direction. *International Journal of Information Management Data Insights*, 1(1), 100002.

Walsh, G. S., & Cunningham, J. A. (2016), Business failure and entrepreneurship: emergence, evolution and future research. *Foundations and Trends® in Entrepreneurship*, 12(3), 163–285. http://dx.doi.org/10.1561/0300000063

Weber, M., Beutter, M., Weking, J., Böhm, M., & Krcmar, H. (2021). AI startup business models. *Business & Information Systems Engineering*, 64, 91–109.

Yin, R.K. (2004). The case study anthology. SAGE Publications.

Yin, R. K. (2009). Case study research: Design and methods (4th ed.). Sage.

7 Integrating AI to Blockchain and Cryptocurrency

A Case Study

Mohamed Bechir Chenguel

7.1 Introduction

Blockchain is a technology that should transform our societies in depth, and this, by providing a decentralized and ultra-secure system to authenticate any financial transaction or personal document (diplomas, contracts, etc.) (Mikalef, P. and Gupta, M. 2021). Blockchain is currently known to follow the emergence of cryptocurrencies since blockchain is the basic technology for using cryptocurrencies. In fact, this technology allows to decentralize the interventions and develop a world where the users are masters of their data. The absence of an intermediary in this process raises doubts about the use of this new technology (Hu, S., Liang, Y. C., Xiong, Z., and Niyato, D. 2021). Both artificial intelligence and blockchain are technologies that are helping to change the world, but their applications are currently very technical and little known to the public, even if artificial intelligence is becoming more and more known. Yet very distinct, these technologies could work together to offer a wider range of applications, from the economic, social, and financial levels. Indeed, the combination of blockchain technology with artificial intelligence can offer companies new growth opportunities. A new stage in the digital revolution is underway, likely to increase the challenge for SME managers to seize these new opportunities and quickly recreate value; Brune (2020) shows how the combination of blockchain technologies and artificial intelligence will disrupt certain established business models. Both artificial intelligence and blockchain are technologies that are helping to change the world, but their applications are currently very technical and little known to the general public, even if artificial intelligence is becoming more and more known. Yet very distinct, these two technologies could work together to offer a wider range of applications. The question is: can Artificial intelligence and blockchain combine in order to bypass certain constraints?

The contribution of our work is to try to improve the notion of the use of these two new technologies while trying to reveal the impact that can be generated on the financial, economic, and social levels. Our work will be organized as follows, in the first section, we will define the two basic concepts, namely blockchain technology, and artificial intelligence. In the

DOI: 10.4324/9781003304616-10

next part, we will present the common fields of action between these two technologies. The third part will be devoted to the relationship between artificial intelligence and cryptocurrencies, and finally the conclusion.

7.2 Concepts Definitions

7.2.1 Defining the Blockchain

The blockchain is a decentralized database, where each participant has information that is distributed to all users of the network. In the form of blocks linked to each other, successive transactions are stored and authenticated (AlShamsi, M., Salloum, S. A., Alshurideh, M., and Abdallah, S. 2021). A blockchain is a technological system based on a blockchain for storing and transmitting information. This information chain constitutes a global database accessible to all users. The blockchain works without any regulatory body. To guarantee the authenticity of the information, each user validates it using cryptography. As soon as a user performs a transaction by implementing information through the blockchain, it is grouped with other related information within the same block. It will be verified and approved by other members of the blockchain using cryptographic techniques. Members who ensure the technical structure of the blockchain implementation by checking and validating consistency with the other information in the block are compensated. As soon as it is validated, the block is time stamped and added to the blockchain. The information will then be visible and accessible to everyone, but it can no longer be changed. In the event of an error, the correction is made with a new transaction (Hu, S., Liang, Y. C., Xiong, Z., and Niyato, D. 2021). A blockchain is a register, a large database that has the particularity of being shared simultaneously with all its users, all of whom are also holders of this register, and who also all have the capacity to enter data according to specific rules.

It is about a "ledger", that is to say a ledger, or better a large register, where is kept the trace of all the exchanges, of all the transactions which have already been carried out between the members of the network since its creation. The advantage is that it is tamper-proof and safe from hackers: since the registry is decentralized, and stored on users' servers, it cannot be hacked. Everything is constantly checked by all users. There is therefore not "one" blockchain, but blockchains, all different, created by anonymous people as well as by large institutions, for a wide variety of uses. Within modern blockchains, there are programs called "Smart Contracts" which aim to control part of the blockchain by organizing the relations between the different parts, by establishing actions to be implemented in order to improve the existing one with the aim to correspond to new market expectations such as transparency of information. Cryptocurrency and Bitcoin in particular is indeed the most telling and well-known example of the use of blockchain (Singh, S., Sharma, P. K., Yoon, B., Shojafar, M., Cho, G. H., and Ra, I. H. 2020). But spinoffs are expected very quickly and in many areas: banking, insurance, medical data, and patents. This is what leads us to see this technology. AlShamsi, M., Salloum, SA, Alshurideh, M., and Abdallah, S. (2021) explain that blockchains, like any multi-agent system, create a competitive environment that can test the effectiveness of artificial intelligence. In turn, this needs algorithms that are equally interpreted by all members of a system, regardless of their differing interests.

7.2.2 Blockchain: The Technology of Tomorrow

Blockchain is one of the most promising new disruptive technologies. It can be defined as transparent and secure information storage and transmission technology that operates without a central control body. Concretely, the exchange is done peer to peer, that is to say without an intermediary, the register which lists all the transactions allows traceability and the conservation of registers by all users, constant verification of transactions is called a distributed consensus (Bamakan, S. M. H., Moghaddam, S. G., and Manshadi, S. D. 2021). The first use case of the technology emerged in 2008 in a context of crisis, by Satoshi Nakamoto to exchange goods and services in Bitcoin (a virtual currency). In 2009, this technology enabled users to transfer virtual currency in a secure, traceable, and unmediated manner. Blockchain should not be confused with cryptocurrency, which is a use case of Blockchain technology (Deebak, B. D., and Fadi, A. T. 2021); the main use cases are:

- Secure transfer of assets between two players: transfer of crypto-currencies, financial assets, ICO…
- Smart contracts are contracts that are self-executing automatically as soon as the condition is met: insurance indemnities, the example of drones in agriculture making it possible to raise the level of rain to trigger insurance indemnities.
- The keeping of a register that allows the sharing of authenticated and immutable data: For example, in some countries, there are problems linked to the absence or irregularity of certain registers and cadastres.

Some countries have registered in the Blockchain a kind of cadastre (Honduras, Ghana…) to ensure the authenticity of documents and information like diplomas for example, and it is, for this reason, several Councils of the Order of Chartered Accountants have set up a diploma registration prototype using Blockchain technology.

7.2.3 Blockchain Types

Blockchain can be public or private. A public Blockchain can be illustrated as an open ledger, which anyone can write on, anyone can read, but which is impossible to erase and indestructible, for example, Bitcoin. The private blockchain allows access only to those authorized by a private company or a consortium. Example: Ripple is a private (consortium) blockchain (Hu, S., Liang, Y. C., Xiong, Z., and Niyato, D. 2021)

7.2.4 Blockchain and Smart Contracts

Blockchain technology allows the implementation of smart contracts, contracts that automatically self-execute once predefined conditions have been met. Enrolling smart contracts in a blockchain guarantees that the terms of the contract cannot be changed (Deebak, B. D., and Fadi, A. T. 2021). For example, smart insurance Fizzy, (a subsidiary of Axa group), compensates its customers for delays as soon as their plane arrives. In fact, the principle is that compensation is triggered automatically in the event of a flight delay of two hours or more, without having to make a claim.

7.2.5 Blockchain and ICO (Initial Coin Offering)

It is a method of raising funds in cryptocurrencies. It works by issuing digital assets called "tokens" or tokens, in exchange for a cryptocurrency (ether or Bitcoin). Indeed, the issuing company issues tokens in pre-sale, against a virtual currency, accepted as a means of payment (Belitski, M., and Boreiko, D. 2021). Tokens, which are at the center of the operating mechanism of ICOs, are subsequently admitted to buying and selling on exchange platforms whose value depends on supply and demand (Agarwal, J. D., Agarwal, M., Agarwal, A., and Agarwal, Y. 2021). Ethereum is the source of one of the first notable ICOs in history: In 2014, Ethereum raised more than $18 million (issuing $60 million of ether redeemable for Bitcoins). Professionals are brought to meet this technology among clients who use cryptocurrencies to carry out transactions, those who are fundraising in ICOs, and those whose application is based on Blockchain technology.

7.2.6 Blockchain the Future Key

Blockchain technology is a real revolution. The impact of blockchain can be compared to that of the Internet, as this technology has changed the way things are done since its establishment in the 1990s. Treiblmaier, H., Swan, M., De Filippi, P., Lacity, M., Hardjono, T., and Kim, H. (2021) consider that the financial world is upset by blockchain, in fact, everyone can become their bank. But this revolution extends far beyond the financial sector. Indeed, some professions will disappear, and others will categorically change, such as the profession of a computer engineer. In fact, the profession of computer engineering has changed very quickly in recent years, as have several other professions that will adapt to these new realities (Majeed, U., Khan, L. U., Yaqoob, I., Kazmi, S. A., Salah, K., and Hong, C. S. 2021). Companies also have to adapt and adjust to the impact of blockchain on their environment and their business models (Bamakan, S. M. H., Moghaddam, S. G., and Manshadi, S. D. 2021). The blockchain will lead to a decentralization of platforms, where users will find greater simplicity and freedom. The implementation of these new technologies is not so simple, since the businesses and societies of tomorrow will not be similar to those of today.

7.3 Defining Artificial Intelligence

Artificial intelligence is a scientific discipline aimed at making a machine reproduce human cognitive abilities (reasoning, language, perception, etc.). With learning methods, artificial intelligence analyzes data in order to organize information and learn how to solve problems, but in systems based on rules of logic, problem-solving is programmed by humans (Mikalef, P., and Gupta, M. 2021). It is crucial to avoid errors that may arise from machine learning, as demonstrated by the unfortunate incident of Microsoft's "Nazi chatbot," which was designed to learn to adapt its language to the behavior of Internet users through the latter's exchanges. The exchanges of the chatbot (conversational robot: an automatic conversation software capable of responding to a human interlocutor in the most natural way possible) of Microsoft becomes Nazi by learning provocative messages from Internet users (Zemčík, T. 2021). So artificial intelligence needs a lot of reliable data, but that depends on the data repository to which the artificial intelligence has access. Nowadays, the concept of Artificial Intelligence is ubiquitous, and it is often promoted as a miracle solution to enhance the productivity and efficiency of various professionals. Artificial intelligence can even herald the end of several professions and trades because of its simplicity and its facilitating role between economic agents. The ultimate goal of Artificial Intelligence is to mimic the workings of the human brain. Artificial intelligence uses very advanced predictive analytics algorithms, using a quantity of data provided every day by the users themselves. This is called self-learning. To define artificial intelligence, we must define the different levels of artificial intelligence:

- First- and second-level Artificial Intelligence: IBM's 1997 Deep Blue computer beat the world chess champion. It is a hyper-specialized Artificial Intelligence in a specific context. This is Artificial Intelligence that we encounter on a daily basis, mainly in the calculation of data.
- Third-level Artificial Intelligence: In addition to performing the calculations, Artificial Intelligence level three anticipates the outcome. Based on the results of the (past) operations it performs, it can predict what will happen next.
- Fourth-level Artificial Intelligence: This is self-learning Artificial Intelligence capable of reacting to the world around it and making decisions accordingly (Zemčík, T. 2021).

7.3.1 Algorithms and Artificial Intelligence

We hear a lot about artificial intelligence integrated into certain tools such as algorithms. Let us first define the notion of algorithm, which is defined as being a finite and unambiguous sequence of operations or instructions allowing to solve a class of problems (Mollaret, S. 2021). A recipe, for example, can be considered an algorithm because it makes it possible to obtain the requested result while scrupulously following the recipe. Artificial intelligence makes it possible to accomplish tasks that classical algorithms cannot, such as the ability of the machine to learn itself from the data injected into it. There are two concepts that are important in artificial intelligence: machine learning and deep learning.

7.3.2 Machine Learning

Machine Learning is the field of study that gives computers the ability to learn without being explicitly programmed to learn. Machine learning or machine learning of the computer is the ability to inject data into the machine so that it can use to learn and detect (Awotunde, J. B., Ogundokun, R. O., Jimoh, R. G., Misra, S., and Aro, T. O. 2021). For example in radiology medicine, the machine is taught to locate images of cancer by injecting it with a large quantity of data and images. In some cases, she has been able to overtake a man. We can even design and imagine an algorithm for detecting VAT fraud; this is based on the ability of this algorithm to be able to learn from its data and be able to correct it (Mohanta, B. K., Jena, D., Satapathy, U., and Patnaik, S. 2020).

7.3.3 Deep Learning

This is deep learning, which was born in 2010 with the idea of being inspired by the functioning of the human brain, namely the connections of neurons, which will allow the machine to have an in-depth analysis and to be able to extract the data itself (Gupta, R., Srivastava, D., Sahu, M., Tiwari, S., Ambasta, R. K., and Kumar, P. 2021). Facebook already uses deep learning technology to recognize facial recognition.

7.4 Combining Blockchain and Artificial Intelligence

By giving the possibility of networking data within the same ecosystem of actors, the Blockchain makes it possible to massify access to data securely and to accelerate the machine learning curve for intelligence systems (Finlay, S. 2021). In the long run, this could lead to the democratization of AI algorithms and enable business consortia to leverage their computing power to the same level as tech giants such as Facebook or Google (Shen, Y. 2021).

7.4.1 Artificial Intelligence, A Massive Need for Data

Artificial intelligence could transform the world more than any other technical advance since the Industrial Revolution and fundamentally reinvent the way companies operate and grow (Ekramifard, A., Amintoosi, H., Seno, A. H., Dehghantanha, A., and Parizi, R. M. 2020). To be effective, many artificial intelligence algorithms, and in particular machine learning, require large volumes of data, the value of which depends on its quality. Big Data, whose vocation is to collect, organize, and analyze large volumes of data, is an essential component of artificial intelligence solutions that are deployed in organizations today (Zhang, Z., Song, X., Liu, L., Yin, J., Wang, Y., and Lan, D. 2021). It is in this sense that "data" is often presented as the new precious metal of the 21st century because it is the essential fuel of Artificial Intelligence models which mainly aim to operate classification or prediction. In fact, the two main challenges facing organizations that want to implement an artificial intelligence solution are access to data and the quality of that data for training Artificial Intelligence models. This lack of quality data means that some artificial intelligence solutions do not have a sufficient training dataset and therefore perform poorly or not. This is also a brake on the deployment of artificial intelligence, also creating disparities between companies (depending on their size and resources). Only a few large companies can afford to invest capital and skilled resources to build machine learning models and algorithms in-house. However, if a few large companies have the means to build large databases and invest in the development of artificial intelligence systems, this represents a significant financial investment, which is even more difficult to assume in times of crisis. In addition, their ability to compile this data stops at their scope of activity and the operational cases they encounter daily. It should be noted that it is rare for a single company to be able to respond to a given problem or to present a solution to a problem to which the Artificial Intelligence model claims to respond. The challenge is to collect a volume of data large enough and representative of the different management cases, to introduce them into the models of Artificial Intelligence (Zhang, Z., Song, X., Liu, L., Yin, J., Wang, Y., and Lan, D. 2021). In this context, how do we constitute and qualify large volumes of data, as sufficiently representative, and encourage data holders to share them? How to speed up the training of Artificial Intelligence models and reduce the resulting financial cost? Blockchain may provide the answer to these questions.

7.4.2 The Blockchain, a Factor in the Reliability of Artificial Intelligence

Blockchain is a technology that allows information to be stored and transmitted transparently, securely, and without a central control body. It looks like a large database that contains the history of all the exchanges made and whose users contribute to the system by providing computing power and/

or storage capacity (Gupta, J., Singh, I., and Arjun, K. P. 2021). Some of the essential components of the Blockchain are the token and the smart contract. The token is a digital asset issued and traded on a blockchain that can be sold and bought at any time, in particular on exchange platforms at a price set in real time by supply and demand. Smart contracts are irrevocable computer programs deployed on a blockchain that execute a set of predefined instructions and make it possible to secure an agreement between two or more parties, automate payments, eliminate the risk of non-payment, to drastically reduce the intermediate costs in the development, monitoring, and signing of a contract.

Given these elements, and to respond to the problem of access to quality data, these are used to train an Artificial Intelligence model, it is quite possible to imagine a smart contract that would offer a data holder to share his data within an ecosystem via a blockchain (Singhal, T., Bhargavi, M. S., and Hemavathi, P. 2021). Indeed, many data owners refuse to sell their data to intermediaries or platforms but would not be opposed to sharing it with other organizations. But this is on the condition that this data sharing is done in a secure manner and for a fair remuneration linked to the use and quality of their data. This is enabled by the Blockchain and its smart contracts by guaranteeing that each of the contributors to a blockchain is remunerated according to their actual contribution, within a secure contractual framework. Data holders whose data would be validated would be automatically remunerated in tokens. The controllers who verify that the data is valid and of quality would also be paid in tokens. Organizations that wish to use this data to train their artificial intelligence algorithms would pay in tokens for each use, thus fueling the system, with a drastic effect on the ability of these organizations to accelerate the deployment of their Artificial Intelligence systems. With Blockchain technology, it would also be possible to manage the confidentiality issues of transactions and shared data, especially in very competitive contexts, through the encryption of data that can only be decoded by the organization having the corresponding private key or allowing the establishment of exchange channels in a blockchain such as Hyperledger (Witowski, J., Choi, J., Jeon, S., Kim, D., Chung, J., Conklin, J., and Do, S. 2021). The Blockchain thus makes it possible to share data while preserving the confidentiality of transactions and data. This new economy based on data sharing is already finding concrete applications with several start-ups that can develop decentralized Blockchain platforms for sharing data sets and computing power. By thus facilitating the constitution of large and high-quality databases, the Blockchain can therefore help to accelerate the training of artificial intelligence algorithms and improve their performance. Together, Artificial Intelligence and Blockchain can empower organizations to exceed their current limits and access significant amounts of data and by extension value. In addition, the union of these two new technologies can allow companies to increase their computing power by combining their respective data assets, and together they can reach the levels of large groups like Google or

Facebook. The merger between artificial intelligence and blockchain makes it easier to access artificial intelligence in businesses. They allow small businesses to access a lot of data. The blockchain could also make it possible to restore confidence in the decisions of Artificial Intelligence because it will be easier to carry out an audit of the decision-making process of artificial intelligence by the recovery of all the data collected by the latter in its decision-making.

Finally, the data collected will be used by artificial intelligence and is secured within the blockchain. Thus, the combination of blockchain and artificial intelligence will increase the possibilities of application. They can create a direct link between producers and consumers. The information will then be stored, secured, and used in full transparency. To sum up, Artificial Intelligence could well improve the quality of information transmitted and simplify the execution of tasks, while Blockchain can provide good visibility on the execution of artificial intelligence and thus make it possible to secure information and connections.

7.5 Artificial Intelligence and Cryptocurrencies

Advances in artificial intelligence can greatly benefit blockchain and cryptocurrencies, both in terms of data security and trading. Generally, Artificial Intelligence mainly contributes to simplifying daily life by eliminating or simplifying certain tasks (An, Y. J., Choi, P. M. S., and Huang, S. H. 2021). This technology has also helped in recent years to strengthen the appeal of cryptocurrencies. Emerging after the financial crisis of late 2008, blockchain has steadily captured the attention of investors of all stripes ever since, the latter going on specialized platforms. While the market has had its ups and downs, the development of this industry is currently very promising (Al-Ameer, A., and Fouad, A. S. 2021). Technology can also be the best asset for optimizing Bitcoin and cryptocurrency trading strategy. If the trading algorithms on the financial markets saw the light of day in the 1990s, the cryptocurrency market lends itself perfectly to the democratization of automated trading bots intended for a wide audience ranging from the amateur trader to the pro trader (Awotunde, J. B., Ogundokun, R. O., Jimoh, R. G., Misra, S., and Aro, T. O. 2021).

7.5.1 Artificial Intelligence and Trading

There are different classic trading strategies in the markets already implemented by any professional person. The first distinction to be made when talking about a trading strategy is of a temporal nature; we distinguish short-term strategies generally qualified as speculative. These strategies aim to analyze and anticipate price variations over short periods. Moreover, there are long-term strategies that aim to invest in increasing the value of an asset over a long period (Al-Ameer, A., and Fouad, A. S. 2021). Thus, the use of trading algorithms may be more relevant when opting for the option of a short-term strategy, in a context where technology can be much more efficient than the human brain. The second distinction is made between "Swing Trading" and "Position Trading" strategies. With a "Position Trading" strategy as the name suggests, you will position yourself in an asset or this case in crypto with the objective of benefiting from an upward trend over several weeks or even months. Conversely, when you opt for "Swing Trading", the crypto holding period is much shorter, here we will no longer count in weeks or months but days, or even hours. Once again, you will understand that bots and algorithms bring all their intelligence in the context of "Swing Trading" rather than "Position Trading". While the development of high-frequency trading on the traditional financial markets has greatly developed in recent years to benefit from price variations over a short or very short period, taking transaction costs into account requires reviewing the timing of Swing Trading so as not to be overwhelmed by unforeseen costs (Ganapathy, A., Redwanuzzaman, M., Rahaman, M. M., and Khan, W. 2020). Trading strategies are augmented by the power of algorithms and artificial intelligence. One thing is certain, that technological innovation is a trader's best asset.

These classic trading strategies (not using technological innovation) are revolutionized by super robot traders using the best artificial intelligence algorithms (Sabry, F., Labda, W., Erbad, A., and Malluhi, Q. 2020). This is why when looking for a robot trader for your crypto, the majority of traders will look for robots that are dedicated to unearthing medium and long-term cryptocurrency trends; these robot traders thus minimize the potential risks. The second technological innovation in the financial markets is algorithmic "Quant Trading". Financial engineers have, thus, developed algorithms packed with artificial intelligence that constantly analyze the financial markets by focusing on two main metrics which are the evolution of prices of course, and the volumes traded (Iqbal, M., Iqbal, M. S., Jaskani, F. H., Iqbal, K., and Hassan, A. 2021). Classic financial markets have greeted technological developments with mixed eyes, with established traders for years looking down on the prospect of being replaced by an army of robot traders. The cryptocurrency markets, for their part, offer many more possibilities for deploying technological solutions to optimize your trading strategy. Thus, at first, traders in the cryptocurrency markets mostly went back to classic strategies (Sebastião, H., and Godinho, P. 2021). However, today some companies intend to democratize the use of trading bots and more broadly the deployment of artificial intelligence in the cryptocurrency markets.

7.5.2 Artificial Intelligence and Transaction Security

As investors bet on the blockchain, artificial intelligence has an increasingly important role in cryptocurrency trading. Indeed, traders can have access to more precise analyzes and make well-informed decisions thanks to the robots specially designed for trading, thus resulting in a better return on investment

(Ghosh, A., Gupta, S., Dua, A., and Kumar, N. 2020). Among the problems that the blockchain industry still faces are hacking operations and cyberattacks. Indeed, every day, millions of dollars in cryptocurrencies change hands fraudulently. To remedy this, Artificial Intelligence makes it possible to reinforce security and it is cybersecurity systems using artificial intelligence that prove to be the most effective in protecting the blockchain (Mattos, D. M. F., Krief, F., and Rueda, S. J. 2020). Indeed, they can instantly identify the nature of a threat. Then, they put it on a blacklist to prevent another intrusion. Thus, Artificial Intelligence evolves (Hu, S., Liang, Y. C., Xiong, Z., and Niyato, D. 2021), increasing its effectiveness with each threat, and learning from previous operations (Al-Ameer, A., and Fouad, A. S. 2021). To ensure the security and integrity of the blockchain, each transaction is verified before being added by miners. The latter will thus receive a reward in the form of cryptocurrency. But the only problem is that this process is too energy-consuming and has an impact because of the energy required by the processors and graphics cards that run it (Chenguel, M. B. 2021). Thus, many mining companies have turned to graphic cards equipped with Artificial Intelligence in order to reduce their carbon footprint. And some firms have established artificial intelligence-based ecosystems where miners can share the required energy load. Thus, these algorithms help make Bitcoin mining faster, more efficient, and more profitable. In conclusion, the technology sector as a whole has started to turn towards machine learning. Also, blockchain and cryptocurrencies should benefit from artificial intelligence.

7.5.3 Using AI to Fight Fraud

Cryptocurrencies like Bitcoin have often taken center stage in recent years. These digital tokens share some of the qualities of cash and can be purchased, traded and spent. In fact, an entire market has developed around the trading of digital currencies, with investors and speculators watching closely for the slightest fluctuation. Several digital platforms specializing in digital wallets have emerged, which manage millions of merchants and consumers, and transaction exchanges with billions of dollars in crypto currencies. These financial services companies must offer services with great transparency to their consumers while taking measures to secure the environment in which they trade. For this, several companies in this field rely on artificial intelligence (AI) using machine learning tools. Of course, Artificial Intelligence is the central point on which these digital transaction companies are based, especially in terms of transparency to avoid all types of fraud. Indeed one of the most important risk factors that a cryptocurrency exchange must control is fraud, and machine learning forms the basis of the anti-fraud system. Artificial intelligence software and tools make it easy to create, train, and deploy machine learning models, enabling the creation and refinement of a machine learning-based system that recognizes shifts and anomalies in user identification sources. This allows them to quickly take action against potential sources of fraud. In fact, authenticating online identities is actually a very complex problem, and artificial intelligence uses software like Sagemaker to develop machine learning algorithms to analyze images to detect scammers. For example, a face similarity algorithm automatically extracts faces from IDs that are loaded and then compares a given face to all faces from other IDs that have been loaded. Scammers often use the same photo for multiple pieces of ID. Otherwise, they would have to modify the face in several places. This face similarity algorithm allows the company to quickly detect counterfeiting. The insights gained from building anti-fraud algorithms also allow us to personalize experiences to different types of users. It's about offering services both for private investors who buy and hold and also for sophisticated professional users who trade extensively. However, risk management is not that simple, and given their digital origins cryptocurrencies are characterized by an immense volume of data. These companies that come up with algorithms to manage digital risk have to bring together data from various microservices, including blockchain and user data, which amounts to thousands of terabytes. However, these IT engineering firms need to take extra steps to ensure customer data is protected. Any code that runs on production servers is reviewed and reviewed by multiple groups of people before being released to production. One of the main tenets is that security comes first, as they store cryptocurrencies on behalf of their clients. Restricted access to data in a highly secure environment makes machine learning all the more difficult. To overcome this difficulty, machine learning engineers can access data logs only through code that has been thoroughly examined. In reality, machine learning engineers cannot connect to production servers and run code that has not been reviewed.

7.6 Conclusion

With the simultaneous development of two key technologies: blockchain and artificial intelligence; which are technologies that can be used together (Agarwal, J. D., Agarwal, M., Agarwal, A., and Agarwal, Y. 2021), in order to put a direct link between the customer and the producer or the service provider. Thus, thanks to a blockchain, a company will not only be able to conclude a transaction directly with a customer transparently and securely and thus, saving the commission of a platform. It can also conclude a

> smart contract which is a contract execution with automatic execution, backed by traditional legal contracts that allow the automation of certain execution processes and guarantee all the conditions to be respected between the two parties for the payment to be made. They can also provide compensation, avoiding, thus, to the customers the long and tedious stages of complaints
>
> An, Y. J., Choi, P. M. S., and Huang, S. H. 2021, p. 8).

Consequently, blockchain brings security and predictability; as for artificial intelligence, it contributes with simplicity in interfacing. Indeed, Artificial Intelligence is the missing link in the blockchain to allow it to become widespread and multiply throughout the economy. The combination of these two new technologies opens up promising possibilities for developing all the business models currently existing. Once companies have metabolized the security and predictability that blockchain guarantees them when they have experienced the simplicity offered by artificial intelligence. This is a very important financial and economic step, where the business model will change and evolve (AlShamsi, M., Salloum, S. A., Alshurideh, M., and Abdallah, S. 2021). Without delving into the apparent complexity of these technologies, SME managers should therefore seize upon them now and think about a promising strategy. It is the blockchain that we must focus on primarily, and we must think carefully about the uses that could accelerate the growth of companies. Large groups have already understood this, and have already developed, for the most part, blockchain-based projects with a view to business between companies. But the articulation of these two technologies opens up a range of use cases that will soon also be perceptible to consumers (Singh, S., Sharma, P. K., Yoon, B., Shojafar, M., Cho, G. H., and Ra, I. H. 2020). These mutations that lead to disruption are presented as inevitable, without being sufficiently concerned with their social repercussions. Indeed, these new technologies, with the programs and the robotic combination with artificial intelligence, will allow the massive use of robots, which will adapt and react to their environment, thus replacing a large number of jobs and, ultimately, will transform society. This will result in widening the income inequalities that already exist between the creative class that created these novelties and the immense mass of employees in sectors working classically.

Bibliography

Agarwal, J. D., Agarwal, M., Agarwal, A., & Agarwal, Y. (2021). Economics of cryptocurrencies: Artificial intelligence, blockchain, and digital currency. In Kashi R Balachandran (ed.), *Information for Efficient Decision Making: Big Data, Blockchain and Relevance* (pp. 331–430). New York University Leonard N Stern School of Business, New York.

Al-Ameer, A., & Fouad, A. S. (2021, April). A methodology for securities and cryptocurrency trading using exploratory data analysis and artificial intelligence. In *2021 1st International Conference on Artificial Intelligence and Data Analytics (CAIDA)* (pp. 54–61). IEEE.

AlShamsi, M., Salloum, S. A., Alshurideh, M., & Abdallah, S. (2021). Artificial intelligence and blockchain for transparency in governance. In *Artificial Intelligence for Sustainable Development: Theory, Practice and Future Applications* (pp. 219–230). Springer, Cham.

An, Y. J., Choi, P. M. S., & Huang, S. H. (2021). Blockchain, cryptocurrency, and artificial intelligence in finance. In Choi, P.M.S., & Huang, S.H. (eds) *Fintech with*

Artificial Intelligence, Big Data, and Blockchain, 1. Blockchain Technologies. Springer, Singapore. https://doi.org/10.1007/978-981-33-6137-9_1

Awotunde, J. B., Ogundokun, R. O., Jimoh, R. G., Misra, S., & Aro, T. O. (2021). Machine learning algorithm for cryptocurrencies price prediction. In *Artificial Intelligence for Cyber Security: Methods, Issues and Possible Horizons or Opportunities* (pp. 421–47). Springer, Cham.

Bamakan, S. M. H., Moghaddam, S. G., Manshadi, S. D. (2021). Blockchain-enabled pharmaceutical cold chain: Applications, key challenges, and future trends. *Journal of Cleaner Production*, 302, 127021.

Belitski, M., & Boreiko, D. (2022). Success factors of initial coin offerings. *The Journal of Technology Transfer*, 47, 1690–1706.

Brune, P. (2020). Towards an enterprise-ready implementation of artificial intelligence-enabled, blockchain-based mart contracts. arXiv preprint arXiv:2003.09744.

Chenguel, M. B. (2021). Blockchain and ecological impact: Between reality and accusation? Lecture Notes in Networks and Systems. https://www.springer.com/series/15179

Deebak, B. D., & Fadi, A. T. (2021). Privacy-preserving in smart contracts using blockchain and artificial intelligence for cyber risk measurements. *Journal of Information Security and Applications*, 58, 102749.

Ekramifard, A., Amintoosi, H., Seno, A. H., Dehghantanha, A., & Parizi, R. M. (2020). A systematic literature review of integration of blockchain and artificial intelligence. In: Choo, K. K., Dehghantanha, A., & Parizi, R. (eds.), *Blockchain Cybersecurity, Trust and Privacy. Advances in Information Security*, vol. 79. Springer, Cham. https://doi.org/10.1007/978-3-030-38181-3_8

Finlay, S. (2021). *Artificial Intelligence and Machine Learning for Business: A No-Nonsense Guide to Data Driven Technologies* (No. 4th ed). Relativistic, Preston.

Ganapathy, A., Redwanuzzaman, M., Rahaman, M. M., & Khan, W. (2020). Artificial intelligence driven crypto currencies. *Global Disclosure of Economics and Business*, 9(2), 107–118.

Ghosh, A., Gupta, S., Dua, A., & Kumar, N. (2020). Security of cryptocurrencies in blockchain technology: State-of-art, challenges and future prospects. *Journal of Network and Computer Applications*, 163, 102635.

Gupta, J., Singh, I., & Arjun, K. P. (2021). Artificial intelligence for blockchain I. In *Blockchain, Internet of Things, and Artificial Intelligence* (pp. 109–140). Chapman and Hall/CRC, Boca Raton, FL.

Gupta, R., Srivastava, D., Sahu, M., Tiwari, S., Ambasta, R. K., & Kumar, P. (2021). Artificial intelligence to deep learning: Machine intelligence approach for drug discovery. *Molecular Diversity*, 25, 1315–1360.

Hu, S., Liang, Y. C., Xiong, Z., & Niyato, D. (2021). Blockchain and artificial intelligence for dynamic resource sharing in 6G and beyond. *IEEE Wireless Communications*, 28, 145–151.

Iqbal, M., Iqbal, M. S., Jaskani, F. H., Iqbal, K., & Hassan, A. (2021). Time-series prediction of cryptocurrency market using machine learning techniques. *EAI Endorsed Transactions on Creative Technologies*, 4(4), 6.

Majeed, U., Khan, L. U., Yaqoob, I., Kazmi, S. A., Salah, K., & Hong, C. S. (2021). Blockchain for IoT-based smart cities: Recent advances, requirements, and future challenges. *Journal of Network and Computer Applications*, 181, 103007.

Mattos, D. M. F., Krief, F., & Rueda, S. J. (2020). Blockchain and artificial intelligence for network security. *Annals of Telecommunications*, 75, 101–102.

Mikalef, P., & Gupta, M. (2021). Artificial intelligence capability: Conceptualization, measurement calibration, and empirical study on its impact on organizational creativity and firm performance. *Information & Management*, 58(3), 103434.

Mohanta, B. K., Jena, D., Satapathy, U., & Patnaik, S. (2020). Survey on IoT security: Challenges and solution using machine learning, artificial intelligence and blockchain technology. *Internet of Things*, 11, 100227.

Mollaret, S. (2021). Artificial intelligence algorithms in quantitative finance (Doctoral dissertation, Paris Est).

Sabry, F., Labda, W., Erbad, A., & Malluhi, Q. (2020). Cryptocurrencies and artificial intelligence: Challenges and opportunities. *IEEE Access*, 8, 175840–175858.

Sebastião, H., & Godinho, P. (2021). Forecasting and trading cryptocurrencies with machine learning under changing market conditions. *Financial Innovation*, 7(1), 1–30.

Shen, Y. (2021, April). The application of artificial intelligence in computer network technology in the era of big data. In *2021 International Conference on Computer Technology and Media Convergence Design (CTMCD)* (pp. 173–177). IEEE.

Singh, S., Sharma, P. K., Yoon, B., Shojafar, M., Cho, G. H., & Ra, I. H. (2020). Convergence of blockchain and artificial intelligence in IoT network for the sustainable smart city. *Sustainable Cities and Society*, 63, 102364.

Singhal, T., Bhargavi, M. S., & Hemavathi, P. (2021). Coalescence of artificial intelligence with blockchain: A survey on analytics over blockchain data in different sectors. In Hassanien, A.E., Bhattacharyya, S., Chakrabati, S., Bhattacharya, A., & Dutta, S. (eds), *Emerging Technologies in Data Mining and Information Security* (pp. 703–711). Advances in Intelligent Systems and Computing, vol 1286. Springer, Singapore.

Treiblmaier, H., Swan, M., De Filippi, P., Lacity, M., Hardjono, T., & Kim, H. (2021). What's next in blockchain research? –An identification of key topics using a multidisciplinary perspective. *ACM SIGMIS Database: The Database for Advances in Information Systems*, 52(1), 27–52.

Witowski, J., Choi, J., Jeon, S., Kim, D., Chung, J., Conklin, J., … & Do, S. (2021). MarkIt: A collaborative artificial intelligence annotation platform leveraging blockchain for medical imaging research. *Blockchain in Healthcare Today*, 4, https://blockchainhealthcaretoday.com/index.php/journal/article/view/176.

Zemčík, T. (2021). Failure of chatbot Tay was evil, ugliness and uselessness in its nature or do we judge it through cognitive shortcuts and biases? *AI & Society*, 36(1), 361–367.

Zhang, Z., Song, X., Liu, L., Yin, J., Wang, Y., & Lan, D. (2021). Recent advances in blockchain and artificial intelligence integration: Feasibility analysis, research issues, applications, challenges, and future work. *Security and Communication Networks*, 1–15.

Part 3

The Societal Impact of Artificial Intelligence

8 AI Human Capital, Jobs and Skills

Lea Samek and Mariagrazia Squicciarini

8.1 Introduction

Artificial Intelligence (AI) is considered by many a General Purpose Technology (GPT). It is profoundly transforming the way people work, learn or interact (Bessen, 2019; Georgieff and Hyee, 2021; Acemoglu et al., 2022) and has a strong potential to facilitate innovation (Agrawal, Gans and Goldfarb, 2018; Cockburn, Henderson and Stern, 2018; Gierten et al., 2021) and increase productivity (Brynjolfsson, Rock and Syverson, 2017; Corrado, Haskel and Jona-Lasinio, 2021; Rammer, Czarnitzki and Fernández, 2021). By shaping the way information is generated and processed, AI decision-supporting algorithms can complement or augment a number of tasks that workers perform on the job, such as cancer detection in MRI scans (Bi et al., 2019), and may lead to automate others, especially routine tasks.

AI also contributes to creating new and different types of jobs, and to redefining occupational profiles through shaping skill requirements. As AI development, deployment, and adoption increases and AI technologies evolve, the (sets of) skills that the workers of today and tomorrow need to be endowed with change. This ultimately entails that adapting to and thriving in the AI era requires individuals to not only acquire new skills and competencies but to also engage in lifelong learning.

In what follows, we first review the literature concerned with AI adoption and automation and discuss the possible employment implications, which vary across demographic groups, occupations, and regions (Section 8.2). Overall, existing studies point to both, the possible job offsetting consequences of AI adoption and the creation of new (types of) jobs as AI alters the tasks that workers need to perform on the job. AI offers opportunities to some individuals by contributing to the emergence of new occupational profiles and complementing existing ones but presents challenges to others by making certain tasks obsolete and destroying jobs that are intensive in such tasks.

A section providing an overview of skills that are most frequently required in AI jobs follows (Section 8.3). Analyzing whether and to what extent different (types of) skills bundles are demanded sheds light on skill complementarities and allows identifying those skills that are central for AI transformation.

DOI: 10.4324/9781003304616-12

These studies confirm that technical skills are central to the deployment of AI while highlighting that they go hand in hand with other cognitive and socio-emotional skills.

Section 8.4 discusses how best to form and augment human capital, and to help individuals adapt to AI-induced changes in the labor market, especially through reskilling and upskilling. It highlights the importance of access to quality education for all, independently of, e.g. age or gender, and the need to provide especially girls and women with opportunities to participate in science, technology, engineering, and mathematics (STEM)-related education and training. It further underlines that lifelong learning becomes a must in the digital era, in light of constantly evolving AI-related technologies and changing skill requirements; more frequent job-to-job transitions as job tenures shorten; and workers' heterogeneous skills, competencies, and abilities.

8.1.1 AI and Automation Change Jobs and Skills Demand

The use of AI and robots is often associated with automation, (substantial) workplace transformation, and job destruction, with human intervention, possibly being rendered redundant or obsolete (Aghion, Jones and Jones, 2017; Acemoglu and Restrepo, 2018).[1] In recent years, numerous studies have tried to assess the possible job destruction triggered by AI and the use of robots. Among those studies, Frey and Osborne (2017) estimate that 47% of jobs in the United States are at risk of automation. A very similar outlook emerges from a McKinsey Global Institute report (Manyika et al., 2017), which estimates that almost half of the activities that people are paid to do globally could be automated using current technologies, with less than 5% consisting of activities that can be fully automated.

However, the timing for such redundancies to occur is often mentioned in a very general fashion or overlooked. This creates uncertainty about the urgency or otherwise the time that policy may have to address the possible employment-related challenges that AI deployment and adoption may trigger. Conversely, Arntz, Gregory, and Zierahn (2017) argue that the risk of being automated is often overstated because the substantial heterogeneity that characterizes job tasks and the adaptability of jobs in the digital transformation is often neglected. When taking the task content of jobs into account, they estimate that only 9% and 10% of jobs in the United States (compared to the aforementioned 47%) and the United Kingdom, respectively, are at risk.

In practice, scholars find no discernible effect on employment as of yet. Using US online vacancy data, Acemoglu et al. (2022) argue that AI substitutes humans in a subset of tasks without any detectable aggregate labor market consequences. Squicciarini and Staccioli (2022) find only negligible effects of labor-saving technologies on employment shares in Organisation for Economic Co-operation and Development (OECD) countries over the past decade suggesting that either these technologies have yet to be implemented into production processes in those countries, or that their effect has been offset, on average, by complementary labor-augmenting technologies or by increases in related demand (Bessen, 2019).

The notable differences in the estimated number of individuals at risk of losing their jobs due to automation mainly stem from the assumptions made about the automatability or routineness of different tasks (e.g. Autor and Salomons (2018), Marcolin, Miroudot and Squicciarini (2018)) and the data used to generate the relevant estimates. Despite these differences, all studies concur in underlining that all jobs will see their tasks vary due to automation and AI, although to different extents. For instance, Manyika et al. (2017) argue that in about 60% of occupations, at least a third of activities can be automated.

More recent work exploits this argument to study AI adoption through the human capital lens and uses online vacancy data to provide evidence on AI-related skills demanded by employers. These skills can be found in all occupational categories, thus confirming the potential of this GPT to change every aspect of production and, consequently, to affect all workers (Squicciarini and Nachtigall, 2021). This pattern notwithstanding, some occupational profiles, demographic groups, and regions appear to be more affected by this new technological paradigm than others.

8.1.2 Exposure to the AI Revolution Varies by Occupation, Demography, Ethnicity, and Geography

Samek, Squicciarini and Cammeraat (2021) find that managers, professionals as well as technicians and associate professionals account for 99% of the AI-related vacancies identified in the United States over the period 2012–2019, with the large majority of AI-related jobs being for professional occupations (87%). A similar distribution emerges for the United Kingdom. The authors find a large majority of AI-related companies looking only for professionals, i.e. they do not post any other AI-related vacancies, and therefore argue that professionals can be considered as being more core, while managers and technicians seemingly complement AI-related professional workers.

They nevertheless find that the most AI-intensive jobs, i.e. jobs in which the share of AI skills out of the total number of skills is largest, even include occupational groups where AI skills cannot be taken for granted, such as craft and related trade workers as well as plant/machine operators and assemblers. At the same time, the share of AI skills is increasing over time for most occupations, suggesting that the AI intensity of AI-related jobs is increasing overall, even though highly skilled occupations involving non-routine cognitive tasks, such as lab technicians, engineers, and actuaries, are still considered to be most exposed to AI (Aghion, Jones and Jones, 2017; Brynjolfsson, Mitchell and Rock, 2018; Felten, Raj and Seamans, 2019; Webb, 2019).

One possible explanation refers to Moravec's Paradox, whereby tasks requiring high-level reasoning demand relatively light computational resources while tasks requiring sensor-motor skills (generally associated with lower skill occupations) demand vast computational resources (Gries and

Naudé, 2018). Alternatively, the related Polanyi's Paradox emphasizes the challenge that computers face in performing tasks relying on tacit knowledge, i.e. where people understand intuitively how to perform a seven task but cannot elicit the rules or procedures they follow (Polanyi, 2009). However, the fact that high-skilled occupations are most exposed to automation is new and can be contrasted to past evidence which finds automation to be associated with mostly routine and/or low-skilled tasks (Autor, Levy and Murnane, 2003; Nedelkoska and Quintini, 2018). In fact, Marcolin, Miroudot and Squicciarini (2018) only find a weak negative correlation between skill content and routine intensity, i.e. more routine-intensive occupations tend to be only weakly associated with lower skills, lending support to the ongoing empirical work that relies on skill information.

With tasks being automated or augmented differently across occupations and sectors, it is important to further zoom in on the skills demanded in those occupations. For instance, Stephany (2020) shows that learning Java is of limited economic benefit in the field of data engineering, whereas learning how to program in Python increases the wages of freelancers on online labor platforms significantly. In comparison, for the field of 3D design, Java yields a much higher contribution to wages than the so-called "super star" programming language Python. Samek, Squicciarini and Cammeraat (2021), who focus on AI-related jobs, find that socio-emotional skills, especially related to presentation, planning, budgeting, and business development, are much more important among managers and tend to be more evident in business services and education. Reports published by the World Economic Forum (World Economic Forum, 2016; 2020) find that big data allows for increased sophistication in inventory management or product personalization in wholesale and retail, whereas the finance or information and communication sectors increasingly face consumers' concerns related to labor standards and privacy.

However, with different demographic groups being overrepresented in certain occupations or sectors, labor market segmentation by gender, age, and racial-ethnic identity further contributes to uneven AI exposure (Muro, Maxim and Whiton, 2019). Muro, Maxim and Whiton (2019) suggest that male workers, for instance, are more vulnerable to potential future automation because they are overrepresented in production, transportation, and construction, sectors that have above-average projected automation exposure. Women, in comparison, comprise upward of 70% of the labor force in relatively safe occupations, like health care, personal services, and education. They also suggest that almost every second worker aged 16–24 are exposed to automation due to their overrepresentation in automatable jobs related to food preparation and serving. Although black workers are overrepresented in health and personal care services, which are on average less susceptible to automation, together with Hispanic and American Indian workers they are expected to face more disruptions than other racial and ethnic groups due to their overrepresentation in high-exposure sectors like construction as well as agriculture (Hispanic workers) and transportation (black workers).

A growing literature further investigates the possible consequences that the automation of job tasks, enabled by AI, may have across countries or regions. These studies explore whether the deployment of AI technologies contributes to the erosion of labor cost advantages, which generally motivate foreign direct investments or global value chain-type of production arrangements and, hence, location or relocation in developing countries in the first place. Maloney and Molina (2019) find little evidence of labor market polarization and labor-displacing automation in emerging countries. Conversely, Carbonero, Ernst and Weber (2020) argue that robotization has a much more pronounced negative effect in emerging economies, with robots that contribute to decreasing offshoring from developed countries and, consequently, employment in emerging economies.

Focusing on regional differences, Samek, Squicciarini and Cammeraat (2021) find the demand for AI talent to have increased across many regions but remained concentrated geographically, with a majority located in capitals, e.g. London in the United Kingdom and California in the United States. Muro, Maxim and Whiton (2019) argue that large regions and whole states, which differ less from one another in their overall industrial compositions, will see noticeable but not necessarily radical variations in task exposure to automation. Instead, risks vary with the local industry, task, and skill mix, which in turn determines local susceptibility to task automation.

8.1.3 AI Changes Overall Firms' Demand by Creating New Jobs and Shaping Occupational Profiles

AI also contributes to the emergence of new occupational profiles, such as "trainers" to teach AI systems, "explainers" to translate outputs generated by AI, and "sustainers" to monitor AI to ensure its functioning (Wilson, Daugherty and Bianzino, 2017; Alekseeva et al., 2021), and work modalities, which may or may not be of a high skill or high quality, in terms of pay, tenure, training opportunities or working hours (Agrawal, Gans and Goldfarb, 2019). On the one hand, more job roles will likely involve the ability to identify areas where AI and automation resources will be most effective. On the other hand, "Gig" jobs, entailing the remote provision of digital services through online labor platforms, often offer flexibility and autonomy but tend to result in low pay, irregular working hours or overwork, and social isolation as well as exhaustion (Wood et al., 2018).

With occupations like data scientists emerging, skill re-bundling and cross-skilling strategies, i.e. the combination of skills from different occupational domains, gain in importance. However, the precise skill requirements needed to master emerging technologies have until very recently remained opaque (De Mauro et al., 2018) and – despite growing demand for them – new occupations, in fields like data management, digital design, and autonomous systems, are not yet acknowledged by official employment taxonomies. With new, partly nameless occupations emerging, keeping up to date with skill requirements in these newly emerging jobs can be challenging for workers and educators. This may result in path dependence, i.e. staying on existing (possibly stagnant or even regressing) career paths, and preventing reskilling into these new areas (Escobari, Seyal and Meaney, 2019).

However, AI adoption does not only impact developers, users, and educators of AI but also the entire workforce of firms, regardless of whether they are endowed with AI skills or not. AI-adopting firms tend to increase salaries (Alekseeva et al., 2021) and change hiring behavior also for non-AI jobs, the latter spurred by AI-suitability (Acemoglu et al., 2022). AI-exposed establishments are found to change their skill mix requirements differentially in non-AI positions once AI is adopted – suggesting that non-AI job tasks are affected - and simultaneously reduce hiring in non-AI positions, albeit only modestly. Therefore, the imprint of AI can already be seen at the level of firms and establishments, whose pre-existing task structures make them more suitable for using AI.

With human capital adjusting relatively slowly to changes, i.e. changes in skills endowment and supply take time to materialize, and skill requirements constantly changing, endowing educators with adequate digital competencies becomes instrumental. Educators would need to train individuals for them to work effectively with AI systems and give people a voice in what AI should and should not be designed to do. Many educators are already revisiting how best to integrate new technologies in the curriculum as well as in pedagogical practices, including social robots assisting teachers in their pedagogical tasks (for a detailed discussion, see Baker's chapter (2021) in the OECD Digital Education Outlook 2021).[2] Their physical nature lends them to real-world interactions with learners, and they have an increased social presence, which may enhance learning outcomes (Belpaeme and Tanaka, 2021). Also, for AI to avoid exacerbating or creating new divides, it would be important to endow individuals with ethical awareness competencies. This would entail making individuals aware of the ethical challenges brought about by AI technologies concerning jobs, skills, inclusion, and human rights more generally, as remarked in universal standards such as the UNESCO Recommendation on the Ethics of AI (Ramos, 2022).

8.2 Working with AI: The Human Capital Behind AI

AI-related workers are generally technically skilled people, who need to exhibit a set of AI-related skills in addition to other cognitive and socio-emotional skills, regardless of whether their job entails developing or using AI. Technological advances have always generated new demands for human specialization (Autor, 2022) and AI represents no exception to this rule. In the context of digital transformation, scholars as well as policy interventions have at times solely focused on the importance of digital skills, although recent evidence points to the fact that digital skills alone do not go very far. Navigating and thriving in the digital era call for individuals to also be endowed with a wide array of cognitive (e.g. literacy, numeracy, and problem-solving) and socio-emotional skills, and to be able to learn and update their knowledge throughout life (OECD, 2016; 2017b; 2019). Van Deursen and van Dijk (2014) argue that digital skills even encompass operational, formal, information, communication, content creation, and strategic skills and are altogether essential for people to participate (economically, politically, socially, culturally, institutionally, educationally and spatially) in the information society.

However, with human capital being highly specific to the tasks carried out at work, it is important to distinguish the role played by cognitive, socio-emotional, and tasks-based skills in shaping the ability of individuals to be part of the AI transformation (Gibbons and Waldman, 2004; Gathmann and Schönberg, 2010; Grundke et al., 2017; 2018; Cammeraat, Samek and Squicciarini, 2021a; b). Addressing questions related to the type of skills and the skill compositions that are particularly demanded by employers active in the AI space thus becomes a key step in shedding light on the human capital needed to work with AI. Additionally, given the pace at which AI is evolving, we have to better understand which skills have gained in importance over time and which skills have seemingly experienced a decline in demand, to inform education, skills, and labor market discussions.

8.2.1 *AI-Specialistic Skills are a Must in the AI Era*

Machine learning (ML) and the programming language Python consistently stand out, not only as the most frequently sought-after individual AI-related skills demanded in AI-related jobs, but they are also most frequently demanded together, forming the core set of AI-related workers' skill profiles (Stephany, 2020; Samek, Squicciarini and Cammeraat, 2021; Squicciarini and Nachtigall, 2021). ML refers to computer algorithms that rely on data and experience to improve performance on a set of tasks automatically. Python is at present considered to be the key programming language for data science, which commands a significant wage premium (Stephany, 2020) and is an inter-disciplinary field using scientific methods, processes and algorithms in a view to extracting knowledge from structured and unstructured data (Grus, 2019).

Given the amount of data that is collected and the need for it to be analyzed, it is not surprising that Samek, Squicciarini and Cammeraat (2021) further identify competencies related to the management of big data, namely MapReduce and data mining, to complement the broader set of AI-related skill pairs that represent the foundation of AI-related workers' skill profile. MapReduce is a programming and implementation approach used to process and generate big data sets with parallel distributed algorithms on a cluster. Data mining is a process that helps turn raw data into useful information by looking for patterns or clusters in large data. In job openings posted in more recent years, the two key skills Python and ML also often appear together with deep learning and natural language processing (NLP). The former is a subfield of ML and works iteratively to progressively extract higher-level features from raw inputs while the latter enables machines to read, decipher and derive meaning from human languages.

Although a clear trend toward requiring a broader set of AI skills emerges with some skills losing relative importance and other skills emerging more prominently in more recent years, the composition of these sought-after technical skills appears relatively stable over time (Samek, Squicciarini and Cammeraat, 2021; Squicciarini and Nachtigall, 2021). With AI jobs becoming more AI intensive, i.e. with a growing number of AI jobs progressively requiring greater numbers of AI skills (Lane and Saint-Martin, 2021; Squicciarini and Nachtigall, 2021), it may be desirable to invest in the acquisition of these skills, as they will likely be needed also for the AI talent of the future (Samek, Squicciarini and Cammeraat, 2021; Squicciarini and Nachtigall, 2021).

To shed light on the relative importance of skill bundles and offer insights into the skills required in more "specialized" roles of AI-related work, Samek, Squicciarini and Cammeraat (2021) analyze pairwise correlations to explore how often skills appear together relative to how often they appear separately in job adverts. They identify three main skill bundles, namely one related to developing AI itself, one to AI applications, and one to robotics.[3] Although the skill components of each bundle remain relatively stable over the observation period 2013–2019, skills related to AI development and applications of AI become more intertwined in recent years, resulting in the network shown in Figure 8.1. In this example of recent US online vacancies (2017–2019), skills related to neural networks emerge at the network's center connecting these two clusters of skills, possibly because AI applications related to neural networks and deep learning were typically associated with supervised learning models, whereas AI developments like clustering, NLP and other unsupervised ML models started to use neural networks more recently.

The driver of this growing interconnectedness may be related to the growing reliance on deep learning models and approaches, driven by companies such as AlphaGo and DeepMind and by the acquisition of DeepMind by Google. Alternatively, it could be explained by the emergence of hybrid AI. These are software systems employing a combination of AI-related methods and techniques in parallel, for example combining neural networks and fuzzy logic in neuro-fuzzy systems.[4] This may mirror greater complementarity between AI skills, or result from organizations looking for workers endowed with both method and software-related skills. Job postings often describe them as software developers with AI skills and employers more recently call them "ML engineers". At the same time, some organizations, such as Ocado or Uber, may look for human capital specialized in a particular field, e.g. "computer vision engineers" with NLP or computer vision competencies.

Despite the growing skills interconnectedness observed, AI applications and AI developments feature very distinct skill components. The latter is characterized by very technical and specialistic skills often needed to find

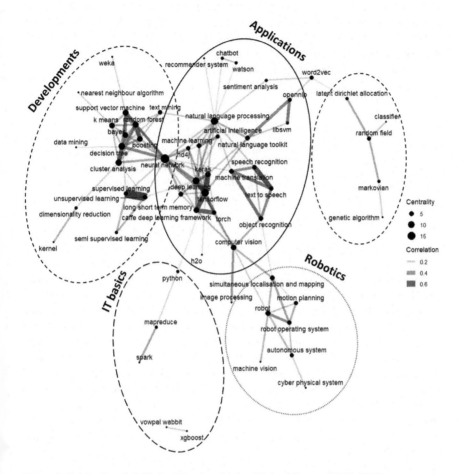

Figure 8.1 AI-related skills in AI-related jobs, United States, 2017–2019.

Note: To aid presentation, only edges with a correlation exceeding 0.1 are shown here. The identified skill bundles are: (1) Skills related to developing and advancing AI; (2) AI applications; (3) robotics; and (4) AI IT basics.

Source: Samek, Squicciarini and Cammeraat (2021) using Lightcast data (June 2021).

logical relationships and analyze patterns from the structure of data related to, for instance, consumer transactions, user behavior, or energy consumption. Typical skills mentioned in those vacancies are related to the probabilistic graphical network model Bayes, powerful variants of decision trees like random forests and gradient/adaptive boosting, or unsupervised learning processes such as cluster analysis and the clustering algorithm k means (commonly used in, e.g. medical imaging and biometrics).

A second, smaller skill group emerges which encompasses competencies mainly associated with computer and information research scientists, who are theorists, designers, or inventors developing solutions to problems in the field of computer hardware and software. It mainly involves the statistical modeling method Markov Random field, used in statistical physics dating back as far as the Ehrenfests (Hernández-Lemus, 2021). Due to its generality, it is now often applied in computational molecular or structural biology, ecology, and pattern recognition, among other fields.

The skill bundle classified as AI applications has deep learning, NLP, and Tensorflow at the center, which are each highly correlated with neural networks. This should come as no surprise given that deep learning is based on neural networks and more recently on software libraries, like Tensorflow, for deep learning coding. Besides computer and information research scientists, these skills tend to be sought in software developers (e.g. database developers or software applications engineers) and, although to a much lesser extent, even in engineers, market research analysts, or accountants. Vacancies requiring NLP-related skills often go beyond computer and mathematical occupations and even extend to detectives and criminal investigators as well as truck and delivery service drivers. They are characterized by competencies related to speech recognition, machine translation, text mining, sentiment analysis, and the Natural Language Toolkit, which is a suite of libraries and programs for NLP written in Python.

As mentioned before, robotics is an example of a field that evokes but does not necessarily rely on AI as such (Baruffaldi et al., 2020). Nevertheless, it is one of the top ten skills Samek, Squicciarini and Cammeraat (2021) identify in US and UK AI-related online vacancies and usually encompasses competencies related to machine vision, autonomous and robot operating systems, motion planning, cyber-physical systems, and simultaneous localization and mapping. Given the frequent application of vision systems in robotics, e.g. in the automotive industry, pharmacy, military, and police equipment, it is not surprising to find the robotics-related skill bundle linked to computer vision, which Samek, Squicciarini and Cammeraat (2021) classify as an AI application. Moreover, several computer vision skills are based on deep learning algorithms and are developed on deep learning frameworks, a fact that explains the proximity of these items to the AI application bundle.

Shedding light on the full set of skills needed to perform AI-related jobs requires looking beyond specialistic AI-related skills, and analyzing the extent to which other cognitive and socio-emotional skills are sought after when recruiting individuals expected to work with AI. The following subsection thus focuses on all skills demanded in such jobs.

8.2.2 Cognitive and Socio-Emotional Skills Complement AI-Specialistic Skills

The importance of cognitive skills such as literacy, numeracy, problem-solving, and socio-emotional skills to thrive in the digital and interconnected global economy has been widely acknowledged (OECD, 2016; 2017b; Muller and Safir, 2019). Evidence shows that this also applies to AI-related jobs.

Overall, a trend towards requiring a set of generic skills emerges, which often relates to "tools of the job".

For instance, De Mauro et al. (2018) analyze big data related to online vacancies and confirm Miller's (2014) findings that skill requirements for data scientists go beyond their expertise in analytical methods. Relying on natural clustering, they distinguish between technology enablers, i.e. technical roles with a focus on systems and applications; and business-impacting professionals, i.e. business-oriented roles concerned with data analysis and economic impact. Stephany (2020) uses an endogenous clustering approach to investigate skill profiles containing AI and finds that competencies tend to be grouped around software and technology but also administrative and support work. Although the most frequently mentioned skills, besides programming languages, relate to ML, data science, NLP, neural networks, and data analysis/mining/visualization, smaller skill groups also emerge around the areas of product design, translation, editing, marketing, and law. Based on research carried out by the venture capital fund MMC Ventures (2019), Lane and Saint-Martin (2021) conclude that in addition to a doctoral degree in mathematics, statistics, or programming, AI jobs at the top end of the market require increasingly sector-specific, engineering and commercial competencies, reaffirming the need to also examine non-AI skills in AI-related jobs. At the same time, Toney and Flagg (2020) find that roughly 80% of all AI jobs require a bachelor's degree with a declining share requiring qualifications beyond that. This may likely stem from catching-up effects, and AI being more widely adopted, rather than only or mostly developed.

Samek, Squicciarini and Cammeraat (2021) analysis of AI talent finds that, over time, individuals required to work with AI need to be endowed with a progressively wider range of competencies related to computer programming and software, the management and visualization of big data, data analysis more broadly as well as socio-economic skills. This is shown in Figure 8.2, which zooms in on the top 30 skills demanded in recent US AI job postings (i.e. both AI specialistic skills and non-AI related skills).

Skills related to big data and data science constitute a considerable part of the skills profiles of AI-related jobs, especially in more recent years, possibly because big data, paired with cloud computing, has enabled breakthroughs in ML (Chen, 2012). In the past, a considerable part of the skillset of AI jobs were related to software engineering and development, including specific programming languages, such as Perl scripting language or Hypertext Preprocessor, and operating systems, such as Unix and Linux. More recently, software engineering and development seem to have lost relative importance although programming-related skills, such as Python and Java, gained prominence due to their role in managing big data. However, to use big data effectively, data science-related abilities and further data analysis tools, such as other programming languages like R and SAS, as well as data mining, are in demand. After all, AI agents are often expected to comb through the vast amount of data collected by, e.g., businesses to help identify business

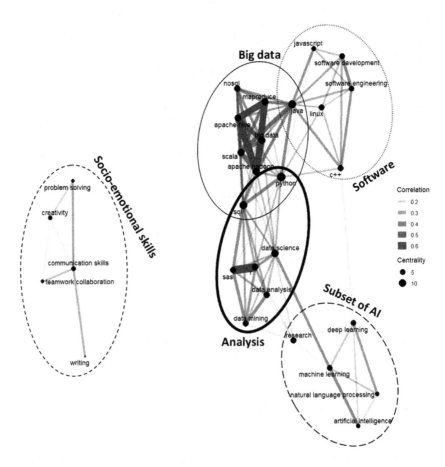

Figure 8.2 Top 30 skills in AI-related jobs, United States, 2017–2019

Note: To aid presentation, only edges with a correlation exceeding 0.1 are shown here. The identified skill bundles are: (1) programming and software-related skills; (2) management of big data; (3) data analysis tools and broader analytical skills, and (4) socio-emotional skills. An additional circled bundle emerges with different subsets of AI technologies.

Source: Samek, Squicciarini and Cammeraat (2021) using Lightcast data (June 2021).

opportunities and optimize product or process development. With data science being an interdisciplinary field, which uses scientific methods and algorithms in a view to extracting knowledge from structured and unstructured data, it serves the purpose of applying those actionable insights from data across a broad range of application domains.

As shown in Figure 8.2, more cognitive skills are consistently demanded in combination with socio-emotional skills, including written and verbal communication, problem-solving, creativity, and teamwork-related competencies. This possibly reflects the need to communicate among and with the team, and to complement AI-specific competencies as well as software-related skills, which amount to about one-third of the skills required in AI jobs, although to different extents in different countries (Squicciarini and Nachtigall, 2021).

Similar conclusions are reached by Van Laar et al. (2017) who argue that 21st-century skills do not necessarily need to be underpinned by information and communication technologies (ICTs). Based on a systematic literature review of more than 1,500 articles, they identify technical, information management, communication, collaboration, creativity, critical thinking, and problem-solving as the seven core skills needed in today's jobs. These are accompanied by ethical awareness, cultural awareness, flexibility, self-direction, and lifelong learning as contextual skills. These findings are very much in line with work relying on survey data finding that self-organization, management, and communication skills are highly rewarded in the labor market, especially in digital-intensive industries, because of their contribution to economic performance (OECD, 2017a; Grundke et al., 2018). Anderson (2017) finds that diverse skill sets are associated with higher wage premia than specialized skills only and that workers with synergistic skill diversity, i.e. skill combinations filling a gap in the market, earn more than workers whose diverse skills can be applied independently on numerous jobs. More generally, recent work exploring productivity and wage premia stemming from skill complementarities provides empirical evidence that skill bundles are more valuable than the sum of their parts (Anderson, 2017; Grundke et al., 2017; 2018; Stephany, 2020).

8.3 Nurturing Human Capital to Adapt to AI-Induced Changes

The aforementioned findings raise important questions for policy in terms of how to best ensure that workers, especially less-skilled workers, are endowed with the skills needed to work with AI and facilitate innovation (Agrawal, Gans and Goldfarb, 2018; Cockburn, Henderson and Stern, 2018; Gierten et al., 2021) as well as increase productivity (Brynjolfsson, Rock and Syverson, 2017; Corrado, Haskel and Jona-Lasinio, 2021; Rammer, Czarnitzki and Fernández, 2021). Moreover, if AI development and adoption pick up, as one would hope for the abovementioned performance reasons, suitable matches in the labor market will need to be fostered to make sure that those, whose skills do not match, can still find, stay or move to suitable jobs.

One possible solution relates to the promotion and facilitation of upskilling, i.e. the improvement of skills within the existing skill portfolio, and reskilling, i.e. the acquisition of new skills outside of the existing skill portfolio (Jaiswal, Arun and Varma, 2021). However, the uptake of training and essentially lifelong learning depends on learners' attitudes and dispositions, which parents and teachers play a big part in shaping (OECD, 2021), and there are no "one-size-fits-all" recipes. Skills needs depend on a number of factors, including initial skill endowment, training needs, and the time and money available to be invested in re- or upskilling (Bechichi et al., 2018; Escobari, Seyal and Meaney, 2019; Stephany, 2021). In other words, previously acquired skills may lower the entry barrier into new skill domains and hence reduce costs. A good example are programming languages which have an underlying similarity to language logic (Stephany, 2021).

Analysis based on the tasks that workers perform on the job, workers' skills endowment, and learning possibilities shows that the cost of moving to a different job (either within the same firm or elsewhere) is non-trivial (Andrieu et al., 2019). Andrieu et al. (2019) estimate that, at the country level, the minimum cost of moving workers in occupations at high risk of automation (assumed to be 14% of the labor force following Arntz, Gregory and Zierahn 2017) to occupations, which the authors call "safe haven", ranges between 1% and 5% of one year GDP in the countries considered. Regardless of the duration of the training needed, which may span several years, and the fact that training does not need to happen at the same time for all workers to be relocated, the costs of such training may prove hard to sustain for countries and firms alike.

To further complicate matters, Ramos (2022) correctly points out that selection into the treatment often applies in two ways. First, evidence shows that workers needing training the most are those who less frequently receive it. Training, especially if sponsored by firms, is often used as a reward mechanism for the best performing and most skilled workers, as this ultimately pays off in terms of firms' returns on investment (Squicciarini, Marcolin and Horvát, 2015; Dostie, 2020). Second, less-skilled individuals are at times those that find it relatively more challenging to engage in education, progress in the education system, or simply go to school and learn (Bechichi et al., 2018; Andrieu et al., 2019).

Overall, these concerns strengthen the fear that those that are already left behind may further suffer from the AI revolution. The new technological paradigm (Dosi, 1982), which AI represents, risks widening already existing divides and inequalities, and to create new ones. At the individual worker level, Andrieu et al. (2019) find that re- and upskilling costs increase with the cognitive skills of workers in the occupation of origin, that is the lower the level of initial skill endowment, the greater the training needed; costs also increase with the proportion of workers at high risk of automation in the manufacturing sector and with the average age of workers in the occupation.

Compared to men, women are even more likely to miss out given girls' relatively lower educational enrolment in disciplines that would allow them to engage with AI (e.g. STEM and ICT), coupled with women's limited use of digital tools (OECD, 2018). At 15 years of age, on average across OECD countries, only 0.5% of girls wish to become ICT professionals, compared to 5% of boys, and twice as many boys as girls expect to become engineers, scientists, or architects.

These expectations persist: Stanford's Institute for Human-Centered Artificial Intelligence (HAI)'s shows that women accounted for less than 19% of all AI and computer science Ph.D. graduates in North America over the past ten years (Jensen, 2021). Moreover, according to the Alan Turing Institute, only 10–15% of ML researchers are women in leading technology companies and, on average, only 12% of authors who had contributed work to the leading three ML conferences in 2017 were women (Young, Wajcman and Sprejer, 2021). At present, lack of diversity triggers fundamental ethical issues of social and economic justice and jeopardizes the value that diversity may bring. In addition, as AI becomes ubiquitous, lack of diversity gets engrained and feeds loops whereby gender biases get built into AI systems and AI-related products, thus making the future even more unequal and gender-biased. However, this discussion is beyond the scope of this chapter. Ramos (2022) provides a detailed discussion on challenges, opportunities, and actionable policies in the era of AI.

The positive takeaway is that all workers if duly trained, can move to a different occupation and perform different tasks. Therefore, even if AI-related jobs require at times new and different sets of skills for workers to be able to accomplish the tasks that working with AI entails, becoming or remaining unemployed is not something that needs to happen. Of course, in the absence of sufficient support, and if (gender-specific) biases and expectations about professions persist, the new technological paradigm that AI represents may further contribute to marginalizing workers that are already on the left-hand side of the distribution in terms of income, skills, or tenure. This would jeopardize their inclusion, not only in the world of work but more generally in society.

8.4 Concluding Remarks

AI and digitalization change the type and distribution of job tasks that workers are asked to perform, and the skills required for the purpose (OECD, 2017b; 2019). While the new technological paradigm (Dosi, 1982), which AI represents, promises to bring about great opportunities, it nevertheless risks widening already existing divides and inequalities and creating new ones. Existing studies point to both, the possible job offsetting consequences of AI adoption and deployment, and the fact that AI creates new (types of) jobs. Therefore, AI offers opportunities to some individuals, by contributing to the emergence of new occupational profiles and complementing existing ones, while presenting challenges to others, by making certain tasks obsolete or redundant and, hence, destroying jobs that are intensive in such tasks. For now, AI does not seem to have any detectable labor market impacts at the aggregate occupation or industry level, though such effects may occur in the future (Acemoglu et al., 2022; Squicciarini and Staccioli, 2022).

The question thus becomes how to nurture and prepare human capital to adapt to AI-induced changes. With AI being a GPT that evolves rapidly and penetrates firms, industries, and countries to different extents at a different speeds (Calvino and Criscuolo, 2019), it becomes as important as challenging to identify the skills needed to succeed today in these new technology-rich work environments and to continue doing so tomorrow as well. This helps prioritize interventions and informs the design of policies fostering the development of the human capital needed for AI to become the economically and societally enhancing technology countries hope for.

Existing evidence suggests that, regardless of whether their job entails developing or adopting AI, AI workers are technically skilled people, who need a set of AI skills related to ML, data mining, cluster analysis, NLP, and robotics. In fact, skills related to the open-source programming software Python and ML represent "must-haves" for working with AI. At the same time, new evidence points to the need of endowing workers with both, technical and socio-emotional skills, if they are to work with AI and be able to benefit from the opportunities offered by digital technologies. Skill bundles related to programming, management of big data, and data analysis are particularly demanded. This is becoming even more important in light of the accelerated adoption and deployment of AI technologies triggered by COVID-19, and the consequent increase in the demand for data scientists and AI experts in both, advanced and developing countries.

However, skill endowment does not stop during early life. Access to quality education for all, independently of age or gender; the need to provide especially girls and women with opportunities to participate in STEM-related education and training; and lifelong learning become a must. It is paramount in light of the constant evolution of AI-related technologies, with the growing need for more or different skills to work with AI, and job-to-job transitions becoming more frequent as job tenures shorten.

All this calls for systemic and systematic approaches bringing together different stakeholders, including education, industry, and community representatives, in order to meet the challenges of the AI era and the fact that individual skills, competencies, and abilities vary importantly. Making sure that nobody is left behind requires endowing individuals with the "right" skills for today's and tomorrow's increasingly digital and globalized world, and making them aware of the possible ethical challenges that the use and abuse of general purpose and pervasive technologies like AI may entail. This is key to ensuring that we have inclusive labor markets that are also conducive to innovation, growth, and well-being.

Notes

1   With automation being a key feature of AI technologies, e.g. by connecting robots, sensors and often using big data for production process optimization (i.e. Industry 4.0), much research considers robotics to be an integral part of AI (European Commission. Joint Research Centre, 2018; Fujii and Managi, 2018; WIPO, 2019).

2   There are no commercial applications yet, due to the considerable technical, economical and logistical challenges of rolling them out in classrooms.

3   They further identify a rather small skill bundle consisting of AI IT, which first encompassed Python and MapReduce. More recently, it expanded into the faster

alternative to MapReduce, namely Spark, and the open-source libraries Vowpal Wabbit, which allows fast learning on big data, and XGBoost, which provides a framework for gradient boosting, signaling a new era of big data.

4 A neuro-fuzzy system is a learning machine that is trained by a learning algorithm derived from neural network theory. Although fuzzy systems and neural networks tend to be used if no mathematical model exists to solve the problem otherwise, a fuzzy system demands linguistic rules as prior knowledge while neural networks rely on learning examples.

Bibliography

Acemoglu, D. et al. (2022), "Artificial Intelligence and Jobs: Evidence from Online Vacancies", *Journal of Labor Economics*, Vol. 40/S1, pp. S293–S340, https://doi.org/10.1086/718327.

Acemoglu, D. and P. Restrepo (2018), "The Race between Man and Machine: Implications of Technology for Growth, Factor Shares, and Employment", *American Economic Review*, Vol. 108/6, pp. 1488–1542, https://doi.org/10.1257/aer.20160696.

Aghion, P., B. Jones and C. Jones (2017), *Artificial Intelligence and Economic Growth*, National Bureau of Economic Research, Cambridge, MA, https://doi.org/10.3386/w23928.

Agrawal, A., J. Gans and A. Goldfarb (2019), "Artificial Intelligence: The Ambiguous Labor Market Impact of Automating Prediction", *Journal of Economic Perspectives*, Vol. 33/2, pp. 31–50, https://doi.org/10.1257/jep.33.2.31.

Agrawal, A., J. Gans and A. Goldfarb (2018), *Prediction Machines: The Simple Economics of Artificial Intelligence*, Harvard Business Review Press, Cambridge, MA.

Alekseeva, L. et al. (2021), "The Demand for AI Skills in the Labor Market", *Labour Economics*, Vol. 71, p. 102002, https://doi.org/10.1016/j.labeco.2021.102002.

Anderson, K. (2017), "Skill Networks and Measures of Complex Human Capital", *Proceedings of the National Academy of Sciences*, Vol. 114/48, pp. 12720–12724, https://doi.org/10.1073/pnas.1706597114.

Andrieu, E. et al. (2019), "Occupational transitions: The cost of moving to a "safe haven"", *OECD Science, Technology and Industry Policy Papers*, No. 61, OECD Publishing, Paris, https://doi.org/10.1787/6d3f9bff-en.

Arntz, M., T. Gregory and U. Zierahn (2017), "Revisiting the Risk of Automation", *Economics Letters*, Vol. 159, pp. 157–160, https://doi.org/10.1016/j.econlet.2017.07.001.

Autor, D. (2022), *The Labor Market Impacts of Technological Change: From Unbridled Enthusiasm to Qualified Optimism to Vast Uncertainty*, National Bureau of Economic Research, Cambridge, MA, https://doi.org/10.3386/w30074.

Autor, D., F. Levy and R. Murnane (2003), "The Skill Content of Recent Technological Change: An Empirical Exploration", *The Quarterly Journal of Economics*, Vol. 118/4, pp. 1279–1333, https://doi.org/10.1162/003355303322552801.

Autor, D. and A. Salomons (2018), *Is Automation Labor-Displacing? Productivity Growth, Employment, and the Labor Share*, National Bureau of Economic Research, Cambridge, MA, https://doi.org/10.3386/w24871.

Baker, R. (2021), "Artificial intelligence in education: Bringing it all together", *OECD Digital Education Outlook 2021: Pushing the Frontiers with Artificial Intelligence, Blockchain and Robots*, OECD Publishing, Paris, https://doi.org/10.1787/f54ea644-en.

Baruffaldi, S. et al. (2020), "Identifying and measuring developments in artificial intelligence: Making the impossible possible", *OECD Science, Technology and Industry Working Papers*, No. 2020/05, OECD Publishing, Paris, https://doi.org/10.1787/5f65ff7e-en.

Bechichi, N. et al. (2018), "Moving between jobs: An analysis of occupation distances and skill needs", *OECD Science, Technology and Industry Policy Papers*, No. 52, OECD Publishing, Paris, https://doi.org/10.1787/d35017ee-en.

Belpaeme, T. and F. Tanaka (2021), "Social Robots as educators", *OECD Digital Education Outlook 2021: Pushing the Frontiers with Artificial Intelligence, Blockchain and Robots*, OECD Publishing, Paris, https://doi.org/10.1787/1c3b1d56-en.

Bessen, J. (2019), "Automation and Jobs: When Technology Boosts Employment★", *Economic Policy*, Vol. 34/100, pp. 589–626, https://doi.org/10.1093/epolic/eiaa001.

Bi, W. et al. (2019), "Artificial Intelligence in Cancer Imaging: Clinical Challenges and Applications", *CA: A Cancer Journal for Clinicians*, Vol. 69, No. 2, pp. 127–157, https://doi.org/10.3322/caac.21552.

Brynjolfsson, E., T. Mitchell and D. Rock (2018), "What Can Machines Learn and What Does It Mean for Occupations and the Economy?", *AEA Papers and Proceedings*, Vol. 108, pp. 43–47, https://doi.org/10.1257/pandp.20181019.

Brynjolfsson, E., D. Rock and C. Syverson (2017), *Artificial Intelligence and the Modern Productivity Paradox: A Clash of Expectations and Statistics*, National Bureau of Economic Research, Cambridge, MA, https://doi.org/10.3386/w24001.

Calvino, F. and C. Criscuolo (2019), "Business dynamics and digitalisation", *OECD Science, Technology and Industry Policy Papers*, No. 62, OECD Publishing, Paris, https://doi.org/10.1787/6e0b011a-en.

Cammeraat, E., L. Samek and M. Squicciarini (2021a), "Management, skills and productivity", *OECD Science, Technology and Industry Policy Papers*, No. 101, OECD Publishing, Paris, https://doi.org/10.1787/007f399e-en.

Cammeraat, E., L. Samek and M. Squicciarini (2021b), "The role of innovation and human capital for the productivity of industries", *OECD Science, Technology and Industry Policy Papers*, No. 103, OECD Publishing, Paris, https://doi.org/10.1787/197c6ae9-en.

Carbonero, F., E. Ernst and E. Weber (2020), "Robots worldwide: The impact of automation on employment and trade", *Institute for Employment Research* IAB-Discussion Paper, No. 7/2020.

Chen, K. (2012), "Building High-Level Features using Large Scale Unsupervised Learning", *arxiv*, July, v5, https://arxiv.org/abs/1112.6209.

Cockburn, I., R. Henderson and S. Stern (2018), *The Impact of Artificial Intelligence on Innovation*, National Bureau of Economic Research, Cambridge, MA, https://doi.org/10.3386/w24449.

Corrado, C., J. Haskel and C. Jona-Lasinio (2021), "Artificial Intelligence and Productivity: An Intangible Assets Approach", *Oxford Review of Economic Policy*, Vol. 37/3, pp. 435–458, https://doi.org/10.1093/oxrep/grab018.

De Mauro, A. et al. (2018), "Human Resources for Big Data Professions: A Systematic Classification of Job Roles and Required Skill Sets", *Information Processing & Management*, Vol. 54/5, pp. 807–817, https://doi.org/10.1016/j.ipm.2017.05.004.

Dosi, G. (1982), "Technological Paradigms and Technological Trajectories", *Research Policy*, Vol. 11/3, pp. 147–162, https://doi.org/10.1016/0048-7333(82)90016-6.

Dostie, B. (2020), "Who Benefits from Firm-Sponsored Training?", *IZA World of Labor*, https://doi.org/10.15185/izawol.145.v2.

Escobari, M., I. Seyal and M. Meaney (2019), *Realism About Reskilling: Upgrading the Career Prospects of America's Low-Wage Workers*, The Brookings Institution, Washington, DC.

European Commission. Joint Research Centre (2018), *Artificial Intelligence: A European Perspective*, Publications Office of the European Union, Luxembourg, https://doi.org/10.2760/936974.

Felten, E., M. Raj and R. Seamans (2019), "The Variable Impact of Artificial Intelligence on Labor: The Role of Complementary Skills and Technologies", *SSRN Electronic Journal*, https://doi.org/10.2139/ssrn.3368605.

Frey, C. and M. Osborne (2017), "The Future of Employment: How Susceptible are Jobs to Computerisation?", *Technological Forecasting and Social Change*, Vol. 114, pp. 254–280, https://doi.org/10.1016/j.techfore.2016.08.019.

Fujii, H. and S. Managi (2018), "Trends and Priority Shifts in Artificial Intelligence Technology Invention: A Global Patent Analysis", *Economic Analysis and Policy*, Vol. 58, pp. 60–69, https://doi.org/10.1016/j.eap.2017.12.006.

Gathmann, C. and U. Schönberg (2010), "How General Is Human Capital? A Task-Based Approach", *Journal of Labor Economics*, Vol. 28/1, pp. 1–49, https://doi.org/10.1086/649786.

Georgieff, A. and R. Hyee (2021), "Artificial intelligence and employment : New cross-country evidence", *OECD Social, Employment and Migration Working Papers*, No. 265, OECD Publishing, Paris, https://doi.org/10.1787/c2c1d276-en.

Gibbons, R. and M. Waldman (2004), "Task-Specific Human Capital", *American Economic Review*, Vol. 94/2, pp. 203–207, https://doi.org/10.1257/0002828041301579.

Gierten, D. et al. (2021), "Firms going digital: Tapping into the potential of data for innovation", *OECD Digital Economy Papers*, No. 320, OECD Publishing, Paris, https://doi.org/10.1787/ee8340c1-en.

Gries, T. and W. Naudé (2018), "Artificial intelligence, Jobs, inequality and productivity: Does aggregate demand matter?", *IZA Discussion Paper Series*, 12005.

Grundke, R. et al. (2017), "Having the right mix: The role of skill bundles for comparative advantage and industry performance in GVCs", *OECD Science, Technology and Industry Working Papers*, No. 2017/03, OECD Publishing, Paris, https://doi.org/10.1787/892a4787-en.

Grundke, R. et al. (2018), "Which skills for the digital era?: Returns to skills analysis", *OECD Science, Technology and Industry Working Papers*, No. 2018/09, OECD Publishing, Paris, https://doi.org/10.1787/9a9479b5-en.

Grus, J. (2019), *Data Science from Scratch*, O'Reilly Media, Inc., Newton, MA.

Hernández-Lemus, E. (2021), "Random Fields in Physics, Biology and Data Science", *Frontiers in Physics*, Vol. 9, pp. 1–19, https://doi.org/10.3389/fphy.2021.641859.

Jaiswal, A., C. Arun and A. Varma (2021), "Rebooting Employees: Upskilling for Artificial Intelligence in Multinational Corporations", *The International Journal of Human Resource Management*, Vol. 33/6, pp. 1179–1208, https://doi.org/10.1080/09585192.2021.1891114.

Jensen, B. (2021), *AI Index Diversity Report: An Unmoving Needle*, https://hai.stanford.edu/news/ai-index-diversity-report-unmoving-needle.

Lane, M. and A. Saint-Martin (2021), "The impact of Artificial Intelligence on the labour market: What do we know so far?", *OECD Social, Employment and Migration Working Papers*, No. 256, OECD Publishing, Paris, https://doi.org/10.1787/7c895724-en.

Maloney, W. and C. Molina (2019), "Is automation labor-displacing in the developing countries, too? robots, polarization, and jobs", *World Bank* Working Paper 08, https://openknowledge.worldbank.org/handle/10986/33301.

Manyika, J. et al. (2017), *Jobs lost, jobs gained: What the future of work will mean for jobs, skills, and wages.*

Marcolin, L., S. Miroudot and M. Squicciarini (2018), "To Be (Routine) or not to Be (Routine), That is the Question: A Cross-Country Task-Based Answer†", *Industrial and Corporate Change*, Vol. 28/3, pp. 477–501, https://doi.org/10.1093/icc/dty020.

Miller, S. (2014), "Collaborative Approaches Needed to Close the Big Data Skills Gap", *Journal of Organization Design*, Vol. 3/1, p. 26, https://doi.org/10.7146/jod.9823.

MMC Ventures (2019), *The State of AI 2019: Divergence*, http://www.stateofai2019.com/.

Muller, N. and A. Safir (2019), "What employers actually want: Skills in demand in online job vacancies in Ukraine", *World Bank Group Working Papers,* No. 1932, http://documents1.worldbank.org/curated/en/344171559904342136/pdf/What-Employers-Actually-Want-Skills-in-Demand-in-Online-Job-Vacancies-in-Ukraine.pdf.

Muro, M., R. Maxim and J. Whiton (2019), *Automation and Artificial Intelligence – How Machines are Affecting People and Places*, https://www.brookings.edu/wp-content/uploads/2019/01/2019.01_BrookingsMetro_Automation-AI_Report_Muro-Maxim-Whiton-FINAL-version.pdf.

Nedelkoska, L. and G. Quintini (2018), "Automation, skills use and training", *OECD Social, Employment and Migration Working Papers*, No. 202, OECD Publishing, Paris, https://doi.org/10.1787/2e2f4eea-en.

OECD (2021), *OECD Skills Outlook 2021: Learning for Life*, OECD Publishing, Paris, https://doi.org/10.1787/0ae365b4-en.

OECD (2019), *OECD Skills Outlook 2019: Thriving in a Digital World*, OECD Publishing, Paris, https://doi.org/10.1787/df80bc12-en.

OECD (2018), *Bridging the Digital Gender Divide*, OECD Publishing, Paris.

OECD (2017a), *OECD Science, Technology and Industry Scoreboard 2017: The Digital Transformation*, OECD Publishing, Paris, https://doi.org/10.1787/9789264268821-en.

OECD (2017b), *OECD Skills Outlook 2017: Skills and Global Value Chains*, OECD Publishing, Paris, https://doi.org/10.1787/9789264273351-en.

OECD (2016), "New Skills for the Digital Economy: Measuring the demand and supply of ICT skills at work", *OECD Digital Economy Papers*, No. 258, OECD Publishing, Paris, https://doi.org/10.1787/5jlwnkm2fc9x-en.

Polanyi, M. (2009), *The Tacit Dimension*, University of Chicago Press, Chicago, IL.

Rammer, C., D. Czarnitzki and G. Fernández (2021), "Artificial Intelligence and Industrial Innovation: Evidence From Firm-Level Data", *SSRN Electronic Journal*, https://doi.org/10.2139/ssrn.3829822.

Ramos, G. (2022), "A.I.'s Impact on Jobs, Skills, and the Future of Work: The UNESCO Perspective on Key Policy Issues and the Ethical Debate", *New England Journal of Public Policy*, Vol. 34/1, pp. 1–13.

Samek, L., M. Squicciarini and E. Cammeraat (2021), "The human capital behind AI: Jobs and skills demand from online job postings", *OECD Science, Technology and Industry Policy Papers*, No. 120, OECD Publishing, Paris, https://doi.org/10.1787/2e278150-en.

Squicciarini, M., L. Marcolin and P. Horvát (2015), "Estimating cross-country investment in training: An experimental methodology using PIAAC data", *OECD*

Science, Technology and Industry Working Papers, No. 2015/9, OECD Publishing, Paris, https://doi.org/10.1787/5jrs3sftp8nw-en.

Squicciarini, M. and H. Nachtigall (2021), "Demand for AI skills in jobs: Evidence from online job postings", *OECD Science, Technology and Industry Working Papers*, No. 2021/03, OECD Publishing, Paris, https://doi.org/10.1787/3ed32d94-en.

Squicciarini, M. and J. Staccioli (2022), "Labour-saving technologies and employment levels: Are robots really making workers redundant?", *OECD Science, Technology and Industry Policy Papers*, No. 124, OECD Publishing, Paris, https://doi.org/10.1787/9ce86ca5-en.

Stephany, F. (2021), "One Size Does Not Fit All: Constructing Complementary Digital Reskilling Strategies using Online Labour Market Data", *Big Data and Society*, Vol. 8/1, p. 205395172110031, https://doi.org/10.1177/20539517211003120.

Stephany, F. (2020), "Does It Pay Off to Learn a New Skill? Revealing the Economic Benefits of Cross-Skilling", *SSRN Electronic Journal*, https://doi.org/10.2139/ssrn.3717077.

Toney, A. and M. Flagg (2020), *U.S. Demand for AI-Related Talent*, Center for Security and Emerging Technology, Washington, DC, https://doi.org/10.51593/20200027.

van Deursen, A. and J. van Dijk (2014), *Digital Skills: Unlocking the Information Society*, Palgrave Macmillan, New York.

van Laar, E. et al. (2017), "The Relation Between 21st-Century Skills and Digital Skills: A Systematic Literature Review", *Computers in Human Behavior*, Vol. 72, pp. 577–588, https://doi.org/10.1016/j.chb.2017.03.010.

Webb, M. (2019), "The Impact of Artificial Intelligence on the Labor Market", *SSRN Electronic Journal*, https://doi.org/10.2139/ssrn.3482150.

Wilson, H., P. Daugherty and N. Bianzino (2017), "The Jobs That Artificial Intelligence Will Create", *MIT Sloan Management Review*, Vol. 58/4, pp. 13–16.

WIPO (2019), *WIPO Technology Trends 2019 – Artificial Intelligence*, WIPO, Geneva, https://doi.org/10.34667/tind.29086.

Wood, A. et al. (2018), "Good Gig, Bad Gig: Autonomy and Algorithmic Control in the Global Gig Economy", *Work, Employment and Society*, Vol. 33/1, pp. 56–75, https://doi.org/10.1177/0950017018785616.

World Economic Forum (2020), *The Future of Jobs Report 2020*, World Economic Forum, Geneva, http://www3.weforum.org/docs/WEF_Future_of_Jobs_2020.pdf.

World Economic Forum (2016), *The Future of Jobs 2016*, World Economic Forum, Geneva, http://www3.weforum.org/docs/WEF_Future_of_Jobs.pdf.

Young, E., J. Wajcman and L. Sprejer (2021), *Where Are the Women? Mapping the Gender Job Gap in AI*, The Alan Turing Institute, London

9 AI for Sustainability

A Dangerous Fantasy or an Unfulfilled Potential

Daniela Inclezan and Luis I. Prádanos

9.1 Introduction

During the last few years, a proliferation of scientific reports confirms the obvious: the constant global expansion of a fossil fuel-based techno-industrial economic metabolism is incompatible with life on a finite planet. The more this economic system globalizes, the faster the living systems of the planet collapse. In a recent article in *Nature*, Elhacham et al found that human-made things now overweight all biomass on Earth (2020). In other words, global economic activity is transforming life into infrastructure and there-fore destroying the web of life on which human communities depend. The 2018 *WWF Living Planet Report* revealed "that population sizes of wildlife decreased by 60% globally between 1970 and 2014." Similar disturbing conclusions were published in 2019 by the IPBES in their *Global Assessment Report on Biodiversity and Ecosystem Services*. This process of "biological anni-hilation" (Ceballos, Ehrlich, and Dirzo, 2017) seems to be the result of the globalization of an extractivist and growth-oriented economic culture that is clashing with the biophysical limits of Earth (Herrington, 2020). The logic of this dominant economic culture is deeply encoded into our techno-social systems and has lately been automated and amplified by our machine learning technologies.

Our civilization is in a serious ecological overshoot. Machine-learning-based AI systems, which were passively adopted *en masse* in recent years and rapidly deployed by both private and public institutions without time for scrutiny (Truby, 2020, p. 948), have contributed to a significant acceleration of existing trends toward increasing ecological depletion, energy consump-tion, and global inequality. These ongoing AI implementations within the context of a profit-maximizing and growth-oriented economic culture are making our most pressing interrelated issues—ecological breakdown, energy decline, and social corrosion—much worse.

Sustainable Development Goals (SDGs) were incorporated into UN prior-ities in 2015 with a target date of 2030, but these goals are not free from the bias towards the unrealistic idea that constant economic development is possible on a finite planet. SDG 8 for example strives to achieve "sustainable economic

DOI: 10.4324/9781003304616-13

growth," while SDG 9 advocates for "sustainable industrialization."[1] SDGs have been criticized for reflecting a top-down approach that ignores local realities and different ways of thinking. They mirror the belief that the environment is just a resource to be used and managed (see SDG 14 to "conserve and use the oceans, seas, and marine resources for sustainable development"), which contradicts indigenous worldviews that attribute agency not only to humans but to nonhumans as well.

An extensive empirical review of AI contributions to SDGs, followed by a consensus-based expert elicitation process, reported by Vinuesa et al (2020) indicates that AI can act as both an enabler and an inhibitor of SDG targets. The authors find that AI can support the accomplishment of 134 of the 169 targets (79%) associated with the 17 SDGs, while it may simultaneously negatively impact progress towards 59 targets (35%). When SDGs are divided into the three areas of Society, Economy, and Environment, AI is determined to have the greatest enabling effect on Environment goals (93%) and the highest inhibitor effect on Society goals (38%). Jon Truby (2020) considers examples from the finance world and similarly concludes that unchecked AI advances that may promote SDGs may be manipulated and misused in a way that damages progress towards them. Henrik Skaug Sætra (2021) critiques the methodology used by Vinuesa et al (2020) and argues that an analysis of the impact of AI on the accomplishment of SDGs must distinguish between direct and indirect effects, and also consider impacts as multiple levels: micro, meso, and macro. With such an analysis, the positive impacts of AI are much smaller (and less generalizable) than its possible negative effects. A common thread in these studies is the push for an ethical, transparent, accountable, and regulated advancement of AI.

We can conclude that, so far, the well-intentioned SDGs have not materialized into a more sustainable and just world. Rather, we are witnessing the *de facto* expansion of neoliberal economic globalization that confuses prosperity with an unchecked economic growth, which is biophysically incompatible with a finite planet. Within this globally dominant growth-oriented economic framework, technological development in general and the rapid evolution of AI applications, in particular, cannot properly address ecological overshoot and global inequality. A number of critical technology scholars find that machine learning implementations, which include the subclass of deep learning algorithms, are rather automating, accelerating, and exacerbating the existing troublesome trends that are making human societies more extinction-driven, extractivist, undemocratic, and unequal. Most importantly, AI technologies, as they are currently applied by corporations and governing agencies, are not only reinforcing and accelerating the unsustainable inertias of the dominant economic cultural paradigm but also making it more and more difficult to sustain alternative ways of perceiving and being in the world that are not inherently unsustainable, extractivist, and exploitative (Crawford, 2021, pp. 11–12).

9.2 Part I. Smart vs. Wise: Why Automating Unsustainable and Unfair Inertias may be Unwise

Making a destructive and unfair techno-social system faster and smarter may not be wise. It would be wiser to first embed the system within regenerative and equalitarian principles and, only then, sophisticate its functions and equip it with AI algorithms. Under the current historical conjunction, the social and ecological costs of wide implementations of machine learning technologies in everyday life are significant.

In terms of ecological costs of AI, we could enumerate the increasing energy demands to run data centers (Bridle, 2018, p. 63), train algorithms (Hao, 2019; Strubell, Ganesh, and McCallum, 2019; Bender et al, 2021), and produce and recharge smart devices of all kinds; the drastic and historically unprecedented acceleration of planetary extractivism facilitated by recent developments in AI (Arboleda, 2020), and the massive proliferation of mismanaged e-waste (more on the ecological downsides of AI in the next section). These costs are hidden by metaphors that create a false pretense of immateriality for our modern technology. We currently work in the intangible "cloud" (Srinivasan, 2017, p. 2), play games in virtual reality, and celebrate decreases in our carbon footprint that are due to working from home, but we tend to ignore the materiality of the devices we depend on for our remote work and entertainment, and the ever-increasing physical infrastructure that supports all of this.

The social costs of AI are somehow more theorized than its ecological costs. However, one cannot ignore the profound relationship between the two. Often the poorer and more marginalized populations pay the highest environmental price of technology, while the more privileged have the means to push forward and disproportionally benefit from a globally imposed extractivist, consumerist, and unsustainable way of life. As scholars working on social and political ecology have concluded, powerful actors mobilize the same "modern" hierarchical distinctions and classifications that perpetuate inequality, to also justify the unsustainable exploitation of nonhumans (Crawford, 2021, pp. 123–149). In other words, under the current economic and political incentives, technology is used by powerful actors to extract and accumulate wealth while simultaneously externalizing the social and ecological costs to others. Thus, as long as AI continues accelerating inequality, it will be an amplifier of unsustainability.

Substantial work still remains to be done to expose the true social costs of AI and undo the misleading public discourses disseminated by well-funded corporate think tanks and marketing strategies that emphasize and exaggerate the unfulfilled social promises of these technologies while grossly ignoring the factual negative consequences of its implementations. For instance, Cathy O'Neil describes in her 2016 book—*Weapons of Math Destruction. How Big Data Increase Inequality and Threatens Democracy*—the way in which the broad implementation of opaque machine processing technologies ends up punishing the poor and making the rich richer (O'Neil, 2016, p. 3). These technologies are highly biased and "often punish individuals that happen to *be* the exception" (O'Neil, 2016, p. 6), as these automated systems often perpetuate "many poisonous assumptions [that] are camouflaged by math and go largely untested and unquestioned" (O'Neil, 2016, p. 7). Virginia Eubanks arrives to similar conclusions in *Automating Inequality. How High-tech Tools Profile, Police, and Punish the Poor* (2017). Eubanks found that "Automated decision-making shatters the social safety net, criminalizes the poor, intensifies discrimination, and compromises democracy" (Eubanks, 2017, p. 12). The most vulnerable people are in fact "targets rather than beneficiaries of these systems" of data-based technologies when they are applied to public services (Eubanks, 2017, p. 9).

Both studies confirm that AI is automating and amplifying existing inequalities and power asymmetries. One of the reasons, as Sasha Costanza-Chock explains in *Design Justice. Community-Led Practices to Build the Worlds We Need* (2020), may be that "machine learning is intersectionally biased" (Costanza-Chock, 2020, p. 19) as most algorithmic decision support systems are designed and trained with selective data that reproduce the existing systemic oppression and societal prejudices. "Most design processes today therefore are structured in ways that make it impossible to see, engage with, account for, or attempt to remedy the unequal distribution of benefits and burdens that they reproduce" (Costanza-Chock, 2020, p. 19). Although unintentionally, machine learning processes happen to be unfair by design as existing asymmetrical power relations and biases "are encoded in and reproduced through the design of sociotechnical systems" (Costanza-Chock, 2020, p. 4). Fortunately, there is a "rapidly growing community of researchers... focused on challenging the ways that inequality is reproduced through the design of AI and algorithmic decision support systems" (Costanza-Chock, 2020, p. 9). We applaud these efforts and invite AI scholars to contribute to this much needed research to expose and correct the effects of algorithmic injustices.

Many other critical technology scholars and research journalists also agree that "Technology is in fact a key driver of inequality across many sectors" (Bridle, 2018, p. 113), which is true for AI specifically as well (Vinuesa et al., 2020; Sætra, 2021). This is bad news, considering that studies in epidemiology found out that growing inequality is socially damaging, undermines democracy, and makes more difficult to effectively address environmental issues (Wilkinson and Pickett, 2010). A number of recent studies suggest that the combination of widening inequality with increasing social polarization and political radicalization that is currently threatening democracies worldwide is exacerbated by machine learning technologies. This "algorithmic radicalisation" (Bridle, 2018, p. 212) is exemplified by YouTube recommendation algorithms that work by identifying what viewers like and increasing its "discoverability" (Bridle, 2018, p. 217). This means that each subsequent recommendation introduces a more radical content in relation to the previous one. Zeynep Tufekci goes as far as calling YouTube "the Great

Radicalizer" due to the fact that its recommender algorithms favor extremist and inflammatory content (2018). According to Tufekci, this troublesome escalation of extremist content likely has to do "with the nexus of artificial intelligence and Google's business model" that consists of "selling our attention to companies that will pay for it". As Bridle points out, "It is not about intention, but about a kind of violence inherent in the combination of digital systems and capitalist incentives" (Bridle, 2018, p. 230). Similarly, Facebook algorithms reward extremist content, facilitate radicalization of unstable people, and amplify misinformation campaigns because its business model is based on addiction and surveillance (Peirano, 2022, p. 55). In short, Big Tech companies do not design machine learning techniques to enhance the common good but to generate profit by amplifying what is popular and maximizing engagement. The unintended consequence is that "Entire cultural industries become feedback loops for an increasingly dominant narrative of fear and violence" (Bridle, 2018, p. 131) and, as a result, AI risks empowering dangerous political and corporate actors who deny or minimize the environmental crisis, disregard human rights, and even criminalize and target environmental activists (Dauvergne, 2020, pp. 17, 146, 196). This diverts our attention away from humanity's most existential and pressing socioecological problems, which prevents us from effectively dealing with these issues (Dauvergne, 2020, p. 9).

One of the main businesses of Big Tech corporations is to store massive databases and process them with machine learning algorithms to sell it to third parties. The more information they store and process the more powerful they become (Peirano, 2019, p. 119; Crawford, 2021, pp. 89–121). As these large firms dominate the market, they use their power to evade regulation and undermine innovation outside their sphere of influence by monopolizing the knowledge they gain in their opaque processes (Bessen, 2022). This increasing datafication and automation of everyday life does not make labor conditions better for most workers, as it was supposed to, but rather it is doing the opposite (Crawford, 2021, pp. 53–87), as it results in more concentration of power, increasing global inequality, and volatile labor markets (Kaplan, 2016). In fact, "Automation does not translate in leisure time", but in less labor bargaining power for the working class (Greenfield, 2017, p. 184). In other words, it seems that "Exploitation is encoded into the systems we are building" (Bridle, 2018, p. 229). These technologies are even colonizing our sleeping time and disrupting our resting patterns in many disturbing and unsustainable ways whose unintended consequences are impossible to foresee (Crary, 2013).

9.3 Part II. AI Material and Energy Intensities: The Inherent Unsustainability of High-tech Systems

The previous section suggests that the current implementation of AI technologies may be socially unsustainable if not significantly corrected. In this section, we explore how it may also be ecologically unviable. One of the most comprehensive books dealing with AI and sustainability is arguably Peter Dauvergne's *AI in the Wild. Sustainability in the Age of Artificial Intelligence* (2020). It provides a critical political economy lens that recognizes AI "not as benign or neutral but as a reflection of capitalism and an instrument of power" (Dauvergne, 2020, p. 7) due to high investments in its development from military and commercial interests (Dauvergne, 2020, p. 11). Dauvergne recognizes that AI is also a "valuable tool for fine-tuning environmental learning and management" (Dauvergne, 2020, p. 12). However, given how sociotechnical systems operate within our existing economic and political incentives, "the environmental applications of artificial intelligence have limited capacity to alter the political and economic forces underlying the escalating global sustainability crisis and tend to reflect the same anthropocentric and technocratic biases common to state management" (Dauvergne, 2020, p. 14).

Although most AI technologies are developed for commercial and military purposes, there are some machine learning projects focusing explicitly on sustainability issues (e.g., Global Fishing Watch, Rainforest Connection). However, as Dauvergne observes, "the primary energy underlying the upsurge in the use of AI for environmental research, conservation, and management is coming not from governments or transnational corporations but from a diverse array of nonprofits, startups, universities, and environmental advocacy organization" (Dauvergne, 2020, p. 68). Solutions coming from academia and nonprofit organizations suffer from a lack of connectivity, a smaller scope, and limitations in the number of contributors and resources. In academia in particular, there are more projects focusing on applications related to social justice than on sustainability issues (although the two problems are interdependent, as shown in the previous section). Most of them deal only with symptoms of environmental decline rather than its root causes. The two top-tier AI conferences—the conference of the Association for the Advancement of Artificial Intelligence (AAAI) and the International Joint Conferences on Artificial Intelligence (IJCAI)—have special tracks for research on socio-environmental issues, but the percentage of accepted papers that have a sustainability focus is relatively small. AAAI's "AI for Social Impact" track promotes research that addresses "pressing societal challenges, e.g., health, food, environment, education, governance, among others."[2] Out of the 50 papers accepted in this track in 2022,[3] roughly 24% have an environmental focus. IJCAI's track on "AI for Good" publishes research related to the UN's Sustainable Development Goals.[4] Only 21% of the 33 papers, project proposals, and demos accepted in 2022 targeted environmental goals.[5]

Most importantly, a majority of sustainability-focused projects are designed to manage more efficiently the highly entropic metabolism of growth-oriented, techno-industrial societies and to mitigate its increasingly disruptive environmental effects. Almost none of these projects are designed to reduce overall material and energy throughput in the global economy. Microsoft's

AI for Earth initiative, for instance, strives to build a Planetary Computer that "enables global-scale environmental monitoring by combining petabytes of data and spatial analysis tools"[6] by using "the power of the cloud."[7] This celebratory discourse fails to acknowledge the materiality and high environmental costs of storing and processing data while praising the results of the "digital revolution." According to Ramesh Srinivasan, the dominant technological culture suffers from a "recency-bias" (Srinivasan, 2017, p. 4), where new AI solutions are seen as the panacea for sustainability problems, in disfavor of history and context, including existing indigenous solutions that benefit from a long tradition of use, address root causes, and reflect systemic thinking. In contrast, the main goal of mainstream AI projects is to improve management practices rather than to promote and facilitate a transition to a socioeconomic metabolism decoupled from the obsession with growth that could be sustained in the long term by our finite and already overstressed planetary ecosystems.

This dominant techno-managerial approach to environmental issues strives to make an inherently unsustainable system more efficient rather than to transform it. As such, most AI technologies are currently intensifying and accelerating ongoing unsustainable forces. This means that basic needs of societies are getting more hyper-dependent on interconnected complex techno-industrial systems that are increasingly more difficult to sustain ecologically, energetically, economically, and geopolitically. This is especially disturbing when both the functionality of our food systems and our cities are getting increasingly dependent on technologies that are materially and energy intensive and will be biophysically unviable in the context of global energy decline, geopolitical instability, and ecological overshoot.

Radically transforming the global industrial food system and the dominant urban model are "the world's greatest sustainability needs" (Dauvergne, 2020, p. 15). The agroindustry is currently the main driver of biodiversity loss, topsoil depletion, and water pollution on a global scale. Modern urban processes are energy hyper-intensive systems that require massive continuous inputs of fossil fuels, materials, water, and food, and produce unmanageable quantities of waste and pollution. Urban and agroindustrial processes are two sides of the same interdependent linear extractivist metabolism that is rapidly destroying the web of life at a planetary scale (Brenner and Katsikis, 2020). Most AI projects targeting agricultural and urban issues are in fact intensifying and accelerating, rather than deescalating and transforming, the unsustainable and highly entropic urban-agro-industrial metabolism (Fernández Durán, 2010). Tech corporations are "empowering the agrifood industry" (Dauvergne, 2020, pp. 15–16) and promoting the development of smart cities—making these unsustainable high-tech models the default—rather than contesting the biophysical impossibility of universalizing these extractive and energy-devouring ways of producing food and organizing human societies.

The industrial food system is a threat in itself (Peirano, 2022, pp. 104–106) because it is unsustainable and extractivist by design—the more it is used the faster all the things that are needed to produce food are depleted (topsoil, water, agricultural biodiversity, available nutrients, traditional knowledge)—and so is the urban model that prioritizes consumerism and individual vehicles while segregating spaces by functions. Under this techno-managerial approach, "technologies are the protagonists and people are points on the map that are trapped in optimization processes designed to extract data" (Peirano, 2022, p. 139). "The smart city ideology is the one embraced by logistic corporations such as Amazon and Uber" (Peirano, 2022, p. 139). It is always a failure when implemented and it ultimately consumes more energy than what it saves (Peirano, 2022, pp. 140–144; for a critique of smart cities see Inclezan and Prádanos, 2017; Greenfield, 2013; Mattern, 2021).

Smart agriculture and smart city projects are mostly intended to make inherently unsustainable systems more efficient, rather than questioning and contesting their social desirability and environmental viability. High-tech "smart" projects absorb a disproportionate amount of public funds as corporate publicity claims that these projects provide the solution to complex social and ecological issues. This prevents society from supporting and developing "non-smart" readily available solutions that empower communities rather than big corporations, are less risky and less energy-intensive, are based on systems thinking and the understanding of the interdependency of agro-urban processes, and function by regenerating rather than by depleting the ecological systems in which they are integrated. Regenerative agriculture, agroecology, indigenous food systems, and permaculture, for instance, offer tested techniques and design processes able to produce healthy and highly nutritious food, sequester carbon, regenerate the soil, clean and retain water, support biodiversity, and empower local communities. Similarly, Transition Town's urban models as well as permaculture sites are designed for walkability and human scale, are integrated into their ecological and agrarian bioregions, favor public and multifunctional spaces, and promote locally managed clean energy sources (see https://transitionnetwork.org). These alternatives to the unsustainable high-tech agroindustry and high-tech urbanism strive to meet the needs of local communities while promoting social cohesion and environmental regeneration (see Inclezan and Prádanos, 2017). The question remains, can AI be repurposed so it can support these alternative, holistic, and transformative agro-urban models that are challenging the inherent unsustainability of our dominant modern techno-industrial designs, or is the field too enmeshed and invested in the dominant economic paradigm that it cannot operate beyond its extractivist mandates? How the field confronts and responds to this question will be key to understanding if AI could ever become a tool for conviviality and sustainability or will continue being an unintended driver of inequality, extractivism, radicalization, energy intensification, and ecological depletion.

AI is highly implicated in climate change, not only because the rapidly increasing global computing infrastructure has an expanding energy footprint but also because the tech industry is crucial in sustaining fossil fuel markets (Dobbe and Whittaker, 2019). AI has immense and ever-growing, but often ignored, material entanglements and energy intensities that could not be maintained by the post-carbon and post-extractive civilization that we need to create to avert the worse consequences of climate breakdown. In fact, critical energy studies found that humanity is fully immersed in a progressive and irreversible energy decline, as the energy return on energy invested in renewable technologies is way too low to replace fossil fuels and sustain the energy requirements of a techno-industrial civilization (Prieto and Hall, 2013; Fernández Durán and Reyes, 2018; Turiel, 2020; Seibert and Rees, 2021). In other words, it is unclear where the massive energy requirements of the AI global infrastructure are going to come from in a context of climate change and energy decline.

The amount of materials, water, and energy required to produce only one computer is enormous (even without considering its life cycle analysis). The illusion of digital dematerialization has been largely debunked by ecological economics. Similarly, MIT researchers Emma Strubell, Ananya Ganesh, and Andrew McCallum (2019), raised the alarm about the environmental cost of training neural networks for research in natural language processing. They estimate the required energy to be comparable to that necessary for a trans-American flight, while Karen Hao (2019) compared the carbon emissions of one single language model to those emitted by five cars in their lifetimes. In addition to the high carbon footprint and energy usage, Bender et al (2021) highlighted the role of these neural network models in furthering environmental racism, as the environmental cost for training English language models is "impacting the world's marginalized communities first," for instance communities in the Maldives or Sudan, "when similar large-scale models aren't being produced for Dhivehi or Sudanese Arabic" (Bender et al., 2021, p. 612).

Moreover, the implementation of more and faster technology always means more material extraction and more energy usage, not less (Alexander and Rutherford, 2020) and is therefore more unsustainable from an ecological perspective (Bridle, 2018, p. 64). In the context of a consumerist and growth-oriented economic culture, even improvements in eco-efficiency result in an overall increase in energy and material extraction, because the gains achieved by these technologies are reinvested to trigger further economic growth (Alexander and Rutherford, 2020). This is known as the rebound effect. Techno-optimism is often an ecology and energy blind perspective. The power that we attribute to machines is directly proportional to our ecological and energy illiteracy (Vindel, 2020, pp. 306–307). If we consider energy decline and ecological overshoot into the equation when we discuss high-tech agriculture and high-tech urbanism, for instance, the senselessness of smart agriculture and smart cities becomes clear.

Kate Crawford's recent book, *Atlas of AI* (2021), offers an "expanded view of artificial intelligence as an *extractive industry*" (Crawford, 2021, p. 15) made out of "physical infrastructures that are reshaping the Earth, while simultaneously shifting how the world is seen and understood" (Crawford, 2021, p. 19). The tech industry is currently fueling a planetary extractivism of terraforming proportions (Crawford, 2021, pp. 23–51). The vast environmental implications of this resource-intensive industry are obviously unsustainable not only because their extractivist practices exacerbate our current ecological overshoot but also because the energy and minerals that make global computation possible are becoming increasingly scarce. Crawford's book maps the materialities of AI and the "topographies of extraction that connects them" (Crawford, 2021, p. 49). As Crawford compellingly points out, AI is not autonomous at all, it depends on rapidly increasing levels of violent exploitation and extraction of human and nonhuman labor and health that are shadowed by abstract and immaterial metaphors (e.g., the cloud) as well as the dematerialization fantasies promoted by the tech industry.

Once high-tech systems are implemented in a school, building, farm, city, or administrative process, a new level of high maintenance requirements is also introduced. The maintenance of high-tech systems is usually much more cumbersome, expensive and labor and energy intensive than what their corporate advocates recognize (Broussard, 2019, p. 193; Mattern, 2021, pp. 106–139). The issues of maintenance and repair tend to be overlooked—if not completely ignored—by "smart" technology promoters. The initial implementation of many of these systems in public administrative, educational, or medical services is often accompanied by celebratory discourses and promises that almost never materialize. The consequences of these failures leave behind an increased social dysfunctionality and a large transfer of public funds to private hands.

If everything mentioned in this section is considered together, we could entertain the possibility that a sustainable post-carbon society will likely be a post-digital society or, at the very least, a society that uses computing technologies in less superfluous, less risky, more democratic, and much more selective ways. Perhaps an "open localization" strategy (Velegrakis and Gaitanou, 2019) would achieve a balance between sustainability and high technology. This means re-localizing as much as feasible the ways communities provide for their basic needs (food, water, energy) while keeping all communities culturally open and interconnected by knowledge-sharing digital technologies. This is to be seen. By now, as AI intensifies existing trends, global consumerism, energy consumption, and extractivism are increasing. This triggers a massive and socioecologically deleterious planetary wave of green grabbing enclosures, accumulation by dispossession, displacement, and forced depeasanization (Federici, 2019, pp. 188–197; Arboleda, 2020). In other words, AI within the existing sociohistorical context is a key driver and accelerator of unsustainable patterns and it is in fact "automating the global crisis" (Dauvergne, 2020, p. 137) in an irreflexive way as we will discuss in the next section.

9.4 Part III. The Unsustainable Fallacy of Technological Neutrality

During the last decades, we experienced a troublesome simultaneous depolitization of environmental and technological issues, as critical public discussions around these topics disappeared from civic discourses and were displaced by a techno-managerial rhetoric that pretends that constant increases in efficiency and speed are the solution to all problems, and therefore technological acceleration and economic growth should be the main priority of societies. Support for these ideas comes from the myth of *techno-inevitability* that "naturalizes a belief that technologies should dictate our material and sentient experiences of being" and "transforms a set of political and philosophical agendas into words such as «natural,» «scientific,» and «humane»" (Srinivasan, 2017, p. 9). This manufactured consensus on the political neutrality of technological acceleration confuses irreflexive and unsustainable profit-oriented technological development with social progress and innovation (even in the context of widening global inequality and ecological overshoot). We showed in previous sections how this confusion has lethal social and ecological consequences. Data journalist Meredith Broussard calls this flawed assumption technochauvinism: "the belief that tech is always the solution" (2019, pp. 7–8). This assumption is maintained even in cases where the simplest (low-tech) solution seems to be the most effective (Broussard, 2019, p. 10). Technochauvinism, as we explained previously, is mostly blind to the energy requirements and environmental consequences associated with high-tech processes.

Machine learning developments make this technological depolitization even more problematic. The first AI systems were designed to do whatever we knew how to, but more efficiently and faster. More recent machine learning and deep learning technologies end up identifying and accelerating patterns that we do not even understand anymore (Peirano, 2019, p. 139). As decisions are automated in an opaque way, there is no room for political discussions or public debates about what we want to perpetuate and what we want to change as societies. Decisions are therefore automated without the possibility of ethical and political consideration and contestation. This makes "smart" societies irreflexive by default. But irreflexivity does not entail political neutrality, for politics are already encoded in the design of algorithms—especially given the fact that our automated systems reproduce past stereotypes and biases and therefore perpetuate "the historic prejudices deeply encoded in our data sets" (Bridle, 2018, p. 144). These discriminatory automated systems become deeply ingrained and entangled in the functionality of our institutions and societies due to the fact that AI "is an accelerator of all other technologies" (Dauvergne, 2020, pp. 9–10).

The irreflexive conditioning of automated systems has been noticed by a number of critical technology scholars (Greenfield, 2017, pp. 251–252; Bridle, 2018; Broussard, 2019; Vineusa, 2020; Truby, 2020; Sætra, 2021) and occurs due to the fact that "The combination of opacity and complexity renders much of the computational process illegible; and because computation itself is perceived to be politically and emotionally neutral" (Bridle, 2018, p. 40). The "automation bias" encoded in computational processes entails a default externalization of "both the decision process and the responsibility onto the machine" (Bridle, 2018, p. 43). An automated system that learns from selective data can never solve root problems, because it never interrogates the past from which the data was extracted and only reacts and responds to immediate symptoms in a way that aggravates the problems and makes them more difficult to manage in the future. Modern energy-intensive technology makes possible externalizing the social and ecological costs of our consumerist cultures (this function is irreflexively unfair by definition as we do not see the socioecological damage we inflict) as it hides the ecologically unequal exchange at a global scale (Hornborg, 2022). As Silvia Federici (2019) reminds us, paraphrasing German sociologist Otto Ullrich, "only modern technology's capacity to transfer its costs over considerable times and spaces and our consequent inability to see the suffering caused by our daily usage of technological devices allow the myth that technology generates prosperity to persist" (Federici, 2019, p. 190).

Perhaps, rather than accelerating our technological development, we should put more time and energy in trying to understand the social and ecological implications of our dominant techno-social systems. In other words, it is time to consider alternative cultural imaginaries that help us rethink our relationship with our technologies in completely different ways. We need to be more thoughtful about which kind of technological innovation is desirable and which one is detrimental. To insert reflection into our techno-social systems we need to focus much more on social and cultural innovation rather than blindly focusing on improving technological capabilities without interrogating their unintended consequences. This means substituting the neutrality of technology paradigm for a different approach based on the political ecology of technology.

The dominant accelerationist thought (Bridle, 2018, p. 132), implicit in the neutrality paradigm, assumes that "our only possible act is to accelerate the existing order" (Bridle, 2018, p. 134). Algorithms reproduce existing bias because they are trained in the societal dominant values and they propagate and amplify past mistakes (Peirano, 2019, p. 141). "Computation projects a future that is like the past" (Bridle, 2018, p. 44), excluding possible futures that do not fit the model, assuming that nothing will radically change (Bridle, 2018, pp. 44, 81). The problem we face today is that we need a profound and quick change of course to avert the worse consequences of ecological overshoot and climate breakdown. If nothing changes substantially, the conditions that make our planet humanly inhabitable will be seriously and irreversibly compromised. It seems that our current techno-social systems prevent us from changing direction in the precise historical conjunction in which not doing so is unaffordable. This double bind is due to the fact that our technologies significantly condition the way we can respond to pressing problems and how we envision possible solutions. If our most powerful tools were developed in the context of a growth-oriented economic culture that gave rise to a deeply unsustainable and unfair sociotechnical system, how can these tools help us find a way out of the socioecological crisis that the afore-mentioned economic culture manufactured?

The technology neutrality paradigm is extremely dangerous for the health of our planet's ecosystems as well as our democracies because "New technologies do not merely augment our abilities, but actively shape and direct them" (Bridle, 2018, p. 2). Apparently, many people are looking at computer screens, reading fake news highlighted by biased algorithms, and liking staged friends' photos while our neighbors get digitally radicalized and 70% of our agricultural biodiversity disappears. Political questions should not be avoided if we want to solve this conundrum: who is excluded in the techno-logical designs that affect our daily routines and who decides what kind of data is relevant to train the algorithms that will inform our political opin-ions and absorb our energies and attentions? Often times the same groups that were excluded from the benefits of (neo)colonial exploitation are also excluded from the design of our technology and become the collateral dam-age of its algorithmic injustice. There is no such thing as raw data (Greenfield, 2017, p. 210; Crawford, 2021, p. 221) and with machine learning technolo-gies "certain perspectives on reality are reinforced, and others undermined" (Greenfield, 2017, p. 212). The perspectives that are reinforced are usually the ones embraced by powerful industrial and military interests and are deeply deleterious for the health of our minds, societies, and ecologies (Crawford, 2021, pp. 181–209). Alternative perspectives that embrace regenerative and non-extractive logics tend to be undermined. These perspectives are usually not perceived (or, if they are, it is to stigmatize them) by our technologically entangled institutional and theoretical radars. They remain outside of the official menu of possible solutions and are excluded from significant funding opportunities.

Our society's path dependency, "which is the tendency of a dynamic sys-tem to evolve in ways that are determined by decisions made in its past" (Greenfield, 2017, p. 232), is exacerbated and automated by machine learn-ing technologies in a historical conjunction in which our survival as a spe-cies requires from us nothing less than radically and urgently changing paths. A good example is how dominant discourses around highly complex and extremely risky geoengineering proposals assume that we can solve our eco-logical problems by intensifying the techno-managerial, extractive, anthro-pocentric, and hubristic logic that caused them (Peirano, 2022, p. 112). This is the maximum expression of an irreflexive and addictive path-dependent society that cannot do anything other than keep accelerating in the precise moment in which it should be using the emergency break. Once again, the technology neutrality paradigm traps us into an automated deadly rat race that leaves no room for political and ethical considerations. Under this dominant cultural imaginary, our only possibility is to keep running toward our demise.

The fantasy of technological neutrality excuses societies from the messy business of engaging in politics and public debate regarding how to regulate, design, develop, and implement AI technologies. Corporations—and their unfair algorithms—are happy to make the decisions for us. This passive and unconscious delegation means that we give up our democratic responsibilities and privileges of discussing and deciding collectively what we value as a society, how we distribute technological benefits and risks, responsibilities and vulnerabilities, and what kind of behaviors enhance the common good and need to be incentivized and encoded into our techno-social systems versus which ones are socially and ecologically detrimental and need to be discouraged and deactivated. It is important to remember that "Every unchallenged assertion of the neutral goodness of technology [...] sustains and nourishes uneven power relationships" (Bridle, 2018, pp. 245–247) that are rapidly destroying the planetary web of life (Patel and Moore, 2017). Challenging the neutrality paradigm and escaping the tyranny of efficiency entails "learning to question what motivates the design of our sensemaking tools" (Greenfield, 2017, p. 239).

Since their inception, modern technologies were informed by an extractivist and (neo)colonial cultural paradigm in which the role of "modern" human societies was considered to appropriate and exploit all planetary life (as well as the life of all humans that happened to be registered as "non-modern" by this classification system) in the name of progress. Smart technologies are therefore designed to extract energy, labor, and data (Peirano, 2022, pp. 27–29). We obviously need to contest this dominant extractive imaginary if we are to create convivial and regenerative technologies, but our sociopolitical infrastructures are more difficult to change than our technical ones, because they are made out of ideologies and narratives that are ingrained in our brains (Peirano, 2022, pp. 65–66). Our dominant cultural imaginaries have materialized in a global ecological overshoot and therefore some of the habits and beliefs associated with this cultural paradigm cannot be sustained for much longer. Under current biophysical and social realities, our dominant beliefs become toxic attachments that, quite literally, can kill us. Today's techno-optimism (or technochauvisnism) is a sort of "cruel optimism" (Berlant, 2011) that is inflicting massive damage to our democracies and ecosystems. It is time for envisioning different stories to live by that are more compatible with our finite planet (Stibbe, 2015).

9.5 Part IV. Confronting the Hard Question: Can AI Become a Convivial and Regenerative Tool?

AI technologies, as every sociotechnical system that influences the way we think and the way we do things, are never neutral, value-free tools. The "colonization of everyday life by information processing" (Greenfield, 2017, p. 32) has unknown but deep implications for "our psyches, our societies, or our ways of organizing the world" (Greenfield, 2017, p. 20) as well as for how our economic metabolism reorganizes planetary ecologies in ways that could compromise our survival as a species (Patel and Moore, 2017). Given the unsustainable current inertia exacerbated by AI, should we advocate for not developing certain machine learning capabilities? If so, which ones, why, and how could we encourage broad audiences outside of academic circles to engage in this debate? As Costanza-Chock (2020) points out, "there are many cases where a design justice analysis asks us not to make systems more inclusive, but to refuse to design them at all" (Costanza-Chock, 2020, p. 19). If this is the case, "should sustainability advocates perhaps fight against further development of AI?" (Dauvergne, 2020, p. 11).

This is largely a rhetorical question as not engaging with the already existing AI technologies may not be an option—no matter how dangerous they may currently be—because it would mean to renounce to effective tools for cooperation at our disposal while being vulnerable to the effects of their manipulation by corporate and authoritarian actors (Peirano, 2022, p. 47). However, letting powerful corporations monopolize the innovation and implementation of AI technologies is not an option either. We envision reimagining these tools to make them not just smarter and more efficient, but also wiser and more equalitarian. We also advocate for checks and boundaries for AI technologies, established in a more participatory and transparent way.

It should be clear by now that "AI is never going to produce a sustainability revolution within the contemporary global order" (Dauvergne, 2022, p. 8). So far, "these allegedly disruptive technologies leave existing modes of domination mostly intact, [and therefore we should be] asking if they can ever truly be turned to liberatory ends" (Greenfield, 2017, p. 8). Once again, the politics and ethics of technology are unavoidable. For AI to serve the common good and the regeneration of depleted ecosystems, radically different economic and political cultures as well as diverse leadership paradigms need to be activated. Tellingly, in the process of writing this chapter we noticed that, in the highly male-dominated field of AI, a significant number of the most critical and socioecologically sensitive interventions were made by women and gender non-conforming scholars. Diversifying the field is obviously crucial if it is ever going to serve the common good. This is a necessary but insufficient first step. Overcoming the hubristic, extractivist, and exploitative mindset ingrained in our unsustainable dominant economic culture will take more than diversifying leadership in AI.

As Gregory Bateson brilliantly put it, "The creature that wins against its environment destroys itself" (Bateson, 1972, p. 501). Smart technologies are yet another modern industrial tool designed to control, manage, exploit, and ultimately, win against our environment. The extractivist and hubristic vision that guided its development is at odds with the maintenance of human and ecological health. We need new visions and stories to live by that are more attuned to human and ecological vulnerability and interdependence and prioritize socioecological reciprocity and synergy, whole systems health, and regenerative socionatural relations (Stibbe, 2015). We have to stop fighting a supposedly external nature and start working with it if we do not want to destroy ourselves. We need to learn from ecosystems, where the real intelligence of our planet resides, not from poorly designed human institutions and machines that perpetuate historical prejudices and unsustainable patterns (Walh, 2016; Escobar, 2018; Fry, 2018). Permaculture, biomimesis, and systems thinking should guide not only our design processes but also inform our ethical, legal, economic, and political philosophies (Capra and Luisi, 2014). If we challenge the technochauvinist dominant imaginary, the field of AI could perhaps play a key role in enhancing regenerative design principles and practices. The feasibility for this radical re-direction of the field is to be seen, but changing some of the technological imaginaries of successful male Silicon Valley individuals and venture capitalists' space colonizers for humbler and more socioecologically desirable models of success may be a good starting point. In the words of environmental educator David Orr (2004):

"The planet does not need more successful people. But it does desperately need more peacemakers, healers, restorers, storytellers, and lovers of every kind. It needs people who live well in their places. It needs people of moral courage willing to join the fight to make the world habitable and humane. And these qualities have little to do with success as our culture has defined it" (Orr, 2004, p. 12)

The extractivist and (neo)colonial vision that has dominated technological thinking in general and AI development in particular needs to be displaced by a radically different cultural and technological paradigm (Crawford, 2021, pp. 229–237). We call for a transition to a regenerative-oriented AI paradigm. Guided by a postgrowth cultural imaginary (Prádanos, 2018), the field could engage in an algorithmic re-design process led by bottom-up heterogeneous and diverse thinkers, practitioners, and communities that are well-versed in whole systems thinking, critical energy studies, and political ecology of technology. AI developments could then be publicly discussed and collectively approved. AI implementations could be debated and decided by the affected stakeholders and communities and every project could be designed to ensure algorithmic accountability and transparency, empower local communities, heal the soil, promote biodiversity, and contribute to the common good. Successful projects could be widely shared for the collective intelligence to be enhanced.

A few examples of convivial and regenerative projects that could be tackled by a regenerative-oriented AI paradigm are the following: developing technological applications that could be participatory and collectively managed, improved, shared, and easily repurposed to serve the differentiated needs of diverse local communities and bioregions; engaging in projects that help decentralize and locally manage energy and food systems in a cooperative and regenerative way; redesigning the existing habit-making technologies so that rather than radicalizing people and promoting compulsive consumerism, they make users more ecologically conscious and less energy blind, etc.

We also advocate for opening the space for other voices and views on sustainability that diverge from Western ways of thinking. Srinivasan points out in his book *Whose Global Village? Rethinking How Technology Shapes Our World*

(2017) that "existing approaches toward managing and databasing knowledge significantly contrast with local customs and traditions, particularly those practiced by indigenous peoples engaging in their own environment" (Srinivasan, 2017, p. 9). In some forms of indigenous thinking, there is an intrinsic relationship between biodiversity, culture, and language. As David Turnbull (2009) indicates, "biodiversity does not exist in isolation, biodiversity is inseparably linked to cultural diversity, to indigenous knowledge". Conversely, Wesley Y. Leonard concludes that language revitalization efforts cannot happen without regenerating the ecological context in which a language emerged: "language reclamation entails a resurgence of physical, spiritual, and relational contexts that support language learning" (Leonard, 2021, p. 150). We believe that researchers in the field of AI should engage, with an open mind, in language reclamation and ecological regeneration efforts initiated by indigenous communities. However, current methods for classification and collection based on Western hierarchical systems and ontologies are not compatible with indigenous ways of perceiving the world (Srinivasan, 2017, pp. 130–132). Thus, such scholarly work will require designing and developing new methods and tools in the field to support indigenous thinking. We view this as an exciting opportunity for AI researchers to use their creativity and ingenuity to imagine wiser, fairer, and more ecologically-sound types of technology.

9.6 Concluding Remarks

Should AI scholars advocate for teaching the political ecology of technology—insisting that AI implications are not merely technical issues—not only in Computer Science programs but also in all educational settings? Probably so, for without a broadly promoted and nourished technological and ecological literacy, public opinion about AI and sustainability is nothing but an acritical celebration of the marketing greenwashing fantasies disseminated by tech corporations and other interest groups. Building an informed public and civic discourse around the potentialities and dangers of AI for transitioning from extractivist and exploitative techno-social systems to regenerative and fair ones is probably the most challenging and urgent task—for our field, as well as for the health of human and nonhuman communities everywhere—moving forward. The political ecology of technology can no longer be ignored by AI scholars, educators, and practitioners. As this chapter suggests, the social and ecological costs of avoiding the politics of technology are becoming increasingly unsustainable.

Notes

1 https://sdgs.un.org/goals.
2 https://aaai.org/Conferences/AAAI-22/aiforsocialimpactcall/.
3 https://aaai.org/Conferences/AAAI-22/wp-content/uploads/2021/12/AAAI-22_Accepted_Paper_List_Main_Technical_Track.pdf.

4 https://ijcai-22.org/calls-ai-for-good/.
5 https://ijcai-22.org/special-track-on-ai-for-good-accepted-papers/.
6 https://www.microsoft.com/en-us/ai/ai-for-earth.
7 https://planetarycomputer.microsoft.com/.

Bibliography

Alexander, S. and Rutherford, J.A. (2020). Critique to Techno-Optimism: Efficiency without Sufficiency Is Lost. In: Kalfagianni, D.F. and Hayden, A., eds. *Routledge Handbook of Global Sustainability Governance*. London: Routledge.

Arboleda, M. (2020). *Planetary Mine: Territories of Extraction under Late Capitalism*. London: Verso.

Bateson, G. (1972). *Steps to an Ecology of Mind: Collected Essays in Anthropology, Psychiatry, Evolution, and Epistemology*. Chicago: The University of Chicago Press.

Bender, E.M., Gebru, T., McMillan-Major, A., and Shmitchell, S. (2021). On the Dangers of Stochastic Parrots: Can Language Models Be Too Big? *Proceedings of the 2021 ACM Conference on Fairness, Accountability, and Transparency (FAccT'21)*. New York: ACM, pp. 610–623.

Berlant, L. (2011). *Cruel Optimism*. Durham: Duke University Press.

Bessen, J. (2022). *The New Goliaths: How Corporations Use Software to Dominate Industries, Kill Innovation, and Undermine Regulation*. New Haven: Yale University Press.

Brenner, N. and Katsikis, N. (2020). Operational Landscapes: Hinterlands of the Capitalocene. *Architectural Design*, 90(1), pp. 22–31.

Bridle, J. (2018). *New Dark Age: Technology and the End of the Future*. London: Verso.

Broussard, M. (2019). *Artificial Unintelligence: How Computers Misunderstand the World*. Cambridge: The MIT Press.

Capra, F. and Luisi P.L. (2014). *The Systems View of Life: A Unifying Vision*. Cambridge: Cambridge University Press.

Ceballos, G., Ehrlich, P.R., and Dirzo, R. (2017). Biological Annihilation Via the Ongoing Sixth Mass Extinction Signaled by Vertebrate Population Losses and Declines. *PNAS*, 114(30), pp. 6089–6096.

Costanza-Chock, S. (2020). *Design Justice: Community-Led Practices to Build the Worlds We Need*. Cambridge: The MIT Press.

Crary, J. (2013). *24/7: Late Capitalism and the End of Sleep*. London: Verso.

Crawford, K. (2021). *Atlas of AI: Power, Politics, and the Planetary Costs of Artificial Intelligence*. New Haven: Yale University Press.

Dauvergne, P. (2020). *AI in the Wild. Sustainability in the Age of Artificial Intelligence*. Cambridge: The MIT Press.

Dobbe, R. and Whittaker, M. (2019). AI and Climate Change: How They're Connected, and What We Can Do About It. *Medium, AI Now Institute*. Available from: www.ainowinstitute.org [accessed 23 October 2022].

Elhacham, E., Ben-Uri, L., Grozovski, J., Bar-On, Y.M., and Milo, R. (2020). Global Human-Made Mass Exceeds All Living Biomass. *Nature*, 588, pp. 442–444.

Escobar, A. (2018). *Designs for the Pluriverse: Radical Interdependence, Autonomy, and the Making of Worlds*. Durham: Duke University Press.

Eubanks, V. (2017). *Automating Inequality: How High-tech Tools Profile, Police, and Punish the Poor*. New York: St. Martin's Press.

Federici, S. (2019). *Re-enchanting the World: Feminism and the Politics of the Commons*. San Francisco: PM Press.

Fernández Durán, R. (2010). *El Antropoceno: la crisis ecológica se hace mundial. La expansión del capitalismo global choca con la biosfera.* Madrid: Coeditores Virus y Libros en Acción.

Fernández Durán, R. and Reyes, L.G. (2018). *En la espiral de la energía.* 2nd ed. Madrid: Libros en Acción.

Fry, T. (2018). *Design Futuring: Sustainability, Ethics and New Practice.* London: Bloomsbury Visual Arts.

Greenfield, A. (2013). *Against the Smart City.* New York City: Do projects.

Greenfield, A. (2017). *Radical Technologies.* London: Verso.

Hao, K. (2019). Training a Single AI Model can Emit as Much Carbon as Five Cars in their Lifetimes. *MIT Technology Review* [online]. Available from: MIT Technology Review [accessed 23 October 2022].

Herrington, G. (2020). Update to Limits to Growth: Comparing the World3 Model with Empirical Data. *Journal of Industrial Ecology,* 25(3), pp. 614–626.

Hornborg, A. (2022). Ecologically Unequal Exchange Theory as Genuine Materialism: A Response to Somerville. *Capitalism, Nature, Socialism,* 33(2), pp. 79–84.

Inclezan, D. and Prádanos, L.I. (2017). Viewpoint: A Critical View on Smart Cities and AI. *Journal of Artificial Intelligence Research,* 60. Available from: https://jair.org/index.php/jair/article/view/11094 [accessed 23 October 2022].

IPBES. (2019). *Global Assessment on Biodiversity and Ecosystem Services of the Intergovernmental Science-Policy Platform on Biodiversity and Ecosystem Services.* Bonn: IPBES secretariat. Available from: https://ipbes.net/global-assessment [accessed 23 October 2022].

Kaplan, J. (2016). *Humans Need Not Apply. A Guide to Wealth and Work in the Age of Artificial Intelligence.* New Haven: Yale University Press.

Leonard, W.Y. (2021). Contesting *Extinction* through a Praxis of Language Reclamation. In: McCullagh, S.M., Prádanos, L., Tabusso Marcyan, I., and Wagner, C., eds. *Contesting Extinctions: Decolonial and Regenerative Futures.* London: Lexington Books, pp. 143–159.

Mattern, S. (2021). *A City Is Not a Computer: Other Urban Intelligences.* Princeton: Princeton University Press.

O'Neil, C. (2016). *Weapons of Math Destruction: How Big Data Increase Inequality and Threatens Democracy.* New York: Crown.

Orr, D.W. (2004). *Earth in Mind: On Education, Environment, and the Human Prospect.* Washington, DC: Island Press.

Patel, R. and More, J.W. (2017). *A History of the World in Seven Cheap Things: A Guide to Capitalism, Nature, and the Future of the Planet.* Oakland: University of California Press.

Peirano, M. (2019). *El enemigo conoce el sistema.* Barcelona: Debate.

Peirano, M. (2022). *Contra el futuro.* Barcelona: Debate.

Prádanos, L.I. (2018). *Postgrowth Imaginaries.* Liverpool: Liverpool University Press.

Prieto, P.A. and Hall, C.A.S. (2013). *Spain's Photovoltaic Revolution: The Energy Return on Investment.* Berlin: Springer.

Sætra, H.S. (2021). AI in Context and the Sustainable Development Goals: Factoring in the Unsustainability of the Sociotechnical System. *Sustainability,* 13(4), 1738. Available from: https://doi.org/10.3390/su13041738 [accessed 23 October 2022].

Seibert, M. and Rees, W. (2021). Through the Eye of a Needle: An Eco-Heterodox Perspective on Renewable Energy Transition. *Energies,* 14(15), 4508. Available from: https://doi.org/10.3390/en14154508 [accessed 23 October 2022].

Srinivasan, R. (2017). *Whose Global Village: Rethinking How Technology Shapes Our World*. New York: New York University Press.

Stibbe, A. (2015). *Ecolinguistics: Language, Ecology, and the Stories We Live By*. New York: Routledge.

Strubell, E., Ganesh, A., and McCallum, A. (2019). Energy and Policy Considerations for Deep Learning in NLP. *Proceedings of the 57th Conference of the Association for Computational Linguistics (ACL)*, 1, pp. 3645–3650. Available from https://doi.org/10.18653/v1/P19-1355 [accessed 23 October 2022].

Truby, J. (2020). Governing Artificial Intelligence to benefit the UN Sustainable Development Goals. *Sustainable Development*, 28(4), pp. 946–959.

Tufekci, Z. (2018). YouTube, the Great Radicalizer. *The New York Times* [online]. Available from: https://www.nytimes.com/2018/03/10/opinion/sunday/youtube-politics-radical.html [accessed 23 October 2022].

Turiel, A. (2020). *Petrocalipsis. Crisis energética global y cómo (no) la vamos a solucionar*. Madrid: Alfabeto.

Turnbull, D. (2009). Working with Incommensurable Knowledge: Traditions Assemblage, Diversity, Emergent Knowledge, Narrativity, Performativity, Mobility and Synergy. *Thoughtmesh.net* [online]. Available from: http://thoughtmesh.net/publish/279.php?indigenous [accessed 23 October 2022].

Velegrakis, G. and Gaitanou, E. (2019). Open Localization. In: Kothari, A., Salleh, A., Escobar, A., Demaria, F., and Acosta, A., eds. *Pluriverse: A Post-Development Dictionary*. New Delhi: Tulika Books, pp. 259–262.

Vindel, J. (2020). *Estética Fósil: Imaginarios de la energía y crisis ecosocial*. Barcelona: Arcadia/MACBA.

Vinuesa, R., Azizpour, H., Leite, I., Ballam, M., Dignum, V., Domisch, S., Felländer, A., Langhans, S.D., Tegmark, M., and Fuso Nerini, F. (2020). The Role of Artificial Intelligence in Achieving the Sustainable Development Goals. *Nature Communications*, 11(233). Available from: https://doi.org/10.1038/s41467-019-14108-y [accessed 23 October 2022].

Walh, D.C. (2016). *Designing Regenerative Cultures*. Axminster: Triarchy Press.

Wilkinson, R. and Pickett, K. (2010). *The Spirit Level: Why Greater Equality Makes Societies Stronger*. New York: Bloomsbury Press.

World Wildlife Fund. (2018). *Living Planet Report—2018: Aiming Higher* [online]. Available from: https://www.worldwildlife.org/pages/living-planet-report-2018 [accessed 23 October 2022].

10 AI-Based Technologies in the Phygital Care Journey

Irene Di Bernardo, Marialuisa Marzullo, Cristina Mele and Tiziana Russo Spena

10.1 Introduction

In calling for more people-centered healthcare ecosystems, the World Health Organization (2020) recommends shifting focus, from treating diseases to adopting a wider perspective on patient needs and medical care. In turn, new methods are required to ensure the comprehensive physical and mental well-being of patients throughout all phases of treatment, also known as the patient journey, which spans from symptom perception to disease treatment to care and follow-up interactions (Bjerg, 2011; Chan et al., 2022). To improve healthcare services, digital technologies can provide valuable support to patient-centered health ecosystems, due to their capacity to collect wide-ranging, real-time data (Oldenburg et al., 2015), automate care activities (Fruehwirt and Duckworth, 2021), support decision-making (Osei-Frimpong et al., 2018), and capture clinical information relevant to specific health conditions (Aggarwal et al., 2020). According to emerging literature that documents the contributions of artificial intelligence (AI)–based solutions to patient experiences (Alkire et al., 2020), they can enhance healthcare value co-creation (Lee, 2019) and increase patient well-being (McColl-Kennedy et al., 2017).

Understanding how patients navigate and experience the healthcare ecosystem is critical to improve value co-creation processes (Mele and Russo Spena, 2019). In such an endeavor scholars and practitioners need to identify key moments that affect treatment decision-making, Despite the growing focus on the patient in service research, the concept of the "care journey", has not yet been fully explained (Ponsignon et al., 2018; Leone et al., 2021). There is a need to figure out the journey phases that compose, and the impact of the growing use of technologies on each phase to achieve healthcare goals and foster well-being (Mele et al., 2022)

In this chapter, we focus on the "phygital care journey," which combines physical with digital actions and interactions, involving patients, physicians, formal (i.e. nurses), and informal caregivers (i.e. family and friends).

We offer a framework on the phygital care journey, articulated in frame four connected phases: origination, diagnosis, treatment, and follow-up. We argue that AI-based solutions can offer a pervasive nudge, by amplifying

DOI: 10.4324/9781003304616-14

caregivers' and care receivers' abilities, control, and actions (Mele and Russo Spena, 2019), making them active actors alongside the care journey.

10.2 Literature Review

10.2.1 Patient Journey and Experience

The expression "patient journey" refers to the pathway a person takes to deal with a medical condition or illness, during which the patient encounters diverse actors, tools, and steps (Chan et al., 2022). Simonse et al. (2019, p. 83) define it as a "comprehensible representation of health service and its procedures, including relationships and feelings from a patient perspective." Each journey has a starting point and crucial moments involving discoveries and obstacles, which lead to some point of arrival (Bjerg, 2011). The multiple actors the patient meets along this pathway represent part of the patient's journey too, and their interactions are referred to as service touchpoints (Halvorsrud et al., 2019). From the perspective of the individual patient (Reay et al., 2017; Gualandi et al., 2019; Simonse et al., 2019), the patient journey consists of a series of experiences evoked by interacting with other actors in the healthcare ecosystem (Reay et al., 2017; Simonse et al., 2019).

The final result emerges from the progressive succession of phases (Trebble et al., 2010), though the precise phases that actually constitute the patient journey remain a topic of debate. In particular, some scholars assume the phases are distinct (Ponsignon et al., 2018), but others argue that they are interconnected (Devi et al., 2020). Ponsignon et al. (2018) propose five distinct stages: (1) receive a diagnosis through interactions designed to assess and communicate the patient's condition; (2) provide inpatient care by admitting the patient to a healthcare facility for treatment, stay, and discharge; (3) offer outpatient care, such as when a patient visits a healthcare facility for treatment but does not stay overnight; (4) provide post-treatment care, including follow-up services, check-ups, aftercare, medical support, and complaint handling; and (5) support end-of-life care to terminally ill patients. In contrast, Devi et al. (2020) suggest six progressive, interconnected stages: (1) awareness, related to a trigger event when a patient self-evaluates symptoms, conducts research, and considers potential health conditions that may require treatment; (2) screening and initial contact with a health system through a call center, chat, email, mobile, or in-person visit; (3) diagnosis based on assessment at a medical facility; (4) treatment provided by the health system, both on-site and as follow-up care; (5) adherence and lifestyle changes designed to reduce readmissions and promote long-term well-being; and (6) palliative, ongoing care.

McCarthy et al. (2016) also assert that analyzing each individual patient's stage in the journey is key to exploring or describing the patient experience, which includes tasks performed during encounters, emotional dynamics, physical changes, and various touchpoints. The patient experience thus is "the sum of all interactions that influence patient perceptions across the continuum of care" (Alkire et al., 2020, p. 2). It occurs during moments when the patient interacts with the healthcare service (McCarthy et al., 2016; Alkire et al., 2020). Doyle et al. (2013) and Coulter et al. (2009) argue for making the patient experience one of the three pillars of quality, alongside clinical effectiveness, and patient safety. Paying attention to the overall experience allows actors to define defects in the healthcare ecosystem and implement actions aimed at eliminating these defects.

A useful tool for monitoring the patient experience is patient journey mapping (Borycki et al., 2020; Joseph et al., 2020; Kushniruk et al., 2020; He et al., 2021; Ly et al., 2021). It can capture information about patients' behavior, feelings, and motivations, as well as the attitudes of healthcare professionals across episodes of care (Borycki et al., 2020). Scholars also consider ways to manage emotions during service experiences (McColl-Kennedy et al., 2017). Mapping emotions is critical to understanding patients because their emotions influence their perceptions, adherence to care instructions, intentions, and behaviors (McColl-Kennedy et al., 2017). The growing use of digital and AI-based technologies can empower patients and alter their overall experience (Bolton et al., 2018). Few studies have investigated technologies as integral to patient journeys or their effects on distinct journey phases (Leone et al., 2021). Understanding how emerging technologies influence the patient journey and experience is a central research priority (Alkire et al., 2020; Leone et al., 2021).

10.2.2 AI-Based Technologies in a Phygital Journey

Because AI-based technologies can monitor conditions, engage in real-time data collection, transmit interactive feedback (Wuenderlich et al., 2015), and process vast amounts of data, they strongly influence how collected information prompts particular actions and can promote both connectivity and responsiveness (Larivière et al., 2017; Huang & Rust, 2018). For example, smart devices can collect individual health data (e.g., number of steps, calories, sleep hours, pulse rate) and provide personalized health recommendations (De Keyser et al., 2020). Other AI-based apps support healthcare professionals' daily activities (Wuenderlich et al., 2015; Baker et al., 2017), such that they can perform basic tasks more efficiently, gain access to more resources, and increase the quality of the services they provide (van Doorn et al., 2017; Prakash et al., 2021). In describing the medical decision-making process, Prakash et al. (2021) assert that AI applications and deep-learning algorithms are promising alternatives to increase the accuracy of physicians' diagnoses and treatments.

Digital applications and contexts have become integral to the patient journey (Kraus et al., 2021; Schiavone et al., 2021). According to Leone et al. (2021), AI-based solutions also can guide and improve the patient journey, by enhancing service and operational practices in terms of information transmission, greater flexibility, file preservation, and document reproducibility. Mele et al. (2021) and Mele and Russo Spena (2022) also see smart technologies and AI-based solutions as integral to physical journeys, because digital technologies integrate physical elements and social presence (Mele et al., 2021). In the phygital journey, interactions affect cognitive, emotional, social, and behavioral impacts (Gelsomini et al., 2021; Mele et al., 2021). At each touch-point, physical and digital exchanges of information, data, and sensations take place (Mele et al., 2021), with important impacts on patients' experiences and the quality of the service provided. However, research that applies the notion of a phygital journey to healthcare contexts remains rare, so we seek to conduct a deep, empirical investigation of how AI-based technologies can alter the patient journey and transform it into a phygital patient journey.

10.3 The Phygital Care Journey: A Comprehensive Framework

Due to its advanced capacity, today's AI can process a vast amount of health data and translate useful information into specified actions. The connectivity and responsiveness enabled by AI-based technologies also support high-quality care and personalized patient journeys (van Doorn et al., 2017; Leone et al., 2021; Prakash et al., 2021). The technologies represent add-ons to existing treatments, which can replace some traditional approaches, as well as transform or supplement some activities by caregivers or caretakers. For example, they might increase predictive and diagnostic accuracy and suggest more appropriate therapy options. By detailing how AI-based solutions influence different phases of the care journey, we might identify other potential contributions too. The integration of technologies, including virtual agents, machine and deep learning platforms, virtual reality (VR), and augmented reality (AR), in different phases might establish a more comprehensive framework of the phygital care journey, in terms of how AI-based technologies influence care journeys and patient experiences.

We consider four stages in care journeys: (1) origination, when symptoms appear; (2) diagnosis with medical assistance; (3) treatment, including onsite care, drug treatment, physical therapy, and so forth; and (4) follow-up care, such as information about how to access test results, support for recovery efforts, and prevention education. These phases represent key moments with the greatest impact on patient outcomes. They also represent the unfolding of the care journey.

10.3.1 Origination

Origination is the moment when the patients experience symptoms or notice disorders (Percival and McGregor, 2016). They may experience a sense of perplexity, anxiety, agitation, or fear (Abshire et al., 2015). In some cases, the symptom is identified by technology (Gao et al., 2015), such as when a patient receives a notification on a smartwatch that blood oxygen levels are low or their heart rate has increased precipitously. But in-person conversations about disorders, with friends, family members, or doctors, also might prompt recognition of symptoms and evoke a latent need to investigate them. Patients also may gain deeper understanding of their disorders through consultations with others, such as on social media, with similar concerns. During this symptom discovery stage, AI-based technologies help the patients learn about the origin of their disorders and guide them to the next stage of the journey (Ferreira, 2021). In this starting point of the care journey, AI-based technologies support detection, by enhancing *self-awareness* and *self-control*.

10.3.1.1 Self-Awareness

Self-awareness implies that patients consciously know and understand their own health status, likely by searching for information online and offline and by consulting friends or family members with relevant experiences. By using AI-based technologies, patients can increase this ***self-awareness***, because they can take an active rather than a passive role, such as by setting data alerts or searching for relevant sources of information. Smart devices can be set to offer actionable insights, establish engagement in consistent health-beneficial activities, and advance the discovery process (Gao et al., 2015, Gualandi et al., 2021). Through their data collection capabilities, these technological solutions broaden discovery opportunities for patients and reduce the risk that they might not notice a symptom. Furthermore, they increase self-awareness of disorders and inform subsequent decision-making processes, such as whether to consult a caregiver (Wang & Hajli, 2017).

10.3.1.2 Self-Control

Self-control relates positively to the display of health-promoting behaviors. Patients want to learn more about and seize control over their symptoms.

The Fitbit Smartwatch

The Fitbit Charge 5 can monitor the electrical activity of wearers' hearts to check for irregularities, such as atrial fibrillation; these results can be shared with healthcare providers if desired. Sensors integrated into the device's case combine with a biosensor on the Fitbit Charge 5 to determine if the wearer is exhibiting normal heart rhythm, which implies no irregularities, or atrial fibrillation. During atrial fibrillation, the upper chambers of the heart contract irregularly, increasing the risk of heart attack, blood clots, stroke, and other heart conditions. It can be difficult to detect, but the Fitbit ECG app allows patients to check their heart rhythm directly from their wrists and thus increase the chances of detecting it. This evaluation cannot conclusively diagnose atrial fibrillation, but its results can alert patients to the symptoms, such that they might be motivated to initiate a conversation with their healthcare providers.

When they recognize the possibility of a problem, they likely search for additional information and potential solutions. In these searches, they likely seek to be informed by different sources, which can be facilitated by AI-based devices. Because they continuously collect various data, they can summarize actionable information and help patients keep track of their conditions, as well as reveal new insights or support decisions about next steps (Park et al., 2020). In addition, because technologies can provide continuous feedback, alerts, and recommendations appropriate to each actor's conditions, they can encourage individually appropriate choices (Gao et al., 2015). For example, wearables that monitor wellness parameters, such as sleep and calories, can suggest tactics for getting better sleep or consuming fewer calories; medical devices can help monitor and protect people with physical vulnerabilities (Gao et al., 2015; van Doorn et al., 2017). If the collected data get shared with friends, relatives, or online communities, patients also gain control, in the sense that they obtain more diverse feedback. Such interactions likely improve patients' emotional states, because they feel as if they are in control of their own choices and health, which can overcome initial feelings of fear and confusion.

10.3.2 Diagnosis

The second stage relates to diagnosis, when patients seek medical assistance to evaluate their symptoms (Duits et al., 2016). They likely experience alternating emotions, including agitation and calm, which can be enhanced by receiving a correct diagnosis (Gualandi et al., 2021). In their efforts to evaluate and confirm their potential disorders, patients might consider multiple diagnostic assessments, through physical and digital research. They can interact

---

Xiaomi Mijia ECG

The Xiaomi Mijia T-shirt tracks vital signs, including electrocardiography, body temperature, and movement, using complex signal processing technology, ultra-low-power electronics, and low-power wireless microcontrollers. Its support for an electrocardiogram (ECG) function is unique; it can monitor patients accurately and connect with a Xiaomi Wearable App, then send notifications to smart devices, such that they vibrate if the heart appears overstressed but show a color-coded LED display that recommends a good heart rate zone for training. A COTECH smart sensor, embedded in a special strip of tissue near the chest, can offer a real-time measurement. Together with an analog device, the ADI chip and a module specifically dedicated to bioelectric measures, the shirt helps patients keep their vital parameters under control.

with physicians and caregivers in healthcare facilities but also through online platforms, chatbots, and virtual agents (Ng et al., 2021; Tursunbayeva and Renkema, 2022). These diagnosis channels help patients obtain timely, accurate information and select immediate actions. For example, patients might self-diagnose their condition based on online information, then seek to confirm this diagnosis during physical interactions with a doctor. The AI-based solutions offer two benefits in this stage: *self-diagnosis* and *early diagnosis*.

10.3.2.1 Self-Diagnosis

When they perform self-diagnosis, patients evaluate their symptoms and available information, in terms of the degree of relevance of the symptoms, then seek confirmation, such as through an in-person medical examination. The integration of physical and digital touchpoints lists possible next steps for the patients to take. Comparisons of diagnostic information online and offline might help patients glean insights into suitable treatments for their health condition. With their powerful data analysis capabilities, AI-based technologies can support patients' self-evaluation and facilitate diagnoses (Vyas and Bhargava, 2021). For example, chatbots can provide an informal assessment of health conditions for patients who think they need a medical consultation (Nadarzynski et al., 2019; De Keyser and Kunz, 2022). Virtual doctors interact with patients through an automated chat, then guide them to an assessment of their symptoms, based on automatic analyses of data and information. In addition, the data analysis indicates a list of likely symptoms and their urgency, informing patients about whether they need to see a suitable specialist. Some technologies also offer the convenience of immediate connections to book an in-person or telemedicine visit, depending on patients' needs. Subsequently, patients can obtain confirmation and a more accurate diagnosis by visiting a diagnostic facility and interacting with the staff.

10.3.2.2 Early Diagnosis

Symptoms detected as early as possible represent a valuable goal for patients. By combining data from multiple sources, patients and caregivers can obtain more detailed information, quickly and in a personalized form, which can be extremely helpful for unfamiliar conditions. Using AI-based technologies, they obtain reliable, detailed data in real-time, without time or space constraints, and they can consult and interact with healthcare professionals in informative interactions, which should speed up diagnostic procedures safely. Physicians also can analyze more detailed vital and physiological parameters in less time or connect with other medical providers in real-time. In addition to facilitating disease diagnosis (Dai and Singh, 2020), it can increase accuracy and limit errors (Antoniou et al., 2022). Because patients are guided toward appropriate, timely interventions, the gap between their knowledge and their competence decreases, with positive impacts on their experiences. The clear,

---

Serena

Serena is a virtual assistant featured on Paginemediche (a platform that connects doctors and patients) that helps people diagnose their health concerns online. This AI-based program can assess symptoms and identify possible diseases associated with them, and it offers an opportunity to book an in-person visit if necessary. The virtual doctor refines the diagnosis, informs patients about the degree of relevance of symptoms, and lists possible next steps. Serena also provides quicker answers and a simplified process for obtaining diagnostic feedback.

---

correct, detailed, and immediately available data also support more informed interactions with physicians. In scenarios in which patients feel overwhelmed by the complex health information they receive (Boccia et al., 2020), effective technology tools can reduce their emotional and cognitive burdens and limit the risk of information overload (Bester et al., 2016). Patients experience diminished emotional frustration and in turn move to the next stage.

10.3.3 Treatment

The third stage is the most crucial and complex (Devi et al., 2020). The treatment phase begins when patients start to receive care to address their symptoms. They likely experience feelings of hopefulness mixed with anxiety, though these alternating emotions may be resolved if the treatment provides constant efficacy (Mohr et al., 2018; Gualandi et al., 2021). Patients often enter into intensive interactions with physicians to manage their care and determine if the effects of the treatment are as intended or if another therapy is warranted. This relationship can be facilitated and mediated by technologies (Borycki et al., 2020) that support continuous exchanges through physical and digital touchpoints. An initial step might involve in-person counseling to

---

Augmented Diagnosis: AccuVein

AccuVein is a revolutionary handheld device designed to help providers locate veins for medical procedures and blood draws. It displays a digital map of the vascular system on the surface of the patient's skin in real-time, allowing providers to check vein patency and avoid valves or bifurcations. The displays rely on the hemoglobin in the blood, which preferentially absorbs infrared light. Thus, they can depict the contents of the veins, not the entire vein.

---

define and prescribe care activities. Patients' compliance with the prescribed curative tasks can be facilitated by technological tools, such as AI-prompted reminders to take medications. If integrative care is required, patients also make appointments with another practitioner (e.g., physiotherapy), and they might grant permission for the specialist to share treatment information digitally with their primary doctor, as well as leverage at-home technologies such as VR apps that outline physical therapies (Barteit et al., 2021). However, when symptoms persist without improvement, patients may become discouraged (Sahranavard et al., 2018) and return to the diagnosis stage, such as by changing doctors or healthcare facilities. When AI-based technologies provide solutions, both patients (together with family members) and physicians can improve knowledge and management of therapeutic processes, through two actions: *management* and *upgrade*.

10.3.3.1 Management

Management phase refers to an integrated approach to handle care treatment. To engage in management, patients should follow treatments prescribed by their doctor, often with the support of AI-based solutions such as service robotics, AR, VR, or Internet of Things (IoT) or Internet of Everything (IoE) solutions (Mele and Russo Spena, 2019). Because AI-based solutions can collect data and discover relevant aspects, they give patients insightful details about their care (e.g., correct time to take a drug) and can identify inconsistencies, errors, or anomalies (Meyer, 2019). Alerted to any mistakes, patients can book an in-person consultation to update their physician on the progress of the therapy. Data collected by technological devices also influence the timing of treatments, by complementing caregivers' expertise (formal and informal). For example, doctors might decide whether they need to increase or decrease medication dosages, based on automatic sharing of patients' conditions. In detail, AI-based technologies aid patients and caregivers in determining how to implement the best care solutions or actions, promptly, so they can manage their care effectively and ensure the proper administration of care. In turn, such tools should have positive impacts on patients' sense of hope and reduced anxiety levels.

10.3.3.2 Upgrade

In an upgrade, the treatment adapts to the evolution of the disease and other patient-related conditions. The continuous updating of all data allows for continuous adaptations to ongoing care, in a tailor-made manner (Borycki et al., 2020; McCarthy et al., 2020). Physicians leverage the automated analyses of vast data to monitor patients' treatment compliance, then identify alternative actions if necessary, which should enhance the entire care process (Pradhan and Chawla, 2020). That is, physicians' expertise gets complemented by AI software that assesses vast data from a range of sources (e.g., drug monographs, therapeutic outcomes, disease monographs, scientific articles), as well

---

XR Health: Virtual Reality

XR Health launched the first VR telehealth clinic. While other clinics may assign patients to different therapists, XR Health assigns each patient a dedicated healer. The patient receives a VR viewer to take home. Treatment is delivered through private video consultations and in-app messaging, supported at any time, without having to wait for an appointment. Therapists design customized treatment plans by combining conventional exercises and procedures with state-of-the-art VR technology. The goal is to maximize outcomes by using updated research insights, advanced equipment, and careful monitoring of patients' data. Treatments include functional rehabilitation; memory and cognitive training; options for anxiety, depression, and stress management; therapies to enhance sensory and perceptual processing; postoperative rehabilitation; therapies for movement disorders, neck and back pain, and sports-related problems; and pain care coordination.

---

as by personal smart devices that provide continuous feedback. Both patients and doctors thus learn more about the efficacy of the treatment and required adjustments to the care protocol, which may lower the risk of therapeutic errors (Meyer, 2019; Aggarwal et al., 2020). Furthermore, patients can compare suggestions related to treatment progress received from the device and from the doctor (Pradhan and Chawla, 2020).

10.3.4 Follow Up

The fourth stage is the follow-up, which entails assessments of the outcomes of the treatment (Kwast et al., 2013). Patients who demonstrate poor adherence or report inferior treatment outcomes may present new symptoms and require a new diagnosis, thereby restarting the loop. In this step, the patients may experience confidence and relief, or they might suffer negative emotions if the treatment appears to have failed or the monitoring process is very complex (Gualandi et al., 2021). For example, a patient being discharged from the

---

Micromedex

This AI technology–based software supports drug therapy decisions by generating detailed information about dosages, warnings, and precautions. It gives healthcare professionals recommendations for which medications to use to treat conditions. It also increases the safety and validation of therapeutic pathways.

---

hospital after a heart attack faces a long recovery period, marked by dietary restrictions, medications, exercise regimens, and monitoring of multiple warning signs. At the moment of their discharge, patients should be briefed by nursing staff and receive reference materials related to recovery, but they are responsible for managing the recovery, which can introduce great stress and uncertainty. During this period, patients also may need to interact with multiple professionals (e.g., nutritionist, cardiologist, personal trainer, and home care nurses). Technology can be beneficial, because it can provide support and guidance, in the form of information and insights that should inform decision-making, as well as predictive analyses. Through digital touchpoints, robotic devices and smart apps can gauge vital signs and detect anomalies automatically, so patients should feel safer, even in the absence of caregivers. Rather than visit the hospital for check-ups, patients also might rely on automated technology solutions to receive remote support, monitoring of care, assistance, or surveillance help. Such tools help expedite care services and reduce health risks (Gualandi et al., 2021). In addition, informal caregivers carry out rapid control of patients' actions, with immediate responses to favor the appropriate interventions (Baudier et al., 2019). The simultaneous interactions and phygital follow-up by several actors, together with the possibility to connect at any time and without spatial limits, help patients feel more secure. Follow-up involves *monitoring* and *prevention*.

10.3.4.1 Monitoring

Monitoring of key data and detection of abnormalities or asymptomatic issues (Arias et al., 2020) helps patients address critical concerns in advance (Gatzoulis and Iakovidis, 2007). Self-monitoring in particular is facilitated by technology, which also can send alerts to family members when patients engage in certain activities (e.g., if a patient at risk of falling gets out of bed) (Mele et al., 2021; Ng et al., 2021). Patients affected by diabetes can keep track of their sugar intake levels by using an AI-based smart fork that collects data and transfers this information to patients' family members, who then can intervene by nudging changes to the patients' eating styles and lifestyles. This tool generates positive impacts for both patients' and caregivers' experiences. Therefore, patients may grow more confident, because their health conditions and activities are being continuously checked. In some critical situations, patients seek direct, immediate help and interventions, which can be prompted by alerts sent by AI-based technologies. In turn, patients' family members likely feel some sense of relief and diminished burdens.

10.3.4.2 Prevention

Prevention measures seek to predict and avoid the onset of additional symptoms. In this step, patients seek to eliminate or reduce any factors that might contribute to the recurrence of symptoms. Predictive analyses derived from

EKO: Remote Heart Monitoring Using AI and Sound

EKO brings together advanced stethoscopes and intelligent detection software. The algorithms feature two stethoscope-like devices. The CORE amplifies sound by 40 times, compared with a traditional stethoscope; the DUO combines sound and ECG recording. The latter is available as an in-home device that patients can use to monitor their vital signs. The software relies on sophisticated algorithms to analyze heart health with a single-lead ECG and gauge heartbeats using a deep neural network model trained on multiple heart sound data sets. The sound analysis can detect tissue vibration caused by turbulent blood flow, which is difficult for the human ear to detect, because it overlaps with the heartbeat.

AI-based technologies support this stage. For example, for patients suffering from depression, a social robot can help them avoid situations that tend to evoke depressive episodes or connect them with loved ones by initiating a call through an embedded tablet. Robotic designs that feature big eyes and mimic facial expressions even can prompt emotional bonds during conversations, such that they keep patients engaged and create stronger relationships (Mele et al., 2021). During such engagement, the robot can track and analyze patients' behaviors, feelings, and needs, then tailor advice to those insights. In summary, by leveraging AI-based technologies, patients and their care networks can proactively prevent unwanted effects in the post-treatment phase by taking appropriate measures early (Ng et al., 2021). If the symptoms do recur, the journey begins again.

Mabu (by Catalia Health): The Healthcare Buddy

Mabu is a socially interactive robot that tailors its conversations to facilitate patient follow-up and seeks to help patients deal with chronic diseases, such as by reminding them to maintain their medication regime. The smart platform learns about each patient's personality, interests, and treatment challenges over time. Mabu's conversations then reflect the patients' unique personalities and circumstances. It relies on conversational AI technologies to ask patients key questions that a doctor may have; for example, for patients with heart failure, it might seek to determine if they are experiencing fluid retention, weight increases, or shortness of breath. Anomalous responses that signal a patient may be in danger get sent as alerts to health professionals.

10.4 Conclusions

Care journeys can be marred by late diagnoses, "one-size-fits-all" treatment plans, and limited access that creates bottlenecks in the health system. Treatment traditionally has been location-bound, such that patients had to find access to hospitals, providers, and healthcare facilities. Technological advances have largely eliminated such space, time, and data access limitations, enabling them to connect with doctors and caregivers anytime and anywhere. In this sense, AI has the potential to reshape the healthcare industry completely, including trends in which it provides more significant support for human capabilities and supports healthcare organizations to deliver higher quality services more efficiently.

We present the notion of a phygital care journey, in which physical and digital experiences combine, and we widen our focus to include various involved actors, beyond patients, such as physicians and formal and informal caregivers. This journey extends beyond consulting a website or using a smartwatch; it requires offering actors as many options as possible, efficiently and safely (Mele and Russo Spena, 2022). By enabling remote reservations for patients, better access to information for doctors, and increased service personalization, AI-based technologies can continuously improve patients' experiences; this happens both during the visit and treatment, and also before (e.g., symptom identification, preparing patients for examinations) and after (e.g., sending reminders, providing test results). However, while AI technologies allow utilizing information related to the clinical evidence, the focus is also on the context of the patients' experience, what nudges them to act, and how they are engaged with the whole healthcare treatment. Objective data and patients' voices are not competing information sources.

As in any journey, the connected stages all entail specific care interactions, actions, and actors, and AI-based technologies connect the entire healthcare system to allow the phygital care journey to unfold. It summarizes multiple healthcare interactions and presents a holistic view of the path patients experience as patients navigate the process of getting care and managing their health. By connecting the entire healthcare system, AI-based technologies also provide a pervasive nudge that should amplify actors' abilities and actions (Mele et al., 2019). In sum, technologies enable patients and other actors to enter into an augmented care journey.

10.5 Implications for Practitioners

The concept of the phygital care journey offers important insights for practitioners. First, healthcare organizations need to understand how to create phygital contexts to enable the transition from a paradigm of simple care delivery to an integrated phygital journey where patients exploit all possible touchpoints, physical and digital, for an immediate and interactive care experience. In this endeavor managers should devote more attention to the process of shaping the phygital care journey, by strengthening enablers and removing the obstacles in the origination, diagnosis, treatment, and follow-up stages. Efforts to visualize the care journey are helpful to reduce unpredictability and support the development of the provider's value proposition.

Second, healthcare organizations have to take action to affect patients' experience by improving the interplay between multiple touchpoints to increase and facilitate patient's interactions. In evaluating how AI-based technologies affect patients' experiences, practitioners must also map their emotions.

Third, they should carefully investigate the uses of AI-based technologies and define possibilities for designing and tailoring contexts to the relevant activities of actors by leveraging automatic acquisition and detection of data, which in turn should speed up and optimize the care process. They need to understand how incorporating AI-based technologies into physical contexts might affect various actors' abilities and the broader healthcare ecosystem. In particular, they need more insights into how combinations of digital and physical, machine and human, should be integrated into healthcare.

In summary, practitioners must prioritize strategic, cultural, and social visions of phygital care. They should understand how to exploit opportunities provided by physical and digital integration, consider ways to address challenges (e.g., limited acceptance of technology), and evaluate both economic investments and benefits concerning patients' experiences.

10.6 Implications for Scholars and Future Research

Research into patient experiences increasingly focuses on technological evolutions, and to advance such efforts, the visualization of the phygital care journey can represent an appropriate conceptual framework. Scholars can use the visual phygital care journey to depict how patients, doctors, caregivers, and other actors in healthcare ecosystems interact and engage at different stages, moments, and touchpoints, such that experiences emerge. A focus on AI-based technologies can support investigations of the interplay of social, emotional, and behavioral states along the care journey. Examples of relevant research questions could be: What are the driving forces, connectors, and key pillars of the phygital care experience? How do engage patients and other actors in all four related stages? How can the phygital care journey affect patients' engagement?

Moreover, scholars can analyze how the increasing use of AI-based technologies influences the multiple points of contact, also identifying the enablers and constraints of the four stages. In this sense, further research questions could be: At which stage of the journey can AI-based technology be most useful? What impact do AI-based technologies have on patients' behavior, emotions, and trust during the journey? Are there new ways to capture patients' emotional states (e.g., through extended reality technologies) and their actions in a myriad of real-time touchpoints? What power does digital data have, over physical observations, in physicians' decision-making processes? How can actors of healthcare ecosystems be educated to use AI-based technologies adequately?

Finally, another route to future research could address privacy and ethical challenges. Medical data as confidential information is online, on the cloud, or on edge. The future looks bright for the security and privacy of sensitive medical healthcare data. The research topics, which could be further explored include: What are the ethical implications regarding how data and information from patients and other stakeholders are obtained and managed? How to safeguard and ensure patients' privacy? Will patients want to give sensitive data to benefit from a phygital care experience? What are the ethical boundaries around substituting technologies for human actors and who should set these boundaries?

References

Abshire, M., Xu, J., Dennison Himmelfarb, C., Davidson, P., Sulmasy, D., Kub, J., ... & Nolan, M. (2015). Symptoms and fear in heart failure patients approaching end of life: A mixed methods study. *Journal of Clinical Nursing*, 24(21–22), 3215–3223.

Aggarwal, M., Borycki, E. M., Wagner, E., & Gosselin, K. (2020). The current state of knowledge on mobile health interventions for opioid related harm: Integrating scoping review findings with the patient journey. *Knowledge Management & E-Learning: An International Journal*, 12(4), 448–468.

Alkire, L., O'Connor, G. E., Myrden, S., & Köcher, S. (2020). Patient experience in the digital age: An investigation into the effect of generational cohorts. *Journal of Retailing and Consumer Services*, 57(1–9), 102221.

Antoniou, G., Papadakis, E., & Baryannis, G. (2022). Mental health diagnosis: A case for explainable artificial intelligence. *International Journal on Artificial Intelligence Tools*, 31(3), 2241003.

Arias, M., Rojas, E., Aguirre, S., Cornejo, F., Munoz-Gama, J., Sepúlveda, M., & Capurro, D. (2020). Mapping the patient's journey in healthcare through process mining. *International Journal of Environmental Research and Public Health*, 17(18), 6586.

Baker, S. B., Xiang, W., & Atkinson, I. (2017). Internet of things for smart healthcare: Technologies, challenges, and opportunities. *IEEE Access*, 5, 26521–26544.

Barteit, S., Lanfermann, L., Bärnighausen, T., Neuhann, F., & Beiersmann, C. (2021). Augmented, mixed, and virtual reality-based head-mounted devices for medical education: Systematic review. *JMIR Serious Games*, 9(3), e29080.

Baudier, P., Ammi, C., Lecouteux, A. (2019). Employees' acceptance of the healthcare internet of things: A source of innovation in corporate human resource policies. *Journal of Innovation Economics Management*, 2(3), 89–111.

Bester, J., Cole, C. M., & Kodish, E. (2016). The limits of informed consent for an overwhelmed patient: Clinicians' role in protecting patients and preventing overwhelm. *AMA Journal of Ethics*, 18(9), 869–886.

Bjerg, K. (2011). Dimensions of the patient journey: Charting and sharing the patient journey with long term user-driven support systems. In Rakesh Biswas and Carmel Mary Martin (eds.), *User-Driven Healthcare and Narrative Medicine: Utilizing Collaborative Social Networks and Technologies* (410–432). IGI Global, Hershey, PA.

Boccia, S., Ricciardi, W., & Ioannidis, J. P. (2020). What other countries can learn from Italy during the COVID-19 pandemic. *JAMA Internal Medicine*, 180(7), 927–928.

Bolton, R. N., McColl-Kennedy, J. R., Cheung, L., Gallan, A., Orsingher, C., Witell, L., & Zaki, M. (2018). Customer experience challenges: Bringing together digital, physical and social realms. *Journal of Service Management*, 29(5), 776–808.

Borycki, E. M., Kushniruk, A. W., Wagner, E., & Kletke, R. (2020). Patient journey mapping: Integrating digital technologies into the journey. *Knowledge Management & E-Learning: An International Journal*, 12(4), 521–535.

Chan, T. C., Eberg, M., Forster, K., Holloway, C., Ieraci, L., Shalaby, Y., & Yousefi, N. (2022). An inverse optimization approach to measuring clinical pathway concordance. *Management Science*, 68(3), 1882–1903.

Coulter, A., Fitzpatrick, R., & Cornwell, J. (2009). Measures of patients' experience in hospital: Purpose, methods and uses, King's Fund, 1–32.

Dai, T., & Singh, S. (2020). Conspicuous by its absence: Diagnostic expert testing under uncertainty. *Marketing Science*, 39(3), 540–563.

De Keyser, A., & Kunz, W. H. (2022). Living and working with service robots: A TCCM analysis and considerations for future research. *Journal of Service Management*, 33(2), 165–196.

De Keyser, A., Verleye, K., Lemon, K. N., Keiningham, T. L., & Klaus, P. (2020). Moving the customer experience field forward: Introducing the touchpoints, context, qualities (TCQ) nomenclature. *Journal of Service Research*, 23(4), 433–455.

Devi, R., Kanitkar, K., Narendhar, R., Sehmi, K., & Subramaniam, K. (2020). A narrative review of the patient journey through the lens of non-communicable diseases in low-and middle-income countries. *Advances in Therapy*, 37(12), 4808–4830.

Doyle, C., Lennox, L., & Bell, D. (2013). A systematic review of evidence on the links between patient experience and clinical safety and effectiveness. *BMJ Open*, 3(1), e001570.

Duits, P., Cath, D. C., Heitland, I., & Baas, J. M. (2016). High current anxiety symptoms, but not a past anxiety disorder diagnosis, are associated with impaired fear extinction. *Frontiers in Psychology*, 7(1), 252.

Ferreira, A. (2021). *How To Be A Digital Doctor*. eBook Partnership, London.

Fruehwirt, W., & Duckworth, P. (2021). Towards better healthcare: What could and should be automated?. *Technological Forecasting and Social Change*, 172(1), 120967.

Gao, Y., Li, H., & Luo, Y. (2015). An empirical study of wearable technology acceptance in healthcare. *Industrial Management & Data Systems*, 115(9), 1704–1723.

Gatzoulis, L., & Iakovidis, I. (2007). Wearable and portable eHealth systems. *IEEE Engineering in Medicine and Biology Magazine*, 26(5), 51–56.

Gelsomini, M., Spitale, M., & Garzotto, F. (2021). Phygital interfaces for people with intellectual disability: An exploratory study at a social care center. *Multimedia Tools and Applications*, 80(26), 34843–34874.

Gualandi, R., Masella, C., Piredda, M., Ercoli, M., & Tartaglini, D. (2021). What does the patient have to say? Valuing the patient experience to improve the patient journey. *BMC Health Services Research*, 21(1), 1–12.

Gualandi, R., Masella, C., Viglione, D., & Tartaglini, D. (2019). Exploring the hospital patient journey: What does the patient experience?. *PloS One*, 14(12), e0224899.

Halvorsrud, R., Lillegaard, A. L., Røhne, M., & Jensen, A. M. (2019). Managing complex patient journeys in healthcare. In Pfannstiel, M.A. & Rasche, C. (eds) Service Design and Service Thinking in Healthcare and Hospital Management (329–346). Springer, Cham. https://doi.org/10.1007/978-3-030-00749-2_19

He, Q., Du, F., & Simonse, L. W. (2021). A patient journey map to improve the home isolation experience of persons with mild COVID-19: Design research for service touchpoints of artificial intelligence in eHealth. *JMIR Medical Informatics*, 9(4), e23238.

Huang, M. H., & Rust, R. T. (2018). Artificial intelligence in service. *Journal of Service Research*, 21(2), 155–172.

Joseph, A. L., Kushniruk, A. W., & Borycki, E. M. (2020). Patient journey mapping: Current practices, challenges and future opportunities in healthcare. *Knowledge Management & E-Learning: An International Journal*, 12(4), 387–404.

Kraus, S., Schiavone, F., Pluzhnikova, A., & Invernizzi, A. C. (2021). Digital transformation in healthcare: Analyzing the current state-of-research. *Journal of Business Research*, 123, 557–567.

Kushniruk, A. W., Borycki, E. M., & Parush, A. (2020). A case study of patient journey mapping to identify gaps in healthcare: Learning from experience with cancer diagnosis and treatment. *Knowledge Management & E-Learning: An International Journal*, 12(4), 405–418.

Kwast, A. B. G., Drossaert, C. H., Siesling, S., & Follow-up Working Group. (2013). Breast cancer follow-up: From the perspective of health professionals and patients. *European Journal of Cancer Care*, 22(6), 754–764.

Larivière, B., Bowen, D., Andreassen, T. W., Kunz, W., Sirianni, N. J., Voss, C., … & De Keyser, A. (2017). "Service Encounter 2.0": An investigation into the roles of technology, employees and customers. *Journal of Business Research*, 79(1), 238–246.

Lee, D. (2019). A model for designing healthcare service based on the patient experience. *International Journal of Healthcare Management*, 12(3), 180–188.

Leone, D., Schiavone, F., Appio, F. P., & Chiao, B. (2021). How does artificial intelligence enable and enhance value co-creation in industrial markets? An exploratory case study in the healthcare ecosystem. *Journal of Business Research*, 129(2), 849–859.

Ly, S., Runacres, F., & Poon, P. (2021). Journey mapping as a novel approach to healthcare: A qualitative mixed methods study in palliative care. *BMC Health Services Research*, 21(1), 1–9.

McCarthy, S., O'Raghallaigh, P., Woodworth, S., Lim, Y. L., Kenny, L. C., & Adam, F. (2016). An integrated patient journey mapping tool for embedding quality in healthcare service reform. *Journal of Decision Systems*, 25(sup1), 354–368.

McCarthy, S., O'Raghallaigh, P., Woodworth, S., Lim, Y. Y., Kenny, L. C., & Adam, F. (2020). Embedding the pillars of quality in health information technology solutions using "integrated patient journey mapping"(IPJM): Case study. *JMIR Human Factors*, 7(3), e17416.

McColl-Kennedy, J. R., Danaher, T. S., Gallan, A. S., Orsingher, C., Lervik-Olsen, L., & Verma, R. (2017). How do you feel today? Managing patient emotions during health care experiences to enhance well-being. *Journal of Business Research*, 79(2), 247–259.

Mele, C., & Russo-Spena, T. (2019). Innovation in sociomaterial practices: The case of IoE in the healthcare ecosystem. In Handbook of Service Science, 1(2), 517–544. Springer, Cham.

Mele, C., & Russo-Spena, T. (2022). The architecture of the phygital customer journey: A dynamic interplay between systems of insights and systems of engagement. *European Journal of Marketing*, 56(1), 72–91.

Mele, C., Marzullo, M., Di Bernardo, I., Russo-Spena, T., Massi, R., La Salandra, A., & Cialabrini, S. (2022). A smart tech lever to augment caregivers' touch and foster vulnerable patient engagement and well-being. *Journal of Service Theory and Practice*, 32(1), 52–74.

Mele, C., Russo-Spena, T., Tregua, M., & Amitrano, C. C. (2021). The millennial customer journey: A Phygital mapping of emotional, behavioural, and social experiences. *Journal of Consumer Marketing*, 38(4), 420–433.

Meyer, M. A. (2019). Mapping the patient journey across the continuum: Lessons learned from one patient's experience. *Journal of Patient Experience*, 6(2), 103–107.

Mohr, P., Galderisi, S., Boyer, P., Wasserman, D., Arteel, P., Ieven, A., ... & Gaebel, W. (2018). Value of schizophrenia treatment I: The patient journey. *European Psychiatry*, 53(1), 107–115.

Nadarzynski, T., Miles, O., Cowie, A., & Ridge, D. (2019). Acceptability of artificial intelligence (AI)-led chatbot services in healthcare: A mixed-methods study. *Digital Health*, 5, 2055207619871808.

Ng, Z. Q. P., Ling, L. Y. J., Chew, H. S. J., & Lau, Y. (2021). The role of artificial intelligence in enhancing clinical nursing care: A scoping review. *Journal of Nursing Management*, 3(1), 1–21.

Oldenburg, B., Taylor, C. B., O'Neil, A., Cocker, F., & Cameron, L. D. (2015). Using new technologies to improve the prevention and management of chronic conditions in populations. *Annual Review of Public Health*, 36(1), 483–505.

Osei-Frimpong, K., Wilson, A., & Lemke, F. (2018). Patient co-creation activities in healthcare service delivery at the micro level: The influence of online access to healthcare information. *Technological Forecasting and Social Change*, 126(1), 14–27.

Park, Y. J., & Shin, D. D. (2020). Contextualizing privacy on health-related use of information technology. *Computers in Human Behavior*, 105, 106204.

Percival, J., & McGregor, C. (2016). An evaluation of understandability of patient journey models in mental health. *JMIR Human Factors*, 3(2), e20.

Ponsignon, F., Smart, A., & Phillips, L. (2018). A customer journey perspective on service delivery system design: Insights from healthcare. *International Journal of Quality & Reliability Management*, 35(10), 2328–2347.

Pradhan, K., & Chawla, P. (2020). Medical internet of things using machine learning algorithms for lung cancer detection. *Journal of Management Analytics*, 7(4), 591–623.

Prakash, D. V., Barshe, S., Khade, V., Karmakar, A. (2021). Medical chatbot. *International Journal of Research in Engineering, Science and Management*, 4(3), 161–164.

Reay, S. D., Collier, G., Douglas, R., Hayes, N., Nakarada-Kordic, I., Nair, A., & Kennedy-Good, J. (2017). Prototyping collaborative relationships between design and healthcare experts: Mapping the patient journey. *Design for Health*, 1(1), 65–79.

Sahranavard, S., Esmaeili, A., Dastjerdi, R., & Salehiniya, H. (2018). The effectiveness of stress-management-based cognitive-behavioral treatments on anxiety sensitivity, positive and negative affect and hope. *BioMedicine*, 8(4), 125–142.

Schiavone, F., Mancini, D., Leone, D., & Lavorato, D. (2021). Digital business models and ridesharing for value co-creation in healthcare: A multi-stakeholder ecosystem analysis. *Technological Forecasting and Social Change*, 166(2), 120647.

Simonse, L., Albayrak, A., & Starre, S. (2019). Patient journey method for integrated service design. *Design for Health*, 3(1), 82–97.

Trebble, T. M., Hansi, N., Hydes, T., Smith, M. A., & Baker, M. (2010). Process mapping the patient journey: An introduction. BMJ, 341(1), 12–28.

Tursunbayeva, A., & Renkema, M. (2022). Artificial intelligence in health-care: Implications for the job design of healthcare professionals. *Asia Pacific Journal of Human Resources*, 3(2), 155–189.

Van Doorn, J., Mende, M., Noble, S. M., Hulland, J., Ostrom, A. L., Grewal, D., & Petersen, J. A. (2017). Domo arigato Mr. Roboto: Emergence of automated social presence in organizational frontlines and customers' service experiences. *Journal of Service Research*, 20(1), 43–58.

Vyas, S., & Bhargava, D. (2021). Challenges, opportunities and future trends in smart health. *Smart Health Systems*, 3(1), 113–125.

Wang, Y., & Hajli, N. (2017). Exploring the path to big data analytics success in healthcare. *Journal of Business Research*, 70(3), 287–299.

World Health Organization. (2020). Modes of transmission of virus causing COVID-19: Implications for IPC precaution recommendations: Scientific brief, 29 March 2020 (No. WHO/2019-nCoV/Sci_Brief/Transmission_modes/2020.2). World Health Organization, Geneva.

Wuenderlich, N. V., Heinonen, K., Ostrom, A. L., Patricio, L., Sousa, R., Voss, C. and Lemmink, J. G. A. M. (2015). "Futurizing" smart service: Implications for service researchers and managers. *Journal of Services Marketing*, 29(6/7), 442–447.

11 AI Technologies and Hospital Blood Delivery in Peripheral Regions

Insights from Zipline International

Valentina Cucino and Giulio Ferrigno

11.1 Introduction

Digital and enabling technologies are key drivers in the economic and societal transitions we are currently undergoing (Di Vaio et al., 2020; Loureiro et al., 2021). In the third decade of the 21st Century digitalization support services yield enormous quantities of data and Artificial Intelligence (AI hereafter), machine learning techniques, and data analytics are permeating decision-making. These technologies represent an opportunity for any company working in all kinds of industries as they allow defining new business models and developing new capabilities to integrate, build, and reconfigure internal and external resources/competencies. Albeit the initial skepticism (Barrat, 2013), these technologies are very important for firms willing to reach efficiency, increase productivity, and therefore improve their performance.

In addition to the impact on business performance, these technologies may also have a positive impact on many societal problems in new and unpredictable ways (Dabrowska et al., 2022; Margherita, 2022). Given their potential, they can be an important lever for hybrid organizations, which typically combine charitable and business aspects (Ebrahim et al., 2014). Consider for instance a medical device that uses advanced data science and AI to interpolate physical sensor readings and extrapolate the likelihood of disease (Houfani et al., 2021); or a solar-powered car that uses advanced lighting and touchscreen technology to enhance the driver's comfort and travel safety (Ahmad et al., 2021). Furthermore, the social impact of these technologies becomes exponential if they are contextualized in a peripheral region. Indeed, peripheral regions often suffer from old industries and/or organizational thinness in the sense of a lack of dynamic clusters and support organizations that reduce the chance of developing new industries based on scientific knowledge (Karlsen et al., 2011; Tödtling & Trippl, 2005). Therefore, when exponential technologies are applied to a serious societal challenge, especially in a peripheral region, the chance of creating a viable and sustainable solution may increase dramatically.

However, because of the major advances made in exponential technologies, the complexity of implementing them and the underpinnings they might

DOI: 10.4324/9781003304616-15

have for many aspects of social life are not yet fully understood. Indeed, we are currently struggling with many societal challenges (good health and well-being, i.e. SDG3, responsible consumption and production, i.e. SDG12 and climate change, i.e. SDG13) and we are still far from developing an advanced understanding of how many of these challenges can be partially fulfilled through wide use of exponential technologies.

Building on the literature on AI and hybrid-organization literature innovation, this study examines similar inventions from the digital and AI revolutions, intending to show how these technologies bring about far-reaching changes that will also affect all aspects of our society and life.

11.2 Theoretical Background

11.2.1 AI Technologies-Society Nexus

Digital technologies are defined as combinations of "information, computing, communication, and connectivity technologies" (Bharadwaj et al., 2013, p. 471) or "Social Mobile Analytics Cloud Internet of Things" (Sebastian et al., 2017) have provided both major opportunities and significant challenges to individuals, organizations, ecosystems, and more in general societies (Dabrowska et al., 2022).

In this context, firms develop digital technologies to address grand challenges such as climate change (George et al., 2021) and achieve green growth (Fernandes et al., 2021). Furthermore, new forms of organization, such as digital platforms (e.g., the Next Closet)[1], can enable circular business models, allowing for more efficient usage of resources and the circulation of excess resources across different stakeholders (Bocken & Ritala, 2022), and support sustainable business models (Ferreira et al., 2022). Nonetheless, the intricate nature of digital platforms, which are sometimes social enterprises, hints at the possibility that they may also face the emergence of tensions between social (and environmental) objectives and economic objectives (Kannothra et al., 2018).

The interaction between digital technologies is sustainability is a topic that is currently debated topics for politicians and professionals (Bohnsack et al., 2022). Indeed, although some researchers have supported the negative effects deriving from excessive use of digital technologies on the environment (Bohnsack et al., 2022), several authors discussed the benefits of digital technologies on the environment (Asif et al., 2011; Carnerud et al., 2020). For example, the digitalization of the agri-food sector is proliferating as technologies improve the quality and sustainability of crops.

In the social sphere, it is important that the company supports and assists people with disabilities to provide them with significant hope and life (Cucino et al., 2022). According to the 2030 agenda, the united nations flagships on disabilities and development 2018 reported having reached the milestone for people with disabilities in most SDG pillars such as SDG2 (ending poverty and hunger for all persons with disabilities), SDG3 (guaranteeing a healthy life and promoting well -being), and SDG13 (constructing resilience of people with disabilities and reducing their exposure to any impact from dangers related to climate and other shocks and catastrophes). Therefore, a lot of attention is paid to the socio-technologists of digital technologies that can facilitate the activities of disabled people (Cucino et al., 2022). In fact, there are many digital technologies designed for all types of disabilities, such as assistants for housing technologies, digital and social media games, and mobile applications. However, the development of digital technologies for some types of disabilities (e.g. mental disability) is still low compared to the rest (Pulsiri et al., 2019).

11.2.2 Societal Benefits of AI Technologies in the Periphery

The Covid-19 pandemic has shown the world how economies and businesses can be severely tested by crises. However, it also showed a new side to digital technologies. Indeed, technology coupled with a desire to contribute to helping society enabled companies and organizations more generally to take extraordinary purpose-oriented actions (Cucino et al., 2021; Ferrigno & Cucino, 2021). Indeed, companies like Clinicas de Azucar in Mexico are using AI to analyze data and improve health outcomes for thousands of at-risk diabetic patients. In India, 1mg uses AI to help customers compare prices for medical services from different labs. However, the technology has not only helped several peripheral regions in outlying regions to maintain essential services and keep businesses running during the COVID-19 crisis.

Thus, although the pandemic triggered the deepest global recession since World War II, threatening economies, the development of technology has made it possible to re-evaluate the peripheral regions through the development of new businesses and new jobs. Moreover, although peripheral regions can suffer from lock-in situations due to their limited ability to access new external knowledge, peripheral regions can also contribute with theoretical and practical implications for the advancement of public policy of innovation. An example is the Galician case which helps explain the evolution of the public sector in stimulating innovation, entrepreneurship, and growth, through the use of digital technologies (Zabala-Iturriagagoitia, 2022). Indeed, in times of crisis, businesses in peripheral regions are incredibly flexible, which helps socioeconomic sustainability within the region (Wilson & Anderson, 2004). Moreover, the creation of new enterprises can occur in remote regions often using unique values, connecting and transforming traditional peripheral weaknesses into strengths (Anderson, 2000; Korsgaard et al., 2022).

This phenomenon has also offered a glimpse of a brighter future, where income and employment gains are driven by technologies such as AI. Thus, the strategic adoption of technologies such as AI can be an important part of the rebuilding effort, helping to increase productivity and foster a new generation of innovative companies.

11.3 Methodology

11.3.1 Research Setting

Providing affordable healthcare to people in the low and middle countries is a persistent development problem (Chemouni, 2018). WHO estimated in 2010 that 100 million people are pushed into poverty and 150 million suffer financial catastrophe due to out-of-pocket expenses for health services each year (WHO, 2020, p. 8). However, although universal health coverage is a priority on the global development agenda (as evidenced by its inclusion in the Sustainable Development Goals), how to achieve this in poor countries remains much debated (WHO, 2010).

Rwanda has a serious poverty problem and the nation has an expansive peasant population, which impairs access to health facilities (in line with SDG3), especially for women. Furthermore, many years of civil war and the terrible genocide of the mid-1990s destroyed the nation's health framework. However, despite these difficulties, Rwanda offers itself as a model for improving access to health services (Chemouni, 2018).

Indeed, the Rwandan government has made upgrading family planning services a national priority. In partnership with the World Health Organization, the Rwandan Ministry of Health organized the negotiation and training of health professionals to provide instruction on family planning, family counseling, and similar services to men and women across the nation. This activity has made it possible to significantly reduce the maternal mortality rate, the main causes of which are the high rate of births occurring without qualified assistance (52%) and the reduced use of family planning and basic obstetric care (27%) (Patrick et al., 2022). In addition, greater recognition and health responsibility have made it possible to expand the quantity and quality of assisted births in Rwanda. In addition, the Rwandan government, despite the state of poverty, has been trying for several years to invest in the adoption of new technologies in the health sector (Boch, 2011). This push from political leaders has certainly facilitated the adoption of new technologies. In fact, as early as 2016, the Head of State Paul Kagame affirmed the need to embrace innovation to overcome the achievement of the Sustainable Development Goals

> Rwandans have learned to embrace innovation [...] This attitude has allowed us to overcome great difficulties over the past twenty-two years and makes us optimistic about how much we can still achieve [...] "Good enough" is no longer enough. We have to aim for the best.

Additionally, Rwanda's Kigali International Airport recently welcomed five human-sized robots in July 2020 (WHO, 2020). The machines are intended to screen people's temperatures, send video messages, and detect people not wearing surgical masks. In case of anomalies, the robots report to the officers on duty. These represent just some of the activities aimed at reviving public health in Rwanda.

11.3.2 The Drone Industry: a Focus on Emergency Medical Services and Products

The empirical setting is fundamental from both a theoretical and managerial perspective (Siggelkow, 2007). According to Drones for Development[2], more than 2.5 billion people live in rural and remote areas in peripheral areas. Drones, also known as unmanned aerial vehicles, are advancing into the 21st century and could contribute to the revitalization of some suburban areas because they are an alternative, reliable, and safe option for transporting samples and distributing medical supplies in these areas (Lamptey & Serwaa, 2020). Application areas are diverse and include agriculture, data processing, military, security, and healthcare. Regardless of purpose and use, drones tend to be very flexible in their use, cost-effective, and efficient because they can ship and distribute packages to their destination when needed (Magistretti & Dell'Era, 2019). In addition, drones are environmentally sustainable, with lower carbon emissions, because they run on batteries and travel the skies unimpeded by road infrastructure or traffic networks. Many empirical studies (Figliozzi, 2017; Stolaroff et al., 2018) show that delivery drones are more 'CO2-efficient' than traditional means of delivery, such as motorcycles, cars, vans, lorries, and planes using fossil fuel.

Finally, when drones transport samples or packages, the approximate delivery time is highly predictable (Giones & Brem, 2017). As such, we selected the drone industry to shed light on this topic, corroborated by the fact that this is an emerging technology (Rotolo et al., 2015). Indeed, drone technology is radically new, relatively fast-growing, and uncertain in the future (Magistretti & Dell'Era, 2019). However, looking at different application fields with different perspectives may provide a better understanding of how hidden opportunities for the community can be unveiled. According to Gartner's 2017 Hype Cycle, drone technology is still under development and will be for the next five years. From the practitioner's perspective, we selected the drone industry due to the increasing investments and the growing number of companies that provide emergency medical services and medical products (Table 11.1).

Drone service for medical supplies is a niche market with over 20 players, the most prominent of which are Zipline, Flirtey, Matternet, Volans-i, Drone Delivery Canada, Antworks, and Wingcopter. In this chapter, we investigate a specific type of drone, Zipline International, a California-based automated logistics company that designs, manufactures, and operates drones to deliver vital medical products in Rwanda. The president of Rwanda became famous for having relaunched the country; the deliveries that are made in the country have consistently increased in the last few years. That was possible after the launch of Zipline. In 2016, when the start-up was launched by its

Table 11.1 A Snapshot of Medical Drone Service Providers

Medical drone service providers	Year of fundation	Headquarter	Key partners	Areas covered
Arone	2018	Nigeria	Local Government	Nigeria
Antworks (Terra Drone)	2011	China	Chinese Center for Disease Control and Prevention, Hospitals	China
Drone Delivery Canada (Condor)	2011	Canada	Local Government	Canada
Ehang	2014	China	Lung Biotechnology PBC	Spain, Austria, China, United States
Flirtey (Eagle)	2013	United States	NASA, the City of Reno, Johns Hopkins University of Medicine, EMS provider REMSA	United States, New Zealand, Australia
Helicus	2016	Belgium	Federal Government (EU)	Antwerp
Indro Robotics	2014	Canada	Renfrew County	Ontario
KamomeAir	2015	Japan	Not available	Setouchi
Marut Drones	2019	India	State of Telangana	Telangana, India
Matternet	2011	United States	UPS US hospitals in partnership with UPS, Switzerland in partnership with Swiss Post	Switzerland, United States
Rigitech	2018	Switzerland	Not available	Switzerland
RPS Aerospace	2016	Italy	Not available	Gerenzano, Italy
Skyports	2017	UK	Not available	London, Los Angeles, Singapore
Swoop Aero	2017	Australia	USAID Global Health Supply Chain, UK Aid, and UNICEF	Vanuatu (Oceania), Democratic Republic of the Congo
Unmanned Systems Operations Group (USOG)	2018	United States	SortPak (medication centre)	United States
Volansi	2015	United States	Merck, Direct Relief, Softbox, AT&T	United States, Bahamas, Switzerland, Puerto Rico

(Continued)

Table 11.1 (Continued)

Medical drone service providers	Year of fundation	Headquarter	Key partners	Areas covered
Wing (Google)	2012	United States	FedEx, Walgreens	United States, Australia
Wingcopter	2017	Germany	UPS	Vanuatu (Oceania), United States
Zipline	2014	United States	Novartis, Pfizer, UPS, Bill & Melinda Gates Foundation, the Gavi Alliance	United States, Africa, Maharashtra (India)

Source: Elaboration from authors

founder Keller Rinaudo (a software engineer with an interest in robotics and autonomous systems), the World Health Organization and the World Economic Forum declared it a visionary project. And indeed, the company has grown progressively from 2016 to 2022. Among all drone service providers (DSPs), Zipline has the largest market share, with about 88%; it focuses on delivering lifesaving medical products in multiple countries. It has made around 333,619 deliveries so far[3] and is partnering with pharma companies such as Novartis and Pfizer, along with other associates, to deliver essential medical products to remote regions. Zipline has raised a total of 457M of euros in funding over 10 rounds. The company operates distribution centers in Rwanda, Ghana, Japan, and the United States, with signed agreements to begin service in Nigeria, Côte d'Ivoire, and Kenya. As of April 2022, its drones have made over 20 million miles of flights across 275,000 commercial deliveries. Given the company's growth and that the technology developed by the company will be progressively used in several different industries ranging from the military to other civilian sectors, a deeper understanding of the company is pertinent to practitioners and researchers alike.

11.3.3 Theoretical Sampling: Zipline International

To conduct this study, we have selected the case by following the principles of theoretical sampling (Glaser & Strauss, 1967; Mason, 1996; Pettigrew, 1990). Two main reasons guided us to inspect the case of Zipline International. First, Zipline International is considered one of the most interesting examples as regards the use of autonomous flying robotics to solve the problem of lack of infrastructure. Zipline mainly delivers medical devices, in particular, blood for transfusions, through the use of drones in a country like Rwanda. Moreover, the company selected is also an example that could be easily applied to today's theme of COVID-19 because it allows to deliver remotely and in a very punctual, rapid way medicines and vaccines in unreachable hospitals where there is an urgent need, thereby bypassing human intervention tools. Second, Zipline has developed AI technologies in a country that has suffered severe problems, heavy losses, and a lack of infrastructure such as Rwanda. The country has made a lot of investments for the growth and development of the company. Therefore, Zipline can also be considered a critical example of social innovation worldwide.

11.3.4 Data Source

As discussed earlier, the exploratory nature of this analysis implies the need to inspect the variety and richness of data that help to understand how AI technologies can be developed to satisfy societal needs. To increase the trustworthiness of the data (Ferrigno et al., 2021; Lincoln & Denzin, 1994), as well as the comprehension of the sampling choice (Cook et al., 1979; Ferrigno, 2016), we based our analysis on a system of multiple data sources. More specifically, following previous studies (Dagnino & Ferrigno, 2015; Jick, 1979), we triangulated a variety of information sources, which are reported in Table 11.2.

First, we collected data from various secondary sources such as 45 press releases from different and complementary representative business databases (SDC Platinum, Factiva database, and Lexis-Nexis) and we cross-checked the information gathered through Google News (the keyword used in the search was "Zipline International"). Also, we have included in the data collection the news reported in the blog of the website of the company. Second, we have gathered data from 20 videos, 9 of which were posted on the Zipline International YouTube channel, which have provided further information about how the AI technologies developed by the company can concretely satisfy the societal needs of Rwanda. The videos contained interviews, statements, and stories from managers and founders.

Third, we have integrated the previous sources by using transcripts of interviews or web speeches that we extracted from press releases, reports, and social networks that were reporting information about the development of Zipline International. Finally, we considered more than 30 pages of scientific articles published about the company. English-language articles were

Table 11.2 Variety of Information Sources

Data	Sources
45 press releases	SDC Platinum, Factiva database, Lexis-Nexis, Google News
20 videos (nine of which were posted on the Zipline International YouTube channel)	YouTube; Zipline YouTube channel
30 pages of scientific articles published about the company	Zipline international website

Source: Elaboration from authors

selected given the language skills of the authors. According to these data, the executives involved in the interviews were considered highly knowledgeable informants because they were positioned at various significant managerial levels of the company.

11.4 Data Analysis

The notable amount of data collected about the case of Zipline International provides the basis to use an inferential approach in our empirical analysis (Glynn & Ichino, 2015). Inferential approaches tend to confirm a research-er's preconceived notions and they are well recognized in the literature (Spillman, 2014). In this chapter, we used an approach similar to previous literature (Ferrigno et al., 2022; Wiltshire & Ronkainen, 2021). A summary of the steps used in the data analysis is reported in Figure 11.1.

First, we conducted a content analysis (Weber, 1990) to make sense of the massive amount of documents collected (press releases, data available from the company's websites, blogs, videos, and newspaper articles). The content analysis allowed us to identify similarities and occurrences to identify the right information to conduct the case narrative. The content analysis was carried out in eight steps as suggested by Weber (1990). First, the recording units have been defined. In other words, the authors selected the materials to be encoded. Second, three authors individually defined the coding cate-gories. Third, three authors made a "clarity assessment" by coding a small sample of text. Fourth, the authors compared and reviewed the text sample together to assess the accuracy and reliability of the selected codes. Fifth, the authors examined the unclear codes, unanimously defining and approving the codes. Subsequently, the two authors codified the entire text. When high

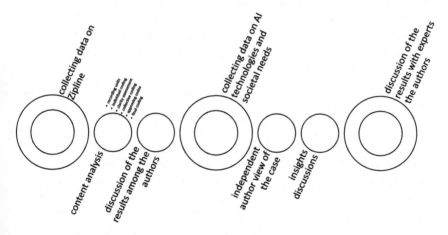

Figure 11.1 Steps conducted in our data analysis.
Source: personal elaboration from authors.

encoder reliability was achieved, the encoding rules were applied to all text. Then, after evaluating the reliability of the coding, the authors gathered and discussed the results.

After conducting the content analysis, we have separately scrutinized the considerable amount of data collected by using the definitions of AI technologies and societal needs and formed an independent view of the case. We then explored the existence of any consistent patterns of relationships within the cases (Yin, 2018). As conceptual insights emerged, we discussed these insights using a devil's advocacy method (Eisenhardt, 1989) to rule out alternative explanations. During the analysis, we iteratively examined the qualitative data by moving back and forth between the theory, data, and literature to adjust for emerging theoretical relationships. As a check, we asked an independent researcher to validate the data analysis.

Last but not least, we contacted five experts of AI technologies to validate our interpretation of results. In the following section, we present the findings of our study.

11.5 Findings and Discussion

Zipline has a long history. Its story begins in 2011 when Keller Rinaudo founded Romotive, which produced an iPhone-controlled robotic toy called the Romo. However, it was only when Romotive closed the company in 2014 that the company focused on providing medical supplies via drones. Co-founders Keenan Wyrobek and William Hetzler have joined forces at this time. Since its founding in 2014, the company has established itself in Ghana and Rwanda, helping to power their national blood delivery network and Covid-19 vaccine distribution, respectively. In 2016, Zipline signed an agreement with the Rwandan government to build a distribution center near Muhanga.

In 2018, the Rwandan government signed a new agreement to build a second distribution center near Kayonza and expand Zipline's service to include smaller health centers as well as hospitals and provide vaccines and other medical products as well as blood products. In April 2018, Zipline announced a second-generation drone, which was placed on Time's "Best Inventions of 2018" list.

In April 2019, Zipline opened its first four planned distribution centers in Ghana to supply 2,500 healthcare facilities. Ghana's fourth distribution center became operational in June 2020. In May 2019, Zipline raised $190 million on a post-money valuation of $1.2 billion. In September 2019, the government of Maharashtra announced Zipline would deliver emergency medicine throughout the country. The proposed deployment includes building ten distribution centers to serve 120 million people. In December 2019, musician Bono joined the board of directors. Zipline was named to CNBC's 2018 (25th place), 2019 (39th place), 2020 (7th place), and 2022 (29th place) lists Disruptor 50 lists.

Along with nine other drone delivery companies, the FAA selected Zipline to participate in a type certification program for drone delivery in 2020. In November 2020, Zipline, along with other manufacturers, began undergoing airworthiness certification with the FAA which would allow their "Sparrow" aircraft model to fly to the United States. The following February, Zipline announced that it would add ultra-low temperature freezers to its distribution centers to allow them to supply temperature-sensitive COVID-19 vaccines.

In February 2021, Zipline announced a plan to construct three distribution centers in Kaduna State, Nigeria. These distribution centers would have ultra-cold storage that is capable of safely storing COVID-19 vaccines, for which health facilities in the state could then place on-demand orders without needing ultra-cold storage of their own. The state also intends to use Zipline's service to transport other health products, including blood, medication, and routine vaccines. In May 2021, Bloomberg reported that Zipline would deliver vaccines to Cross River State and Northern Kaduna State in Nigeria. The following month, Zipline raised $250 million in new funding for a valuation of $2.75 billion.

Zipline was created to meet social needs in Rwanda. Over the years, the company has begun to meet the social needs of other peripheral regions, such as Nigeria, Ghana, and the Ivory Coast. Recently, the company became famous because it was approached by Walmart to make deliveries to the United States. In 2022, the company started a collaboration in Japan, Toyota Tsusho, and opened a center to make deliveries using Zipline equipment in Japan. In February 2022, the company announced an agreement to build a distribution center in Kisumu County, Kenya. Zipline is therefore a paradigmatic case of how it is possible, by helping the poorest countries scale their business internationally. In other words, Zipline is a case of a hybrid company that can balance market goals and social actions. All this has been possible only through the development of AI technologies for the satisfaction of very strong social needs.

11.5.1 *What Makes Zipline So Special?*

The drone delivery system developed by the company made it possible to distribute seven thousand units of blood for transfusion covering 300,000 km of area. The delivery of these units of blood would not have been possible by other means (e.g., by road, as is usually the case in developed countries) because in many cases there are no roads. Through its drone delivery system, Zipline enabled faster blood transfer for transfusions, thus saving the lives of many people. Zipline's drone runs at 100 km per hour and arrives much faster and much cheaper than a pilot-operated transport. There is a fleet of "zips" that have a system of traced routes and these medical products are launched with a small parachute which is then collected by those who have to take it. In this case, we are talking about 20 hospitals and health centers and this fast system practically does not require the cold chain to be able to transport it. The delivery pricing ranges from €15 to €45, decidedly low-cost pricing. It is therefore easy to understand how such an invention can truly have solved a social problem using technology and managing to bypass a huge infrastructural problem. This system, which saves human lives thanks to the use of autonomous flying robotics, is still prohibited in many countries (such as Italy). Nonetheless, this system is instead very important because it can allow the storage and shipping of blood for transfusions and other medicines through logistical tools that involve a take-off area equipped with real launch pads and which allow for the replacement of road transport. This system, of course, involves a collaboration between civil aviation and health authorities so that these blood bags are transported to local hospitals in a very short time with a light, fast, and electric system. Furthermore, this system, within an African country like Rwanda, has also allowed the development of a workforce and jobs of high quality and professionalism that have brought benefits and wealth to the country of Rwanda. The case of Zipline shows how a country that was experiencing difficult situations from an infrastructural point of view became a leader in the healthcare sector by bypassing the problems of the civil war it suffered using AI technology. This led to an 8% growth in gross domestic product from 2001 to 2015 after only 24 years after the Rwandan genocide.

11.5.2 What Takeaways Can We Learn from the Application of AI Technologies in the Relaunch of Rwanda?

Evidence from the world economic forum shows the reasons that partly explain this growth. For example, the agile regulatory system that provides the use of advanced approaches to research, development, clinical trials, and clinical evaluation is an essential element that allows the use of AI technologies and new therapies in healthcare and innovation. Without an appropriate evaluation system of clinical trials and application in public services, AI technologies cannot acquire relevance. This is the first important lesson we learn from Rwanda. Second, the requirements for data platforms and system interoperability from scratch. In many developed countries, such as Italy, we are unable to obtain these requirements because the sharing of clinical data that we would also need to be able to apply AI and other algorithms to our clinical data could infer public health. Last but not least, we should experiment with new reimbursement models that can incentivize the use of precision diagnostics. Innovation is a system based on the assessment of the value of the applications developed for healthcare and on the experimentation of retrospective trials. Clinical systems that work in subpopulations should be understood to develop an awareness of the possible applicability of therapies and drugs developed in Western countries in different populations with different genetic profiles and therefore different reactions to different drugs. In the case of Zipline, it is very important to understand that if we want to apply, for example, the development of AI in the field of medicine and in general if we want to apply it to the innovation of a social type, the element of adaptability to culture, ethnicity, geographical conditions, climatic and also genetic should be considered of fundamental importance. Zipline is a positive case of positive AI that needs a regulatory context, which can be emulated in other cases such as coronavirus.

11.6 Challenges and Opportunities

Two main challenges emerge from the analysis. First, the success of drone operations depends on the weather conditions. Indeed, heat and cold could affect drone performance and remote flight. Strong winds and rain could affect drone flights, battery life, and drone stability. The consequent risk is non-delivery or non-departure until the weather conditions are favorable. A second challenge is not technological but an institutional one. Indeed, in some countries, there may be regulatory problems that could slow the spread of drone technology (Skorup & Haaland, 2020).

Despite these difficulties, two great opportunities emerge (Lamptey & Serwaa, 2020; Skorup & Haaland, 2020). First, it is the relaunch of the peripheral countries. Indeed, drones are contributing immensely to the African revolution, and Ghana has been hailed for supporting this path and, in so doing, has achieved the UN's global goals for universal health care. Second, the development of technology has enabled some peripheral countries such as China to win the pandemic challenge by inspiring innovative ways to increase access to testing and health care for all, even those in remote areas of the country. Thanks to this approach, the Ghanaian government was able to quickly save the lives of the population.

11.7 Contributions

11.7.1 Theoretical Contributions

Digital tools play a key role in changing the way individuals interact (Maiolini et al., 2016). In fact, such technologies help make information explicit and allow participants to keep in touch and solve social and social problems more quickly and effectively. Furthermore, digital technologies reduce the costs of access to innovative ideas (Pisano & Verganti, 2008) and can help companies to increase relationships between individuals and business practices, in relation to ethical issues and social challenges (Vaccaro & Madsen, 2009). Thus, thanks to the emergence of digitized tools, it is possible for many people to actively participate in the generation and implementation of new innovative social ideas (Hutter et al., 2011). However, little evidence has been provided regarding which digital tools are actually used to address social needs (Maiolini et al., 2016). Thus, this chapter offers three contributions to the literature on AI and social innovation. First, in this study, we show that AI technologies can be really powerful to satisfy societal needs. Previous literature on AI has clearly outlined what are the beneficial effects of these technologies on a firm's productivity, organization, and performance (Dabrowska et al., 2022). Moreover, recent studies have started to document the environmental impacts of these technologies (George et al., 2021). However, very few studies have explored the role that these technologies could play for a better society, especially in peripheral regions. By conducting an in-depth qualitative analysis of a representative case of the drone industry (i.e., Zipline International), this study shows how this successful firm has consistently developed AI technologies to satisfy societal needs, especially in peripheral regions such as Rwanda. Second, we also contribute to social innovation literature (Gupta et al., 2020). This study indeed shows that it is possible to generate profits when the social need that is satisfied is very strong. In particular, this study is in line with previous studies that show that through purpose-driven actions it is possible to help solve a collective need even while making profits (Ferrigno & Cucino, 2021). As a result, profits do not become the primary goal of entrepreneurial action but a consequence of solving a societal problem (Craig & Snook, 2014). In fact, by satisfying the societal needs of an underdeveloped country such as Rwanda, the case of Zipline International shows that, when societal needs are satisfied, new business opportunities can emerge and revitalize the business model of the company. Recently Zipline has started to form a plethora of different collaborations with partners (for instance, Walmart) that can impact the growth of the company. Third, we submit a contribution to the literature on innovation in peripheral regions. This study shows that AI technologies can constitute an enabling factor for the development of an underdeveloped country. Rwanda has been traditionally characterized by a lack of infrastructure. Today the country is still without infrastructure but has become the leader in healthcare. Moreover, although peripheral regions are generally considered less favored, Hospers (2005) posited that their advantages come from making a difference, not from doing the same thing as other regions do. This premise indicates that underutilized potential for creating dynamic regional industry may exist within peripheral regions.

11.7.2 Managerial Implications

This study offers three main managerial implications. First, it shows a best practice for entrepreneurs that aim to satisfy societal needs but struggle to generate profits from the social innovation underlying their business. Zipline International was born to meet societal needs in Rwanda. Gradually it began to serve many other peripheral regions, such as Nigeria, Ghana, and Ivory Coast. By doing so, the company has attracted the attention of all media worldwide and became very popular. After five years from its foundation, the company has been contacted by Walmart to operate in the United States and made a partnership in Japan. Therefore, drawing on the case study of Zipline International, we show that it is possible to scale the business internationally when the organization is mainly driven by the intent to satisfy societal needs. Of course, this was possible because the company has developed a very advanced drone that through AI technologies can overcome the lack of infrastructures that characterize peripheral regions to serve many hospitals. The novelty of these technologies has also attracted many investors that provided fuel for the organization, especially in the initial phase. Perhaps, this story could not have been written 20 years ago. However, today is possible because we have AI technologies and we can make noble use of them for the benefit of our society. Second, Zipline has developed an intelligent automated system that delivers blood, vaccines, and medical devices in Rwanda, where access to these precious resources is needed. Nowadays the company operates at an international level by serving many countries, even the developed ones. This story shows that it is also possible to scale the business internationally when at the center of the organization there is a satisfaction of societal needs that are particularly relevant for poor and peripheral regions. Third, this study shows how a country that was experiencing difficult situations from an infrastructural point of view became a leader in the healthcare sector by bypassing the problems of the civil war it suffered using AI technology. This led to an 8% growth in gross domestic product from 2001 to 2015 after only 24 years after the Rwandan genocide.

11.7.3 Limitations and Future Research

This study presents some limitations that may be fertile soil for future research on the topic. First, in this study, we unveiled the role that AI technologies of a specific industry (i.e., the drone industry) play for a better society. Given the single industry setting, the study offers limited generalizability of results as concerns other industries. Hence, further studies may examine the role of AI technologies in other empirical contexts. Second, we analyzed the impact of these technologies in peripheral regions. The analysis may be considered noteworthy for our understanding of the societal benefits that AI technologies may generate in an underexplored research setting. Nonetheless, it could be interesting to offer a comparison with companies mainly operating in developed countries to understand the similarities and differences underlying their business model innovation. For instance, a company that can be studied is Wing, a Google company, which has even surpassed Amazon in its delivery to some areas of the United States. Third, our qualitative analysis is based on observations regarding a single firm (i.e., Zipline International). Future research can elaborate and formalize additional insights by adopting multi-firm research designs (Eisenhardt & Graebner, 2007). More specifically, future studies may confirm, expand, or reduce the validity of the results of this study by conducting multiple comparative case studies research.

Notes

1 https://thenextcloset.com
2 https://dronesfordevelopment.org/
3 https://flyzipline.com/live/

Bibliography

Ahmad, T., Zhang, D., Huang, C., Zhang, H., Dai, N., Song, Y., & Chen, H. (2021). "Artificial intelligence in the sustainable energy industry: Status Quo, challenges and opportunities". *Journal of Cleaner Production*, Vol. *289*, p. 125834.

Anderson, A. R. (2000). "Paradox in the periphery: An entrepreneurial reconstruction?". *Entrepreneurship & Regional Development*, Vol. *12*, No. 2, pp. 91–109.

Asif, M., Searcy, C., Garvare, R., & Ahmad, N. (2011). "Including sustainability in business excellence models". *Total Quality Management & Business Excellence*, Vol. *22*, No. 7, pp. 773–786. https://doi.org/10.1080/14783363.2011.585784

Barrat, J. (2013). "*Our final invention: Artificial intelligence and the end of the human era*". New York: Macmillan.

Bharadwaj, A., El Sawy, O. A., Pavlou, P. A., et al. (2013). "Digital business strategy: toward a next generation of insights". *MIS Quarterly*, Vol. *37*, No. 2, pp. 471–482.

Boch, A. (2011). Culture is "Tight" with Technology Adoption: Cultural and governance factors involved in the acceptance of AI-powered surveillance technology deployed to manage Covid-19.

Bocken, N., & Ritala, P. (2022). "Six ways to build circular business models". *Journal of Business Strategy*, Vol. *43*, No. 3, pp. 184–192.

Bohnsack, R., Bidmon, C. M., & Pinkse, J. (2022). "Sustainability in the digital age: Intended and unintended consequences of digital technologies for sustainable development". *Business Strategy and the Environment*, Vol. *31*, No. 2, pp. 599–602.

Carnerud, D., Mårtensson, A., Ahlin, K., & Slumpi, T. P. (2020). "On the inclusion of sustainability and digitalisation in quality management–an overview from past to present". *Total Quality Management & Business Excellence*, pp. 1–23. https://www.tandfonline.com/doi/full/10.1080/14783363.2020.1848422

Chemouni, B. (2018). "The political path to universal health coverage: Power, ideas and community-based health insurance in Rwanda". *World Development*, Vol. *106*, pp. 87–98.

Cook, T. D., Campbell, D. T., & Day, A. (1979). *Quasi-experimentation: Design & analysis issues for field settings* (Vol. *351*). Boston, MA: Houghton Mifflin.

Craig, N. & Snook, S. (2014). "From purpose to impact". *Harvard Business Review*, Vol. *92*, No. 5, pp. 104–111.

Cucino, V., Ferrigno, G., & Piccaluga, A. (2021). "Recognizing opportunities during the crisis: A longitudinal analysis of Italian SMEs during Covid-19 crisis". In Sinergie (Ed.) *Electronic Conference Proceedings of Sinergie – Sima Management Conference Leveraging Intersections in Management Theory and Practice June 10-11*, Palermo (Italy), pp. 37–41. ISBN: 97888943937-9-8.

Cucino, V., Lungu, D. A., De Rosis, S., & Piccaluga, A. (2022). "Creating value from purpose-based innovation: Starting from frailty". *Academy of Management Proceedings*, Vol. *2022*, No. 1, p. 16792.

Dabrowska, J., Almpanopoulou, A., Brem, A., Chesbrough, H., Cucino, V., Di Minin, A., Giones, F., Hakala, H., Marullo, C., Mention, A., Mortara, L., Nørskov, S., Nylund, P., Oddo, C., Radziwon, A., & Ritala, P. (2022). "Digital transformation, for better or worse: A critical multi-level research agenda". *R&D Management Journal*, Vol. *52*, No. 5, pp. 930–954. https://doi.org/10.1111/radm.12531

Dagnino, G. B., & Ferrigno, G. (2015). "The strategic management of multipartner alliances: Uncovering the triadic alliance problem". In Das, T. K. (Ed.), *Managing multipartner strategic alliances* (pp. 135–169). Charlotte, NC: Information Age Publishing.

Di Vaio, A., Palladino, R., Hassan, R., & Escobar, O. (2020). "Artificial intelligence and business models in the sustainable development goals perspective: A systematic literature review". *Journal of Business Research*, Vol. *121*, pp. 283–314.

Ebrahim, A., Battilana, J., & Mair, J. (2014). "The governance of social enterprises: Mission drift and accountability challenges in hybrid organizations". *Research in Organizational Behavior*, Vol. *34*, pp. 81–100.

Eisenhardt, K. M. (1989). "Building theories from Case Study Research". *Academy of Management Review*, Vol. *14*, No. 4, pp. 532–550.

Eisenhardt, K. M., & Graebner, M. E. (2007). "Theory building from cases: Opportunities and challenges". *Academy of Management Journal*, Vol. *50*, No. 1, pp. 25–32.

Fernandes, C. I., Veiga, P. M., João J.M. Ferreira, & Hughes, M. (2021). "Green growth versus economic growth: Do sustainable technology transfer and innovations lead to an imperfect choice?" *Business Strategy and the Environment*, Vol. *30*, No. 4, 2021–2037.

Ferreira, J. J., Fernandes, C. I., Veiga, P. M., & Hughes, M. (2022), "Prevailing theoretical approaches predicting sustainable business models: a systematic review". *International Journal of Productivity and Performance Management*, Vol. *71*, No. 3, pp. 790–813. https://doi.org/10.1108/IJPPM-12-2020-0653

Ferrigno, G. (2016). "Looking for alliance portfolio characteristics: The case of telecom industry". In Das, T. K. (Ed.), *Managing alliance portfolios and networks*, 177–201. Charlotte, NC: Information Age Publishing.

Ferrigno, G., & Cucino, V. (2021). "Innovating and transforming during COVID-19: Insights from Italian firms". *R&D Management*, Vol. *51*, No. 4, pp. 325–338.

Ferrigno, G., Piccaluga, A., & Dagnino, G. B. (2021). "Managing alliance partner attributes: Lessons from the Ericsson Case Study". In Das, T. K. (Ed.), *Managing the partners in strategic alliances*. Charlotte, NC: Information Age Publishing.

Ferrigno, G., Del Sarto, N., Cucino, V., & Piccaluga, A. (2022). "Connecting organizational learning and open innovation research: An integrative framework and insights from case studies of strategic alliances", *The Learning Organization*, Vol. *29*. https://doi.org/10.1108/TLO-03-2021-0030.

Figliozzi, M. A. (2017). "Lifecycle modeling and assessment of unmanned aerial vehicles (Drones) CO2e emissions". *Transportation Research Part D: Transport and Environment*, Vol. *57*, pp. 251–261.

George, G., Merrill, R. K., & Schillebeeckx, S. J. (2021). "Digital sustainability and entrepreneurship: How digital innovations are helping tackle climate change and sustainable development". *Entrepreneurship Theory and Practice*, Vol. *45*, No. 5, pp. 999–1027.

Glaser, B. G., & Strauss, A. L. (1967). "*The discovery of grounded theory: Strategies for qualitative research*". Chicago, IL: Aldine.

Glynn, A. N., & Ichino, N. (2015). "Using qualitative information to improve causal inference". *American Journal of Political Science*, Vol. *59*, No. 4, pp. 1055–1071.

Gupta, S., Kumar, V., & Karam, E. (2020). "New-age technologies-driven social innovation: What, how, where, and why?". *Industrial Marketing Management*, Vol. *89*, pp. 499–516.

Hospers, G. J. (2005). "Best practices and the dilemma of regional cluster policy in Europe". *Tijdschrift voor Economische en Sociale Geografie*, Vol. *96*, pp. 452–457.

Houfani, D., Slatnia, S., Kazar, O., Saouli, H., & Merizig, A. (2021). "Artificial intelligence in healthcare: A review on predicting clinical needs". *International Journal of Healthcare Management*, Vol. *15*, No. 3, pp. 267–275.

Hutter, K., Hautz, J., Füller, J., Mueller, J., & Matzler, K. (2011). "Communitition: The tension between competition and collaboration in community-based design contests". *Creativity and Innovation Management*, Vol. *20*, No. 1, pp. 3–21.

Jick, T. D. (1979). "Mixing qualitative and quantitative methods: Triangulation in action". *Administrative Science Quarterly*, Vol. *24*, No. 4, pp. 602–611.

Kannothra, C. G., Manning, S., & Haigh, N. (2018). "How hybrids manage growth and social-business tensions in global supply chains: The case of impact sourcing". *Journal of Business Ethics*, Vol. *148*, No. 2, pp. 271–290.

Karlsen, J., Isaksen, A., & Spilling, O. (2011). "The challenge of constructing regional advantages in peripheral areas: The case of marine biotechnology in Tromsø, Norway". *Entrepreneurship and Regional Development*, Vol. *23*, No. 3–4, pp. 235–257.

Korsgaard, S., Wigren-Kristoferson, C., Brundin, E., Hellerstedt, K., Alsos, G. A., & Grande, J. (2022). "Entrepreneurship and embeddedness: Process, context and theoretical foundations". *Entrepreneurship & Regional Development*, Vol. *34*, No. 3–4, pp. 210–221.

Lamptey, E., & Serwaa, D. (2020). "The use of zipline drones technology for COVID-19 samples transportation in Ghana". *HighTech and Innovation Journal*, Vol. *1*, No. 2, pp. 67–71.

Lincoln, Y. S., & Denzin, N. K. (1994). "The fifth moment". In *Handbook of qualitative research* (Vol. *1*, pp. 575–586). Thousand Oaks, CA: Sage.

Loureiro, S. M. C., Guerreiro, J., & Tussyadiah, I. (2021). "Artificial intelligence in business: State of the art and future research agenda." *Journal of Business Research*, Vol. *129*, pp. 911–926.

Magistretti, S., & Dell'Era, C. (2019). "Unveiling opportunities afforded by emerging technologies: Evidences from the drone industry". *Technology Analysis & Strategic Management*, Vol. *31*, No. 5, pp. 606–623.

Maiolini, R., Marra, A., Baldassarri, C., & Carlei, V. (2016). "Digital technologies for social innovation: An empirical recognition on the new enablers". *Journal of Technology Management & Innovation*, Vol. *11*, No. 4, pp. 22–28.

Margherita, A. (2022). "Human resources analytics: A systematization of research topics and directions for future research". *Human Resource Management Review*, Vol. *32*, No. 2, p. 100795.

Mason, J. (1996). "*Qualitative researching*". Newbury Park, CA: Sage.

Patrick, M., Afzal, G., Mahsud, M., & Hanifatu, M. N. (2022). "Factors that affect maternal mortality in Rwanda: A comparative study with India and Bangladesh". *Computational and Mathematical Methods in Medicine*, Vol. *2020*, pp. 1940188. https://doi.org/10.1155/2022/1940188

Pettigrew, A. M. (1990). "Longitudinal field research on change: Theory and practice". *Organization Science*, Vol. *1*, No. 3, pp. 267–292.

Pisano, G. P., & Verganti, R. (2008). "Which kind of collaboration is right for you". *Harvard Business Review*, Vol. *86*, No. 12, pp.78–86.

Pulsiri, N., *et al.* (2019). "Achieving sustainable development goals for people with disabilities through digital technologies". *2019 Portland International Conference* on *Management of Engineering and Technology (PICMET)*, pp. 1–10. https://doi. org/10.23919/PICMET.2019.8893725.

Rotolo, D., Hicks, D., & Martin, B. R. (2015). "What is an emerging technology?". *Research Policy*, Vol. *44*, No. 10, pp. 1827–1843.

Sebastian, I. M., Ross, J. W., Beath, C., et al. (2017). "How big old companies navigate digital transformation". *MIS Quarterly* Executive, Vol. *16*, No. 3, pp. 197–213.

Siggelkow, N. (2007). "Persuasion with Case Studies". *The Academy of Management Journal*, Vol. *50*, No. 1, pp. 20–24.

Skorup, B., & Haaland, C. (2020). "How drones can help fight the coronavirus". *Mercatus Center Research Paper Series, Special Edition Policy Brief.*

Spillman, L. (2014). "Mixed methods and the logic of qualitative inference". *Qualitative Sociology*, Vol. *37*, No 2, pp. 189–205.

Stolaroff, J. K., Samaras, C., O'Neill, E. R., Lubers, A., Mitchell, A. S., & Ceperley, D. (2018). "Energy use and life cycle greenhouse gas emissions of drones for commercial package delivery". *Nature Communications*, Vol. *9*, No. 1, pp. 1–13.

Tödtling, F., & Trippl, M. (2005). "One size fits all? Towards a differentiated regional innovation policy approach". *Research Policy*, Vol. *34*, No. 8, pp. 1203–1219.

Vaccaro, A., & Madsen, P. (2009). ICT and an NGO: Difficulties in attempting to be extremely transparent. *Ethics and Information Technology*, Vol. *11*.No. 3, pp. 221–231.

Weber, R. P. (1990). "*Basic content analysis*" (No. 49). London: Sage.

Wilson, I. & Anderson, A. R. (2004). "Small tourist firms in rural areas: Agility, vulnerability and survival in the face of crisis". *International Journal of Entrepreneurial Behaviour and Research*, Vol. *10*, No. 4, pp. 229–246.

Wiltshire, G., & Ronkainen, N. (2021). "A realist approach to thematic analysis: Making sense of qualitative data through experiential, inferential and dispositional themes". *Journal of Critical Realism*, Vol. *20*, pp. 1–22.

World Health Organization (WHO). (2020). Robots use in Rwanda to fight against COVID-19. WHO | Regional Office for Africa. https://www.afro.who.int/ news/robots-use-rwandafight-against-covid-19.

Yin, R. K. (2018). "*Case study research and applications*", 6th edition. Los Angeles, CA: Sage Publications Inc.

Zabala-Iturriagagoitia, J. M. (2022). "Fostering regional innovation, entrepreneurship and growth through public procurement". *Small Business Economics*, Vol. *58*, No. 2, pp. 1205–1222.

12 Improving Healthcare by Designing AI-Human-Centered Systems

Gaetano Cafiero, Michela De Rosa and Francesco Schiavone

12.1 Introduction

In recent years, given also the scenario foreshadowed by the pandemic, we are gradually witnessing a change of perspective in healthcare. It is in place a stepwise reduction of the focus on the advancement in the field led by technological change, in favor of advancement based on the needs of the users and the healthcare community. Shifting the focus from a technology-centered approach to a human-centered one can aid in the process of creating solutions more efficiently and suitable for specific clinical needs, considering the changes in the context of the application. On the other hand, biomedical research has seen an incredible transition over the past few decades, moving from a well-established hypothesis-driven knowledge discovery paradigm to a unique paradigm of data-driven biomedical science. The development of new computational methodologies is required because of the significant improvements in the automated collecting of massive amounts of molecular and clinical data. Powerful systems for the efficient use of biomedical Big Data in Personalized Medicine will need to be developed. This includes infrastructure, engineering, project management, and financial management (Kitchin, 2014). Accordingly, to fulfill the existing gap, AI and similar technologies are becoming more and more common in business and society, and they are starting increasingly to be used in healthcare. AI is becoming more proficient at completing human tasks more quickly, efficiently, and inexpensively (Tran et al., 2019). Both robotics and AI have enormous potential in the field of healthcare. Like in our daily lives, our healthcare ecosystem is becoming more and more reliant on AI (Leone et al., 2021) and robotics (Kyrarini et al., 2021). Many facets of patient care could be changed by this technology, as well as internal administrative procedures at payer, provider, and pharmaceutical organizations. Numerous research studies have already indicated that AI is capable of doing crucial healthcare jobs including disease diagnosis as well as or better than humans (Hamid, 2016). Healthcare is changing as a result of AI, and many medical specialties and professions are beginning to apply AI. Healthcare stakeholders and medical professionals can now identify healthcare needs and solutions more quickly and accurately with

DOI: 10.4324/9781003304616-16

the help of AI, machine learning (ML), natural language processing (NLP), and deep learning (DL). Data patterns can be used to quickly make decisions about patient care. Accordingly, for example, Kelyon is fully committed to shaping new AI solutions for a patient-centered approach, to improve the health professionals' and patients' daily experiences. At Kelyon, leveraging our experience in the design, development, and management of advanced Digital Health and Software as Medical Devices (SaMDs) solutions, we think that while investing in cutting-edge technology and algorithms is important, doing so alone will not provide you with a significant competitive advantage. We aim at ensuring efficiency and effectiveness in a patient-centered care eco-system. To extract value, it needs to rewire decision-making and operations and invest in human talents to ensure the changes stay. For this reason, we invest twice as much in people and processes as we do in technologies. Spe-cifically, we focus on the application of AI solutions in the field of precision medicine. On one hand, precision medicine methods identify phenotypes of patients with less-common responses to treatment or unique healthcare needs. On the other hand, AI leverages smart computation and inference to provide insights, allow the system to reason and learn, and empowers clinician deci-sion-making through augmented intelligence. In this lens, the convergence of both will help solve the most difficult challenges, especially those in which nongenomic and genomic determinants, combined with information from patient symptoms, clinical history, and lifestyles, will facilitate personalized diagnosis and prognostication. We develop AI models having the ability to predict which patients are likely to need medication based on their genomic data. The key to personalizing medications and dosages is to genotype those patients before that information is needed. The crucial role that healthcare plays in a prosperous, productive society makes it one of the most important industries in the larger big data environment (Panch et al., 2018). The use of AI in the healthcare industry can mean the difference between life and death. AI can help healthcare professionals including doctors, nurses, and others with their regular tasks. AI in healthcare can improve patient outcomes over-all, improve preventative care and quality of life, and create a more precise diagnosis and treatment strategies. Globally, the prevalence of chronic dis-eases is skyrocketing, putting enormous financial pressure on healthcare sys-tems (Liu et al., 2022). Everyone involved in the healthcare delivery chain, including pharmaceutical firms, clinicians, doctors, and patients, is seeking ways to create a more effective healthcare system and improve patient out-comes. Technology advancements in the medical field have the potential to move healthcare from being reactive to proactive. To help enhance patient results and people's lives, AI offers affordable, fundamental technology for safe, low-power, high-performance electronic devices used in healthcare. Of course, in the face of this enormous change in the care ecosystem, it goes without saying that the supply system on the market is also changing, and more and more companies operating in the sector have had to take note of the new needs of their stakeholders, adapting internal competences, skills, and know-how in order to market solutions that could effectively respond to the newly emerging needs (Götz et al., 2022). In this sense, the ability to adapt to radical change that encompasses several aspects of the same organization has proven to be a key factor in remaining competitive. In this chapter, we will take a quick look at the main applications of AI in the field of healthcare and focus on the main medical, social, and economic implications to provide some interesting insights for researchers and practitioners.

12.2 AI in Healthcare: Simple Answers to Complex Questions

A revolution is taking place in the healthcare sector. The increasing expenditure of healthcare sector, mainly due to historical events in the last years, is marking an unprecedented paradigm shift and the need for a real change in terms of organization and resources. Public spending on health in the European Union increased from 7% of GDP in 2019 to 8% in 2020. The 1% increase is due to both a decrease in nominal GDP and an increase in public spending on health (from EUR 978 billion in 2019 to EUR 1,073 billion in 2020), mainly due to the Covid-19 pandemic. During the same period, the expenditure-to-GDP ratio in Italy increased from 6.8% to 7.9%. These are the latest Eurostat data published on 11 March, showing that 'health' remained the second largest function of general government expenditure in the EU, after 'social protection'. The most significant categories of health expenditure were 'hospital services' (3.4% of GDP), 'ambulatory services' (2.5% of GDP), and 'medical products, appliances and equipment' (1.2% of GDP). Italy ranks ninth among the 27 EU countries. Austria and the Czech Republic recorded the highest ratios (both 9.2% of GDP), followed by France (9%). In contrast, Latvia (4.8% of GDP), Poland and Ireland (5.4%) recorded the lowest ratios. The EU Member State with the highest increase in the ratio of public spending on health to GDP was Cyprus, from 3.5 % of GDP in 2019 to 5.9 % in 2020, followed by Malta (from 5.2% to 7.2%) and Hungary (from 4.5% to 6.4%) (Eurostat, 2022). The rising total cost of healthcare and the growing unavailability of medical experts are the driving forces behind this shift, leading to a situation where the healthcare industry wants to adopt new IT-based processes and solutions with cutting-edge technology that could save costs and offer solutions for these new issues. Medical practice is gradually changing because of AI and a variety of medical specialties, including clinical, diagnostic, rehabilitative, surgical, and prognostic techniques, can benefit from a number of AI applications in medicine. AI acts as a key tool for solving complex problems, enabling the care paradigm to effectively leverage empirical evidence, and scientific knowledge and thus be responsive to the real needs to be met while guaranteeing qualitatively high standards of performance. In this section, an examination of the main applications of AI in healthcare is shown.

12.3 Human-Centered Decision-Making Process

Every second, an exponential amount of healthcare data is generated and mined for valuable insights. Today, approximately 30% of the world's data volume is being generated by the healthcare industry. By 2025, the compound annual growth rate of data for healthcare will reach 36%. That's 6% faster than manufacturing, 10% faster than financial services, and 11% faster than media & entertainment (Rbc Capital Market, 2022). Large amounts of information about daily bias are provided and collected by healthcare organizations and their implementation using information technologies enables the automation of pathways and regularities for knowledge extraction operations (Rong et al., 2020). In the healthcare industry, where judgments are generally based on the expertise of the doctors, this results in a reduction in manual activities and smarter data extraction to support the decision-making process. As an outcome, for managing processes in the context of healthcare, a decision support system model based on the exploitation of data can outperform conventional experience-driven techniques (Moreira et al., 2019). In fact, data mining enables professionals to identify links and relationships among seemingly unconnected pieces of information, enabling healthcare organizations to predict trends in patient situations and their implications. In this regard, raw data must be gathered and stored in orderly formats, but their integration opens up a world of opportunities for the search for hidden insights. Healthcare professionals can utilize the resulting patterns to determine diagnoses, prognoses, and therapies for patients under their care. Complex decisions in healthcare may go wrong due to data being unavailable or being too massive to review, information being missed, or suggestions being disregarded, leading to ineffective and expensive procedures and poor clinical outcomes (Kaplan and Frosch, 2005). According to this perspective, the accessibility, accuracy, and integration of the underlying data are strongly correlated with the effectiveness of decision-making in today's digitalized healthcare sector.

To identify the disease and direct clinical decisions, AI systems can collect, analyze, and report massive volumes of data from several modalities (Cho, 2020). AI can support diagnosis, therapeutic, and prognosis results in many medical scenarios because it can find significant associations in raw data (Jiang et al., 2017). Making it more affordable for more people to have their genomes sequenced gives researchers the knowledge they need to design drugs with greater accuracy and speed. The doctor's office requires low-power, even battery-powered, solutions due to equipment downsizing and sequencing technology. In order to dramatically increase processing speed and scalability for genome sequencing and enable personalized medical analysis and therapy, healthcare professionals are employing algorithms to drive additional performance optimizations (Goetz and Schork, 2018). It enables medical practitioners to embrace preventative disease management. It is also possible to forecast risk variables and drivers for each patient, which can assist focus healthcare measures for better results. Additionally, AI techniques can be used to create and develop new medications, monitor patients, and customize patient treatment programs (Mehta et al., 2019). The ability to make better patient decisions requires more time and concise information for doctors. AI could revolutionize medicine by enabling the creation of prediction models for medications and tests that track patients over the course of their whole lifetimes.

The potential use of AI systems to assist physicians and medical researchers in making clinical decisions is one of the major themes. AI can assist doctors in making better clinical decisions or possibly take the role of human judgment in functional areas that are specialized in the healthcare industry, (Jiang et al., 2017). Algorithms can help clinical judgments by expediting the procedure and the amount of care given, which has a favorable effect on the cost of healthcare services (Bennett and Hauser, 2013). As a result, AI technology can assist and streamline the work of medical professionals. Finally, algorithmic platforms can offer virtual aid to help clinicians understand the semantics of language and learn to resolve business process queries like a human would (Redondo and Sandoval, 2016). AI systems are capable of managing the data produced by clinical processes like screening, diagnosis, and treatment assignment. Health professionals can learn about related topics and correlations between subject characteristics and desirable outcomes in this way. These tools can analyze raw data and offer insightful information that can be applied to patient care. They can aid clinicians in the diagnosis procedure; for instance, it will be easier to carry out a high-speed body scan if you have an overall picture of the patient's condition (Anthony, 2020).

12.4 Patient Engagement and Adherence Applications

Traditional, one-way patient interaction has recently been proven to be relatively lacking (Lau, 2019). According to research, people have higher expectations now. To stay competitive in a market where there is increasing industry competition, particularly from franchised multinationals, healthcare providers must give better patient experiences (Lambrinou et al., 2019). When doctors prescribe drugs, people may decide not to take them or use them improperly. Often, poor prescription adherence isn't discovered until something goes wrong. Technology, however, can aid in early intervention, and AI offers the computing capacity required for a successful closed-loop system that encourages participation, from physicians, pharmaceutical firms, and family members. Modern diagnostic tools and healthcare technologies can deliver insightful data in real-time to assist improve patient outcomes (Pekonen et al., 2020). Patient involvement frequently referred to as the final mile of healthcare delivery and a vital element that can mean the difference between positive and unfavorable health outcomes as well as customer satisfaction might benefit from AI and ML in potentially profound ways. Without increasing the workloads of healthcare professionals, AI enables clinicians to engage patients more fully in the correct ways, filling in for care gaps and encouraging patients to change their behavior (and, in some cases, lessening those workloads). AI is helping to improve patient engagement in several ways, including utilizing ML to find the most effective methods of reaching patients at the ideal moment and with the ideal message (Agner and Braun, 2018). In those circumstances, ML can learn from patient behavior to engage them more successfully. For instance, some patients may have a history of reacting solely to SMS messages at a specific time of day. Due to the reduced engagement costs and cost savings, this also benefits providers; using NLP, chatbots may guide patients through routine tasks that were previously completed by personnel with a level of empathy that was unthinkable even a few years ago. When engaging with patients, emotional appropriateness is crucial since patients will soon lose interest in a provider who has poor to no digital bedside manner. In fact, providers have shown that including algorithmic empathy to chatbot ontologies improves engagement and, in turn, health outcomes. A chatbot powered by AI can also save on overhead costs and free up staff for other duties, modifying suggested treatment regimens and other follow-up measures by analyzing vast volumes of historical patient and treatment data, such as EHRs, for cohorts of patients with comparable conditions. Although patient noncompliance is a persistent issue that adversely affects health outcomes, healthcare professionals can utilize ML to develop treatment programs that have the highest likelihood of success for specific patients. By using the right messaging and content, as previously noted, at the appropriate times, and with suitable distribution methods, providers can also quietly affect patient behavior. Other uses include synchronizing patient information tools, enabling suitable conclusions for health risk alarms, and predicting health outcomes (Agrawal et al., 2019). As patients prefer convenience and quick feedback, AI is becoming more and more popular in the field of mental health therapy. Psychiatric professionals have typically relied on therapeutic discourse and patient narrative to gauge mental health because our emotional and mental well-being is mostly represented via language. By enabling technology to infer emotional meaning from a larger range of data sources, recent advancements in artificial intelligence (AI) have opened up new vistas in the subject (Lovejoy, 2019). Sentiment analysis and computational languages have been crucial to this process. The study of, interpretation of, and response to vocal representations of human emotions is known as sentiment analysis in the field of AI (Graham et al., 2019). With a special combination of NLP and sentiment analysis, data scientists have been able to develop computers that can discern human emotion from written text. Currently, these models are used in medicine to offer comprehensive data on a patient's emotional and psychological health (Abualigah et al., 2020). Furthermore, AI has the potential to empower us as individuals to make wiser choices regarding our health. People all across the world are already using wearable devices to gather common data like heart rate and sleep patterns. People who are at risk of contracting certain diseases could be warned well in advance of them becoming serious by using ML to assess this data. The usage of smartphone apps that offer granular-level patient profile information may help patients with certain chronic diseases better manage their conditions and lead healthier lives. All of this could lead to population health improvements and decreased overall expenditures (Vollmer et al., 2020).

12.5 Health Services Management

AI is a broad term for computing innovations that mimic human intelligence's supporting systems, including cognition, DL, engagement, adaptation, and sensory perception (Tran et al., 2019). Recently, interest in and developments in medical AI applications have grown due to current computers' greatly enhanced processing capacity and a large amount of digital data that is available for collection and utilization. In the healthcare industry, there are also a ton of administrative apps. Compared to patient care, the use of AI in this field has relatively less potential for revolution, but it still can produce significant savings. It can be applied in a number of healthcare settings, including claims processing, clinical documentation, revenue cycle management, and management of medical records (Connelly, 2020).

Chatbots have also been tested by several healthcare organizations for telehealth, mental health, and patient engagement. Simple transactions like scheduling an appointment or renewing a prescription may benefit from the use of these NLP-based applications. ML, which can be used for probabilistic database matching, is another AI technique that is relevant to claims and payment administration. Fascinating applications can also aid in the education of staff members who work in the healthcare industry. The disparity between urban and rural health services may be closed with the use of this evidence. Last but not least, AI could help health services management make use of the abundance of data in electronic health records by anticipating data heterogeneity across hospitals and outpatient clinics, looking for outliers, conducting clinical tests on the data, standardizing patient representation, improving future models that can predict diagnostic tests and analyses, and establishing transparency with benchmark data for analyzing services provided (Aisyah and Cockcroft, 2014). Medical big data is created in enormous quantities, and AI algorithms can handle this data and uncover novel information that would otherwise be lost in the clutter (Massaro et al., 2016). These technologies can help find novel medications for managing healthcare services and treating patients. Accordingly, AI has aided doctors and other medical professionals in the fields of medical imaging, geographic geocoding of health data, epidemic and syndromic surveillance, predictive modeling, decision assistance, and health information systems with its advanced algorithms. The effectiveness of these apps is becoming even more crucial during the COVID-19 period when information interchange is continuously required to effectively control the pandemic globally (Hussain et al., 2020).

12.6 AI and Robotics in the Service of Care

In the field of medicine, AI has a wide range of applications. The accuracy and predictability of surgery have risen because of surgical robots. Among other applications, there are bioprinting, diabetes, retinopathy, spine imaging, and radiology are among the other applications (Hashimoto et al., 2020). On the other hand, augmented reality overlays a computer-generated image on a patient's perception of the physical world to produce a consolidated perspective of the operating room. Remote surgery and senior surgeon control of surgeons in the outpatient setting are now both possible thanks to AI-powered telesurgical techniques. In instances when there is limited access to clinics, travel restrictions, or pandemics, intraoperative guidance via video images and communication technologies has been shown to be effective (Fekri et al., 2018). Many surgeons are finding that less invasive surgical procedures and AI and AR-powered surgical mentorship are viable alternatives. On the operator's screen, skilled surgeons can offer real-time advice on the best incision or equipment to utilize, assisting the surgeon while they perform the procedure. Using data and computer vision tools, the surgical workflow can also be examined (Kim and Kim, 2021). Before surgery, robots assist in the analysis of the patient's medical records in order to guide the surgical instruments. Robot-assisted surgery has been shown to significantly reduce the time of a patient's hospital stay because it is minimally intrusive (Prabu et al., 2014). Robots can also use AI to suggest more modern surgical techniques depending on a patient's prior surgical experience. AI methods can improve surgery and rehabilitation therapy for diagnosis. Many robots have been created to assist with and control such jobs. For instance, during motor therapy, a patient's limb can be physically supported and guided by a rehabilitation robot (Tarassoli, 2019). Through tools that can conduct semiautomated surgical activities with growing efficiency, AI offers a significant possibility to alter surgical robotics in the field of surgery. Automating processes to eliminate human error while retaining a high level of accuracy and precision is the ultimate goal of this technology. Some medical robots help patients in addition to medical staff. Exoskeleton robots, for instance, can help paralyzed individuals regain their ability to walk and become independent. Another example of technology in use is a smart prosthesis. These sensor-equipped bionic limbs can be covered with bionic skin and connected to the user's muscles, making them more accurate and responsive than natural body parts (Shortliffe and Sepulveda, 2018).

12.7 Lights and Shadows of AI in Healthcare

It is important to consider that beyond the AI potential benefits, there also is a number of drawbacks. Prejudices and inequality are risks in healthcare AI. AI systems can pick up biases from the data they are given and learn from it. For instance, if AI data is predominantly gathered in academic medical facilities, the ensuing AI systems will learn less about — and subsequently treat — patients from communities who do not frequently visit academic medical facilities and will thus treat them less effectively. Similar to this, if a provider belongs to a race or gender that is underrepresented in the training data, speech-recognition AI systems may perform worse when transcribing encounter notes. Even if AI systems are trained on trustworthy, accurate data, there can be problems if the data shows biases and imbalances that are already present in the healthcare system. Allocating limited resources to patients who are viewed by health systems as less attractive or lucrative for a variety of reasons could exacerbate inequality. Moreover, the most obvious risk is that occasionally inaccurate AI systems can cause patient harm or other problems with healthcare. An AI system might harm a patient by prescribing the incorrect medication, failing to spot a tumor on a radiological test, or choosing one patient over another for a medical bed because it predicted the wrong patient would benefit more. Even without the use of AI, a lot of injuries occur in the modern healthcare system as a result of medical mistakes. AI faults may be distinct for at least two causes. To begin with, patients and caregivers may react differently to software-caused injuries compared to those brought on by human error. Second, instead of the few patients hurt by a single provider's mistake, thousands of patients could be hurt by a defect in one AI system if AI technologies are deployed more broadly. Furthermore, to train AI algorithms, a lot of data is required from sources like electronic health records, pharmacy records, insurance claim paperwork, or consumer-generated data like activity trackers or purchase histories. Health statistics might be hard to find, though. Frequently, data is scattered across various platforms. In addition to the aforementioned variety, patients frequently switch doctors and insurance providers, which fragments data across many systems and formats. This fragmentation increases the risk of error, decreases the dataset's comprehensiveness, and increases the expense of data gathering, all of which limit the types of entities that could successfully develop healthcare AI (Hu et al., 2016).

12.8 Implications for the Healthcare Professionals

The adoption and use of new technologies routinely reshape work, the workforce, and the workplace. The risk that AI will cause significant workforce displacement and job automation has received a lot of attention. While some job automation is possible, there are many outside factors that could prevent widespread job loss. These include the price of automation technologies, the expansion and cost of the labor market, the advantages of automation that go beyond simple labor replacement, and societal and regulatory acceptance (Forliano et al., 2021). As far as one is aware, AI has not yet resulted in the loss of any healthcare jobs. The lack of job consequences has been partially attributed to the industry's slow adoption of AI thus far and the challenges associated with incorporating it into clinical procedures and E HR systems.

The positions in healthcare that are most likely to be automated are those that deal with digital information, like radiology and pathology, as opposed to those that have direct patient interaction (Secundo et al., 2020). However, the adoption of AI in occupations like radiology and pathology is probably going to be gradual. The ability to analyze and categorize images is being improved by technologies like DL but positions in radiology, for example, will not go away anytime soon for a number of reasons (Dal Mas et al., 2019). First, radiologists perform more than just picture reading and interpretation. Radiology AI systems carry execute solitary jobs, much like other AI systems. DL models are trained for specialized image identification tasks in labs and startups. To properly identify all probable findings in medical photos, however, thousands of these specific detection jobs are required, and only a small number of these can currently be completed by AI. The technical specifications of imaging examinations to be performed are defined by radiologists and are tailored to the patient's condition. Radiologists also consult with other doctors on diagnosis and treatment, treat diseases (for example, by providing local ablative therapies), perform image-guided medical interventions like cancer biopsies and vascular stents, relate research results from images to other health records and test results, and discuss procedures and results with patients. Second, there is still a long way to go before clinical image processing techniques are ready for routine use. The probability of a lesion, the probability of cancer, a nodule's characteristic, or its location is some of the different focuses that DL algorithms and imaging technology providers focus on. Integrating DL systems into existing clinical practice would be extremely challenging due to these unique focuses. Third, "labeled data"—the millions of photographs from patients who have obtained a firm diagnosis of cancer, a broken bone, or another pathology—is necessary for DL algorithms for image recognition. However, there isn't a collection of radiology images that are labeled or otherwise. Finally, for automated image analysis to catch on, significant adjustments to medical law and health insurance are necessary. For pathology and other digitally focused elements of medicine, similar factors exist. They make it improbable that during the next 20 years or so, AI will significantly alter the nature of the healthcare workforce. Another potential is the creation of new jobs in the field of AI research and development. Of course, this also means that, over that period, AI technologies are unlikely to significantly lower the costs of medical diagnosis and treatment due to stagnant or rising human employment. Regardless of the specific scope of application, IV cannot fully replace the work of health professionals. Some skills and capabilities can hardly be integrated into an AI system and that can make a difference in the patient's pathway.

12.9 Quality Control and Security Implications

The development of AI in health is a promising area of research, but it is challenging to determine how accurate these systems might be in clinical practice or how reproducible they are in various clinical contexts due to the rapid pace of change, diversity of different techniques, and multiplicity of tuning parameters. We may be crossing a very delicate balance if we become overly dependent on technology without fully comprehending its ramifications and implications if AI is used to make diagnosis, operate specific equipment, and give advice to a patient (Parikh et al., 2019). When a healthcare practitioner is taken out of the process of providing a healthcare service, this could lead to complications in terms of quality control. If an AI system makes a mistake, the practitioner, patients, and institution all stand to lose significantly. Although it is stated that AI can lessen the possibility of human mistakes when analyzing data, worries have been expressed that the systems could perhaps turn biased and result in stigmatization if they are not appropriately designed to reflect the unique characteristics of a demographic group (The Nuffield Council on Bioethics, 2018). The algorithms used by AI systems may reflect the preconceptions and opinions of their designers, and the outcomes they produce may also reflect these biases and ideas. The security of data generated by or contained within the AI system is complicated by the ongoing attention that privacy violations involving healthcare data are receiving (Kupwade and Seshadri, 2014). The AI system itself could be compromised, tricked, or inundated with "false" data, which could be disastrous if not discovered in time. AI's potential misuse has also been cited as a cause for concern. Although AI ought to be used for good, it may also be mishandled and utilized maliciously. AI might be used, for instance, to launch widespread cyberattacks or to covertly divulge private health information about a person. As with any debate on clinical safety, we must keep things in perspective. Without or with AI support, suboptimal decisions will be made, thus we must weigh the likelihood of an improvement against the possibility of unfavorable results (Nelson, 2019).

12.10 Ethical Implications

The employment of AI in healthcare is also subject to a number of ethical considerations. None of this implies that AI, despite being incredibly promising, is a magic bullet for patient engagement. When technology makes judgments or engages in dialogues that are typically handled by humans, especially when people's health (and lives) are at risk, ethical considerations can come into play (Keskinbora, 2019). It can be difficult for doctors to explain to patients how an algorithm identified them when AI-driven diagnostics are used. When AI drives patient interaction, concerns about privacy, responsibility, patient autonomy, and informed permission may surface. Some patients are hesitant to divulge private health information to an algorithm, which may or may not be sensitive to privacy and confidentiality in the same way that a doctor is. The use of intelligent robots to make or assist with healthcare decisions involves questions of accountability, transparency, permission, and privacy (McLennan et al., 2020). Historically, healthcare decisions have been made nearly exclusively by humans. Given the tools of today, transparency may be the most challenging problem to solve. Many AI algorithms are nearly impossible to understand or interpret, in particular DL algorithms used for picture analysis. A patient will probably want to know why if they are told that an image led to their cancer diagnosis. DL algorithms and even doctors with a general understanding of how they work would be unable to explain. AI systems will certainly make mistakes while diagnosing and treating patients, and it might be challenging to hold them accountable (Mirbabaie et al., 2021). Additionally, it's conceivable that there may be instances where AI systems provide patients with medical knowledge that they would rather get from a compassionate doctor. Healthcare ML algorithms may also be prone to algorithmic bias, maybe predicting greater disease likelihood based on race or gender even when those are not the real cause factors (Baima et al., 2021). AI in healthcare is projected to bring about a number of ethical, medical, occupational, and technological developments. The establishment of systems to monitor major issues, act responsibly, and build governance procedures to prevent harmful effects is crucial for healthcare organizations as well as governmental and regulatory agencies. Since this technology has a significant and lasting impact on human society, it will need ongoing care and careful policymaking for many years. Despite these problems, AI will continue to be a technology that is crucial for patient involvement and healthcare in general. While it's unlikely that AI and ML models will ever replace doctors and their staff, they have already shown themselves to be effective tools for patient involvement, and this trend will undoubtedly continue.

12.10.1 Legal Implications

The ethical debate on AI revolves around two fundamental considerations: the first refuses to see any form of intelligence in a subject devoid of conscience and critical spirit, and thus reduces AI to a complex system of rules for the operation of certain technologies; the second, then, denies the idea of granting decision-making capacity to computers (which, once they have received input, are free to enrich and apply it from situation to situation) because they lack conscience and social/emotional intelligence. We begin with the assumption that algorithms used for automated decision-making "produce generally dependable (but subjective and not necessarily accurate) conclusions based upon complicated rules that challenge or confound human capacities for action and comprehension" (Mittelstadt et al., 2016, p. 3). Automated decision-making systems can have an impact on people and society as a whole, posing fresh ethical problems that raise fundamental issues with regard to accountability, respect for human decency, and the relationship between humans and machines (Coeckelbergh, 2020; Latonero, 2018; Matthias, 2004). Legally speaking, a response to automated decision-making systems' possible negative effects on people and society is necessary. Many (legal) academics have questioned whether such systems should have a right to access the rationale used in decision-making as well as how transparent they should be (among others Casey et al., 2019; Edwards and Veale, 2018; Kaminski, 2019). Legally speaking, a response to automated decision-making systems' possible negative effects on people and society is necessary. Many (legal) academics have questioned whether such systems should have a right to access the rationale used in decision-making as well as how transparent they should be. Patients have strong opinions on how their data are secured and how data flow is transparent. Patients and their clinicians must comprehend the interconnections between public, not-for-profit, and industrial sector organizations as well as those within them in order to have confidence in ML and AI models. Compliance with the aforementioned legal frameworks, such as the GDPR of the European Union, is crucial yet insufficient to demonstrate the transparency necessary to produce reliable ML/AI research. Depending on the institutions involved and the type of work being done, different levels of information will be required. Developers of ML/AI algorithms and those responsible for accessing, sharing, or maintaining the data therefore have a duty to consult with relevant parties to determine what is needed in each specific situation. Clear declarations of interest from all parties involved are one component of the reporting process that can assist guarantee transparency regarding the interactions stated above. The topic of privacy is introduced here almost immediately. If we now risk entrusting our personal data to technological devices, let us imagine the implications of showing them how we think, and what our habits, needs, or preferences are (Murdoch, 2021). And let us then imagine that they are free to dispose of this information in order to deduce more and behave accordingly. The enormous importance of systems that protect our personal data is obvious, but it is also easy to see how, in the face of a world where AI is widespread, they would prove insufficient. In terms of privacy, there are often three parties involved: the data owner, the person getting permission to process the data, and third parties who will only receive the data in certain circumstances and for clear purposes. Each of these three parties has a distinct position with associated responsibilities. The system does not yet foresee a "sentient" gadget holding a user's private information. It is up for argument how this device should be structured and what obligations it should have. The privacy policy clearly outlines the purposes for data collection and processing, and these purposes cannot be amended without a new request for consent from the data subjects. However, an AI-equipped computer might change these goals on its own as it adapts to its environment and modifies its behavior. The only option would be to include a rule that had the ability to veto all decisions made by the device, largely restricting its intended use. The GDPR states that data processing may occur in addition to the purposes specified in the information notice if it is "strictly necessary" to use a requested service. Until now, this criterion has always been determined by humans on the basis of reasonable and legal grounds; it would be out of our control if we left it to the judgment of AI-equipped devices. Each person is in charge of their own privacy. In other words, everyone has the freedom to choose which of their personal data to disclose or not, with whom, and how, outside of the bounds of citizenship. However, it has already been mentioned that AI-enabled gadgets can infer considerably more information from the data given to them, including information that is completely private and that the user may have opted not to reveal. Additionally, consent to processing only applies to the data that are the topic of the information and not to any additional data that may be shared in the future. Preventing computers from using cross-referencing to determine a person's health state using the data provided to them (safeguarded by very stringent regulations! Here they are), political opinions, religious convictions, or moral decisions made by individuals would once more limit how they can be used. Finally, unlike people and institutions that currently retain other people's personal data, AI-based systems would not be subject to regulation. In the event of non-compliance, they would become uncontrollable, unpunishable, unpredictable, and maybe harmful for the private information of their owners. The discussion spans the disciplines of ethics, politics, philosophy, and electronic law. It seems likely that until many of the difficulties we have covered are resolved, the dissemination of AI into daily life will not be conceivable. Talking about it and thinking about it can help us get more familiar with a subject that is just superficially futuristic in the interim.

12.10.2 Economic Implications

Since this technology has a significant and lasting impact on human society, it will need ongoing care and careful policymaking for many years. First of all, the reduction of expenditures associated with post-treatment problems. Nowadays, practically every industry benefits from more effective decision-making because of the ability to effectively and accurately show the potential of data. This is also true in healthcare. As healthcare providers move toward a consistent framework for recording patient outcomes, massive amounts of data will become available for analysis by AI-powered systems. These technologies will be able to examine post-treatment result patterns and identify the best remedies based on patient profiles. AI enables clinical decision-making as a result, ensuring that each patient receives the proper interventions and therapies, leading to a more personalized approach to care. As a result of the instant improvement in outcomes, one of the main cost drivers in the majority of healthcare ecosystems around the world—post-treatment problems—will no longer be a factor (Le Nguyen and Do, 2019). Secondly, the cost-cutting through early diagnostics. AI-enabled devices can carry out routine, straightforward tasks more accurately, such as processing CT scans and performing some tests, which reduces physician errors and speeds up diagnosis and remediation before problems get worse. When it comes to evaluating and analyzing mammograms, AI has proven to be much more accurate and quick than humans, enabling much earlier breast cancer detection than humans. The cost of this condition to health services can be significantly reduced in cases like osteoporosis if vertebral fractures are recognized as an early sign of the disease that is frequently missed by human diagnosis. Third, the cost minimization with enhanced clinical trials. AI has the potential to speed up the development of potentially life-saving medications, saving the health care systems billions of dollars in costs.

12.11 Using AI to Advance Healthcare in the Future: Agenda for Researchers and Practitioners

As observed, there are numerous application cases where AI approaches can be applied to improve healthcare systems. Utilizing AI can: cut down on time spent on medical tasks; provide correct diagnoses; conclude medical records and photos; track health status and forecast the onset or progression of diseases; Increase the quality of care; reduce surgical operation complications control prescription abuse and poor medical adherence; support the clinical judgment. Future healthcare options will likely include a significant amount of AI. It is the main capability underlying the development of precision medicine, which is universally acknowledged to be a critically needed improvement in healthcare. It takes the form of ML. Although early attempts at making recommendations for diagnosis and therapy have been difficult, we anticipate that AI will eventually become proficient in that field as well. It will become more common to use speech and text recognition for purposes like patient communication and clinical note transcription. Not determining whether the tools will be capable enough to be beneficial, but rather guaranteeing their acceptance in routine clinical practice, is the biggest hurdle for AI in various healthcare sectors. In order for AI systems to be widely adopted, they need to be endorsed by regulatory bodies, integrated with EHR systems, sufficiently standardized so that similar products function, similarly, taught to clinicians, paid for by public or private payer organizations, and improved over time in the field. These difficulties will eventually be resolved, but it will take considerably longer than it will for the technology to advance. Furthermore, it is increasingly obvious that AI systems will not substantially replace human clinicians in patient care but rather support them. Human physicians may eventually gravitate toward duties and work arrangements that make use of particularly human abilities like empathy, persuasion, and big-picture integration. Perhaps the only healthcare professionals who will eventually lose their employment are those who reject the use of AI. Medical practitioners' workloads may be lighter, healthcare expenses could be reduced, preventive care could be offered, and more accurate diagnoses could be made more quickly and easily thanks to AI. Given that healthcare expenditures are continually rising, AI services are required. Additionally, as the population age structure shifts, particularly in industrialized nations, there will be an increase in chronic diseases affecting the elderly that require high-cost care. Additionally, there will be a shortage of qualified nurses and medical specialists. Moreover, the majority of the population in developing countries, as well as the impoverished and old, lack access to modern, efficient healthcare services. We can achieve considerable reductions in overall healthcare expenditures while also enhancing health outcomes and quality of life when AI methods are fully used in healthcare research and IT procedures. Every examined aspect of healthcare provision shows a need for improvement, which AI approaches may give. Additionally, it is demonstrated that there is a very significant potential for cutting-edge AI solutions in virtually every area of healthcare to save costs, lighten the strain of healthcare personnel, enhance patient quality of life, offer preventive health, and enhance overall health outcomes. For people in developing nations, there are also AI-based solutions available. Preliminary diagnoses, preventive care, patient health monitoring, and virtual nurse assistants are a few of these services. It must be noted that by 2026 (Accenture Consulting, 2017), AI solutions will save the global healthcare industry $150 billion. Based on these data we can assert that investing in AI in healthcare will pay for itself. We advise all research and development organizations and enterprises working on healthcare IT services to completely incorporate AI techniques that have been verified by science into their work. Safety and service quality are also essential components for a new service's effective implementation when it is developed and implemented for industrial reasons, particularly in the healthcare business. Developers of AI methods must adhere to standards, laws, and any potential future legal restrictions in order to preserve and improve their methods' quality. The US Food and Drug Administration has suggested a regulatory framework for AI and ML-based technologies, which includes new concerns in applying AI in healthcare (Food and Drug Administration, 2019). Until the EU Medical Device Regulation (MDR) creates its own regulatory framework for AI and ML-based technologies, this new approach should be used for creating new AI-based products for EU markets. Moreover, when AI methods must be implemented, it is recommended to healthcare AI service developers to join interest group and assessment frameworks. Accordingly, the World Health Organization and International Telecommunications Union have established the Focus Group on AI for Health, which brings together academic, industrial, and governmental stakeholders to advance the application of AI in health by creating an evaluation framework (ITU, 2018). Encouraged by the emerging pieces of evidence, as future work, scholars should continue the research and design of a novel platform where AI techniques and trained AI techniques can be applied and adapted to healthcare information technology (HIT) services by cloud-based, open access, easily integrated platform which uses open access and even proprietary health data repositories, national health databases, hospital information systems, and imaging databases as learning data and constantly evolving AI methods. As AI will continue supporting and affecting the future of healthcare systems in industrialized countries, we must also study how similar AI technologies can be implemented for underdeveloped countries or rural areas to benefit from better healthcare. In order to accomplish so, AI systems should be drawn out to match the requirements of healthcare in these developing countries. AI might therefore be used to boost healthcare personnel's productivity, promote accessibility, and raise quality. AI's capacity to enhance clinical decision-making and even develop remedies based on patient data input can support healthcare organizations' initiatives and programs aimed at enhancing medical resources in low-resource situations. As it is increasingly employed in business and daily life, AI is being used in healthcare. Healthcare professionals could benefit from AI in a number of areas, including patient care and office work. Most AI and healthcare advances are beneficial to the healthcare sector, although the approaches they support may differ greatly. It will be a while before AI in healthcare replaces people for a variety of medical vocations, despite claims made in some publications on the subject that AI is capable of doing just as well as or better than humans at some tasks, like diagnosing illness. Despite these notable advancements, the use of AI in healthcare is still very much in its infancy. Continuous research keeps enhancing the technology's capabilities, leading to more breakthroughs in the upcoming years across a range of industries. The vital healthcare industry, which is undergoing one of the fastest digital transitions right now, has a lot to gain from AI and ML, and facilities have the potential to significantly raise the patient's quality of life.

References

Abualigah, L., Alfar, H. E., Shehab, M., & Hussein, A. M. A. (2020). Sentiment analysis in healthcare: a brief review. In Abd Elaziz, M., Al-qaness, M., Ewees, A., Dahou, A. (eds), *Recent Advances in NLP: The Case of Arabic Language*. Studies in Computational Intelligence, vol. 874. Springer. 129–141.

Accenture Consulting (2017). Artificial intelligence: Healthcare's new nervous system. https://www.accenture.com/_acnmedia/pdf-49/accenture-health-artificial-intelligence.pdf

Agner, J., & Braun, K. L. (2018). Patient empowerment: A critique of individualism and systematic review of patient perspectives. *Patient Education and Counseling*, 101(12), 2054–2064.

Agrawal, A., Gans, J. S., Goldfarb, A. (2019). Exploring the impact of artificial intelligence: Prediction versus judgment. *Information Economics and Policy*, 1(47), 1–6.

Aisyah, M., Cockcroft, S. (2014). A snapshot of data quality issues in Indonesian community health. *International Journal of Networking and Virtual Organisations*, 14(3), 280–297.

Anthony Jr., B. (2020). Use of telemedicine and virtual care for remote treatment in response to COVID-19 pandemic. *Journal of Medical Systems*, 44(7), 132.

Baima, G., Forliano, C., Santoro, G., Vrontis, D. (2021). Intellectual capital and business model: A systematic literature review to explore their linkages. *Journal of Intellectual Capital*, 22(3), 653–679.

Bennett, C. C., Hauser, K. (2013). Artificial intelligence framework for simulating clinical decision-making: A Markov decision process approach. *Artificial Intelligence in Medicine*, 57(1), 9–19.

Casey, B., Farhangi, A., & Vogl, R. (2019). Rethinking explainable machines: The GDPR's right to explanation debate and the rise of algorithmic audits in enterprise. *Berkeley Technology Law Journal*, 34(1), 143–188.

Cho, B.-J., Choi, Y. J., Lee, M.-J., Kim, J. H., Son, G.-H., Park, S.-H., et al. (2020). Classification of cervical neoplasms on colposcopic photography using deep learning. *Scientific Reports*, 10(1), 13652.

Coeckelbergh, M. (2020). Artifcial intelligence, responsibility attribution, and a relational justifcation of explainability. *Science and Engineering Ethics*, 26(4), 2051–2068.

Connelly, T. M., Malik, Z., Sehgal, R., Byrnes, G., Coffey, J. C., Peirce, C. (2020). The 10 most influential manuscripts in robotic surgery: A bibliometric analysis. *Journal of Robotic Surgery*, 14(1), 155–165.

Dal Mas, F., Massaro, M., Lombardi, R., Garlatti, A. (2020). From output to outcome measures in the public sector: A structured literature review. *International Journal of Organizational Analysis*, 27(5), 1631–1656.

Edwards, L., & Veale, M. (2018). Enslaving the algorithm: From a "right to an explanation" to a "right to better decisions"? *IEEE Security and Privacy*, 16(3), 46–54.

Eurostat (2022). Database accessible at https://ec.europa.eu/eurostat/web/main/data/database

Fekri, P., Setoodeh, P., Khosravian, F., Safavi, A. A., & Zadeh, M. H. (2018). Towards deep secure tele-surgery. *Proceedings of the International Conference on Scientific Computing (CSC)*, 81–86.

Food and Drug Administration (2019). Proposed regulatory framework for modifications to artificial intelligence/machine learning (AI/ML)-based software as a medical device (SaMD)-Discussion paper.

Forliano, C., De Bernardi, P., Yahiaoui, D. (2021). Entrepreneurial universities: A bibliometric analysis within the business and management domains. *Technological Forecasting and Social Change*, 1(165), 120522.

Goetz, L. H., & Schork, N. J. (2018). Personalized medicine: Motivation, challenges, and progress. *Fertility and Sterility*, 109(6), 952–963.

Götz, F., Reelitz, C., Buck, C., Eymann, T., & Meckl, R. (2022). Potentials of digital business ecosystems in the healthcare market. In Baumann, S. (ed.), *Handbook on Digital Business Ecosystems*: Strategies, Platforms, Technologies, Governance and Societal Challenges. Edward Elgar Publishing, 662–679.

Graham, S., Depp, C., Lee, E. E., Nebeker, C., Tu, X., Kim, H.-C., & Jeste, D. V. (2019). Artificial intelligence for mental health and mental illnesses: An overview. *Current Psychiatry Reports*, 21(11), 1–18.

Hamid, S. (2016). The opportunities and risks of artificial intelligence in medicine and healthcare [Available Online at: http://www.cuspe.org/wp-content/uploads/2016/09/Hamid_2016.pdf]

Hashimoto, R., Requa, J., Dao, T., Ninh, A., Tran, E., Mai, D., et al. (2020). Artificial intelligence using convolutional neural networks for real-time detection of early esophageal neoplasia in Barrett's esophagus (with video). *Gastrointestinal Endoscopy*, 91(6), 1264–1271.

Hu, J., Perer, A., & Wang, F. (2016). Data driven analytics for personalized healthcare. In Weaver, C., Ball, M., Kim, G., & Kiel, J. (eds), *Healthcare Information Management Systems. Health Informatics*, Springer, 529–554.

Hussain, A. A., Bouachir, O., Al-Turjman, F., Aloqaily, M. (2020). AI techniques for COVID-19. *IEEE Access*, 8, 128776–128795.

International Telecommunications Union (ITU) (2018). Focus group on artificial intelligence for health (FG-AI4H). https://www.itu.int/en/ITU-T/focusgroups/ai4h/Pages/default.aspx

Jiang, F., Jiang, Y., Zhi, H., Dong, Y., Li, H., Ma, S., et al. (2017). Artificial intelligence in healthcare: Past, present and future. *Stroke and Vascular Neurology*, 2(4), 230–243.

Kaminski, M. E. (2019). The right to explanation, explained. *Berkeley Technology Law Journal*, 34(1), 189–218.

Kaplan, R. M., & Frosch, D. L. (2005). Decision making in medicine and health care. *Annual Review of Clinical Psychology*, 1(1), 525–556.

Keskinbora, K. H. (2019). Medical ethics considerations on artificial intelligence. *Journal of Clinical Neuroscience*, 64, 277–282.

Kim, D. K. D., & Kim, S. (2021). What if you have a humanoid AI robot doctor? An investigation of public trust in South Korea. *Journal of Communication in Healthcare*, 15(4), 276–285.

Kitchin, R. (2014). Big data, new epistemologies and paradigm shifts. *Big Data & Society*, 1(1), 1–12.

Kupwade Patil, H., Seshadri, R. (2014). Big data security and privacy issues in healthcare. *IEEE International Congress on Big Data*, Anchorage, AK, 762–765.

Kyrarini, M., Lygerakis, F., Rajavenkatanarayanan, A., Sevastopoulos, C., Nambiappan, H. R., Chaitanya, K. K., et al. (2021). A survey of robots in healthcare. *Technologies*, 9(1), 8.

Lambrinou, E., Hansen, T. B., & Beulens, J. W. (2019). Lifestyle factors, self-management and patient empowerment in diabetes care. *European Journal of Preventive Cardiology*, 26(2_suppl), 55–63.

Latonero, M. (2018). Governing artificial intelligence: Upholding human rights & dignity. https://datasociety.net/wpcontent/uploads/2018/10/DataSociety_Governing_Artificial_Intelligence_Upholding_Human_Rights.pdf

Lau, F. (2019). Patient empowerment: The role of technology. In *Improving Usability, Safety and Patient Outcomes with Health Information Technology: From Research to Practice*, IOS Press, 257, 270.

Le Nguyen, T., & Do, T. T. H. (2019). Artificial intelligence in healthcare: A new technology benefit for both patients and doctors. *2019 Portland International Conference on Management of Engineering and Technology (PICMET)*, 1–15.

Leone, D., Schiavone, F., Appio, F. P., & Chiao, B. (2021). How does artificial intelligence enable and enhance value co-creation in industrial markets? An exploratory case study in the healthcare ecosystem. *Journal of Business Research*, 129, 849–859.

Liu, H., Wu, W., & Yao, P. (2022). Assessing the financial efficiency of healthcare services and its influencing factors of financial development: Fresh evidences from three-stage DEA model based on Chinese provincial level data. *Environmental Science and Pollution Research*, 29(15), 21955–21967.

Lovejoy, C. A. (2019). Technology and mental health: The role of artificial intelligence. *European Psychiatry*, 55, 1–3.

Massaro, M., Dumay, J., Guthrie, J. (2016). On the shoulders of giants: Undertaking a structured literature review in accounting. *Accounting, Auditing & Accountability Journal*, 29(5), 767–801.

Matthias, A. (2004). The responsibility gap: Ascribing responsibility for the actions of learning automata. *Ethics and Information Technology*, 6(3), 175–183.

McLennan, S., Fiske, A., Celi, L. A., Müller, R., Harder, J., Ritt, K., et al. (2020). An embedded ethics approach for AI development. *Nature Machine Intelligence*, 2(9), 488–490.

Mehta, N., Pandit, A., Shukla, S. (2019). Transforming healthcare with big data analytics and artificial intelligence: A systematic mapping study. *Journal of Biomedical Informatics*, 1(100), 103311.

Mirbabaie, M., Stieglitz, S., & Frick, N. R. (2021). Artificial intelligence in disease diagnostics: A critical review and classification on the current state of research guiding future direction. *Health and Technology*, 11(4), 693–731.

Mittelstadt, B. D., Allo, P., Taddeo, M., Wachter, S., & Floridi, L. (2016). The ethics of algorithms: Mapping the debate. *Big Data & Society*, 3(2), 1–21.

Moreira, M. W., Rodrigues, J. J., Korotaev, V., Al-Muhtadi, J., & Kumar, N. (2019). A comprehensive review on smart decision support systems for health care. *IEEE Systems Journal*, 13(3), 3536–3545.

Murdoch, B. (2021). Privacy and artificial intelligence: Challenges for protecting health information in a new era. *BMC Medical Ethics*, 22(1), 1–5.

Nelson, G. S. (2019). Bias in artificial intelligence. *North Carolina Medical Journal*, 80(4), 220–222.

Panch, T., Szolovits, P., Atun, R. (2018). Artificial intelligence, machine learning and health systems. *Journal of Global Health*, 8(2), 020303.

Parikh, R. B., Teeple, S., & Navathe, A. S. (2019). Addressing bias in artificial intelligence in health care. *JAMA*, 322(24), 2377–2378.

Pekonen, A., Eloranta, S., Stolt, M., Virolainen, P., & Leino-Kilpi, H. (2020). Measuring patient empowerment–A systematic review. *Patient Education and Counseling*, 103(4), 777–787.

Prabu, A. J., Narmadha, J., & Jeyaprakash, K. (2014). Artificial intelligence robotically assisted brain surgery. *IOSR Journal of Engineering*, 4(05), 9–14.

Rbc Capital Market. (2022). A healthy outlook for data. https://www.rbccm.com/en/gib/healthcare/episode/the_healthcare_data_explosion

Redondo, T., Sandoval, A. M. (2016). Text analytics: The convergence of big data and artificial intelligence. *International Journal of Interactive Multimedia and Artificial Intelligence*, 3(6), 57–64.

Rong, G., Mendez, A., Assi, E. B., Zhao, B., & Sawan, M. (2020). Artificial intelligence in healthcare: Review and prediction case studies. *Engineering*, 6(3), 291–301.

Secundo, G., Del Vecchio, P., Mele, G. (2020). Social media for entrepreneurship: Myth or reality? A structured literature review and a future research agenda. *International Journal of Entrepreneurial Behavior & Research*, 27(1), 149–177.

Shortliffe, E. H., Sepulveda, M. J. (2018). Clinical decision support in the era of artificial intelligence. *JAMA*, 320(21), 2199–2200.

Tarassoli, S. P. (2019). Artificial intelligence, regenerative surgery, robotics? What is realistic for the future of surgery? *Annals of Medicine and Surgery*, 17(41), 53 –55.

The Nuffield Council on Bioethics. (2018). Artificial intelligence (AI) in healthcare and research. http://nuffieldbioethics.org/project/briefing-notes/artificialintelligence-ai-healthcare-research

Tran, B. X., Vu, G. T., Ha, G. H., Vuong, Q.-H., Ho, M.-T., Vuong, T.-T., et al. (2019). Global evolution of research in artificial intelligence in health and medicine: A bibliometric study. *Journal of Clinical Medicine*, 8(3), 360.

Vollmer, S., Mateen, B. A., Bohner, G., Király, F. J., Ghani, R., Jonsson, P., et al. (2020). Machine learning and artificial intelligence research for patient benefit: 20 critical questions on transparency, replicability, ethics, and effectiveness. *BMJ*, 368, l6927.

Index

Note: **Bold** page numbers refer to tables; *italic* page numbers refer to figures and page numbers followed by "n" denote endnotes.

Abdallah, S. 155
AccuVein 219–220
Acemoglu, D. 172
activation functions 23, 59, 60, 62–69, 73, 75–77
adherence applications 254–256
adoption and application of AI/ML 33–34, *34*, **49**, 49–50; AIOps 52–56; business metrics 41; in finance 24; literature review 34–35; in marketing 26; in medicine *25*, 25–26; model deployment 50–52; performance metrics 41–44; QoE and QoS 29–30; in remote sensing and landmine detection 28–29; supply chain management: 27–28; in tourism and hospitality 27
agile regulatory system 242
agroindustry 198
AIOps 34, 49, 52–56
AI-powered bot 27
AI-powered telesurgical techniques 257
AlexNet 75
algorithmic radicalisation 195
AlphaGo 178
AlShamsi, M. 155
Alshurideh, M. 155
ambulatory services 252
Anderson, K. 183
Andrieu, E. 184
anti-fraud system 163, 164
An, Y.J. 164
Apache airflow 55
Application Programming Interfaces (APIs) 109
Arifovic, J. 68

Arntz, M. 172
Aroussi, S. 30
artificial intelligence (AI) 1, 49–50; algorithms 158; blockchain and cryptocurrency 153–165; business adoption 3; data-centric methods 16; deep learning (DL) 5; definition 136–137, 157; digitalization 185; ethics and human-machine interaction 20; explainable and interpretable 22; facial recognition and image analysis 21; functional applications 2; in healthcare *25*, 25–26, 251, 252, 257–258, 260, 265, 266; hospital blood delivery 231–246; human capital, jobs and skills 171–187; innovation 2; innovative application 49, **49**; interdisciplinary 16, *17*; labor-productivity 15; levels 157; machine learning 5; material and energy intensities 196–201; model deployment 50–51; pervasiveness 2; phygital care journey 212–226; privacy 4; quantum ML 20–21; relationships 16, *16*; RPA 113; social scoring system 4–5; sustainability 1, 3, 6, 192–209; voice and facial recognition 4; working 176–183; *see also* startups
Artificial Intelligence Patent Dataset (AIPD) 1
artificial neural networks (ANNs) 16, 18, 23, 39, 59; activation functions 62–66; architectures 62; business processes 60; consumers and enterprises 60; and DL 61–62
Asatiani, A. 109
Asokan, A.K. 111

Association for the Advancement of
  Artificial Intelligence (AAAI) 197
association rule learning 37
Atlas of AI (book) 6, 201
atrial fibrillation 216
attended bots 111
augmented reality (AR) 215, 220, 257
Autodesk Fusion 360 58
automated decision-making systems
  261–262
automation: job ads 94; in payroll
  systems 94; potential criteria 116, **117**;
  replacement 105; *see also* Robotic
  Process Automation (RPA)
Automation Anywhere 108, 110, *110*
autonomous weapons 5
axons 59
Ayxon AI logo 139, *143*

backpropagation algorithm 59, 61
backpropagation through time
  (BPTT) 78
Baker, M.J. 138
Bampis, C.G. 30
batch learning 19
Bateson, G. 206
Bender, E.M. 200
Bessen, J. 138
big data 21–22, 35, 36, 44, 159, 174, 177,
  181, 186
Big Tech corporations 196
biodiversity 199, 207, 208
biological annihilation process 192
Bitcoin 154, 155, 161, 163
black box 7, 22, 54
Blanchette, S. 111
Blank, S. 135
blockchain: AI 157–161; decentralized
  and ultra-secure system 153; definition
  154–155; digital revolution 153;
  financial, economic and social levels
  153; future key 156–157; ICO 156;
  multi-agent system 155; need for data
  159; reliability 159–161; security and
  predictability 165; smart contracts 156;
  technology 155, 164; types 155–156;
  user data 164; *see also* cryptocurrency
Blue Prism 108, 110, *110*
Bovik, A.C. 30
Bridle, J. 196
Broussard, M. 202
Brune, P. 153
business metrics 33, 41
business process management (BPM) 107,
  109, 110, 114, 118–121, 130

business process management system
  (BPMS) 109
business value 34, 116–118, **117**, 120,
  124, 126

Cammeraat, E. 173–175, 177, 178, *179*,
  180, 181, *182*
Carbonero, F. 175
Castellacci, F. 96
Cewe, C. 109
chatbots 24, 27, 85, 88, 94–96, 218,
  255, 256
Chavlis, S. 71
Choi, P.M.S. 164
clarity assessment 239
cloud computing 181
cluster analysis 179, 186
clustering 18, 37, 39, 94, 178, 181
clutter reduction strategies 28–29
Cogisen logo 145, *148*
cognitive biases 5
Columbus, L. 24
Computer Vision 60, 62, 70, 71, 75, 76,
  113, 114, 180, 257
computer vision: applications 60, 71;
  CNN architectures 70; competencies
  178; engineers 178; RPA tooling 113;
  skills 180
consumption 51, 106, 179, 192, 232
content analysis 239, 240
convolutional neural networks (CNNs)
  23, 49, 60, 61, 71–76, *72–74*, *76*, 77;
  computer vision applications 71;
  feature detectors 69; layer types 73, *74*;
  ODL approaches 29; R-CNN 29
Cooper, L.A. 113
Costanza-Chock, S. 195, 206
cost-effective decisions 25, 26
Coulter, A. 214
Crawford, K. 201
cross-skilling strategies 175
Crunchbase dataset 139
cryptocurrency: AI 161–164; Bitcoin
  154; data security 161; emergence 153;
  fraud 163–164; markets 162; trading
  161–162; transaction security 162–163;
  see also blockchain
cryptography 154
cultural diversity 208
Cunningham, J.A. 135
cybercriminals 4

data-based technologies 195
data mining 177, 181, 186, 253
datasets 4, 5, 36, 53–54, 258

Dauvergne, P. 197
Davenport, T.H. 3
decision-making process: actionable
  information 15; ANN 60; audit 161;
  augmented intelligence 251; biases
  22; blockchain 161; efficiency 138;
  HRM 95; human-centered 253–254;
  ML 28; multiple medical domains 25;
  predictive analyses 222; social safety
  net 195
decision trees 18, 37–39, 179
deep learning (DL) 3, 5, 16, *16*, 49–50,
  158, 177, 178, 180, 202, 215, 251;
  ANNs 22–23, 59, 61–62; CNN 23;
  and machine learning 49; multilayer
  perceptron (MLP) 24; neural network
  architecture 22, *23*; ResNet 24
DeepMind 178
De Filippi, P. 156
delay-and-sum (DAS) algorithm 28–29
De Mauro, A. 181
demography 173–175
devil's advocacy method 240
Devi, R. 213
DevOps 34
Digital Health 251
digital-intensive industries 183
digital technologies 138, 186, 201, 212,
  232, 233, 243
digital tools 123, 129, 184, 243
digital transformation 172, 176
Dijk, J. van 177
discoverability 195
distributed consensus 155
Doyle, C. 214
drone delivery system 241
drone service providers (DSPs) 237
drone technology 235–237, 243
Drop-Off MINI-batch Online
  Dictionary Learning (DOMINODL)
  techniqu 29
Dumas, M. 106, 118, 124, 125

economic metabolism 192, 206
EKO, remote heart monitoring 223
electronic-HRM (e-HRM) 87, 88,
  90–93, 100
Elhacham, E. 192
ELSE Corp logo 143, *144–145*
emergency medical services/products
  235–237
emotional appropriateness 255
endogenous clustering approach 181
end-to-end machine learning 44–49;
  advantages and values 48; data

ingestion 45–46; data splitting 46;
  deployment 47; model evaluation
  46–47; model training 46; monitoring
  model performance 47
entrepreneurship 134, 135, 233
Ernst, E. 175
ethereum 156
ethnicity 173–175
Eubanks, V. 195
EU Medical Device Regulation
  (MDR) 265
explainable AI (XAI) 22
Exponential Linear Unit (ELU) function
  64–65

Facebook 2, 15, 21, 158, 161, 196
face-to-face interview process 94
facial recognition 4, 21, 158
Fairlearn 54
fake media 3
Federated Learning (FL) 18
Federici, S. 203
Feedforward Artificial Neural Network
  (FANN) 62, 66–71, *68*, 77; acyclic
  graph 67; direct graph 67
feedforward networks 23, 60, 67
financial markets 161, 162
financing and banking industries 24
Fitbit Smartwatch 216
Flagg, M. 181
Flick, U. 138, 139
Flux 59
Foy, A. 138
frequency-domain SLIM 29
Frey, C.B. 105, 172
functionalities of RPA 113–114,
  114, 115
fundamentals of AI and ML 45, 48,
  50–51, 159, 185, 261
fuzzy matching 113

Ganesh, A. 200
Garr, S.S. **93**
gated recurrent unit (GRU) 78
Gencay, R. 68
general purpose technology (GPT)
  138, 171
generative adversarial networks (GANs)
  4, 78
generative neural network 60
geography 173–175
Geyer-Klingeberg, J. 106
Ghosh, M. 30
Gig jobs 175
Giovanneschi, F. 29

Global Assessment Report on Biodiversity and Ecosystem Services 192
Google 15, 62, 108, 113, 158, 160, 178, 245; business model 196
Graphical User Interface (GUI) 109
Great Radicalizer 195–196
Gregory, T. 172
grey literature 107–109, 120, 130
Ground Penetrating Radar (GPR) 28, 29
group composition 123; input session 124–125; NBS 125–126; output session 126; process identification 124, *124*; roles 121, 123; setting 123–124

habit-making technologies 207
Hao, K. 200
Hardjono, T. 156
healthcare information technology (HIT) 265
healthcare organizations 224–225, 253, 256, 261, 266
healthcare professionals 214, 218, 251, 253–255, 258–259, 264, 266
health services management 256
He, K. 69, 70
Hetzler, W. 240
high-tech systems 196–201
Hinton, G.E. 69
histogram 16, 17
Hospers, G.J. 244
hospitality 15, 27
hospital services 252
HR information systems (HRIS) 85
HR lifecycle phase 87, **90–93**; data handling and analysis 99; human-centeredness 99; operational objectives/consequences of AI 94–95; relational objectives/consequences of AI 95–97; research implications 100; transformational objectives/ consequences of AI 97–98
Huang, A. 137
Huang, S.H. 164
human capital: AI-induced changes 183–185; AI-specialistic skills 177–180, *179*; cognitive and socio-emotional skills 176, 177, 180–183; digital transformation 176; online vacancy data 173; tasks-based skills 177
human-centered artificial intelligence (HAI) 184
human-centered systems: biomedical research 250; computational methodologies 250; data patterns 251; decision-making process 253–254; economic implications 263–264; ethical implications 260–264; healthcare professionals 258–259; healthcare sector 252; health services management 256; legal implications 261–263; lights and shadows 257–258; patient engagement and adherence applications 254–256; powerful systems 250; precision medicine 251; quality control and security implications 259–260; researchers and practitioners 264–266; service of care 257; technology-centered approach 250
human-centric AI 16, 17
human intelligence 3, 15, 16, 85, 137, 256
human-machine interactions 2, 3, 20
human recruiters by AI 96
human resource (HR) 31, 85; technologies 85, 87–89; *see also* human resource management (HRM)
human resource management (HRM) 85–88, 98; algorithmic management 86; analytics 88; data handling and analysis 99; electronic-HRM 87; human intelligence 85; integrated framework 89, *89*; life cycle stages 85, *86*, 89; objectives/ consequences 87; operational objectives/consequences 94–95; and organizations 89; practices 88, 89; relational objectives/consequences 95–97; research implications 100; theoretical framework 87–89, 89, **90–93**; transformational objectives/ consequences 97–98; vendor solutions 99
Hyperledger 160
Hypertext Preprocessor 181

iGenius logo 145, *145*
image-centric methods 17
impact on business 21, 231
impact on society 231, 261, 263
Inception-V3 76
incremental learning 19
indigenous knowledge 208
Industrial Revolution 159
inequality 165, 184, 185, 195, 257, 258
inferential approaches 239
influence factors (IFs) 30
information and communication technologies (ICTs) 183
initial coin offering (ICO) 156

innovative startups 134–136, 138, 143
intelligent robots 260
International Campaign to Ban Landmines 28
International Data Corporation (IDC) 58
International Joint Conferences on
    Artificial Intelligence (IJCAI) 197
International Telecommunications Union
    (ITU) 265
Internet of Everything (IoE) 220
Internet of Things (IoT) 27, 35, 220
interpretable AI 22
InterpretML 54

Jackson, C. **93**
job automation 258
job offsetting 171, 185

Kafedziski, V. 29
Kellify logo 145, *148–149*
Kelyon 251
kernel function 29, 75
Kim, H. 156
k-means clustering 18, 39, 179
K-nearest neighbors' model 30, 39
Kokina, J. 111
Kubeflow pipelines 55

labor-displacing automation 175
labor market: detectable impacts 185;
    digital-intensive industries 183;
    economy 15; expansion and cost
    258; polarization 175; reskilling and
    upskilling 172; segmentation 174
labor-productivity 15
labor-saving technologies 172
Lacity, M. 156
Lameri, S. 29
landmine detection 28–29
Lane, M. 181
Le Clair, C. 111
LeCun, Y. 76
ledger 154
LeNet-5 75, 76
Leno, V. 110
Leonard, W.Y. 208
Leone, D. 214
Lillicrap, T.P. 59
linear regression 18, 38, 67
logistic regression 18, 37, 38, 67
long short-term memory (LSTM) 78

Mabu, Catalia Health 223
machine learning (ML) 5, 15, 136, 138,
    158, 159, 163, 164, 177, 186, 195,
    196, 215, 251; adoption process 33,
    34; ANNs 16; computer program
    learning 35; decision process 36;
    in diagnostics 25; error function
    36; incremental *vs.* batch learning
    19; model optimization process 36;
    one-class classification 19; predictive
    analytics model 39, *40*; regression
    vs. classification 18; relationships
    16, *16*; supervised learning 36–37;
    unsupervised 37–39
macroeconomic growth 134
macro-level interventions 149, 193
Maia, O.B. 30
Maloney, W. 175
mammograms 263
Manyika, J. 173
mapping 62, 70, 73, 78, 110, *110*,
    180, 214
mapping emotions 214
MapReduce 177, 186n3
Marcolin, L. 174
marketing 21, 26, 143, 194
Marks, J. 17
Maxim, R. 174, 175
McCallum, A. 200
McCarthy, J. 136
McCarthy, S. 213
MDOTM logo 139, *142*
medical drone service providers **236–237**
Mele, C. 214
Mellouk, A. 30
mental disability 233
mental health therapy 255
meso-level interventions 193
micro-level interventions 149, 193
Micromedex 221
microservices 164
Microsoft's Nazi chatbot 157
Miller, S. 181
MindSphere 58
Miroudot, S. 174
ML engineers 178
MLOps 34, 35
model deployment 47–54, 94
Moh, M. 34, 35
Molina, C. 175
Moravec's Paradox 173
Mullukara, N. 111
multi-feature fusion (MFF) 30
multi-firm research designs 245
multi-layer perceptron (MLP) 23, 25, 66
Muro, M. 174, 175
Musixmatch logo 145, *147*

National Fund for Innovation (FNI) 134
National Security Entry-Exit
    Registration System (NSEERS) 21
natural language processing (NLP) 6, 24,
    113, 177, 178, 180, 186, 251, 255, 256
Natural Language Toolkit 180
neoliberal economic globalization 193
Netflix 29
neural network (NN) *23*, 30, 33, 37,
    187n4; ANNs (*see* artificial neural
    networks (ANNs)); CNNs (*see*
    convolutional neural networks
    (CNNs)); FANNs 66–71; in ML 77;
    OLMs 30; ONNX format 54; single-
    layer 61; *see also* deep learning (DL)
neuro-fuzzy systems 178, 187n4
neurons 23, 39, 59, 60, 62, 65, 67, 69,
    77, 158
Nieto, M. 139
non-compliance event 263
non-routine cognitive tasks 173

occupation 171, 173–176, 180, 184,
    185, 259
one-class classification 19
O'Neil, C. 194
Online Dictionary Learning (ODL) 29
opaque machine processing
    technologies 194
open neural network exchange (ONNX)
    format 54
operating systems 54, 181
operationalization 50
operational objectives/consequences of
    AI: acquisition 94; deployment 94;
    development 94–95; identification and
    attraction 94; separation 95
optimized learning models (OLMs) 30
ordinary least square (OLS) estimator 67
Organisation for Economic
    Co-operation and Development
    (OECD) 172
Orr, D. 207
Osborne, M.A. 105, 172

padding approach 72
parameters sharing 74–75
patient-centered health ecosystems 212
patient engagement 254–256, 260
patient journey 212–215
Peak Signal-to-Noise Ratio (PSNR) 30
Penttinen, E. 109
perceptron 23, 59, 61, 63, 66, 67, 69

Pérez, W. 139
performance metrics: measurement
    44; ML 41, **42–43**; predictive
    maintenance 43
peripheral regions: business performance
    231; challenges and opportunities
    243; data analysis *239*, 239–240; data
    source **238**, 238–239; economic and
    societal transitions 231; exponential
    technologies 231–232; findings
    240–243; hybrid organizations
    231; limitations and research 245;
    managerial implications 244–245;
    methodology 234–239; relaunch of
    Rwanda 242–243; research setting
    234–235; social impact 231; societal
    benefits 233; society nexus 232–233;
    theoretical contributions 243–244;
    Zipline International 237–238,
    241–242
Perl scripting language 181
phygital care journey: AI-based
    technologies 214–215; comprehensive
    framework 215–223; concept 212;
    diagnosis 217–219, 224; early diagnosis
    218–219; follow up 221–223;
    management 220; monitoring 222;
    notion 224; origination 215–217;
    patient journey and experiences
    212–214; people-centered healthcare
    ecosystems 212; phases 212;
    practitioners 224–225; prevention
    222–223; scholars and future research
    225–226; self-diagnosis 218; treatment
    219–221; upgrade 220–221; value
    co-creation processes 212
pipeline technology 55
Poirazi, P. 71
Polanyi's Paradox 174
political neutrality 202
Ponsignon, F. 213
pooling methodology 75
Position Trading 162
Prakash, D.V. 214
process discovery/analysis: input session
    126, *127*; NBS 128; output session 128
process-selection method 106, 107
psychiatric professionals 255
Python 54, 174, 177, 180, 186n3
Pytorch 53, 59, 68, 76

quality of experience (QoE) 29–30
quality of service (QoS) 29–30

Quant Trading 162
quantum ML/quantum-enhanced ML 20–21

radiology medicine 158
Ramos, G. 184, 185
random forest (RF) model 30, 37, 39
RAY 53, 54
Rectified Linear Unit (ReLU) 63–64
recurrent neural networks (RNNs) 39, 49, 60, 61, 78
recursive side-lobe minimization (RSM) algorithm 29
regression algorithms 18, 37
reinforcement learning (RL) 19–20, 37–38, 49, 53
Reinkemeyer, L. 113
remote sensing 28–29
residual network 70, *70*
ResNet 24, 70, 76
Rinaudo, K. 237, 240
risk management 164
RLlib 53–54
Roberts, D.A. 69
Robotic Process Automation (RPA) 109–110; AI 113; attended and unattended bots 111; automation potential 116; brainstorming technique 119–121; business value 116; conducting interviews 106; digital colleagues and twins 111–113, *112*; functions 113–114, **114, 115**; process mapping interfaces 110, *110*; process selection criteria 114, **117**, 118; project deadlines 106; relevant literature 108–109; sentences, concepts and keywords 108; software 105; suitability 106; tools 107–108; vendors 108; workshop design 118, 119
robotics 2, 178, 180, 186, 237, 250, 257
robotization 175
Romotive 240
Root Mean Squared Error (RMSE) 67
Rosenblatt, F. 59
routine tasks 137, 171, 255
RPA-suited processes 106
Russo-Spena, T. 214
Rutaganda, L. 106
Rwandan government 234, 240
Rwandan Ministry of Health 234

Saint-Martin, A. 181
Salloum, S.A. 155

Samek, L. 173–175, 177, 178, *179*, 180, 181, *182*
Sætra, H.S. 193
scalable business model 135
Schulte-Althoff, M. 138
science, technology, engineering and mathematics (STEM) 172
scientific knowledge 231, 252
Scopus 107, 108
self-awareness 216
self-control 216–217
self-driving cars 105
self-learning 27, 157
self-monitoring 222
sensor-motor skills 173
Serena 219
shortcut connections 24, 70, *70*
Siegle, D. 129
Simonse, L. 213
Singhal, C. 30
skills: 21st-century 183; acquisition 183; AI-related jobs *182*; automation change jobs and demand 172–173; big data and data science 181; bundles 171, 178, 180, 186; capabilities 259; cognitive and socio-emotional 172; competencies 171; compositions 177; computer vision 180; interconnectedness 178; opportunities 97; organizational training 94; psychometric assessment 95; re-bundling 175; substantial software development 105; technology-rich work environments 186
smart contracts 154–156, 160, 164
smart technologies 138, 201, 205, 206, 214
social costs 194
social protection 252
social repercussions 165
social robots 85, 88, 176, 223
societal needs 238, 240, 244–245
sociotechnical systems 6, 195, 197, 204, 205
Softmax 65–66
Soft Sign activation function 65
Software as Medical Devices (SaMDs) 251
Sparrow aircraft model 241
sparse learning via iterative minimization (SLIM) approach 29
sparse representation (SR) 29
sparsity 74–75
speech-recognition AI systems 258

Spotify 4, 60
Squicciarini, M. 172, 173–175, 177, 178, *179*, 180, 181, *182*
Srinivasan, R. 198, 207
Staccioli, J. 172
startups: AI 136–138; case studies 139, **140**; data collection and analysis 139–145; data for business 139–143; data for marketing 143–145; development 137–138; entrepreneurial culture 134; findings 139; implementation 145–147; implications 147–149; limitations and research 149–150; macroeconomic growth 134; methodology and research process 138; requirements 136; scalability 134; temporary and scalable business model 135; wicked societal problems 135
Stephany, F. 174, 181
Stochastic Neural Analog Reinforcement Calculator (SNARC) 61
Strubell, E. 6, 200
supervised learning machine learning 36–37
supervised learning models 178
supply chain management: 27–28
support vector machines (SVMs) 18, 29, 30, 37–39, 61
sustainability 1, 3, 6; AI material and energy intensities 196–201; automating unsustainable and unfair inertias 194–196; biological annihilation 192; consensus-based expert elicitation process 193; convivial and regenerative tool 205–208; digital technologies 232; ecological overshoot 192; political ecology 208; public opinion 208; social justice 197; technological neutrality 202–205; techno-social systems 192
Sustainable Development Goals (SDGs) 6, 192, 197, 234
sustainable economic growth 192–193
sustainable industrialization 193
Swan, M. 156
Swing Trading 162
Syed, R. 109, 114

Tasaka, S. 30
tasks-based skills 177
technochauvinism 202
technochauvinist dominant imaginary 207
techno-inevitability 202

technological neutrality: algorithmic injustice 204; automation bias 203; civic discourses 202; corporations 205; cruel optimism 205; discriminatory automated systems 202; dominant accelerationist thought 203; energy-intensive technology 203; extractivist and (neo)colonial cultural paradigm 205; growth-oriented economic culture 204; irreflexivity 202; machine learning developments 202; planet's ecosystems 204; social and cultural innovation 203; society's path dependency 204
techno-optimism 200, 205
temporary business model 135
TensorFlow 53, 54, 59, 62, 68, 76, 180
TensorFlow Extended (TFX) 53
Thron logo 143, *144*
time-domain SLIM (TD-SLIM) 29
tokens, digital asset 156, 160, 163
Toney, A. 181
tourism 27
trading strategy 161–162
transaction security 162–163
Transfer Functions (TFs) 16, 17
transformational objectives/consequences of AI: acquisition 97; deployment 97–98; identification and attraction 97; retention 98; separation 98
translated logo 139, *141*
Travel Appeal logo 139, *141–142*
Treiblmaier, H. 156
Tufekci, Z. 195–196
Tune 53–54
Turian, J. 65
Turnbull, D. 208
Twitter 21

UIpath 108, 110, 111, *112*
UIpath Orchestrator 111, *112*
Ullrich, O. 203
unattended bots 111
United Nations Conference on Trade and Development 15
University of Toronto 61
unmanned aerial vehicles *see* drone technology
unsustainability: academia and nonprofit organizations 197; agroindustry 198; agro-urban processes 199; amplifier 194; digital dematerialization 200; digital

revolution 198; eco-efficiency
200; entropic metabolism 197;
extractive industry 201; industrial
food system 199; open localization
strategy 201; political economy 197;
post-carbon and post-extractive
civilization 200; recency-bias
198; socio-environmental issues
197; sociotechnical systems 197;
technological neutrality 202–205;
techno-managerial approach 198,
199; top-tier AI conferences 197
use of AI-based technologies 225, 242
Userbot logo 145, *146*
US Food and Drug Administration 265

Van der Aalst, W.M. 109, 110
Van Deursen, A. 177
Van Laar, E. 183
Viñas-Bardolet, C. 96
Vinuesa, R. 193
virtual agents 215, 218
virtual reality (VR) 95, 194, 215,
220, 221

Walsh, G.S. 135
Wanner, J. 106, 109
Weber, M. 138
Weber, R.P. 239

Weber, W. 175
Whiton, J. 174, 175
Wieringa, R.J. 107
Willcocks, L. 109
WIPO report 1–2
workforce displacement 258
workshop 121, *122*, 123; input session
124–125; NBS 125–126; output
session 126; process discovery and
process analysis 126–128; process
identification 124, *124*; roles 121, 123;
setting 123–124; tooling and setting
128–129, *129*
World Economic Forum 174, 237, 242
World Health Organization (WHO) 212,
234, 237, 265
WorldLift logo 145, *146–147*
WWF Living Planet Report 192
Wyrobek, K. 240

XGBoost (XGB) 30
Xiaomi Mijia ECG 217
XR Health 221

YouTube 29, 195, 238

Zierahn, U. 172
Zipline International 237–239, 241–242,
244, 245

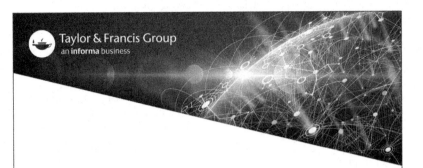

Printed in the United States
by Baker & Taylor Publisher Services